Introducing Linguistics

This outstanding series is an indispensable resource for students and teachers – a concise and engaging introduction to the central subjects of contemporary linguistics. Presupposing no prior knowledge on the part of the reader, each volume sets out the fundamental skills and knowledge of the field, and so provides the ideal educational platform for further study in linguistics.

1   Andrew Spencer   *Phonology*

2   John Saeed   *Semantics*

3   Barbara Johnstone   *Discourse Analysis*

4   Andrew Carnie   *Syntax*

Syntax
A Generative Introduction

Andrew Carnie

Blackwell Publishers

© 2002 by Andrew Carnie

Editorial Offices:
108 Cowley Road, Oxford OX4 1JF, UK. Tel: +44 (0)1865 791100
Osney Mead, Oxford OX2 0EL, UK. Tel: +44 (0)1865 206206
Blackwell Publishing USA, 350 Main Street, Malden, MA 02148-5018, USA.
Tel: +1 781 388 8250
Iowa State Press, a Blackwell Publishing company, 2121 State Avenue, Ames, Iowa
50014-8300, USA. Tel: +1 515 292 0140
Blackwell Munksgaard, Nørre Søgade 35, PO Box 2148, Copenhagen, DK-1016, Denmark.
Tel: +45 77 33 33 33
Blackwell Publishing Asia, 54 University Street, Carlton, Victoria 3053, Australia.
Tel: +61 (0)3 9347 0300
Blackwell Verlag, Kurfürstendamm 57, 10707 Berlin, Germany. Tel: +49 (0)30 32 79 060
Blackwell Publishing, 10, rue Casimir Delavigne, 75006 Paris, France. Tel: +331 5310 3310

First published 2002 by Blackwell Publishers Ltd, a Blackwell Publishing company

Library of Congress Cataloging-in-Publication Data

Carnie, Andrew.
Syntax : a generative introduction / Andrew Carnie.
p. cm. — (Introducing linguistics ; 4)
Includes bibliographical references and index.
ISBN 0-631-22543-9 (alk. paper) — ISBN 0-631-22544-7 (pb. : alk. paper)
1. Grammar, Comparative and general—Syntax. 2. Generative grammar. I. Title. II.
Series

P291 .C33 2002
415—dc21
2001043226

A catalogue record for this title is available from the British Library.

Set in Times Roman by the author
Printed and bound in Great Britain by T. J. International Ltd, Padstow, Cornwall

For further information on
Blackwell Publishers, visit our website: www.blackwellpublishers.co.uk

Dedicated with love to my parents, Robert and Jean
and in memory of my teacher and mentor, Ken Hale

Contents

Contents

Contents

Preface and Acknowledgements

Almost every preface to every syntax textbook out there starts out by telling the reader how different this book is from every other syntax textbook. On one hand, this is often the truth: each author shows their own particular spin or emphasis. This is certainly true of this textbook. For example, you'll be hard pressed to find another textbook on Principles and Parameters syntax that uses as many Irish examples as this one does. Nor will you find another P&P textbook with a supplementary discussion of alternative theoretical approaches like LFG or HPSG. On the other hand, let's face facts. The basic material to be covered in an introductory textbook doesn't really vary much. One linguist may prefer a little more on binding theory, and a little less on control, etc. In this text, I've attempted to provide a relatively balanced presentation of most of the major issues and I've tried to do this in a student-friendly way. I've occasionally abstracted away from some of the thornier controversies, where I felt they weren't crucial to a student understanding the basics. This may, to a certain extent, make the professional syntactician feel that I've cut corners or laid out too rosy a picture. I did this on purpose, however, to give students a chance to absorb the fundamentals before challenging the issues. This doesn't mean I don't want the students to challenge the material I've presented here. Throughout the book, you'll find gray "textboxes" that contain issues for further discussion, or interesting tidbits. Many of the problem sets also invite the student to challenge the black and white presentation I've given in the text. I encourage instructors to assign these, and students to do them, as they form an important part of the textbook. Instructors may note that if a favorite topic is not dealt with in the body of the text, a problem set may very well treat the question.

A quick word on the level of this textbook. This book is intended as an introduction to syntactic theory. It takes the student through most of the major issues in Principles and Parameters, from tree drawing to constraints on movement. While this book is written as an introduction, some students have reported it to be challenging. I use this text in my undergraduate introduction to syntax with success, but I can certainly see it being used in more advanced classes. I hope instructors will flesh out the book, and walk their students through some of the thornier issues.

This textbook has grown out of my lecture notes for my own classes. Needless to say, the form and shape of these notes have been influenced in terms of choice of material and presentation by the textbooks my own students have used. While the book you are reading is entirely my fault, it does owe a particular intellectual debt to the following three textbooks, which I have used in teaching at various times:

Cowper, Elizabeth (1992) *A Concise Introduction to Syntactic Theory: The Government and Binding Approach*. Chicago: Chicago University Press.

Haegeman, Liliane (1994) *Introduction to Government and Binding Theory* (2nd edition). Oxford: Blackwell.

Radford, Andrew (1988) *Transformational Grammar: A First Course*. Cambridge: Cambridge University Press.

I'd like to thank the authors of these books for breaking ground in presenting a complicated and integrated theory to the beginner. Writing this book has given me new appreciation for the difficulty of this task and their presentation of the material has undoubtedly influenced mine.

Sadly, during the final stages of putting this text together, my dissertation director, teacher, mentor, and academic hero, Ken Hale passed away after a long illness. Ken always pushed the idea that theoretical syntax is best informed by cross-linguistic research; while at the same time, the accurate documentation of languages requires a sophisticated understanding of grammatical theory. These were important lessons that I learned from Ken and I hope students will glean the significance of both by reading this text. While I was writing this book (and much other work) Ken gave me many comments and his unfettered support. He was a great man and I will miss him terribly.

Many other thanks are in order. First, let me thank the many people who taught me syntax: Barb Brunson, Noam Chomsky, Elizabeth Cowper, Alec Marantz, Diane Massam, Jim McCloskey, Shigeru Miyagawa, and David Pesetsky. A number of people have read through this book or large portions of it and given me extensive and helpful comments: Ash Asudeh, Andy Barss, Mark Baltin, Emily Bender, Joan Bresnan, Barbara Citko, Sheila Dooley Collberg, Yehuda Falk, Jila Ghomeshi, Paul Hagstrom, Ken Hale, Heidi Harley, Rachel Hayes, Andreas Kathol, Simin Karimi, Sarah Longstaff, Ahmad Reza Lotfi, Martha McGinnis, Peter Norquest, Colin Phillips, Carl Pollard, Kazutoshi Ohno, Heidi Orcutt, Hyeson Park, Frank Richter, Ivan Sag, Theresa Satterfield, Enwei Wang, and several anonymous Blackwell reviewers. The students in my *Introduction to Syntax* classes in Michigan in 1997, and in Arizona in 1998, 1999, 2000, and 2001 used parts or all of this textbook as their reading. Thanks to them for their patience. A number of problem sets in this book were graciously contributed by Sheila Dooley Collberg, Jila Ghomeshi, Heidi Harley, Chris Kennedy, Simin Karimi, and Betsy Ritter. I also owe a great debt to all my colleagues here at the University of Arizona for their help and support. In particular, Diana Archangeli, Andy Barss, Tom Bever, Heidi Harley, Mike Hammond, Eloise Jelinek, and Simin Karimi deserve special mention. My sisters and parents are not only owed a debt of thanks for being so patient and supportive, but also for letting me ruin a perfectly good summer vacation by bringing this book along with us. Simon Eckley, Tami Kaplan, Becky Kennison, Anna Oxbury, Beth Remmes, and Steve Smith of Blackwell, all deserve many thanks for encouraging me to write this up, and then smoothing its way towards production.

Go raibh maith agaibh!

Tucson, Arizona

rative Grammar

h we all have strong opinions about its
stop to think about the wonder of lan-
illiam Safire tell us about the misuse of
f the word *boondoggle*, but surprisingly,
ge: how it actually works. Think about it
erstanding it but you have no conscious
dy of this mystery is the science of lin-
ow language works – how sentences are

cognitive, property of humans. That is,
ng madly away that allows me to sit here
some other set of neurons in your head
hese squiggles into coherent ideas and
work here. If you were listening to me
ith my vocal cords and articulating par-
s, and vocal cords. On the other end of
and translating them into speech sounds
f the acoustics and articulation of speech
d the waves of sound into mental repre-
them into syllables and pattern them
glish know that the made-up word *bluve*
bnuck is not. This is part of the science

called **phonology**. Then you take these groups of sounds and organize them into meaningful units (called morphemes) and words. For example, the word *dancer* is made up of two meaningful bits: *dance* and the suffix *-er*. The study of this level of Language is called **morphology**. Next you organize the words into phrases and sentences. **Syntax** is the cover term for studies of this level of Language. Finally, you take the sentences and phrases you hear and translate them into thoughts and ideas. This last step is what we refer to as the **semantic** level of Language.

Syntax, then, studies the level of Language that lies between words and the meaning of utterances: sentences. It is the level that mediates between sounds that someone produces (organized into words) and what they intended to say.

Perhaps one of the *truly* amazing aspects of the study of Language is not the origins of the word *demerit,* or how to properly punctuate a quote inside parentheses, or how kids have, like, destroyed the English language, eh? Instead it's the question of how we subconsciously get from sounds to meaning. This is the study of syntax.

> ### Language vs. language
> When I utter the term *language*, most people immediately think of some particular language such as English, French, or KiSwahili. But this is not the way linguists use the term; when linguists talk about **Language**, they are generally talking about the *ability* of humans to speak any (particular) language. Some people (most notably Noam Chomsky) also call this the **Human Language Capacity**. Language (written with a capital L) is the part of the mind or brain that allows you to speak, whereas *language* (with a lower case l) is an instantiation of this ability (like French or English). In this book we'll be using language as our primary data, but we'll be trying to come up with a model of Language.

1.   SYNTAX AS A COGNITIVE SCIENCE

Cognitive science is a cover term for a group of disciplines that all aim for the same goal: describing and explaining human beings' ability to think (or more particularly, to think about abstract notions like subatomic particles, the possibility of life on other planets or even how many angels can fit on the head of a pin, etc.). One thing that distinguishes us from other animals, even relatively smart ones like chimps and elephants, is our ability to use Language. Language plays an important role in how we think about abstract notions, or, at the very least, Language appears to be structured in such a way that it allows us to express abstract notions.[1] The discipline of linguistics, along with psychology, philosophy, and computer science, thus forms an important subdiscipline within cognitive science. Sentences are how we get at expressing abstract thought processes, so the study of syntax is an important foundation

---

[1] Whether language constrains what abstract things we can think about (this idea is called the Sapir-Whorf hypothesis) is a matter of great debate and one that lies outside the domain of syntax per se.

stone for understanding how we communicate and interact with each other as humans.

2.   MODELING SYNTAX

The dominant theory of syntax is due to Noam Chomsky and his colleagues, starting in the mid 1950s and continuing to this day. This theory, which has had many different names through its development (Transformational Grammar (TG), Transformational Generative Grammar, Standard Theory, Extended Standard Theory, Government and Binding Theory (GB), Principles and Parameters approach (P&P) and Minimalism (MP)), is often given the blanket name *Generative Grammar*. A number of alternate theories of syntax have also branched off of this research program; these include Lexical-Functional Grammar (LFG) and Head-Driven Phrase Structure Grammar (HPSG). These are also considered part of generative grammar; but we won't cover them extensively in this book, except in chapters 13 and 14. The particular version of generative grammar that we will mostly look at here is roughly the *Principles and Parameters* approach, although we will occasional stray from this into *Minimalism*.

The underlying thesis of generative grammar is that sentences are generated by a subconscious set of procedures (like computer programs). These procedures are part of our minds (or of our cognitive abilities if you prefer). The goal of syntactic theory is to model these procedures. In other words, we are trying to figure out what we subconsciously know about the syntax of our language.

In generative grammar, the means for modeling these procedures is through a set of formal grammatical *rules*. Note that these rules are nothing like the rules of grammar you might have learned in school. These rules don't tell you how to properly punctuate a sentence or not to split an infinitive. Instead, they tell you the order in which to put your words (in English, for example, we put the subject of a sentence before its verb; this is the kind of information encoded in generative rules). These rules are thought to generate the sentences of a language, hence the name *generative* grammar. You can think of these rules as being like the command lines in a computer program. They tell you step by step how to put together words into a sentence. We'll look at precise examples of these rules in the next chapter. But before we can get into the nitty-gritty of sentence structure, let's look at some of the underlying assumptions of generative grammar.

Noam Chomsky

Avram Noam Chomsky was born on the 7th of December 1928, in Philadelphia. His father was a Hebrew grammarian and his mother a teacher.
Chomsky got his Ph.D. from the University of Pennsylvania, where he
studied linguistics under Zellig Harris. He took a position in machine
translation and language teaching at the Massachusetts Institute of
Technology. Eventually his ideas about the structure of language trans-
formed the field of linguistics. Reviled by some and admired by others,
Chomsky's ideas have laid the groundwork for the discipline of linguistics,
and have been very influential in computer science, and philosophy.

Chomsky is also one of the leading intellectuals in the anarchist
socialist movement. His political writings about the media and political
injustice have profoundly influenced many.

Chomsky is among the most quoted authors in the world (among
the top ten and the only living person on the list). He continues his publishing about linguistics and politics to this day from his office at MIT.

For more information on the life of Noam Chomsky, read Robert
Barsky's (1997) *Noam Chomsky: A Life of Dissent*.

3.   SYNTAX AS SCIENCE – THE SCIENTIFIC METHOD

To many people the study of language properly belongs in the domain of the hu-
manities. That is, the study of language is all about the beauty of its usage in fine
(and not so fine) literature. However, there is no particular reason, other than our
biases, that the study of language should be confined to a humanistic approach. It is
also possible to approach the study of language from a scientific perspective; this is
the domain of linguistics. People who study literature often accuse linguists of abstracting away from the richness of good prose and obscuring the beauty of
language. Nothing could be further from the truth. Most linguists, including the present author, enjoy nothing more than reading a finely crafted piece of fiction, and
many linguists often study, as a sideline, the more humanistic aspects of language.
This doesn't mean, however, that one can't appreciate and study the formal properties (or rules) of language and do it from a scientific perspective. The two approaches
to language study are both valid, and neither takes away from the other.

Science is perhaps one of the most poorly defined words of the English language. We regularly talk of scientists as people who study bacteria, particle physics,
and the formation of chemical compounds, but ask your average Joe or Jill on the
street what science means, and you'll be hard pressed to get a decent definition. Science refers to a particular methodology for study: the scientific method. The
scientific method dates backs to the ancient Greeks, such as Aristotle, Euclid, and
Archimedes. The method involves observing some data, making some generalizations about patterns in the data, developing hypotheses that account for these
generalizations, and testing the hypotheses against more data. Finally, the hypotheses

are revised to account for any new data and then tested again. A flow chart showing the method is given in (1):

1)

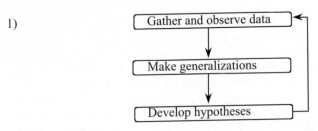

In syntax, we apply this methodology to sentence structure. Syntacticians start by observing data about the language they are studying, then they make generalizations about patterns in the data (e.g., in simple English declarative sentences, the subject precedes the verb). They then generate a hypothesis – preferably one that makes predictions – and test the hypothesis against more syntactic data, and if necessary go back and re-evaluate their hypotheses. The hypotheses are called **rules,** and the group of hypotheses that describe a language's syntax is called a **grammar**.

The term *grammar* strikes terror into the hearts of many people. But you should note that there are two ways to go about writing grammatical rules. One is to tell people how they should speak (this is of course the domain of English teachers and copy-editors); we call these kinds of rule **prescriptive rules** (as they prescribe how people should speak according to some standard). Some examples of prescriptive rules include "never end a sentence with a preposition," "use *whom* not *who*," "don't split infinitives." These rules tell us how we are supposed to use our language. The other approach is to write rules that describe how people *actually* speak, whether or not they are speaking "correctly." These are called **descriptive rules**. Consider for a moment the approach we're taking in this book; which of the two types (descriptive or prescriptive) is more scientific? Which kind of rule is more likely to give us insight into how the mind uses Language? For these reasons, we focus on descriptive rules. This doesn't mean that prescriptive rules aren't important (in fact, in the exercises section of this chapter you are asked to critically examine the question of descriptive vs. prescriptive rules), but for our purposes descriptive rules are more important. For an interesting discussion of the prescriptive/descriptive debate, see Pinker's 1995 book: *The Language Instinct*.

Let's turn now to a real world application of the scientific method to some language data. The following data concern the form of a specific kind of noun, called an **anaphor** (plural: **anaphors**, the phenomenon is called **anaphora**). These are the nouns that end with -*self* (e.g., *himself, herself, itself,* etc.). In chapter 4, we look at the distribution of anaphora in detail; here we'll only consider one superficial aspect of them. In the following sentences, as is standard in the syntactic literature, a sentence that isn't well-formed is marked with an **asterisk** (*) before it. For these sentences assume that *Bill* is male and *Sally* is female.

2)   a)   Bill kissed himself.
         b)   *Bill kissed herself.

c)   Sally kissed herself.
d)   *Sally kissed himself.

To the unskilled eye, the ill-formed sentences in (2b and d) just look silly. It is obvious that Bill can't kiss herself, because Bill is male. However, no matter how matter-
of-factly obvious this is, it is part of a bigger generalization about the distribution of
anaphors. In particular, the generalization we can draw about the sentences in (2) is
that an anaphor must agree in **gender** with the noun it refers to (its ***antecedent***). So in
(2a and b) we see that the anaphor must agree in gender with *Bill*, its antecedent. The
anaphor must take the masculine form *himself*. The situation in (2c and d) is the
same; the anaphor must take the form *herself* so that it agrees in gender with the
feminine *Sally*. A plausible hypothesis (or rule) given the data in (2), then, is stated
in (3):

3)   An anaphor must (i) have an antecedent and (ii) agree in gender with that
          antecedent.

The next step in the scientific method is to test this hypothesis against more data.
Consider the additional data in (4):

4)   a)   The robot kissed itself.
       b)   She knocked herself on the head with a zucchini.
       c)   *She knocked himself on the head with a zucchini.
       d)   The snake flattened itself against the rock.
       e)   ?The snake flattened himself/herself against the rock.
       f)   The Joneses think themselves the best family on the block.
       g)   *The Joneses think himself the most wealthy guy on the block.
       h)   Gary and Kevin ran themselves into exhaustion.
       i)   *Gary and Kevin ran himself into exhaustion.

Sentences (4a, b, and c) are all consistent with our hypothesis that anaphors must
agree in gender with their antecedents, which at least confirms that the hypothesis is
on the right track. What about the data in (4d and e)? It appears as if any gender is
compatible with the antecedent *the snake*. This appears, on the surface, to be a contradiction to our hypothesis. Think about these examples a little more closely,
however. Whether or not sentence (4e) is well-formed or not depends upon your assumptions about the gender of the snake. If you assume (or know) the snake to be
male, then *The snake flattened himself against the rock* is perfectly well-formed. But
under the same assumption, the sentence *The snake flattened herself against the rock*
seems very odd indeed, although it is fine if you assume the snake is female. So it
appears as if this example also meets the generalization in (3); the vagueness about
its well-formedness has to do with the fact that we are rarely sure what gender a
snake is and not with the actual structure of the sentence.
          Now, look at the sentences in (4f–i); note that the ill-formedness of (g) and
(i) is not predicted by our generalization. In fact, our generalization predicts that
sentence (4i) should be perfectly grammatical, since *himself* agrees in gender (mas-

culine) with its antecedents *Gary* and *Kevin*. Yet there is clearly something wrong with this sentence. The hypothesis needs revision. It appears as if the anaphor must agree in gender and **number** with the antecedent. Number refers to the quantity of individuals involved in the sentence; English primarily distinguishes singular number from plural number. (5) reflects our revised hypothesis.

5)   An anaphor must agree in gender and number with its antecedent.

If there is more than one person or object mentioned in the antecedent, then the anaphor must be plural (i.e., *themselves*).
        Testing this against more data, we can see that this partially makes the right predictions (6a), but it doesn't properly predict the grammaticality of sentences (6b–e):

6)   a)   People from Tucson think very highly of themselves.
        b)   *I gave yourself the bucket of ice cream.
        c)   I gave myself the bucket of ice cream.
        d)   *She hit myself with a hammer.
        e)   She hit herself with a hammer.

Even more revision is in order. The phenomenon seen in (6b–e) revolves around a grammatical distinction called **person**. Person refers to the perspective of the speaker with respect to the other participants in the speech act. First person refers to the speaker. Second person refers to the listener. Third person refers to people being discussed that aren't participating in the conversation. Here are the English pronouns associated with each person: (**Nominative** refers to the **case** form the pronouns take when in subject position like *I* in "*I* love peanut butter;" **accusative** refers to the form they take when in object positions like *me* in "John loves *me*." We will look at case in much more detail in chapter 9, so don't worry if you don't understand it right now.)

7)

	Nominative		Accusative		Anaphoric	
	Singular	Plural	Singular	Plural	Singular	Plural
1st	I	we	me	us	myself	ourselves
2nd	you	you	you	you	yourself	yourselves
3rd masc	he		him		himself	
3rd fem	she	they	her	them	herself	themselves
3rd neut	it		it		itself	

As you can see from this chart, the form of the anaphor seems also to agree in person with its antecedent. So once again we revise our hypothesis (rule):

8)   An anaphor must agree in person, gender and number with its antecedent.

With this hypothesis, we have a straightforward statement of the distribution of this noun type, derived using the scientific method. In the exercises section below, and in chapter 4, you'll have an opportunity to revise the rule in (8) with even more data.

Do Rules Really Exist?

Generative Grammar claims to be a theory of cognitive psychology, so the natural question to ask at this point is whether formal rules really exist in the brain/minds of speakers. After all, a brain is a mass of neurons firing away, how can formal mathematical rules exist up there? Remember, however, that we are attempting to *model* Language, we aren't trying to describe Language exactly. This question confuses two disciplines: psychology and neurology. Psychology is concerned with the mind, which represents the output and the abstract organization of the brain. Neurology is concerned with the actual firing of the neurons and the physiology of the brain. Generative grammar doesn't try to be a theory of neurology. Instead it is a model of the psychology of Language. Obviously, the rules don't exist, per se in our brains, but they do represent the external behavior of the mind. For more discussion of this issue, look at the readings in the further reading section of this chapter.

3.1   Sources of Data

If we are going to apply the scientific method to syntax, it is important to consider the sources of data. One obvious source is in collections of either spoken or written texts. Such data are called ***corpora*** (singular is ***corpus***). There are many corpora available, including some searchable through the World Wide Web. For languages without a literary tradition or ones spoken by a small minority, it is often necessary for the linguist to go and gather data and compile a corpus in the field. In the early part of this century, this was the primary occupation of linguists, and it is proudly carried on today by many researchers.

While corpora are unquestionably invaluable sources of data, they can only be a partial representation of what goes on in the mind. More particularly, corpora will only contain instances of grammatical (or more precisely well-formed) sentences (sentences that sound "OK" to a native speaker). You might think this would be enough for a linguist to do her job. But corpora are just not enough: there is no way of knowing whether a corpus has *all* possible forms of grammatical sentences. In fact, as we will see in the next chapter, due to the infinite and productive nature of language, a corpus could *never* contain all the grammatical forms of a language, nor could it even contain a representative sample. To really get at what we know about our languages (remember syntax is a cognitive science), we have to know what sentences are *not* well-formed. That is, in order to know the range of what are acceptable sentences of English, Italian or Igbo, we *first* have to know what are *not* acceptable sentences in English, Italian or Igbo. This kind of negative information is not available in corpora, which mostly provide grammatical, or well-formed, sentences.

Consider the following sentence:

9)   *Who do you wonder what bought?

For most speakers of English, this sentence borders on word salad – it is not a good sentence of English. How do you know that? Were you ever taught in school that you can't say sentences like (9)? Has anyone ever uttered this sentence in your presence before? I seriously doubt it. The fact that a sentence like (9) sounds weird, but similar sentences like (10a and b) *do* sound OK is not reflected anywhere in a corpus:

10)   a) Who do you think bought the bread machine?
        b) I wonder what Fiona bought.

Instead we have to rely on our knowledge of our native language (or on the knowledge of a native speaker consultant for languages that we don't speak natively). Notice that this is *not* conscious knowledge. I doubt there are many native speakers of English that could tell you why sentence (9) is terrible, but most can tell you that it is. This is subconscious knowledge. The trick is to get at and describe this subconscious knowledge.

The psychological experiment used to get this subconscious kind of knowledge is called the ***grammaticality judgment task***. The judgment task involves asking a native speaker to read a sentence, and judge whether it is well-formed (grammatical), marginally well-formed, or ill-formed (unacceptable or ungrammatical).

There are actually several different kinds of grammaticality judgments. Both of the following sentences are ill-formed for different reasons:

11)   a) #The toothbrush is pregnant.
        b) *Toothbrush the is blue.

Sentence (11a) sounds bizarre (cf. *the toothbrush is blue*) because we know that toothbrushes (except in the world of fantasy/science fiction) cannot be pregnant. The meaning of the sentence is strange, but the form is OK. We call this ***semantic ill-formedness*** and mark the sentence with a #. By contrast, we can glean the meaning of sentence (11b); it seems semantically reasonable (toothbrushes can be blue), but it is ill-formed from a structural point of view. That is, the determiner *the* is in the wrong place in the sentence. This is a ***syntactically ill-formed*** sentence. A native speaker of English will judge both these sentences as ill-formed, but for very different reasons. In this text, we will be concerned primarily with syntactic well-formedness.

Intuitions as Science?

Many linguists refer to the grammaticality judgment task as "drawing upon our native speaker intuitions." The word "intuition" here is slightly misleading. The last thing that pops into our heads when we hear the term "intuition" is science. Generative grammar has been severely criticized by many for relying on "unscientific" intuitions. But this is based primarily on a misunderstanding of the term. To the lay person, the term "intuition" brings to mind guesses and luck. This usage of the term is certainly standard. When a generative grammarian refers to 'intuition' however, she is using the term to mean "tapping into our subconscious knowledge." The term "intuition" may have been badly chosen, but in this circumstance it refers to a real psychological effect. Intuition (as a grammaticality judgment) has an entirely scientific basis. It is replicable under strictly controlled experimental conditions (these conditions are rarely applied, but the validity of the task is well established). Other disciplines also use intuitions or judgment tasks. For example, within the study of vision, it has been determined that people can accurately judge differences in light intensity, drawing upon their subconscious knowledge (Bard et al. 1996).

4.   WHERE DO THE RULES COME FROM?

In this chapter we've been talking about our subconscious knowledge of syntactic rules, but we haven't dealt with how we get this knowledge. This is sort of a side issue, but it may affect the shape of our theory. If we know how children acquire their rules, then we are in a better position for a proper formalization of them. The way by which children develop knowledge is an important question in cognitive science. The theory of generative grammar makes some very specific (and very surprising) claims about this.

4.1   Learning vs. Acquisition

One of the most common misconceptions about Language is the idea that children and adults "learn" languages. Recall that the basic kind of knowledge we are talking about here is subconscious knowledge. When producing a sentence you don't consciously think about where to put the subject, where to put the verb, etc. Your subconscious language faculty does that for you. Cognitive scientists make a distinction in how we get conscious and subconscious knowledge. Conscious knowledge (like the rules of algebra, syntactic theory, principles of organic chemistry, or how to take apart a carburetor) is *learned*. Subconscious knowledge, like how to speak or the ability to visually identify discrete objects, is *acquired*. In part, this explains why classes in the formal grammar of a foreign language often fail abysmally to train people to speak those languages. By contrast, being immersed in an environment where you can subconsciously acquire a language is much more effective. In this text we'll be primarily interested in how people acquire the rules of their language. Not all rules of grammar are acquired, however. Some facts about Language seem to be built into our brains, or *innate*.

4.2   Innateness: Language as an Instinct

If you think about the other types of knowledge that are subconscious, you'll see that many[2] of them (for example, the ability to walk) are built directly into our brains – they are instincts. No one had to teach you to walk (despite what your parents might think!). Kids start walking on their own. Walking is an instinct. Probably the most controversial claim of Noam Chomsky's is that Language is also an instinct. Many parts of Language are built in, or *innate*. Much of Language is an ability hard-wired into our brains by our genes.

Obviously, particular languages are not innate. It isn't the case that a child of Slovak parents growing up in North America who is never spoken to in Slovak, grows up speaking Slovak. They'll speak English (or whatever other language is spoken around them). So on the surface it seems crazy to claim that Language is an instinct. There are very good reasons to believe, however, that a human facility for Language (perhaps in the form of a "Language organ" in the brain) is innate. We call this facility **Universal Grammar** (or **UG**).

4.3   The Logical Problem of Language Acquisition

Before exploring the psychological arguments for UG, I want to show you that from a logical perspective, an infinitely productive system like the rules of Language *cannot* have been learned or acquired. Infinite systems are both unlearnable and unacquirable. Since we all have such an infinite system in our heads, and we can't have learned it, it must be the case that it is built in. The argument presented here is based on an unpublished paper by Alec Marantz.

Language is an infinitely productive system. That is, you can produce and understand sentences you have never heard before. For example, I can practically guarantee you have never heard the following sentence:

12)   The dancing chorus line of elephants broke my television set.

The magic of syntax is that it can generate forms that have never been produced before. Another example of the infinite quality lies in what is called **recursion**. It is possible to utter a sentence like (13):

---

[2] but not all!

13)   Rosie loves magazine ads.

It is also possible to put this sentence inside another sentence, like (14):

14)   I think [Rosie loves magazine ads].

Similarly you can put this larger sentence inside of another one:

15)   Drew believes [I think [Rosie loves magazine ads]].

and of course you can put this bigger sentence inside of another one:

16)   Dana doubts that [Drew believes [I think [Rosie loves magazine ads]]].

and so on, and so on ad infinitum. It is always possible to embed a sentence inside of a larger one. This means that Language is an infinite system. There are no limits on what we can talk about.

It turns out that rule-generated infinite systems like Language are not learn-able, as a simple fact of logic. Consider the following simplified situation:

Imagine that the task of a child is to determine the rules by which her lan-guage is constructed. Further, let's simplify the task, and say a child simply has to match up situations in the real world with utterances she hears.[3] So upon hearing the utterance *the cat spots the kissing fishes*, she identifies it with an appropriate situa-tion in the context around her (as represented by the picture).

17)   "the cat spots the kissing fishes" =

Her job, then, is to correctly match up the sentences with the situation.[4] More cru-cially she has to make sure that she does *not* match it up with all the other possible alternatives, such as the things going on around her (like her older brother kicking the furniture, or her mother making her breakfast, etc.). This matching of situations with expressions is a kind of mathematical relation (or function) that *maps* sentences

---

[3] The task is actually several magnitudes more difficult than this, as the child has to work out the phonology, etc., too, but for argument's sake, let's stick with this simplified example.
[4] Note that this is the job of the child who is using universal grammar, not the job of UG itself.

onto particular situations. Another way of putting it is that she has to figure out the rule(s) that decode(s) the meaning of the sentences. It turns out that this task is quite impossible.

Let's make this even more abstract to get at the mathematics of the situation. Assign each sentence some number. This number will represent the input to the rule. Similarly we will assign each situation a number. The function (or rule) modeling language acquisition maps from the set of sentence numbers to the set of situation numbers. Now let's assume that the child has the following set of inputs and correctly matched situations (perhaps explicitly pointed out to her by her parents). The x value represents the sentences she hears, the y the number correctly associated with the situation.

18)

Sentence (input)	*Situation* (output)
x	y
1	1
2	2
3	3
4	4
5	5

Given this input, what do you suppose that the output where $x=6$ will be?

6	?

Most people will jump to the conclusion that the output will be 6 as well. That is, they assume that the function (the rule) mapping between inputs and outputs is $x = y$. But in fact, in the hypothetical situation I envision here, the correct answer is situation number 126. The rule that generated the table in (18) is actually:

19) $[(x-5)*(x-4)*(x-3)*(x-2)*(x-1)]+x = y$

With this rule, all inputs equal to or less than 5 will give an output equal to the input, but for all inputs greater than 5, will give some large number.

When you hypothesized the rule was $x = y$, you didn't have all the crucial information; you only had part of the data. This seems to mean that if you hear only the first five pieces of data in our table then you won't get the rule, but if you learn the sixth you will figure it out. Is this necessarily the case? Unfortunately not: Even if you add a sixth line, you have no way of being sure that you have the right function until you have heard *all* the possible inputs. You have no way of knowing if you have heard all the relevant data (like the sixth input) until you have heard them all.

Now we know that Language is creative; almost every time you speak you generate a sentence that has never been uttered before. As discussed above there are an infinite number of possible sentences, thus an infinite number of inputs. If there are an infinite number of inputs it is *impossible* to hear them all in your lifetime (let alone in the four to six years that it takes you to master your native language). Infinite systems are unlearnable, because you never have enough input to be sure you have all the relevant facts. This is called *the logical problem of language acquisi-tion*.

Generative grammar gets around this logical puzzle by claiming that the child acquiring English, Irish, or Yoruba has some help: a flexible blueprint to use in constructing her knowledge of language called Universal Grammar. Universal Grammar restricts the number of possible functions that map between situations and utterances, thus making language learnable.

4.4   Other Arguments for UG

The evidence for UG doesn't rely on the logical problem alone, however. There are many other arguments that support the hypothesis that at least a certain amount of language is built in.

An argument that is directly related to the logical problem of language ac-quisition discussed above has to do with the fact that we know things about the grammar of our language that we couldn't possibly have learned. Start with the data in (20). A child might plausibly have heard sentences of these types:

20)   a)   Who do you think that Ciaran   will question first?
       b)   Who do you think   Ciaran   will question first?
       c)   Who do you think   will question Seamus first?

The child has to draw a hypothesis about the distribution of the word *that* in English sentences. One conclusion consistent with this observed data is that the word *that* in English is optional. You can either have it or not. Unfortunately this conclusion is not accurate. Consider the fourth sentence in the paradigm in (20). This sentence is the same as (20c) but with a *that*:

       d)   *Who do you think that   will question Seamus first?

It appears as if *that* is only optional when the question word (*who* in this case) starts in object position (as in 20a and b) It is obligatorily absent when the question word starts in subject position (as in 20c and d) (don't worry about the details of this gen-eralization, we'll return to it in chapter 11). What is important to note is that *no one* has ever taught you that (20d) is ungrammatical. Nor could you have come to that conclusion on the basis of the data you've heard. The logical hypothesis on the basis of the data in (20a–c) predicts sentence (20d) to be grammatical. There is nothing in the input a child hears that would lead them to the conclusion that (20d) is ungram-matical, yet every English-speaking child knows it is. One solution to this conundrum is that we are born with the knowledge that sentences like (20d) are ungrammatical.[5] This kind of argument is often called the **underdetermination of the data** argument for UG.

Most parents raising a toddler will swear up and down that they are teaching their children to speak; that they actively engage in instructing their child in the proper form of the language. That overt instruction by parents plays any role in language development is easily falsified. The evidence from the experimental language acquisition literature is very clear: parents, despite their best intentions, do not, for the most part, correct ungrammatical utterances by their children. More generally, they correct the content rather than the form of their child's utterance (see for example the extensive discussion in Holzman 1997).

21)   (from Marcus et al. 1992)
        Adult: Where is that big piece of paper I gave you yesterday?
        Child: Remember? I writed on it.
        Adult: Oh that's right, don't you have any paper down here, buddy?

When a parent does try to correct a child's sentence structure, it is more often than not ignored by the child:

22)   (from Pinker 1995: 281 – attributed to Martin Braine)
        Child: Want other one spoon, Daddy
        Adult: You mean, you want the other spoon.
        Child: Yes, I want other one spoon, please Daddy.
        Adult: Can you say "the other spoon"?
        Child: Other ... one ... spoon
        Adult: Say "other".
        Child: other
        Adult: "spoon"
        Child: spoon
        Adult: "other ... spoon"
        Child: other ... spoon. Now give me other one spoon.

This humorous example is typical of parental attempts to "instruct" their children in language. When they do occur, they fail. However, children still acquire language in the face of a complete lack of instruction. Perhaps one of the most convincing

---

[5] The data in example (20) is a particularly interesting case. This phenomenon is sometimes called the **that-*trace* effect** (for reasons that need not concern us here) and we'll discuss it some more in chapter 11. There is no disputing the fact that this phenomenon is not learnable. However, it is also a fact that it is not a universal property of all languages. For example, French and Irish don't seem to have the *that*-trace effect. Here is a challenge for those of you who like to do logic puzzles: If the *that*-trace effect is not learnable and thus must be biologically built in, how is it possible for a speaker of French or Irish to violate it? Think carefully about what kind of input a child might have to have in order to learn an "exception" to a built-in principle. This is a hard problem, but there is a solution. It may become clearer below when we discuss parameters.

explanations for this is UG. In the problem set part of this textbook, you are asked to consider other possible explanations and evaluate which are the most convincing.

There are also typological arguments for the existence of an innate language faculty. All the languages of the world share certain properties (for example they *all* have subjects and predicates – other examples will be seen throughout the rest of this book). These properties are called **universals** of Language. If we assume UG, then the explanation for these language universals is straightforward – they exist because all speakers of human languages share the same basic innate materials for building their language's grammar. In addition to sharing many similar characteristics, recent research into Language acquisition has begun to show that there is a certain amount of consistency cross-linguistically in the way children acquire Language. For example, children seem to go through the same stages and make the same kinds of mistakes when acquiring their language, no matter what their cultural background.

Finally, there are a number of biological arguments in favor of UG. As noted above, Language seems to be both human-specific and pervasive across the species. All humans, unless they have some kind of physical impairment, seem to have Language as we know it. This points towards it being a genetically endowed instinct. Additionally, research from neurolinguistics seems to point towards certain parts of the brain being linked to specific linguistic functions.

4.5   Explaining Language Variation

The evidence for UG seems to be overwhelming. However, we are still left with the annoying problem that languages differ from one another. This problem is what makes the study of linguistics so interesting. It is also not an unsolvable one. One way in which languages differ is in terms of the words used in the language. These clearly have to be learned or memorized. Other differences between languages (such as the fact that basic English word order is subject-verb-object (SVO), but the order of an Irish sentence is verb-subject-object (VSO) and the order of a Turkish sentence is subject-object-verb (SOV)) must also be acquired. The explanation for this kind of fact will be explored in chapter 5. Foreshadowing slightly, we'll claim there that differences in the grammars of languages can be boiled down to the setting of certain innate **parameters** (or switches) that select among possible variants. Language variation thus reduces to learning the correct set of words and selecting from a predetermined set of options.

Oversimplifying slightly, most languages put the order of elements in a sentence in one of the following word orders:

23)   a)   Subject Verb Object (SVO)   (e.g., English)
        b)   Subject Object Verb (SOV)   (e.g., Turkish)
        c)   Verb Subject Object (VSO)   (e.g., Irish)

A few languages use:

        d)   Verb Object Subject (VOS)   (e.g., Malagasy)

No (or almost no)[6] languages use

e) Object Subject Verb (OSV)
f) Object Verb Subject (OVS)

Let us imagine that part of UG is a parameter that determines the basic word order. Four of the options (SVO, SOV, VSO, and VOS) are innately available as possible settings. Two of the possible word orders are not part of UG. The child who is acquiring English is innately biased towards one of the common orders, when she hears a sentence like "Mommy loves Kirsten," if the child knows the meaning of each of the words, then she might hypothesize two possible word orders for English: SVO and OVS. None of the others are consistent with the data. The child thus rejects all the other hypotheses. OVS is not allowed, since it isn't one of the innately available forms. This leaves SVO, which is the correct order for English. So children acquiring English will choose to set the word order parameter at the innately available SVO setting.

5.   CHOOSING AMONG THEORIES ABOUT SYNTAX

There is one last preliminary we have to touch on before actually doing syntax. In this book we are going to posit many hypotheses. Some of these we'll keep, others we'll revise, and still others we'll reject. How do we know what is a good hypothesis and what is a bad? Chomsky (1965) proposed that we can evaluate how good theories of syntax are, using what are called the *levels of adequacy*. Chomsky claimed that there are three stages that a grammar (the collection of descriptive rules that constitute your theory) can attain in terms of adequacy.

If your theory only accounts for the data in a corpus (say a series of printed texts) and nothing more it is said to be an *observationally adequate grammar*: Needless to say, this isn't much use if we are trying to account for the cognition of Language. As we discussed above, it doesn't tell us the whole picture. We also need to know what kinds of sentences are unacceptable, or ill-formed. A theory that accounts for both corpora and native speaker intuitions about well-formedness is called a *descriptively adequate grammar*: On the surface this may seem to be all we need. Chomsky, however, has claimed that we can go one step better. He points out that a theory that also accounts for how children acquire their language is the best. He calls this an *explanatorily adequate grammar*. The simple theory of parameters might get this label. Generative grammar strives towards explanatorily adequate grammars.

---

[6] This is a matter of some debate. Derbyshire (1985) has claimed that the language Hixkaryana has object initial order.

6.   SUMMARY

In this chapter, we've done very little syntax but talked a lot about the assumptions underlying the approach we're going to take to the study of sentence structure. The basic approach to syntax that we'll be using here is generative grammar; we've seen that this approach is scientific in that it uses the scientific method. It is descriptive and rule based. Further, it assumes that a certain amount of grammar is built in and the rest is acquired.

IDEAS, RULES, AND CONSTRAINTS INTRODUCED IN THIS CHAPTER

i)   ***Syntax***
      The level of linguistic organization that mediates between sounds and meaning, where words are organized into phrases and sentences.

ii)   ***Language*** *(capital L)*
      The psychological ability of humans to produce and understand a particular language. Also called the ***Human Language Capacity***. This is the object of study in this book.

iii) ***language*** *(lower-case l)*
      A language like English or French. These are the particular instances of the human Language. The data source we use to examine Language is language.

iv)   ***Generative Grammar***
      A theory of linguistics in which grammar is viewed as a cognitive faculty. Language is generated by a set of rules or procedures. The version of generative grammar we are looking at here is primarily the ***Principles and Parameters approach*** (P&P) touching occasionally on ***Minimalism***.

v)   ***The Scientific Method***
      Observe some data, make generalizations about that data, draw a hypothesis, test the hypothesis against more data.

vi)   ***Grammar***
      Not what you learned in school. This is the set of rules that generate a language.

vii) ***Prescriptive Grammar***
      The grammar rules as taught by so called "language experts." These rules, often inaccurate descriptively, prescribe how people should talk/write, rather than describe what they actually do.

viii)   ***Descriptive Grammar***
        A scientific grammar that describes, rather than prescribes, how people talk/write.

ix)   ***Anaphor***
        A word that ends in *-self* or *-selves* (a better definition will be given in chapter 4).

x)   ***Gender (Grammatical)***
        Masculine vs. Feminine vs. Neuter. Does not have to be identical to the actual sex of the referent. For example, a dog might be female, but we can refer to it with the neuter pronoun *it*. Similarly, boats don't have a sex, but are grammatically feminine.

xi)   ***Antecedent***
        The noun an anaphor refers to.

xii)   ***Asterisk***
        * used to mark syntactically ill-formed (unacceptable or ungrammatical) sentences. The hash mark, pound, or number sign (#) is used to mark semantically strange, but syntactically well-formed, sentences.

xiii)   ***Number***
        The quantity of individuals or things described by a noun. English distinguishes singular (e.g., *a cat*) from plural (e.g., *the cats*). Other languages have more or less complicated number systems.

xiv)   ***Person***
        The perspective of the participants in the conversation. The speaker or speakers (*I, me, we, us*) are called first person. The listener(s) (*you*), are called the second person. Anyone else (those not involved in the conversation) (*he, him, she, her, it, they, them*), are called the third person.

xv)   ***Case***
        The form a noun takes depending upon its position in the sentence. We discuss this more in chapter 9.

xvi)   ***Nominative***
        The form of a noun in subject position (*I, you, he, she, it, we, they*).

xvii)   ***Accusative***
        The form of a noun in object position (*me, you, him, her, it, us, them*).

xviii) ***Corpus (pl. Corpora)***
        A collection of real-world language data.

xix)   ***Native Speaker Judgments (intuitions)***
        Information about the subconscious knowledge of a language. This information is tapped by means of the grammaticality judgment task.

xx)   ***Semantic Judgment***
        A judgment about the meaning of a sentence, often relying on our knowledge of the real world.

xxi)   ***Syntactic Judgment***
        A judgment about the form or structure of a sentence.

xxii)   ***Learning***
        The gathering of conscious knowledge (like linguistics or chemistry).

xxiii) ***Acquisition***
        The gathering of subconscious information (like language).

xxiv)   ***Recursion***
        The ability to embed structures iteratively inside one another. Allows us to produce sentences we've never heard before.

xxv)   ***Observationally Adequate Grammar***
        A grammar that accounts for observed real-world data (like corpora).

xxvi)   ***Descriptively Adequate Grammar***
        A grammar that accounts for observed real-world data and native speaker judgments.

xxvii) ***Explanatorily Adequate Grammar***
        A grammar that accounts for observed real-world data and native speaker intuitions and offers an explanation for the facts of language acquisition.

xxviii) ***Innate***
        Hard-wired or built in, an instinct.

xxix)   ***Universal Grammar (UG)***
        The innate (or instinctual) part of each language's grammar.

xxx)   ***The Logical Problem of Language Acquisition***
        The proof that an infinite system like human language cannot be learned on the basis of observed data – an argument for UG.

xxxi)   ***Underdetermination of the Data***
        The idea that we know things about our language that we could not have possibly learned – an argument for UG.

xxxii) ***Universal***
A property found in all the languages of the world.

FURTHER READING

Pinker, Steven (1995) *The Language Instinct*. New York: Harper Perennial.
[This book was a New York Times best-seller. It offers a very down to earth and readable survey of the Chomskyan approach to linguistics, and touches on, among other things, issues in language acquisition and prescriptivism.]

Sampson, Geoffrey (1997) *Educating Eve: The Language Instinct Debate*. London: Cassell.
[This book is a response to Pinker's The Language Instinct. It offers an anti-innatist perspective. Novice readers should be warned that many of the arguments, while on the surface seeming reasonable, don't always stand up to careful scrutiny.]

Chomsky, Noam (1965) *Aspects of the Theory of Syntax*. Cambridge: MIT Press.
[This book contains many of the original arguments for innateness. It also discusses at length the philosophical perspective taken by generative grammar.]

Barsky, Robert (1997) *Noam Chomsky: A Life of Dissent*. Cambridge: MIT Press.
[This is a fine biography of Noam Chomsky. It focuses primarily on his background and political work rather than on his linguistics, but has some nice descriptions of his intellectual development and can give some insight into the origins of generative grammar.]

Jackendoff, Ray (1993) *Patterns in the Mind*. London: Harvester-Wheatsheaf.
[This is a very accessible introduction to Cognitive Science.]

Uriagereka, Juan (1998) *Rhyme and Reason: An Introduction to Minimalist Syntax*. Cambridge: MIT press.
[The first chapter of this book provides an interesting expansion of many of the ideas expressed in this chapter. Warning to the novice: it is written in the form of a dialog between a linguist and another scientist. It is not the book to start your study of syntax with.]

PROBLEM SETS

1.   INTUITIONS

All of the following sentences have been claimed to be ungrammatical or un-acceptable by someone at some time. For each sentence, indicate whether this unacceptability is

i)   a prescriptive or a descriptive judgment, and
ii)   for all descriptive judgments indicate whether the ungrammaticality has to do with syntax or semantics.

One- or two-word answers are appropriate. If you are not a native speaker of English, enlist the help of someone who is. If you are not familiar with the *prescriptive* rules of English grammar, you may want to consult a writing guide or English grammar or look at Pinker's *The Language Instinct*.

a)   Who did you see in Las Vegas?
b)   You are taller than me.
c)   My red is refrigerator.
d)   Who do you think that saw Bill?
e)   Hopefully, we'll make it through the winter without needing the snow-blower.
f)   My friends wanted to quickly leave the party.
g)   Bunnies carrots eat.
h)   John's sister is not his sibling.

2.   INNATENESS

Above, we argued that some amount of syntax is innate (inborn). Can you think of an argument that might be raised against innateness? (It doesn't have to be an argument that works, just a plausible one.) Alternately, could you come up with a hypothetical experiment that could disprove innateness? What would such an experiment have to show? Remember that cross-linguistic variation (differences between languages) is *not* an argument against innateness or UG, because UG contains parameters that allow minute variations.

3.   PRESCRIPTIVE RULES

In the text above, we argued that descriptive rules are the primary focus of syntactic theory. This doesn't mean that prescriptive rules don't have their uses. What are these uses? Why do we maintain prescriptive rules in our society?

4.   UNIVERSALS

Pretend for a moment that you don't believe Chomsky and that you don't believe in the innateness of syntax (but only *pretend*!). How might you account for the existence of universals (see definition above) across languages?

5.   LEARNING VS. ACQUISITION

We have distinguished between learning and acquiring knowledge. Learning is conscious, acquisition is automatic and subconscious. (Note that acquired things are *not* necessarily innate. They are just subconsciously obtained.) Other than language are there other things we acquire? What other things do we learn? What about walking? or reading? or sexual identity? An important point in answering this question is to talk about what kind of evidence is necessary to distinguish between learning and acquisition.

6.   LEVELS OF ADEQUACY

Below, you'll find the description of several different linguists' work. Attribute a level of adequacy to them (state whether the grammars they developed are observationally adequate, descriptively adequate, or explanatorily adequate. Explain *why* you assigned the level of adequacy that you did.

a) Juan Martínez has been working with speakers of Chicano English in the barrios of Los Angeles. He has been looking both at corpora (rap music, recorded snatches of speech) and working with adult native speakers.

b) Fredrike Schwarz has been looking at the structure of sentences in eleventh-century Welsh poems. She has been working at the national archives of Wales in Cardiff.

c) Boris Dimitrov has been working with adults and corpora on the formation of questions in Rhodopian Bulgarian. He is also con-

ducting a longitudinal study of some two-year-old children learning the language to test his hypotheses.

7.   ANAPHORA

In this chapter, as an example of the scientific method, we looked at the distribution of anaphora (nouns like *himself*, *herself*, etc.). We came to the
following conclusion about their distribution:

> An anaphor must agree in person, gender, and number with its antece-
> dent.

However, there is much more to say about the distribution of these nouns (in
fact, chapter 4 of this book is entirely devoted to the question).

Part 1: Consider the data below. Can you make an addition to the above
statement that explains the distribution of anaphors and antecedents in the
very limited data below?

a)   Geordi sang to himself.
b)   *Himself sang to Geordi.
c)   Betsy loves herself in blue leather.
d)   *Blue leather shows herself that Betsy is pretty.

Part 2: Now consider the following sentences:[7]

e)   Everyone should be able to defend himself/herself/themselves.
f)   I hope nobody will hurt themselves/himself/?herself.

Do these sentences obey your revised generalization? Why or why not? Is
there something special about the antecedents that forces an exception here,
or can you modify your generalization to fit these cases?

---

[7] Thanks to Ahmad Lotfi for suggesting this part of the question.

chapter 2

Fundamentals: Rules, Trees, and Parts of Speech

0.   INTRODUCTION

This book is all about the study of sentence *structure*. So let's start by defining what we mean by "structure." Consider the sentence in (1):

1)   The students loved their syntax assignments.

One way to describe this sentence is as a simple linear string of words. Certainly this is how it is represented on the page. We could describe the sentence as consisting of the words *the, students, loved, their, syntax, assignments* in that order. As you can probably figure out, if that were all there was to syntax, you could put down this book here and not bother with the next thirteen chapters. But that isn't all there is to syntax. The statement that sentence (1) consists of a linear string of words misses several important generalizations about the internal structure of sentences and how these structures are represented in our minds. In point of fact we are going to claim that the words in sentence (1) are grouped into units (called constituents) and that these constituents are grouped into larger constituents, and so on until you get a sentence. Needless to say, however, before we can look at these phrases, we have to briefly look at the kinds of words that compose them. This is the topic of section 1 below.

1.   PARTS OF SPEECH

Many of us learned in school that words are grouped into categories like nouns, verbs, adjectives, etc. There is actually a good solid scientific basis for this categorization. Ideally, we want to be able to talk about what kinds of words appear in different positions in a sentence. We can only do this if we have ways of talking about what the "kinds of words" are. For this, we are going to borrow a set of names from traditional grammars. These are the **parts of speech** (also called **syntactic categories**). The most important of these are the **noun, verb, preposition,** and **adverb/adjective**.

Consider the sentences in (2). Notice that we can substitute various words that are of the type *noun* for the second word in the sentence:

2)   a)   The *man* loved peanut butter cookies.
        b)   The *puppy* loved peanut butter cookies.
        c)   The *king* loved peanut butter cookies.

but we cannot substitute words that aren't nouns:[1]

3)   a)   *The *green* loved peanut butter cookies.
        b)   *The *in* loved peanut butter cookies.
        c)   *The *sing* loved peanut butter cookies.

The same holds true for larger groups of words (the square brackets [...] mark off the relevant groups of words).

4)   a)   *[John]* went to the store.
        b)   *[The man]* went to the store.
        c)   *[Quickly walks]* went to the store.

5)   a)   *[Norvel]* kissed the blarney stone.
        b)   *[To the washroom]* kissed the blarney stone.

If we have categories for words that can appear in certain positions and categories for those that don't we can make generalizations (scientific ones) about the behavior of different word types. This is why we need parts of speech.

If you were taught any formal grammar in school, you may have been told that a noun is a "person, place, or thing," or that a verb is "an action, state, or state of being." Alas, this is a very over-simplistic way to characterize various parts of speech. It also isn't terribly scientific or accurate. The first thing to notice about definitions like this is that they are based on semantic criteria. It doesn't take much effort to find counterexamples to these semantic definitions. One generalization that

---

[1] Remember, the * symbol means that a sentence is syntactically ill-formed.

we can make is that nouns are the typical subject of sentences. Nouns also often follow words like "the," so in the following sentence *man* is a noun:

6)   The *man* danced a lively jig.

Consider now the following:

7)   The *destruction* of the city bothered the Mongols.

The meaning of *destruction* is *not* a "person, place, or thing." It is an action. By semantic criteria, this word should be a verb. But in fact, it is clearly a noun. It is the subject of the sentence and it follows the word *the*. Similar cases are seen in (8):

8)   a)   *Sincerity* is an important quality.
         b)   The *assassination* of the president.
         c)   *Tucson* is a great place to live.

Sincerity is an attribute, a property normally associated with adjectives. Yet in (8a), *sincerity* is a noun. Similarly in (8b) *assassination*, an action, is functioning as a noun. (8c) is a little more subtle. The semantic property of identifying a location is usually attributed to a preposition; in (8c) however, the noun *Tucson*, refers to a location, but isn't itself a preposition. It thus seems difficult (if not impossible) to rigorously define the parts of speech based solely on semantic criteria. This is made even clearer when we see that a word can change its part of speech depending upon where it appears in a sentence:

9)   a)   Gabrielle's *father* is an axe-murderer.   (N)
         b)   Anteaters *father* attractive offspring.   (V)
         c)   ?Wendy's *father* country is Iceland.   (A)

The situation gets even worse when we consider languages other than English. Consider the following data from Warlpiri:

10)   Wita-ngku   ka   maliki wajilipinyi.
         small-SUBJ   AUX dog   chase.PRES
         "The small (one) is chasing the dog."

In this sentence, we have a thing we'd normally call an adjective (the word *wita* 'small') functioning like a noun (e.g., taking subject marking). Is this a noun or an adjective?
        Perhaps the most striking evidence that we can't use semantic definitions for parts of speech comes from the fact that you can know the part of speech of a word without even knowing what it means:

11)   The yinkish dripner blorked quastofically into the nindin with the pidibs.

Every native speaker of English will tell you that *yinkish* is an adjective, *dripner* a noun, *blorked* a verb, *quastofically* an adverb, and *nindin* and *pidibs* both nouns, but they'd be very hard pressed to tell you what these words actually mean. How then can you know the part of speech of a word without knowing its meaning? The answer is simple: The definitions for the various parts of speech are not semantically defined. Instead they depend on where the words appear in the sentence and what kinds of suffixes they take. Nouns are things that that appear in "noun positions" and take "noun affixes" (endings). The same is true for verbs, adjectives, etc. Here are the criteria that we used to determine the parts of speech in sentence (11):

12)   a)   yinkish   between *the* and a noun
                                takes -*ish* adjective ending
       b)   dripner   after an adjective (and *the*)
                                takes -*er* noun ending
                                subject of the sentence
       c)   blorked   after subject noun
                                takes -*ed* verb ending
       d)   quastofically   after a verb
                                takes -*ly* adverb ending
       e)   nindin   after *the* and after a preposition
       f)   pidibs   after *the* and after a preposition
                                takes -*s* noun plural ending

The part of speech of a word is determined by its place in the sentence and by its morphology, *not* by its meaning. In the appendix to this chapter, there is a list of rules and distributional criteria that you can use to determine the part of speech of a word.

2.   STRUCTURE

Look again at the sentence we have in (1) (repeated here as (13)):

13)   The students loved their syntax assignments.

Notice that on a purely intuitive level there is some notion that certain words are more closely related to one another. For example, the word *the* seems to be tied more to the meaning of *students* than it is to *loved* or *syntax*. A related intuition can be seen by looking at the sentences in (14).

14)   a)   The students loved their phonology readings.
       b)   The students hated their morphology professor.

Compare these sentences to the ones in (13). You'll see right away that the relationship between *the students* and *their syntax assignments* in (13) and *the students* and *their phonology readings* in (14a) is the same. Similarly, the relation between *the students* and *their morphology professor* in (14b), while of a different kind (hating instead of loving), is of a similar type: There is one group (*the students*) who are either hating or loving another entity (*their syntax assignments* or *their morphology professor*). In order to capture these intuitions (the intuition that certain words are more closely connected than others, and the intuitions about relationships between words in the sentence), we need a more complex notion. The notions we use to capture these intuitions are **constituency** and **hierarchical structure**. The notion that *the* and *students* are closely related to one another is captured by the fact that we treat them as part of a bigger unit that contains them, but not other words. We have two different ways to represent this bigger unit. One of them is to put square brackets around units:

15)   [the students]

The other is to represent the units with a group of lines called a tree structure:

16)
        the students

These bigger units are called constituents. A definition for a constituent is given in (17):

17)   *Constituent*
        A group of words that functions together as a unit.

The Psychological Reality of Constituency

In the 1960s, Merrill Garrett and his colleagues showed that constituency has some reality in the minds of speakers. The researchers developed a series of experiments that involved placing a click in a neutral place in the stream of sounds. People tend to perceive these clicks not in the place where they actually occur, but at the edges of constituents. The italicized strings of words in the following sentences differ only in how the constituents are arranged.

i)   [In her *hope of marrying*] *An/na was impractical.*
                                 ↑

ii)   [Harry's *hope of marrying An/na*] *was impractical.*
                                      ↑

Syntactic constituency is marked with square brackets [ ]; the placement of the click is marked with a slash /. People perceive the click in different places (marked with a ↑) in the two sentences, corresponding to the constituent boundaries – even though the click actually appears in the same place in each sentence (in the middle of the word *Anna*).

Constituency is the most important and basic notion in syntactic theory. Constituents form the backbone of the rest of this book. They capture the intuitions mentioned above. The "relatedness" is captured by membership in a constituent. As we will see it also allows us to capture the relationships between constituents exemplified to in (14).

Constituents don't float out in space. Instead they are embedded one inside another to form larger and larger constituents. This is *hierarchical structure.* Foreshadowing the discussion below a bit, here is the structure we'll develop for a sentence like (13):

18)

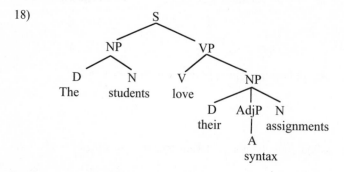

This is a typical hierarchical tree structure. The sentence constituent (represented by the symbol S) consists of two constituents: a subject *noun phrase* (NP) *[the students]* and a predicate or *verb phrase* (VP) *[love their syntax assignments].* The subject NP in turn contains a *noun* (N) *students* and a *determiner* (or article) (D) *the.* Similarly the VP contains a *verb* (V), and an object NP *[their syntax assignments].* The object NP is further broken down into three bits: a determiner *their*, an adjective *syntax*, and a noun *assignments*. As you can see this tree has constituents (each represented by the point where lines come together) which are inside other constituents. This is hierarchical structure. Hierarchical constituent structure can also be represented with brackets. Each pair of brackets ([ ]) represents a constituent. We normally put the label of the constituent on the left member of the pair. The bracketed diagram for (13) is given in (19):

19) [s[np[pThe] [nstudents]] [vp[vloved] [np[ptheir] [ap[asyntax]] [n assignments]]]].

As you can see, bracketed diagrams are much harder to read, so for the most part we will use tree diagrams in this book. However, sometimes bracketed diagrams have their uses, so you should be able to translate back and forth between trees and bracketed diagrams.

Constituents, Phrases, Clauses, Sentences

Many students have trouble distinguishing phrases from clauses or constituents. A **constituent** is any group of words (or even a single word) that functions as a unit. Phrases and clauses are types of constituents. **Phrases** are generally constituents that are built up around a particular word. For example, a noun phrase consists of a noun and all the words that modify it. We'll look at **clauses** in more detail in chapter 6, but they are roughly constituents equivalent to simple sentences – that is, a subject and a predicate.

---

3.   RULES AND TREES

Now we have the tools necessary to develop a simple theory of sentence structure. We have a notion of constituent, which is a group of words that functions as a unit, and we have labels (parts of speech) that we can use to describe the parts of those units. Let's put the two of these together and try to develop a description of a possible English sentence. In generative grammar, generalizations about structure are represented by rules. These rules are said to "generate" the tree in the mind. So if we draw a tree a particular way, we need a rule to generate that tree. The rules we are going to consider in this chapter are called *phrase structure rules* (PSRs) because they generate the phrase structure tree of a sentence.

3.1   Noun Phrases (NPs)

Let's start with the constituents we call noun phrases (or NPs) and explore the range of material that can appear in them. The simplest NPs contain only a noun (usually a proper noun or a plural noun):

20)   a)   John   b)   people

Our rule must minimally generate NPs then that contain only a N. The format for PSRs is shown in (21a), we use X, Y, and Z here as variables to stand for any category. (21b) shows our first pass at an NP rule:

21)   a)   XP   →   X Y Z
                  ↑   ↑   ↑
            the label   "consists of"   the elements that make up
            for the constituent   the constituent

        b)   NP → N

This rule says that an NP is composed of (written as →) an N. This rule would generate a tree like (22):

22)   NP
         |
         N

There are many NPs that are more complex than this of course:

23)   a)   the box
         b)   his binder
         c)   that pink fluffy cushion

Words like *the*, *his*, and *that* are called determiners (also known as articles). We abbreviate determiner as D. We must revise our rule to account for the presence of determiners:

24)   a)   NP → D N

This generates a tree like:

b)   NP
       /   \
      D   N
     the   box

Compare the NPs in (20) and (23): You'll see that determiners are optional. As such we must indicate their optionality in the rule. We do this with parentheses ( ) around the optional elements:

25)   NP → (D) N

Nouns can also be optionally modified by adjectives, so we will need to revise our rule as in (26).

26)   a)   the big box   b)   his yellow binder

27)   NP → (D) (A) N

Nouns can also take prepositional phrase (PP) modifiers (see below where we discuss the structure of these constituents), so once again we'll have to revise our rule:

28)   a)   the big box of crayons
         b)   his yellow binder with the red stripe

29)   NP → (D) (A) N (PP)

For concreteness, let's apply the rule in (29):

30)

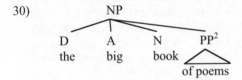

The NP constituent in (30) consists of four subconstituents: the D, A, N and PP.

     We need to make one more major revision to our NP rule. It turns out that you can have more than one adjective and more than one PP in an English NP:

31)   The [A big] [A yellow] box [PP of cookies] [PP with the pink lid].

In this NP, the noun *box* is modified by *big, yellow, of cookies*, and *with the pink lid*. The rule must be changed then to account for this. It must allow more than one adjective and more than one PP modifier. We indicate this with a +, which means "repeat this category as many times as needed":

32)   NP → (D) (A+) N (PP+)

We will have cause to slightly revise this rule in later sections of this chapter, and completely revise it in later chapters, but for now we can use this rule as a working hypothesis.

3.2   *Adjective Phrases and Adverb Phrases (APs)*

Consider the following two NPs:

33)   a)   the big yellow book
          b)   the very yellow book

On the surface, these two NPs look very similar. They both consist of a determiner, followed by two adjectives[3] and then a noun. But consider what modifies what in these NPs. In (33a) *big* modifies *book*, as does *yellow*. In (33b) on the other hand only *yellow* modifies book; *very* does not modify *book* (**very book*) – it modifies *yellow*. On an intuitive level then, the structures of these two phrases are actually quite different. (33a) has two adjective constituents that modify the N, whereas (33b) has only one *[very yellow]*. This constituent is called an adjective phrase (AP). The rule for the adjective phrase is given in (34a):

---

[2] We use a triangle here to obscure the details of the PP. Students should avoid using triangles when drawing trees, as you want to be as explicit as possible. I use it here only to draw attention to other aspects of the structure.
[3] Or if you prefer: in (33b) an adverb (*very*) followed by an adjective (*big*).

Adjectives and Adverbs: Part of the Same Category?
In much work on syntactic theory, there is no significant distinction made between adjectives and adverbs. This is because it isn't clear that they are really distinct categories. While it is true that adverbs take the *-ly* ending and many adjectives don't, there are other distributional criteria that suggest they might be the same category. They both can be modified by the word *very*, and they both have the same basic function in the grammar – to attribute properties to the items they modify. The issue is still up for debate. To remain agnostic about the whole thing, I use A for both adjectives and adverbs, with the caveat that this might be wrong. If you want to distinguish them, use Adj for adjectives and Adv to abbreviate for adverbs. If you do make a distinction between adjectives and adverbs, you will have to slightly modify the phrase structure rules I have given in the text. What would these rules look like?

34)   a)   AP → (AP) A

        b)
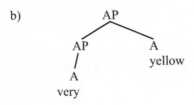

The existence of an AP category requires that we slightly modify our NP rule too:

35)   NP → (D) (AP+) N (PP+)

This will give us the following structures for the two NPs in (33):

36)   a)
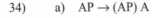

b)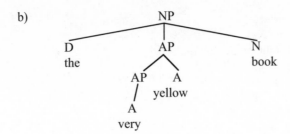

So despite their surface similarity, these two NPs have radically different structures. In (36a) the N is modified by two APs, in (36b) by only one. This leads us to an important observation about tree structures. This is the golden rule of tree structures:

37)   *The Golden Rule of Tree Structures*
        Modifiers are always attached within the phrase they modify.

The adjective *very* modifies *yellow*, so it is part of the *yellow* AP in (36b). In (36a) by contrast, *big* doesn't modify *yellow*, it modifies *book*, so it is attached directly to the NP containing *book*.
        We use the same category (A) and rule AP → (AP) A to account for adverbs:

38)   very quickly

39)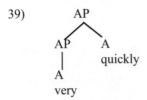

Here is a common mistake to avoid: Notice that the AP rule specifies that its modifier is another AP: AP → (AP) A. The rule does NOT say *AP → (A) A, so you will never get trees of the form shown in (40):

40)

3.3   *Prepositional Phrases (PPs)*

The next major kind of constituent we consider is the prepositional phrase (PP). Most PPs take the form of a preposition followed by an NP:

41)   a)   [_PP to [_NP the store]]
          b)   [_PP with [_NP an axe]]
          c)   [_PP behind [_NP the rubber tree]]

The PP rule appears to be:

42)   a)   PP → P NP

          b)   PP

                P   NP
              with   ◿◺
                    an axe

There might actually be some evidence for treating the NP in PPs as optional. There is a class of prepositions, traditionally called particles, that don't require a following NP:

43)   a)   I haven't seen him *before*.
          b)   I blew it *up*.
          c)   I threw the garbage *out*.

If these are prepositions, then it appears as if the NP in the PP rule is optional:

44)   a)   PP → P (NP)

Even though all these particles look similar to prepositions (or are at least homo-phonous with them), there is some debate about whether they are or not. As an exercise you might try to think about the kinds of phenomena that would distinguish particles from prepositions without NPs.

3.4   Verb Phrases (VPs)

The last major constituent type to consider is the verb phrase (VP). Minimally a VP consists of a single verb:

45)   VP → V
46)   Ignacious [_VP left].

Verbs may be modified by adverbs (APs), which are, of course, optional:

47)   Ignacious [_VP left quickly].
48)   VP → V (AP)

Interestingly, many of these adverbs can appear on either side of the V, and you can have as many APs as you like:

49)   Ignacious [$_{VP}$ quickly left].
50)   Ignacious [$_{VP}$ often left quickly].
51)   VP → (AP+) V (AP)

Verbs can also take an NP (called the direct object in traditional grammar):

52)   VP → (AP+) V (NP) (AP+)
53)   Bill [$_{VP}$ frequently kissed *his mother-in-law*].

They can also take multiple PPs:

54)   Bill [$_{VP}$frequently got his buckets [$_{PP}$ *from the store*] [$_{PP}$ *for a dollar*]].
55)   VP → (AP+) V (NP) (PP+) (AP+)

Let's draw the tree for the VP in (54), using the rule in (55):

56)

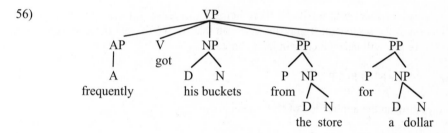

3.5   Clauses

Thus far, we have NPs, VPs, APs, and PPs, and we've seen how they can be hierarchically organized with respect to one another. One thing that we haven't accounted for is the structure of the sentence (or more accurately ***clause***).[4] A sentence consists of a subject NP and a VP:

57)   [$_S$[$_{NP}$ Bill] [$_{VP}$ frequently got his buckets from the store for a dollar]].

This can be represented by the rule in (58):

58)   S → NP VP

A tree for (57) is given in (59):

---

[4] We'll give a proper definition for clause in a later chapter.

59)

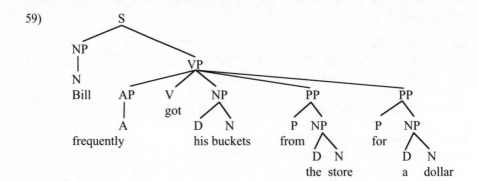

Clauses can also include other items, including modal verbs and auxiliary verbs like those in (60):

60)   a)   Cedric *might* crash the longboat.
       b)   Gustaf *has* crashed the semi-truck.

For lack of a better term, we'll call these items T (for tense, since they bear the tense inflection in the sentence). It may surprise you that we won't treat these as verbs, the reason for this will become clear in later chapters.

61)   S → NP (T) VP

A tree showing the application of this rule is given in (62):

62)

Clauses don't always have to stand on their own. There are times when clauses are embedded inside other clauses:

63)   [s Shawn said [s he decked the janitor]].

In sentence (63) the clause *he decked the janitor*, lies inside the larger main clause. Sometimes these clauses take a special introductory word, which we call a complementizer:

64)   [s Shawn said [s' [COMP that] [s he decked the janitor]]].

We need a special rule to introduce complementizers (C):

65)   S' → (C) S

For the moment we will assume that all embedded clauses are S', whether or not they have a complementizer. We'll show evidence for this in chapter 6.

Embedded clauses appear in a variety of positions. In (63), the embedded clause appears in essentially the same slot as the direct object. Embedded clauses can also appear in subject position:

66)   [s [s' That he decked the janitor] is obvious].

Because of this we are going to have to modify our S and VP rules to allow embedded clauses. Syntacticians use curly brackets { } to indicate a choice. In the following rules you are allowed *either* an NP or an S' but not both:

67)   S → {NP/S'} (T) VP
68)   VP → (AP+) V ({NP/S'}) (PP+) (AP+)

3.6   *Summary*

In this section we've been looking at the PSRs needed to generate trees that account for English sentences. As we'll see in later chapters, this is nothing but a first pass at a very complex set of data. It is probably worth repeating the final form of each of the rules here:

69)   a)   S' → (C) S
         b)   S → {NP/S'} (T) VP
         c)   VP → (AP+) V ({NP/S'}) (PP+) (AP+)
         d)   NP → (D) (AP+) N (PP+)
         e)   PP → P (NP)
         f)   AP → (AP) A

These rules account for a wide variety of English sentences. A sentence using each of these rules is shown in (70):

70)   The big man from NY has often said that he gave peanuts to elephants.

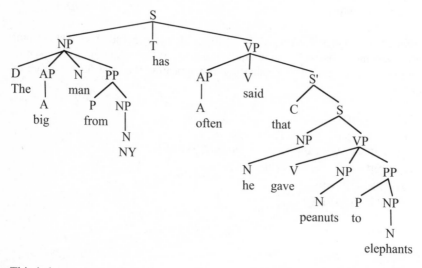

This is by no means the only tree that can be drawn by these rules. In fact, the possibilities are infinite.

4.   HOW TO DRAW A TREE

You now have the tools you need to start drawing trees. You have the rules, and you have the parts of speech. I suspect that you'll find drawing trees much more difficult than you expect. It takes a lot of practice to know which rules to apply and apply them consistently and accurately to a sentence. You won't be able to draw trees easily until you literally do dozens of them. Drawing syntactic trees is a learned skill that needs lots of practice, just like learning to play the piano.

There are actually two ways to go about drawing a tree. You can start at the bottom and work your way up to the S, or you can start with the S and work your way down. Which technique you use depends upon your individual style. For most people who are just starting out, starting at the bottom of the tree with the words works best. When you become more practiced and experienced you may find starting at the top quicker. Below, I give step-by-step instructions for both of these techniques

4.1   *Bottom-up Trees*

This method for tree drawing often works best for beginners. Here are some (hopefully helpful) steps to go through when drawing trees.

1   Write out the sentence and identify the parts of speech:

D   A   A   N   V   D   N
The very small boy kissed the platypus.

2   Identify what modifies what. Remember the golden rule of trees. If the word modifies something then it is contained in the same constituent as that thing.

Very modifies *small.*
Very small modifies *boy.*
The modifies *boy.*
The modifies *platypus.*
The platypus modifies *kissed.*

3   Start linking together items that modify one another. It often helps to start at the right edge. Always start with adjacent words. If the modifier is modifying a noun, then the rule you must apply is the NP rule:

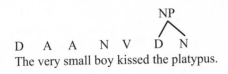

NP

D   A   A   N   V   D   N
The very small boy kissed the platypus.

Similarly if the word that is being modified is an adjective, then you must apply the AP rule:

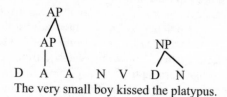
The very small boy kissed the platypus.

4   Make sure you apply the rule *exactly* as it is written. For example the AP rule reads AP → (AP) A. This means that in the tree above, both adjectives have to have an AP on top of them. It is tempting to draw a tree without the embedded AP. Remember that the rule that generates this (*AP → A A) is <u>not</u> one of our PSRs.

5   Keep applying the rules until you have attached all the modifiers to the modified constituents. Apply one rule at a time. Work from right to left (from the end of the sentence to the beginning.) Try doing the rules in the following order:

a)   the AP rule.
b)   NPs and PPs (you sometimes have to alternate between these).
c)   VPs.
d)   S.
e)   If your sentence has more than one clause in it, it is usually best to start with the one on the right edge of the sentence. *Unless* there is an embedded sentence in subject position, in which case you start with that one.

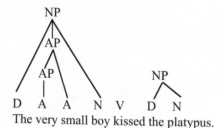
The very small boy kissed the platypus.

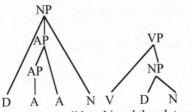

The very small boy kissed the platypus.

6   When you've built up the subject NP and the VP, apply the S (and S') rule:

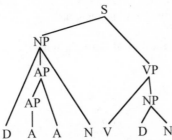

The very small boy kissed the platypus.

7   *This is the most important step of all*: Now go back and make sure that your tree is really generated by the rules. Check each level in the tree and make sure your rules will generate it. If they don't, apply the rule correctly and fix the structure.

8   Some important considerations:
    a)   Make sure that everything is attached to the tree.
    b)   Make sure that every category has only *one* line immediately on top of it (it can have more than one under it, but only one immediately on top of it).
    c)   Don't cross lines.
    d)   Make sure all branches in the tree have a part of speech label.
    e)   Avoid triangles.

Skill at tree drawing comes only with practice. At the end of this chapter are a number of sentences that you can practice on. Use the suggestions above if you find them helpful. Another helpful idea is to model your trees on ones that you can find in this chapter. Look carefully at them, and use them as a starting point. Finally, don't forget: Always check your trees against the rules that generate them.

4.2   *The Top-down Method of Drawing Trees*

Most professional syntacticians use a slightly quicker means of drawing trees. Once you are practiced at identifying tree structures, you will probably want to use this technique. But be warned, sometimes this technique can lead you astray if you are not careful.

1   This method starts out the same way as the other: write out the sentence and identify the parts of speech.

D   A   A   N   V   D   N
The very small boy kissed the platypus.

2   Next draw the S node at the top of the tree, with the subject NP and VP underneath:

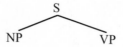

D   A   A   N   V   D   N
The very small boy kissed the platypus.

3   Using the NP rule, flesh out the subject NP. You will have to look ahead here. If there is a P, you will probably need a PP. Similarly, if there is an A, you'll need at least one AP, maybe more. Remember the golden rule: elements that modify one another are part of the same constituent.

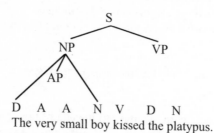

D   A   A   N   V   D   N
The very small boy kissed the platypus.

4   Fill in the APs and PPs as necessary. You may need to do other NPs inside
         PPs

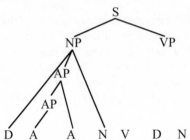

The very small boy kissed the platypus.

5   Next do constituents inside the VP, including object NPs, and any APs and
         PPs inside them.

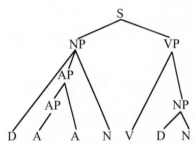

The very small boy kissed the platypus.

6   Again, the most important step is to go back and make sure that your tree
         obeys all the rules, as well as the golden rule of tree structures.

7   Some important considerations:
         a)   Make sure that everything is attached.
         b)   Make sure that every category has only *one* line immediately on top of
              it. (It can have more than one under it, but only one immediately on top
              of it.)
         c)   Don't cross lines.
         d)   Make sure all branches in the tree have a part of speech label.
         e)   Avoid triangles.

Again, I strongly recommend that you start your tree drawing using the bottom-up
method, but after some practice, you may find this latter method quicker.

4.3   *Bracketed Diagrams*

Sometimes it is preferable to use the bracketed notation instead of the tree notation. This is especially true when there are large parts of the sentence that are irrelevant to the discussion at hand. Drawing bracketed diagrams essentially follows the same principles for tree drawing (see 4.1 or 4.2 above). The exception is that instead of drawing to lines connecting at the top, you put square brackets on either side of the constituent. A label is usually put on the left member of the bracket pair as a subscript.

71)

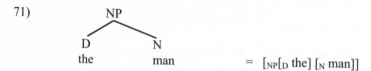

= [$_{NP}$[$_D$ the] [$_N$ man]]

Both words and phrases are bracketed this way. For each point where you have a bunch of lines connecting, you have a pair of brackets.

To see how this works, let's take our sentence from section 4.1 and 4.2 above and do it again in brackets:

1   First we mark the parts of speech. This time with labeled brackets:

[$_D$ The] [$_A$ very] [$_A$ small] [$_N$ boy] [$_V$ kissed] [$_D$ the] [$_N$ platypus].

2   Next we apply the AP rule, NP and PP rules:

AP:
[$_D$ The] [$_{AP}$[$_A$ very]] [$_A$ small] [$_N$ boy] [$_V$ kissed] [$_D$ the] [$_N$ platypus].
[$_D$ The] [$_{AP}$[$_{AP}$[$_A$ very]] [$_A$ small]] [$_N$ boy] [$_V$ kissed] [$_D$ the] [$_N$ platypus].

NP:
[$_{NP}$[$_D$ The]][$_{AP}$[$_{AP}$[$_A$ very]][$_A$ small]][$_N$ boy]] [$_V$ kissed] [$_D$ the] [$_N$ platypus].
[$_{NP}$[$_D$ The]][$_{AP}$[$_{AP}$[$_A$ very]][$_A$ small]][$_N$ boy]][$_V$ kissed][$_{NP}$[$_D$the][$_N$platypus]].

3   Now the VP and S rules:

VP:
[$_{NP}$[$_D$The]][$_{AP}$[$_{AP}$[$_A$very]][$_A$small]][$_N$boy]][$_{VP}$[$_V$kissed][$_{NP}$[$_D$the][$_N$platypus]]].

S:
[$_S$[$_{NP}$[$_D$The]][$_{AP}$[$_{AP}$[$_A$very]][$_A$small]][$_N$boy]][$_{VP}$[$_V$kissed][$_{NP}$[$_D$the][$_N$platypus]]]].

4   Finally, go back and check that the structure can be generated by the rules.

5.   MODIFICATION AND AMBIGUITY

Syntactic trees allow us to capture another remarkable fact about language. Let's start with the following two sentences:

72)   a)   The man killed the king with a knife.
       b)   The man killed the king with the red hair.

Each of these sentences turns out to have more than one meaning, but for the moment consider only the least difficult reading for each (the phrases in quotes in (73) are called **paraphrases**, which is the technical term for "another way of saying the same thing"):

73)   a)   (72a) meaning "the man used a knife to kill the king."
       b)   (72b) meaning "the king with red hair was killed by the man."

The two sentences in (72) have very similar surface forms. But when we take into account the meanings in (73), we'll claim that they have very different structures. Remember the golden rule: **Modifiers are always attached within the phrase they modify**. In (72a) the PP *with a knife* modifies *killed*, so the structure will look like (74):

74)

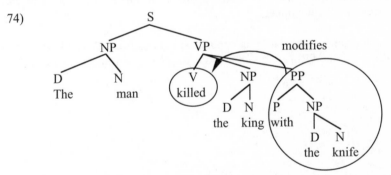

[With a knife] describes how the man killed the king. It modifies the verb *killed*, so it is attached under the VP. Now contrast that with the tree for (72b). Here the PP modifies the noun *king*, so it will be attached under the NP.

75)

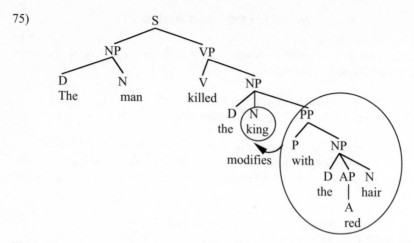

These are two very similar sentences, but they have quite different structures. As noted above, these sentences are actually ambiguous. The other readings for the two sentences are given in (76).

76)   a)   (72a) meaning "the king with the knife was killed by the man (who used a gun)."
       b)   (72b) meaning "the man used the red hair to kill the king (perhaps by strangling him with it)."

These alternate meanings have the exact opposite structures from (74) and (75). The meaning in (76a) has the PP *with the knife* modifying *king,* and thus attached to the NP:

77)

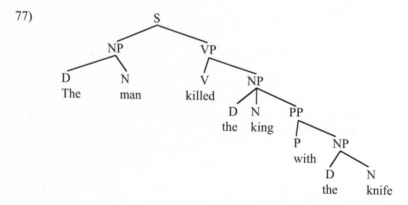

The meaning in (77b) has the PP *with the red hair* modifying the verb *kill,* so it is attached to the VP:

78)

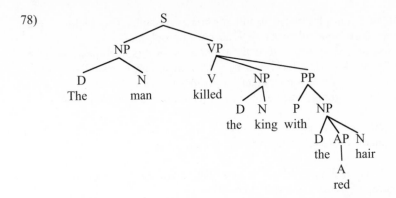

These examples illustrate an important property of syntactic trees. Trees allow us to capture the differences between ambiguous readings of the same surface sentence.

6.   CONSTITUENCY TESTS

In chapter 1, we held linguistics in general (and syntax specifically) up to the criterion of the scientific method. That is, if we make a hypothesis about something, we must be able to test that hypothesis. In this chapter, we have proposed the hypothesis that sentences are composed of higher-level groupings called constituents. Constituents are represented in tree structures and are generated by rules. If the hypothesis of constituency is correct, we should be able to test it in general (as well as test the specific instances of the rules).

In order to figure out what kinds of tests we need, it is helpful to reconsider the specifics of the hypothesis. The definition of constituents states that they are groups of words which function as a unit. If this is the case, then we should find instances where groups of words behave as single units. These instances can serve as tests for the hypothesis. In other words, they are **tests for constituency**. There are a lot of constituency tests listed in the syntactic literature. We are going to look at only four here: replacement, stand alone, movement, and coordination.

First, the smallest constituent is a single word, so it follows that if you can replace a group of words with a single word then we know that group forms a constituent. Consider the italicized NP in (79), it can be replaced with a single word (in this case a pronoun). This is the **replacement** test.

79)   a)   *The man from NY* flew only ultra-light planes.
       b)   *He* flew only ultra-light planes.

There is one important caveat to the test of replacement: There are many cases in our rules of optional items (those things marked in parentheses like the AP in NP → (D) (AP) NP). When we replace a string of words with a single word, how do we know that we aren't just leaving off the optional items? To avoid this problem, we have to keep the meaning as closely related to the original as possible. This requires some judgment on your part. None of these tests is absolute or foolproof.

The second test we will use is the **stand alone** test (sometimes also called the **sentence fragment** test). If the words can stand alone in response to a question, then they probably constitute a constituent. Consider the sentence in (80a) and repeated in (80b). We are going to test for the constituency of the italicized phrases.

80)   a)   Paul *ate at a really fancy restaurant.*
        b)   Paul *ate at* a really fancy restaurant.

If we ask the question "What did Paul do yesterday afternoon?" we can answer with the italicized group of words in (80a), but not in (80b):

81)   a)   Ate in a really fancy restaurant.
        b)   *Ate at.

Neither of these responses is proper English in prescriptive terms, but you can easily tell that (81a) is better than (81b).

Movement is our third test of constituency. If you can move a group of words around in the sentence, then they are a constituent because you can move them as a unit. Some typical examples are shown in (82). **Clefting** (82a) involves putting a string of words between *It was* (or *It is*) and a *that* at the beginning of the sentence. **Preposing** (82b) (also called **pseudoclefting**) involves putting the string of words before a *is/are what* or *is/are who* at the front of the sentence. We discuss the **passive** (82c) at length in chapter 9. Briefly, it involves putting the object in the subject position, the subject in a "by phrase" (after the word *by*) and changing the verb form (for example from *kiss* to *was kissed*).

82)   a)   Clefting: It was [a brand new car] that he bought.
                            (from *He bought a brand new car.*)

        b)   Preposing: [Big bowls of beans] are what I like.
                            (from *I like big bowls of beans.*)

        c)   Passive: [The big boy] was kissed by [the slobbering dog].
                            (from *The slobbering dog kissed the big boy.*)

Again, the movement test is only reliable when you keep the meaning roughly the same as the original sentence.

When Constituency Tests Fail

Unfortunately, sometimes it is the case that constituency tests give false results (which is one of the reasons we haven't spent much time on them in this text). Consider the case of the subject of a sentence and its verb. These do not form a constituent:

i)

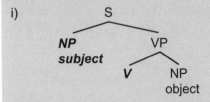

However, under certain circumstances you can conjoin a subject and verb to the exclusion of the object:

ii) Bruce loved and Kelly hated phonology class.

Sentence (ii) seems to indicate that the verb and subject form a constituent, which they don't according to the tree in (i). As you will see in later chapters, it turns out that things can move around in sentences. This means that sometimes the constituency is obscured by other factors. For this reason, to be sure that a test is working correctly you have to apply more than one test to a given structure. Always perform at least two different tests to check constituency; as one alone may give you a false result.

Finally, we have the test of ***coordination*** (also called ***conjunction***). Coordinate structures are constituents linked by a conjunction like *and* or *or*. Only constituents of the same syntactic category can be conjoined:

83)   a)   [John] and [the man] went to the store.
        b)   *John and very blue went to the store.

If you can coordinate a group of words with a similar group of words, then they form a constituent.

PSRs for Conjunction

In order to draw trees with conjunction in them, we need two more rules. These rules are slightly different than the ones we have looked at up to now. These rules are not category specific. Instead they use a variable (X). This X can stand for N or V or A or P etc. Just like in algebra, it is a variable that can stand for different categories. We need two rules, one to conjoin phrases (*[The Flintstones] and [the Rubbles]*) and one to conjoin words (*the [dancer] and [singer]*):

i)   XP → XP conj XP
ii)   X → X conj X

These result in trees like:

iii)   NP
      ╱ │ ╲
   NP conj NP

iv)   V
      ╱ │ ╲
   V   conj V

7.   SUMMARY AND CONCLUSION

We've done a lot in this chapter. We looked at the idea that sentences are hierarchically organized into constituent structures. We represented these constituent structures in trees and bracketed diagrams. We also developed a set of rules to generate those structures, and finally we looked at constituency tests that can be used to test the structures. Parts of speech are the labeling system for constituent structure. We showed that parts of speech can't be determined by meaning alone. In the appendix to this chapter, we sketch out some distributional tests for part of speech class.

APPENDIX: PARTS OF SPEECH TESTS

In this appendix, we return to the question of how to scientifically determine what part of speech (or word class or syntactic category) a word is. Recall from the discussion above that we assign part of speech category based upon linguistic distribution. That is, based upon where in the sentence the word appears, and what affixes (morphology) the word takes. For each major part of speech, you'll find the traditional definition based (incorrectly) on meaning, then some of the distributional criteria you could use in English. Notice that these are language specific: each language will have its own distributional criteria, so for each language linguists have to develop a list like the one below. Finally each entry contains a "frame." If you can insert the word into that frame, at least one instance of that word is that part of speech (but note that many words can fit into frames for different parts of speech).

NOUNS:

> *Traditionally:* Person, place, or thing
> *Distributionally*:
> - the subject or object of a sentence
> - modified by adjectives
> - follow determiners (*the, a, this*)
> - marked with case, number (singular, plural), gender endings
> - formed by adding derivational endings like *-ment, -ness, -ing, -er*
> *Frame*   X is a pain in the neck.

VERBS:

> *Traditionally:* Action (sometimes state)
> *Distributionally:*
> b)   the predicate of the clause
> c)   modified by adverbs and take auxiliaries
> d)   follow subject, precede object
> e)   take tense (-ed), aspect (-en), mood endings
> f)   can be negated
> *Frame*:   They can X *or* They X-ed the banana.

ADJECTIVES:

> *Traditionally*: State (modifying), qualities, attributes
> *Distributionally*:
> - follow *very*
> - modify nouns (and follow determiners)
> - formed by adding derivational endings like *-ish, -some*
> *Frames:* She is very X
>   I want the X book.

ADVERBS:

> *Traditionally*: Modifier of anything other than a noun
> *Distributionally:*
> - formed by adding *-ly* ending
> - appear at beginning of sentence, or at the very end
> *Frames:* Bill treats Fred X.
>   X the women go to work.

Open vs. Closed Classes of Speech

Linguistic theory distinguishes two kinds of lexical items (words). Parts of speech are divided into **open** and **closed class** items. Membership in open class categories (N, V, A) is unlimited. New words may be coined at any time, if they are open class (e.g., *fax, internet, grody*). Membership in closed classes, by contrast, is limited and coinages are rare. While it is certainly possible to define distributional criteria for closed class categories, their membership is so limited that it is simply easier to list them. We give a partial listing of some closed class items here:

PREPOSITIONS (P): *to, from, under, over, with, by,* etc.
CONJUNCTIONS (Conj): *and, or,* etc.
DETERMINERS (D): *This, that, the, a, my, your, our, his, her, their, each, every, some,* etc.
COMPLEMENTIZERS (C): *that, which, for* (all followed by a clause)
AUXILIARIES/MODALS (T): *is, have, can, must, should, would,* etc.

IDEAS, RULES, AND CONSTRAINTS INTRODUCED IN THIS CHAPTER

i)   ***Constituent***
        A group of words that functions together as a unit.

ii)   ***Hierarchical Structure***
        Constituents in a sentence are embedded inside of other constituents.

iii)   ***Parts of Speech*** (*a.k.a.* ***word class***, ***syntactic categories***)
        The labels we give to constituents (N, V, A, P, NP, VP, etc.). Assigned distributionally.

iv)   ***Syntactic Trees and Bracketed Diagrams***
        These are means of representing constituency. They are generated by rules.

v)   **Phrase Structure Rules**
        a)   S' → C S
        b)   S → {NP/S'} (T) VP
        c)   VP → (AP+) V ({NP/S'}) (PP+) (AP+)
        d)   NP → (D) (AP+) N (PP+)
        e)   PP → P (NP)
        f)   AP → (AP) A
        g)   XP → XP conj XP
        h)   X → X conj X

vi)   **Recursivity**
        The property of loops in the phrase structure rules that allow infinitely long
        sentences, and explain the creativity of language.

vii)   **The Golden Rule of Tree Structure (The Principle of Modification)**
        Modifiers are always attached within the phrase they modify.

viii)   **Constituency tests**
        Tests that show that a group of words function as a unit. There are four
        major constituency tests: **movement, coordination, stand alone**, and **re-
        placement**.

ix)   **Open Class**
        Parts of speech that are open class can take new members or coinages: N,
        V, A.

x)   **Closed Class**
        Parts of speech that are closed class don't allow new coinages: D, P, Conj,
        C, etc.

FURTHER READING

Chomsky, Noam (1957) *Syntactic Structures*. The Hague: Janua Linguarum 4.

Chomsky, Noam (1965) *Aspects of the Theory of Syntax*: Cambridge: MIT Press.

[The following books are other introductory syntax textbooks that have extensive discussion of the issues discussed in this chapter:]

Aarts, Bas (1997) *English Syntax and Argumentation*. New York: St. Martin's Press.

Fabb, Nigel (1994) *Sentence Structure*. London: Routledge.

Radford, Andrew (1988) *Transformational Grammar: A First Course*. Cambridge: Cambridge University Press.

PROBLEM SETS

1.   PART OF SPEECH 1[5]

Identify the main parts of speech (i.e., Nouns, Verbs, Adjectives/Adverbs, and Prepositions) in the following sentences. Treat hyphenated words as single words:

a) The old rusty pot-belly stove has been replaced.
b) The red-haired assistant put the vital documents through the new efficient shredder.
c) The large evil leathery alligator complained to his aging keeper about his extremely unattractive description.
d) I've just eaten the last piece of chocolate cake.

2.   PART OF SPEECH 2

Consider the following selection from *Jabberwocky*, a poem by Lewis Carroll:

> Twas brillig and the slithy toves
> Did gyre and gimble in the <u>wabe</u>;
> All mimsy <u>were</u> the borogoves,
> And the mome raths <u>outgrabe</u>.
>
> "Beware the Jabberwock, my son!
> The jaws that bite, the claws that catch!
> Beware the <u>Jubjub</u> bird, and shun
> The <u>frumious bandersnatch</u>!"
>
> He took his <u>vorpal</u> sword in hand:
> Long time the <u>manxone</u> foe he sought –
> So rested he by the <u>tumtum</u> tree
> <u>And</u> stood a while <u>in</u> <u>thought</u>.

---

[5] Problem set contributed by Sheila Dooley-Collberg.

And as in <u>uffish</u> thought <u>he</u> stood
The <u>Jabberwock</u> with eyes of flame,
Came <u>whiffling</u> through <u>the</u> <u>tulgey</u> wood,
and <u>burbled</u> as it came.

For each underlined word, indicate its part of speech (word class), and explain the *distributional* criteria by which you came up with that classification. Do not try to use a dictionary. Most of these words are nonsense words. You will need to figure out what part of speech they are based upon what suffixes and prefixes they take, along with where they appear relative to other words. (See the appendix above.)

3.   NOOTKA

(Data from Sapir and Swadesh 1939)

Consider the following data from Nootka, a language spoken in British Columbia, Canada. (The : mark indicates a long vowel. ? is a glottal stop. PRES in the second line means "present tense," DEF means "definite determiner" (the).)

a)   Mamu:k-ma   qu:?as-?i.
       working-PRES   man-DEF
       "The man is working."

b)   Qu:?as-ma   mamu:k-?i.
       man-PRES   working-DEF
       "The working one is a man."

Reading Foreign Language Examples
There are three parts to all foreign language examples used in syntax. Look at the sentences above. The first line is the sentence or phrase in the language under consideration. The second line, which is the most important for our purposes, contains a word-by-word translation of the sentence. Finally, there is a colloquial English translation. The second line, called the **gloss**, is the most useful if you don't speak the language. It shows you the order of elements in the sentence. When reading about the syntax of foreign languages, concentrate on the order of elements in this second line.

Questions about Nootka:
1) In sentence a, is *Qu:ʔas* a verb or a noun?
2) In sentence a, is *Mamu:k* a verb or a noun?
3) In sentence b, is *Qu:ʔas* a verb or a noun?
4) In sentence b, is *Mamu:k* a verb or a noun?
5) What criteria did you use to tell what is a noun in Nootka and what is a verb?
6) How does this data support the idea that there are no semantic criteria involved in determining the part of speech?

4.   ENGLISH

Draw phrase structure trees *and* bracketed diagrams for each of the following sentences, indicate all the categories (phrase (e.g., NP) and word level (e.g., N)) on the tree. Use the rules given above in the summary of this chapter. Be careful that items which modify one another are part of the same constituent. Treat words like *can, should, might, was*, as instances of the category T (tense).[6]

a) The very young child walked from school to the store.
b) John paid a dollar for a head of lettuce.
c) Teenagers drive rather quickly.
d) A clever magician with the right equipment can fool the audience easily.
e) The police might plant the drugs in the apartment.
f) Those Olympic hopefuls should practice diligently every day.
g) The latest research on dieting always warns people about the dangers of too much cholesterol.
h) That annoying faucet was dripping constantly every day for months.

5.   AMBIGUITY

The following English sentences are all ambiguous. Provide a paraphrase (a sentence with roughly the same meaning) for each of the possible meanings, and then draw (two) trees of the *original* sentence that distinguish the two meanings. Be careful not to draw the tree of the paraphrase. Your two trees should be different from one another, where the difference reflects which elements modify what. (For sentence (b) ignore the issue of capitalization.)

a) John said Mary went to the store quickly.
b) I discovered an old English poem.

---

[6] Thanks to Sheila Dooley Collberg for contributing sentences d–h.

6.   STRUCTURE

In the following sentences a sequence of words is marked as a constituent with square brackets. State whether or not it is a real constituent, and what criteria (that is constituency tests) you applied to determine that result.

a) Susanne gave [the minivan to Petunia].
b) Clyde got [a passionate love letter from Stacy].

7.   CONSTITUENCY TESTS (ADVANCED) [7]

Do the words in boldface in the following sentence form a *single* constituent? That is, is there a *[Barbie and Ken kissing]* constituent? How do you know? Use all the tests available to you.

Barbie and Ken were seen by everyone at the party **kissing**.

A couple of things may help you in this problem. (1) Remember, that constituents can be inside other constituents. (2) This sentence is a passive, which means that some movement has happened, so don't let the fact that there is other stuff in between the two bits throw you off.

8.   ENGLISH PREPOSITIONS

In the text, we claimed that perhaps the NP in PPs was optional, explaining why we can say *He passed out*, where the preposition *out* has no object. Consider an alternative: the expression *[passed out]* is really a "complex" verb. Using constituency tests, provide arguments that the structure of expressions like:

a) He blew out the candle.
b) He turned off the light.
c) He blew up the building.
d) He rode out the storm.

is really [[V P] NP] rather than: [V [P NP]].

---

[7] Sheila Dooley Collberg is the source of this problem set.

9.   BAMBARA

(Data from Koopman 1992)

Consider the following data from Bambara, a Mande language spoken in
Mali. (The glosses have been slightly simplified.) Pay careful attention to the
second line, where the word order of Bambara is shown.

a) A   kasi-ra.
    he   cried
     "He cried."

b) A   kaa-ra.
    she went
     "She went."

c) Den   ye   ji   min.
    child   PAST   water   drink
     "The child drank water."

d) N son-na a ma.
    I agreed it to
     "I agreed to it."

Answer the following questions about Bambara:

1) Is there a gender distinction in Bambara?
2) Do you need a T category in Bambara?
3) Is there a Determiner category in Bambara?
4) What is the NP (if you need one) for Bambara?
5) What is the PP rule for Bambara?
6) What is the VP rule for Bambara?
7) What is the S rule for Bambara? (Keep in mind your answers to the
    above questions – be consistent.)
8) Draw trees for (a), (c), and (d) using your rules.
9) Draw bracketed diagrams for (b) and (c).

10.   HIXKARYANA

(Data from Derbyshire 1985)

Look carefully at the following data from a Carib language from Brazil (the glosses have been slightly simplified from the original):

a) Kuraha   yonyhoryeno   biyekomo.
    bow   made   boy
    "The boy made a bow."

b) Newehyatxhe   woriskomo komo.
    take-bath   women   all
    "All the women take a bath."

c) Toto   heno komo   yonoye kamara.
    person   dead all   ate   jaguar
    "The jaguar ate all the people."

Now answer the following questions about Hixkaryana:

1) Is there any evidence for a determiner category in Hixkaryana? Be sure to consider quantifier words as possible determiners (like *some* and *all*).
2) Is there evidence for an AP rule in Hixkaryana?
3) Posit an NP rule to account for Hixkaryana. (Be careful to do it for the second line, the word-by-word gloss, in these examples not the third line.)
4) Posit a VP rule for Hixkaryana.
5) Posit an S rule for Hixkaryana.
6) What is the part of speech of *newehyatxhe*? How do you know?
7) Draw the trees for (a) and (c) using the rules you posited above. (Hint: if your trees don't work, then you have probably made a mistake in the rules.)
8) Give bracketed diagrams for the same sentences.

11.   IRISH

(Data from Carnie field notes)

Consider the following data from Modern Irish Gaelic.

a) Phóg Liam   Séan.
    kissed William John
    "William kissed John."

b) Phóg   Seán Liam.
    Kissed John William
    "John kissed William."

c) Phóg an fear an mhuc.
    kissed the man the pig
    "The man kissed the pig."

d) Chonaic mé an mhuc mhór.
    Saw   I the pig   big
    "I saw the big pig."

e) Rince   an bheán.
    Danced   the woman
    "The woman danced."

On the basis of this data answer the following questions:

1) Is there any evidence for an AP category in Irish?
2) Write the NP rule for Irish, be sure to mark optional things in parenthe-
    ses.
3) Can you write a VP rule for Irish? Assume that object NPs (like *William* in
    (b) and *the big pig* in (d)) *must* be part of the VP, and that subject NPs
    (like *John* in (b) and *I* in (d)) are *never* part of VPs.
4) What is the S rule for Irish? (Be careful that your S rule is consistent with
    your answer in (3).)
5) Using the rules you developed, draw trees for sentences (c), (d) and (e).

chapter 3

Structural Relations

0. INTRODUCTION

In chapter 2, we developed the notion of constituency. Constituents are groups of words that function as single units. In order to systematically identify these, we proposed a set of rules. These rules generate trees, which in turn represent constituency. Take a careful look at any tree in the last chapter and you'll notice that it is a collection of labels and lines; within this collection of labels there is an organization. In particular, various parts of the tree are organized hierarchically with respect to one another. A collection of lines and labels with an internal organization like syntactic trees is a geometric object. It isn't a geometric object like a circle or a square, but nonetheless it has bits that are spatially organized with respect to one another. If syntactic trees are geometric objects, they can be studied and described mathematically – the focus of this chapter. This chapter differs from all the others in this book. You won't see many sentences or phrases here, and there is very little data. This chapter is about the purely formal properties of trees. But don't think you can skip it. The terminology we develop here is a fundamental part of syntactic theory and will play an important role in subsequent chapters.

> ### Why Study the Geometry of Trees?
> It is worth considering whether it is necessary to concern ourselves with the mathematics of tree diagrams. There are actually two very good reasons why we should do this. First, by considering the geometry of trees, we can assign names to the various parts and describe how the parts relate to one another. For example, in the last chapter we were only able to give a vague definition of the term *constituent*. In this chapter, we'll be able to give a precise description. Second, it turns out that there are many syntactic phenomena that make explicit reference to the geometry of trees. One of the most obvious of these refers to anaphors. Anaphors can only appear in certain positions in the geometry of the tree. The distribution of anaphors and other types of nouns is the focus of the next chapter.

1.   THE PARTS OF A TREE

Let's start with a very abstract tree drawing:

1)

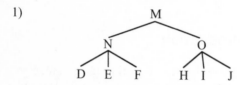

This tree would be generated by the rules in (2):

2) $M \rightarrow N\,O$
           $N \rightarrow D\,E\,F$
           $O \rightarrow H\,I\,J$

You can check this by applying each of the rules to the tree in (1). I'm using an abstract tree here because I don't want the content of each of the nodes to interfere with the underlying abstract mathematics. (But if you find this confusing, you can substitute S for M, NP for N, VP for O, etc., and you'll see that this is just a normal tree.) Now we can describe the various parts of this tree. The lines in the tree are called **branches**. A formal definition of branch is given in (3), and the branches are marked in (4):

3)   *Branch*
           A line connecting two parts of a tree.

4)
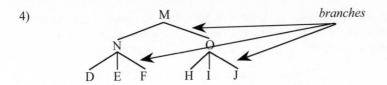

The end of any branch is called a **node**. Both ends are called nodes. For example, N and F are both called nodes of a branch. Any time two or more branches come together, this is also called a node:

5)   *Node*
        The end of a branch.

Nodes in a tree are labeled. In the tree above, M, N, O, D, E, F, H, I, J are the **labels** for the nodes that make up the tree. This is very abstract of course. In the last chapter, we looked at the various parts of speech (N, V, A, P, etc.) and the phrasal categories associated with them (NP, VP, AP, PP, etc.). These are the labels in a real syntactic tree.

6)   *Label*
        The name given to a node.

There are actually different kinds of nodes that we'll want to make reference to. The first of these is called the **root node**. The root node doesn't have any branch on top of it. There is only ever one root node in a sentence. (The term root is a little confusing, but try turning the trees upside down and you'll see that they actually do look like a tree (or a bush at least). In most trees we looked at in the last chapter, the root node is almost always the S (sentence) or S' node.

7)   *Root node*
        The node with no line on top of it.

At the opposite end of the tree are the nodes that don't have any lines underneath them. If the tree analogy were to really hold up, we should call these "leaves." More commonly, however, these are called **terminal nodes**.

8)   *Terminal node*
        Any node with no branch underneath it.

Any node that isn't a terminal node is called a **non-terminal node**:

9)   *Non-terminal node*
        Any node with a branch underneath it.

Notice that the root node is also a non-terminal node by this definition. After we add some definitions in the next chapter, we'll have reason to reformulate the definitions of root, terminal and non-terminal nodes, but for now these should give you the basic idea. In (10), we have a tree where the root node, the terminal nodes, and the non-terminal nodes are all marked.

(10)

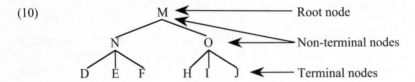

M ← Root node

N   O ← Non-terminal nodes

D   E   F   H I   J ← Terminal nodes

In this tree, M is the root node. M, N, and O are non-terminals, and D, E, F, H, I, and J are terminal nodes.

We now have all the terms we need to describe the various parts of a tree. The lines are called branches. The ends of the lines are called nodes, and each of the nodes has a label. Depending upon where the node is in the tree, it can be a root node (the top), a terminal (the bottom), or a non-terminal (any node except the bottom). Next we turn to a set of terms and descriptions that will allow us to describe the relations that hold between these parts. Because we are talking about a tree structure here, these relations are often called ***structural relations***.

2.   DOMINANCE

Some nodes are higher in the tree than others. This reflects the fact that trees show a hierarchy of constituents. In particular, we want to talk about nodes that are higher than one another *and* are connected by a branch. The relation that describes two nodes that stand in this configuration is called ***dominance***. A node that sits atop another and is connected to it by a branch is said to dominate that node.

11)   *Dominance*
        Node A dominates node B if and only if A is higher up in the tree than B
        and if you can trace a line from A to B going only downwards.

In (12), M dominates all the other nodes (N, O, D, E, F, H, I, J). N dominates D, E, and F, and O dominates H, I, J. O does not dominate F, as you can see by virtue of the fact that there is no branch connecting them.

12)   M

                    N   O

            D   E   F   H I   J

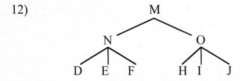

Dominance is essentially a containment relation. The phrasal category N contains the terminal nodes D, E, and F. Containment is seen more clearly when the tree is converted into a bracketed diagram:

13)   [$_M$ [$_N$ D E F] [$_O$ H I J]]

In (13) the brackets associated with N ([$_N$ D E F]) contains the nodes D, E, and F. The same holds true for O which contains H, I, and J. M contains both N and O and all the nodes that they contain. So dominance is a technical way of expressing which categories belong to larger categories.

Axioms of Dominance

There is actually more to the math of dominance than what we've given in the main body of the text. Higginbotham (1985) developed a set of axioms that describe this. If you are interested in the details, here are his axioms and a brief description of what they mean.

where $x \leq y$ means x dominates y
a) $x \leq x$
b)   if $x \leq y \leq z$ then $x \leq z$
c)   if $x \leq y \leq x$ then $x = y$
d)   if $x \leq z$ and $y \leq z$ then either $x \leq y$ or $y \leq x$ (or both if $x = y = z$)

(a) means that every node dominates itself. (b) means that the dominance relation is transitive (if A dominates B and B dominates C, then A also dominates C). (c) means that the relation is unidirectional (if you are dominated by a node, you cannot also dominate that node). Finally axiom (d) rules out multiple mothers for a node.

There is an informal set of terms that we frequently use to refer to dominance. This set of terms is based on the fact that syntactic trees look a bit like family trees. If one node dominates another, it is said to be the ***mother***; the node that is dominated is called the ***daughter***. In the tree above in (12), N is D's mother and D is N's daughter. We can even extend the analogy (although this is pushing things a bit) and call M D's grandmother.

14)   *Mother*
         A is the mother of B if A dominates B *(to be revised)*.

15)   *Daughter*
         B is the daughter of A if B is dominated by A *(to be revised)*.

With this set of terms in place we can now redefine our definitions of root nodes, terminal nodes, and non-terminals a little more rigorously:

16)   *Root node (revised)*
        The node that dominates everything, but is dominated by nothing. (The
        node that is no node's daughter.)

17)   *Terminal node (revised)*
        A node that dominates nothing. (A node that is not a mother.)

18)   *Non-terminal node (revised)*
        A node that dominates something. (A node that is a mother.)

Dominance is actually quite a general notion: In (12), M dominates all of
the nodes under it. In certain circumstances we might want to talk about
relationships that are smaller and more local. This is the relationship of ***immediate
dominance.*** A node immediately dominates another if there is only one branch
between them.

19)   *Immediately dominate*
        Node A immediately dominates node B if there is no intervening node G
        that is dominated by A, but dominates B. (In other words, A is the first node
        that dominates B.)

In (12), M dominates all the other nodes in the tree, but it only immediately
dominates N and O. It does not immediately dominate any of the other nodes
because N and O intervene. To be really strict, the relation of motherhood is one of
immediate dominance – not dominance.

20)   *Mother*
        A is the mother of B if A immediately dominates B.

21)   *Daughter*
        B is the daughter of A if B is immediately dominated by A.

Closely related to these definitions is the definition of ***sister***:

22)   *Sisters*
        Two nodes that share the same mother.

In the last chapter, we developed an intuitive notion of constituent. The
relation of dominance actually allows us to be a little more rigorous and develop a
formal notion of constituency. In order to do this, we need yet another definition,
exhaustive domination:

23)   *Exhaustive domination*
        Node A exhaustively dominates a *set* of nodes {B, C, ..., D}, provided it
        immediately dominates all the members of the set (so that there is no

member of the set that is not dominated by A) *and* there is no node G immediately dominated by A that is not a member of the set.

This is a rather laborious definition. Let's tease it apart by considering an example.

24)

What we are concerned with here is a *set* of nodes and whether or not a given node dominates the entire set. Sets are indicated with curly brackets {}. Start with the set {B,C,D} and look at the tree in (24). In (24) all members of the set {B,C,D} are immediately dominated by A; there is no member of the set that isn't dominated by A. This satisfies the first part of the definition in (23). Turning to the second part, A *only* dominates these nodes and no others. There is no node G dominated by A that is not a member of the set. This being the case we can say of the tree in (24) that A exhaustively dominates the set {B, C, D}. Let's turn to a different tree now.

25)

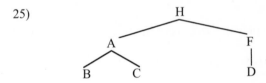

Again let's consider whether A exhaustively dominates the set {B,C,D}. In (25), one member of the set, D, is not immediately dominated by A. As such the set {B,C,D} is *not* exhaustively dominated by A. The reverse situation is seen in (26):

26)

While it is the case that in (26), B, C, and D are all immediately dominated by A, there is also the node G, which is not a member of the set {B,C,D}, so the set {B,C,D} is not exhaustively dominated by A (although the set {B,C,D,G} is). On a more intuitive level, exhaustive domination holds between a set of nodes and their mother. Only when the entire set and only that set are immediately dominated by their mother can we say that the mother exhaustively dominates the set.

Look carefully at the structures in (24), (25), and (26). In (24) you'll see that the set {B,C,D} forms a constituent (labeled A). In (25), that set does not form a constituent, nor does it form a constituent in (26) (although the set is part of a larger constituent in that tree). In (26), there is no sense in which B, C, D form a unit that excludes G. It seems then that the notion of constituency is closely related to the relation of exhaustive domination. This is reflected in the following formal definition of a constituent.

27)   *Constituent*
          A set of nodes exhaustively dominated by a single node.

Before turning to some other structural relations, it is important to look at one confusing piece of terminology. This is the distinction between *constituent* and *constituent of*. A constituent, as defined in (27), is a set of nodes exhaustively dominated by a single node. A **constituent of**, by contrast, is a *member* of the constituent set. Consider the tree in (28):

28)

Here we have the constituent A, which exhaustively dominates the set {B,C,D}. Each member of this set is called a "constituent of A." So B is a constituent of A. "Constituent of" boils down to domination. A dominates B therefore B is a constituent of A:

29)   *Constituent of*
          B is a constituent of A if and only if A dominates B.

There is, of course, the more local variety:

30)   *Immediate constituent of*
          B is an immediate constituent of A if and only if A immediately dominates B.

This ends our discussion of the up and down axis of syntactic trees. Next we consider the left to right relations that hold of trees.

3.   PRECEDENCE

Syntactic trees don't only encode the hierarchical organization of sentences, they also encode the linear order of the constituents. Linear order refers to the order in which words are spoken or written (left to right if you are writing in English). Consider the following rule:

31)   M → A B

This rule not only says that M dominates A and B and is composed of A and B. It also says that A must precede B in linear order. A must be said before B, because it appears to the left of B in the rule. The relation of "what is said first" is called **precedence**:

32) *Precedence*

Node A precedes node B if and only if A is to the left of B and neither A dominates B nor B dominates A *and* every node dominating A either appears to the left of B or dominates B.

This definition is pretty complex, so let's break it apart. The first bit says that if A appears to the left of B (i.e., is said first), then it precedes B. This can be seen in the tree in (33), which is generated by the rule in (31):

33)

A appears to the left of B and correctly precedes it. The second bit of the definition says "neither A dominates B nor B dominates A." The reason for this should be obvious on an intuitive level. Remember, domination is a containment relation. If A contains B, there is no obvious way in which A could be to the left of B. Think of it this way. If you have a box, and the box has a ball in it, you can't say that the box is to the left of the ball. That is physically impossible. The box surrounds the ball. The same holds true for dominance. You can't both dominate and precede/follow. The final part of the definition says "every node dominating A either precedes B or dominates B." There is a reason why we have to add this clause to the definition. This has to do with the fact that the terminals of a tree don't float out in space, they are dominated by other nodes that might precede or follow. Consider the following tree drawn by a sloppy tree-drawer:

34)

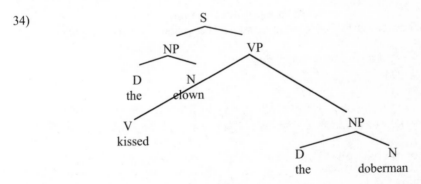

In this sloppily drawn tree, the verb *kissed* actually appears to the *left* of the noun *clown*. However, we wouldn't want to say that *kissed* precedes *clown*; this is clearly wrong. The sentence is said "The clown kissed the doberman," where *kissed* follows *clown*. We rule this possibility out by making reference to the stuff that dominates the nodes we are looking at. Let A = *clown* and B = *kissed*. Now let's apply the final clause of the definition:

35)   *and* every node dominating *clown* either appears to the left of *kissed* or
        dominates *kissed*.

Look at the tree in (34): The nodes dominating the N *clown* either precede *kissed*
(NP) or dominate *kissed* (S). This part of the definition also allows us to explain an
important restriction on syntactic trees: ***You cannot allow branches to cross.*** Trees
like (36) are completely unacceptable (they are also impossible to generate with
phrase structure rules – try to write one and you'll see):

36)

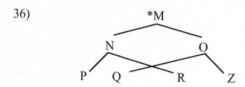

In this tree, Q is written to the left of R, apparently preceding R, but by the definition
of precedence given above, this tree is ruled out. Q is to the left of R, but O *which
dominates Q* is not. In other words, you can't cross branches. Another way of
phrasing this is given below in (37):

37)   *No crossing branches constraint*
        If one node X precedes another node Y then X and all nodes dominated by
        X must precede Y and all nodes dominated by Y.

Axioms of Precedence

Higginbotham (1985) also developed a set of axioms for precedence.

> where ¬ means "precedes"
> a) if $x¬y$, then $NOT(y¬x)$
> b) if $x¬y¬z$, then $x¬z$
> c) if $x¬y$ or $y¬x$, then $NOT(x \leq y)$ and $NOT(y \leq x)$
> d) $x¬y$ iff for all terminals $u, v, x \leq u$ and $y \leq v$ jointly imply $u¬v$

(a) means that you cannot both precede and follow. (b) means that the
precedence relation is transitive. (c) shows that dominance and
precedence are mutually exclusive (if you precede y, you cannot
dominate y and vice versa). (d) is the same as the no-crossing branches
constraint. It claims that constituents may not be discontinuous.

Just as in the dominance relation, where there is the special local definition
called "immediate dominance," there is a special local form of precedence called
immediate precedence:

38)   *Immediate precedence*
        A immediately precedes B if there is no node G that follows A but precedes
        B.

Consider the string given in (39) (assume that the nodes dominating this string meet
all the criteria set out in (32)):

39)   A   B   G

In this linear string, A immediately precedes B, because A precedes B and there is
nothing in between them. Contrast this with (40):

40)   A   G   B

In this string, A does **not** immediately precede B. It does precede B, but G intervenes
between them, so the relation is not immediate.

4.   C-COMMAND

Perhaps the most important of the structural relations is the one we call *c-command*.
Although c-command takes a little getting used to, it is actually the most useful of all
the relations. In the next chapter, we'll look at the phenomenon of **binding**, which
makes explicit reference to the c-command relation. C-command is defined
intuitively in (41) and more formally in (42):

41)   *C-command (informal)*
        A node c-commands its sisters and all the daughters (and granddaughters
        and great-granddaughters, etc.) of its sisters.

42)   *C-command (formal)*
        Node A c-commands node B if every branching node dominating A also
        dominates B, and neither A nor B dominate the other.

Look at the tree in (43). The node A c-commands all the nodes in the circle. It
doesn't c-command any others:

43)

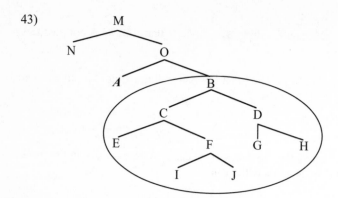

That is, A c-commands its sister (B) and all the nodes dominated by its sister (C, D, E, F, G, H, I, J). Consider now the same tree without the circle, and look at the nodes c-commanded by G:

44)

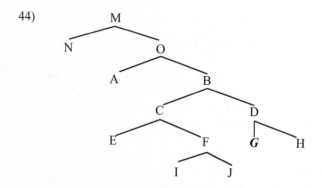

G c-commands *only* H (its sister). Notice that it does not c-command C, E, F, I, or J. C-command is a relation that holds between sisters and aunts and nieces. It *never* holds between cousins or between a mother and daughter.

There are various kinds of c-command. The first of these is when two nodes c-command one another. This is called **symmetric c-command** and is defined in (45):

45)   *Symmetric c-command*
        A symmetrically c-commands B, if A c-commands B *and* B c-commands A.

This relation holds only between sisters. The other kind of c-command is the kind that holds between an aunt and her nieces. This is called (unsurprisingly) **asymmetric c-command**:

46)   *Asymmetric c-command*
        A asymmetrically c-commands B if A c-commands B but B does *not* c-
        command A.

How Did C-command Get Its Name?

C-command is kind of a strange name for this relation, and there is not a lot of agreement about where the name comes from. *Command* is a notion stolen from traditional grammar, but implemented on our kind of trees. Some people claim that the *c-* in *c-command* comes from the notion that c-command involves constituency and means *constituent command*. Other scholars in the field trace the name to a slightly more inventive origin. At one point in generative grammar, there were two notions of command: *command* and *kommand* (the difference between them need not concern us). Of course, these are said the same way, even though written differently. So, the story goes, people giving talks at conferences needed a way to distinguish them, so they referred to *k-command* (command starting with a *k*) and *c-command* (command starting with a *c*). So the *c-* in *c-command* refers to the fact that *command* starts with the letter *c*. Whether or not this etymology is correct is one for the historians to decide.

Consider again the tree in (44) (repeated here as (47)):

47)

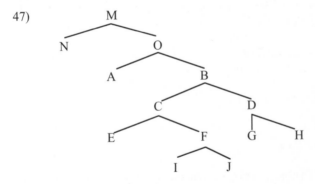

In this tree N and O symmetrically c-command each other (as do all other pairs of sisters). However, N asymmetrically c-commands A, B, C, D, E, F, G, H, I, and J, since none of these c-command N.

> ## Immediate C-command: Government
> Maybe to your surprise, we haven't defined a notion of c-command parallel to the notions of immediate dominance and immediate precedence. That is, we haven't defined a "local" version of c-command. Such a notion exists, but with a different name. Local c-command is frequently called **government**. The study of the government relation was extremely popular in the version of generative grammar that existed between about 1981 and 1991. In fact, that version of the theory was often called Government and Binding Theory or GB. In GB theory, extremely refined definitions of government were developed. Later versions of generative grammar (such as the Minimalist approach espoused in Chomsky 1993) have done away with government. To find out more about the definitions and uses of government, see Haegeman (1994).

5.   GRAMMATICAL RELATIONS

In addition to the structural relations that hold between items in a tree, there are also some traditional grammatical terms that can be defined structurally. These are useful terms, and we will frequently make reference to them. We call these *grammatical relations*. Technically speaking, grammatical relations are not structural relations. Some theories of grammar (for example Lexical Functional Grammar and Relational Grammar) posit primitive grammatical relations (meaning they are not structurally defined). In the approach we are developing here, however, grammatical relations are defined structurally.

The first of these is the *subject* of a sentence. In English, this is always the NP that appears before the verb or auxiliary:

48)   a)   *The puppy* licked the kitten's face.
        b)   *It* is raining.
        c)   *Fred* feels fine.
        d)   *The kitten* was licked.

Notice that the definition of subject is not a semantic one. It is not necessarily the doer of the action. In (48c) for example, Fred is not deliberately feeling fine. In sentence (48d), the kitten is the one being licked, not the licker. Different semantic types[1] of noun phrases appear to be allowed to function as the subject. There is a straightforward structural definition of the subject:

---

[1] In chapter 7, we will look at different semantic types of noun phrases. These types are called *thematic relations*.

49)   *Subject (preliminary)*
        NP daughter of S

In later chapters, we will have cause to refine this definition somewhat, but for now, this will do.

There are two other grammatical relations that we will consider. One of these is the **object** of the verb and the **object of a preposition**. Examples of these are seen in (50) and (51) respectively:

50)   *Object*
        a)   Susan kissed *the clown's nose.*
        b)   Cedric danced *a jolly jig.*

51)   *Object of a preposition*
        a)   Gilgamesh cut the steak with *a knife.*
        b)   We drove all the way to *Buenos Aires.*

Preliminary definitions of these are given in (52) and (53), again we will have reason to revise these in later chapters.

52)   *(direct) Object*
        NP daughter of VP

53)   *Object of preposition*
        NP daughter of PP

Indirect Object

There is another grammatical relation that we won't consider here, because it is quite difficult to structurally define (at this point). It is the relation of **indirect object**. Examples of indirect objects are italicized below:

i)   I gave *Jennifer* the jujoobs.
ii)   I gave the jujoobs *to Jennifer.*

As you can see, indirect objects can both be NPs and PPs. They also appear in positions similar to direct objects. For this reason, we'll leave them aside for the moment.

In addition to subjects, objects, and indirect objects, you may also occasionally see reference made to **obliques**. In English, obliques are almost always marked with a preposition. The PPs in the following sentence are obliques:

54)   John tagged Lewis *with a regulation baseball on Tuesday.*

In many languages, such as Finnish, obliques aren't marked with prepositions, instead they get special suffixes that mark them as oblique; so obliqueness is not necessarily defined by being a preposition, that is just a convenient definition for now.

6.   SUMMARY AND CONCLUSIONS

This chapter has been a bit different from the rest of this book. It hasn't been about Language per se, but rather about the mathematical properties of the system we use to describe language. We looked at the various parts of a syntactic tree and then at the three relations that can hold between these parts: dominance, precedence, and c-command. In all the subsequent chapters of this book, you'll find much utility for the terms and the relations described here.

IDEAS, RULES, AND CONSTRAINTS INTRODUCED IN THIS CHAPTER

i)   ***Branch***
        A line connecting two parts of a tree.

ii)   ***Node***
        The end of a branch.

iii)   ***Label***
        The name given to a node (e.g., N, NP, S, etc.).

iv)   ***Root Node*** *(revised)*
        The node that dominates everything, but is dominated by nothing. (The node that is no node's daughter.)

v)   ***Terminal Node*** *(revised)*
        A node that dominates nothing. (A node that is not a mother.)

        ..   *de (revised)*
                                    nates something. (A node that is a mother.)

                                    s node B if and only if A is higher up in the tree than B
                                    a branch from A to B going only downwards.

viii)   ***Mother***
         A is the mother of B if A immediately dominates B.

ix)   ***Daughter***
         B is the daughter of A if B is immediately dominated by A.

x)   ***Sisters***
         Two nodes that share the same mother.

xi)   ***Immediately Dominate***
         Node A immediately dominates node B if there is no intervening node G
         that is dominated by A, but dominates B. (In other words, A is the first node
         that dominates B.)

xii)   ***Exhaustive Domination***
         Node A exhaustively dominates a *set* of nodes {B, C, ... , D}, provided it
         dominates all the members of the set (so that there is no member of the set
         that is not dominated by A) *and* there is no node G dominated by A that is
         not a member of the set.

xiii)   ***Constituent***
         A set of nodes exhaustively dominated by a single node.

xiv)   ***Constituent of***
         A is a constituent of B if and only if B dominates A.

xv)   ***Immediate Constituent of***
         A is an immediate constituent of B if and only if B immediately dominates
         A.

xvi)   ***Precedence***
         Node A precedes node B if and only if A is to the left of B and neither A
         dominates B nor B dominates A *and* every node dominating A either
         appears to the left of B or dominates B.

xvii)   ***No Crossing Branches Constraint***
         If node X precedes another node Y then X and all nodes dominated by X
         must precede Y and all nodes dominated by Y.

xviii)   ***Immediate Precedence***
         A immediately precedes B if there is no node G that follows A but precedes
         B.

xix)   ***C-command*** *(informal)*
         A node c-commands its sisters and all the daughters (and granddaughters,
         and great-granddaughters, etc.) of its sisters.

xx)   ***C-command*** *(formal)*
        Node A c-commands node B if every branching node dominating A also
        dominates B *and* neither A nor B dominates the other.

xxi)   ***Symmetric C-command***
        A symmetrically c-commands B if A c-commands B *and* B c-commands A.

xxii)   ***Asymmetric C-command***
        A asymmetrically c-commands B if A c-commands B but B does *not* c-
        command A.

xxiii) ***Subject*** *(preliminary)*
        NP daughter of S.

xxiv)   *(direct)* ***Object*** *(preliminary)*
        NP daughter of VP.

xxv)   ***Object of Preposition*** *(preliminary)*
        NP daughter of PP.

FURTHER READING

Chomsky, Noam (1975) *The Logical Structure of Linguistic Theory*. New York:
    Plenum.

Higginbotham, James (1985) A Note on Phrase Markers. *MIT Working Papers in
    Linguistics* 6, 87–101.

Reinhart, Tanya (1976) The Syntactic Domain of Anaphora. Ph.D. dissertation. MIT.

Reinhart, Tanya (1983) *Anaphora and Semantic Interpretation*. London: Croom
    Helm.

PROBLEM SETS

1.   STRUCTURAL RELATIONS I[2]

Consider the following tree:

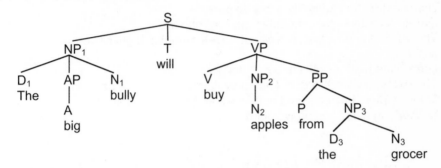

1) What node(s) dominate *grocer*?
2) What node(s) immediately dominate D_3 *the*?
3) Do *will* and *buy* form a constituent?
4) What nodes does N_1 *bully* c-command?
5) What nodes does NP_1 *the big bully* c-command?
6) What is V *buy's* mother?
7) What nodes does *will* precede?
8) List all the sets of sisters in the tree.
9) What is the PP's mother?
10) Do NP_1 and VP asymmetrically or symmetrically c-command one another?
11) List all the nodes c-commanded by V.
12) What is the subject of the sentence?
13) What is the object of the sentence?
14) What is the object of the preposition?
15) Is NP_3 a constituent of VP?
16) What node(s) is NP_3 an immediate constituent of?
17) What node(s) does VP exhaustively dominate?
18) What is the root node?
19) List all the terminal nodes.
20) What immediately precedes N_3 *grocer*?

---

[2] The idea for this problem set is borrowed from Radford (1988).

2.   TREES

Using the rules we developed in chapter 2, draw the trees for the following
sentences:

a)   The big man from New York loves bagels with cream cheese.
b)   Susan rode a bright blue train from New York.
c)   The plucky platypus kicked a can of soup from New York to Tucson.
d)   John said Martha sang the aria with gusto.
e)   Martha said John sang the aria from *La Bohème*.
f)   The book of poems from the city of Angels with the bright red cover
     stinks.
g)   Louis hinted Mary stole the purse deftly.
h)   The extremely tired students hated syntactic trees with a passion.
i)   Many soldiers have claimed bottled water quenches thirst best.
j)   Networking helps you grow your business.

3.   STRUCTURAL RELATIONS II

Look at your tree for sentence (a) of question 2.

1) List all the nodes that the subject NP c-commands.
2) List all the nodes that the subject NP asymmetrically c-commands.
3) List all the nodes that the subject NP dominates.
4) List all the nodes that the subject NP immediately dominates.
5) List all the nodes that the subject NP precedes.
6) List all the nodes that the VP node c-commands.
7) List all the nodes that the VP asymmetrically c-commands.
8) List all the nodes that the VP dominates.
9) List all the nodes that the VP immediately dominates.
10) List all the nodes that the VP precedes.
11) List all the nodes that the VP follows (i.e., is preceded by).

4.   NEGATIVE POLARITY ITEMS

There is a class of phrase, such as [a red cent] and [a single thing], that are
called Negative Polarity Items (NPI). These are only allowed in sentences
with a negative word like *not*. So for example, in sentences (a) and (c) the
NPI is fine, in the (b) and (d) sentences, however, the sentence is at best
strange.

a)   I didn't have a red cent.
b)   *I had a red cent.   (ungrammatical with idiomatic reading)

c)   I didn't read a single book the whole time I was in the library.
d)   *I read a single book the whole time I was in the library.

It turns out that sentences with NPIs not only must have a word like *not*, they also have to be in a particular structural relationship with that *not* word. On the basis of the following sentences figure out what that relationship is. There are two possible answers consistent with this data.

e)   I did not have a red cent.
f)   *A red cent was not found in the box.

5.   GRAMMATICAL RELATIONS[3]

For each of the following sentences, identify the subject, the object (if there is one), the indirect object (if there is one), any objects of prepositions, the verb, and any adverbs.

a)   It never rains violently in southern California.
b)   Soon we should give the family dog another bath.
c)   The quiz show contestant bravely made a wild guess about the answer.

6.   TZOTZIL

(Data from Aissen 1987)

Tzotzil is a Mayan language spoken in Mexico. Consider the following sentences, then answer the questions that follow. Glosses have been simplified and the orthography altered from the original source.

a)   'ispet   lok'el 'antz   ti   t'ule.
     carry   away woman   the rabbit
     "The rabbit carried away (the) woman."

b)   'ibat xchi'uk smalal   li Maruche.
     go   with   her-husband the Maruch
     "(the) Maruch went with her husband." (Maruch is a proper name.)

c)   Pas ti   'eklixa'une.
     built the church
     "The church was built."

---

[3] Problem set contributed by Sheila Dooley Collberg.

1) What is the NP rule for Tzotzil?
2) What is the PP rule for Tzotzil?
3) What is the VP rule for Tzotzil?
4) What is the S rule for Tzotzil?
5) What is the subject of sentence (b)?
6) Is [the church] a subject or an object of sentence (c)?
7) Does the verb precede the subject in Tzotzil?
8) Does the object precede the subject in Tzotzil?
9) Does the verb precede the object in Tzotzil?
10) Using the rules you developed in (1)–(4) above, draw the trees for (b) and (c).

7.   HIAKI

(Data from Dedrick and Casad 1999)

Consider the data from the following sentences of Hiaki (also known as Yaqui), an Uto-Atzecan language from Arizona and Mexico. Data have been simplified.

a) Tékil   né-u   'aáyu-k.
   work   me-for   is
   "There is work for me." (literally: "Work is for me.")

b) Hunáa'a yá'uraa hunáka'a hámutta nokriak.
   that   chief   that   woman defend
   "That chief defended that woman."

c) Taáwe tótoi'asó'olam káamomólim híba-tu'ure.
   Hawk   chickens   young   like
   "(The) hawk likes young chickens."

d) Tá'abwikasu   'áma   yépsak.
   different-person   there   arrived
   "A different person arrived there."
                        (assume *there* is an adverb)

1) What is the NP rule for Hiaki?
2) Do you need a PP rule for Hiaki? Why or why not?
3) What is the VP rule for Hiaki?
4) What is the S rule for Hiaki?
5) Using the rules you developed in questions 1–4, draw the tree for sentences (b, c, d).
6) What is the subject of sentence (b)?
7) Is there an object in (d)? If so, what is it?

8)   What node(s) does *hunáa'a* c-command in (b)?

9)   What node(s) does *hunáa'a yá'uraa* c-command in (b)?

10) What does *'áma* precede in (d)?

11) What node immediately dominates *káamomólim* in (c)?

12) What nodes dominate *káamomólim* in (c)?

13) What node immediately precedes *káamomólim* in (c)?

14) What nodes precede *káamomólim* in (c)?

15) Does *káamomólim* c-command *táawe* in (c)?

16) Do *hunáka'a* and *hámutta* symmetrically c-command one another in (b)?

Binding Theory

chapter 4

0. INTRODUCTION

Let's leave syntax for a moment and consider some facts about the meaning of NPs in English. There are some NPs that get their meaning from the context and discourse around them. For example, in the sentence in (1), the meaning of the word *Felicia* comes from the situation in which the sentence is uttered:

1)   Felicia wrote a fine paper on Zapotec.

If you heard this sentence said in the real world, the speaker is assuming that you know who Felicia is and that there is somebody called Felicia who is contextually relevant. Although you may not have already known that she wrote a paper on Zapotec,[1] this sentence informs you that there is some paper in the world that Felicia wrote, it's about Zapotec. It presupposes that there is a paper in the real world and that this paper is the meaning of the phrase *a fine paper on Zapotec*. Both *a fine paper on Zapotec* and *Felicia* get their meaning by referring to objects in the world.[2] This kind of NP is called a ***referring expression*** (or ***R-expression***):

---

[1] Zapotec is a language spoken in southern Mexico.
[2] This is true whether the world being referred to is the actual world, or some fictional imaginary world created by the speaker/hearer.

2)   *R-expression*
        An NP that gets its meaning by referring to an entity in the world.

The vast majority of NPs are R-expressions. But it is by no means the case that all NPs are R-expressions. Consider the case of the NP *herself* in the following sentence:

3)   Heidi bopped *herself* on the head with a zucchini.

In this sentence, *Heidi* is an R-expression and gets its meaning from the context, but *herself* must refer back to *Heidi*. It cannot refer to Arthur, Miriam, or Andrea. It must get its meaning from a previous word in the sentence (in this case *Heidi*). This kind of NP, one that obligatorily gets its meaning from another NP in the sentence, is called an ***anaphor*** (as we saw in chapter 1).

4)   *Anaphor*
        An NP that obligatorily gets its meaning from another NP in the sentence.

Typical anaphors are *himself, herself, themselves, myself, yourself,* and *each other*.

Types of Anaphors
There are actually (at least) two different kinds of anaphors. One type is the reflexive pronouns like *herself, himself,* and *themselves*. The other kind are called ***reciprocals***, and include words like *each other*. For our purposes, we'll just treat this group like a single class, although there are differences between the distribution of reflexives and reciprocals.

There is yet another kind of NP. These are NPs that can optionally get their meaning from another NP in the sentence, but may also optionally get it from somewhere else (including context or previous sentences in the discourse). These NPs are called ***pronouns***.[3] Look at the sentence in (5):

5)   Art said that he played basketball.

In this sentence, the word *he* can optionally refer to Art (i.e., the sentence can mean "Art said that Art played basketball") or it can refer to someone else (i.e. "Art said that Noam played basketball"). Typical pronouns include: *he, she, it, I, you, me, we, they, us, him, her, them, his, her, your, my, our, their, one*. A definition of pronoun is given in (6):

---

[3] There is some discrepancy among linguists in the use of this term. Some linguists use the term ***pronominal*** instead of pronoun and use the term pronoun to cover both anaphors and pronominals. This distinction, while more precise, is confusing to the beginner, so for our purposes we'll just contrast pronouns to anaphors, and avoid the term pronominal.

6)   *Pronoun*
        An NP that may (but need not) get its meaning from another word in the
        sentence.

        Getting back to syntax, it turns out that these different semantic types of
NPs can only appear in certain syntactic positions that are defined using the structural relations we developed in the last chapter. Anaphors, R-expressions, and
pronouns can only appear in specific parts of the sentence. For example, an anaphor
may not appear in the subject position of sentence:

7)   *Herself bopped Heidi on the head with a zucchini.

The theory of the syntactic restrictions on where these different NP types can appear
in a sentence is called **Binding Theory** and is the focus of this chapter.

1.   THE NOTIONS *COINDEX* AND *ANTECEDENT*

We're going to start with the distribution of anaphors. First, we need some terminology to set out the facts. An NP that gives its meaning to an anaphor (or pronoun) is
called an **antecedent**:

8)   *Antecedent*
        An NP that gives its meaning to a pronoun or anaphor.

For example, in sentence (3) (repeated here as 9), the NP *Heidi* is the source of the
meaning for the anaphor *herself*, so *Heidi* is called the antecedent:

9)   Heidi bopped   herself on the head with a zucchini.
          ↑   ↑

        antecedent   *anaphor*

We use a special mechanism to indicate that two NPs refer to the same entity. After
each NP we write a subscript letter. If the NPs refer to the same entity, then they get
the same letter. If they refer to different entities they get different letters. Usually we
start (as a matter of tradition) with the letter *i* and work our way down the alphabet.
These subscript letters are called **indices** or **indexes** (singular: **index**).

10)   a)   [Colin]$_i$ gave [Andrea]$_j$ [a basketball]$_k$.
        b)   [Art]$_i$ said that [he]$_j$ played [basketball]$_k$ in [the dark]$_l$.
        c)   [Art]$_i$ said that [he]$_i$ played [basketball]$_k$ in [the dark]$_l$.
        d)   [Heidi]$_i$ bopped [herself]$_i$ on [the head]$_j$ with [a zucchini]$_k$.

In (10a), all the NPs refer to different entities in the world, so they all get different
indexes. The same is true for (10b). Note that with this indexing, the sentence only

has the meaning where *he* is not *Art*, but someone else – the pronoun *he* and *Art* have different indexes. Sentence (10c), by contrast, has *he* and *Art* referring to the same person. In this sentence, *Art* is the antecedent of the pronoun *he,* so they have the same index. Finally in (10d), the anaphor *herself,* by definition, refers back to *Heidi* so they get the same index. Two NPs that get the same index are said to be **coindexed**. NPs that are coindexed with each other are said to **corefer** (i.e., refer to the same entity in the world).

11)   *Coindexed*
         Two NPs are said to be coindexed if they have the same index.

2.   BINDING

The notions of coindexation, coreference, and antecedence are actually quite general ones. They hold no matter what structural position an NP is in the sentence. It turns out, however, that the relations between an antecedent and a pronoun or anaphor must bear particular structural relations. Contrast the three sentences in (12).[4]

12) .   a)   Heidi$_i$ bopped herself$_i$ on the head with a zucchini.
         b)   [Heidi$_i$'s mother]$_j$ bopped herself$_j$ on the head with a zucchini.
         c)   *[Heidi$_i$'s mother]$_j$ bopped herself$_i$ on the head with a zucchini.

In particular notice the pattern of indexes on (12b) and (12c). These sentences show, that while the word *herself* can refer to the whole subject NP *Heidi's mother*, it can't refer to an NP embedded inside the subject NP, such as *Heidi*. Similar facts are seen in (13).

13)   a)   The mother of Heidi$_i$]$_j$ bopped herself$_j$ on the head with a zucchini.
         b)   [*[The mother of Heidi$_i$]$_j$ bopped herself$_i$ on the head with a zucchini.

Look at the trees for (12a and b), shown in (14a and b) below, and you will notice a significant difference in terms of the position where the NP immediately dominating *Heidi* is placed.

---

[4] In order to account for these sentences we'll have to slightly modify our NP rule:
         NP → (D) (NP) (AP+) N (PP+)

14)   a)(=12a)

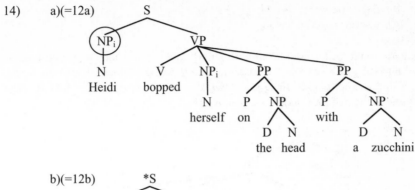

b)(=12b)

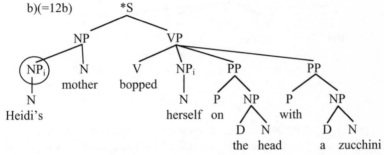

In (14a) the circled NP c-commands the NP dominating *herself*, but in (14b) it does not. It appears that the crucial relationship between an anaphor and its antecedent involves c-command. So in describing the relationship between an anaphor and an antecedent we need a more specific notion than simple coindexation. This is **binding**:

15)   *Binds*
         A binds B if and only if
                  A c-commands B *and*
                  A and B are coindexed.

Binding is a kind of coindexation. It is coindexation that happens when one of the two NPs c-commands the other. Notice that coindexation alone does not constitute binding. Binding requires *both* coindexation and c-command.

         Now we can make the following generalization, which explains the ungrammaticality of sentences (16a)(=7) and (16b)(=12c).

16)   a) (=7)   *Herself bopped Heidi on the head with a zucchini.
         b) (=12c) *[Heidi$_i$'s mother]$_j$ bopped herself$_i$ on the head with a zucchini.

In neither of these sentences is the anaphor bound. In other words, it is not c-commanded by the NP it is coindexed with. This generalization is called **Binding Principle A**. Principle A determines the distribution of anaphors:

17)   *Binding Principle A (preliminary)*
       An anaphor must be bound.

Remember, bound means coindexed with an NP that c-commands it. If you look at
the tree in (14b) you'll see that the anaphor *herself*, and the NP *Heidi* are coindexed.
However they are not bound, since *[NP Heidi]* does not c-command *[NP herself]*. The
same is true in the tree for (16a)(=7) shown in (18):

18)

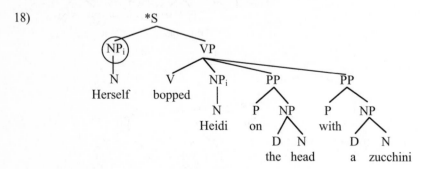

Even though the two NPs are coindexed, they do not form a binding relation, since
the antecedent doesn't c-command the anaphor. You might think that these are in a
binding relation, since the anaphor c-commands the antecedent. But notice that this
is not the way binding is defined. Binding is *not* a symmetric relationship. The
binder (or antecedent) must do the c-commanding of the bindee (anaphor or pronoun), not the reverse.

3.   LOCALITY CONDITIONS ON THE BINDING OF ANAPHORS

Consider now the following fact about anaphors:

19)   *Heidi$_i$ said that herself$_i$ discoed with Art.
       (cf. Heidi$_i$ said that she$_i$ discoed with Art.)

A tree for sentence (19) is given below:

20)   *   S

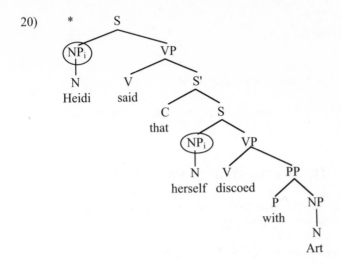

As you can see from this tree, the anaphor is bound by its antecedent: *[NP Heidi]* c-commands *[NP herself]* and is coindexed with it. This sentence is predicted to be grammatical by the version of Principle A presented in (17), since it meets the requirement that anaphors be bound. Surprisingly, however, the sentence is ungrammatical. Notice that the difference between a sentence like (19) and a sentence like (12a) is that in the ungrammatical (19), the anaphor is in an embedded clause. The anaphor seems to need to find its antecedent in the same clause. This is called a *locality constraint*. The anaphor's antecedent must be near it or "local" in some way. The syntactic space in which an anaphor must find its antecedent is called a *binding domain*. For the moment let's just assume that the binding domain is the clause.

21)   *Binding domain*
         The clause containing the NP (anaphor, pronoun, or R-expression).

Binding Domain

The definition we've given here for "binding domain" is clearly over-simplistic. For example, when there is an NP that contains an anaphor and an NP marked with 's, that NP seems to function as a binding domain.

i)   Heidi$_i$ believes any description of herself$_i$.
ii)   *Heidi$_i$ believes Martha$_j$'s description of herself$_i$.
iii)   Heidi$_i$ believes Martha$_j$'s description of herself$_j$.

The literature on this is extensive and beyond the scope of this textbook. But you should be aware that the definition given here needs extensive revision.

With this in mind, let's revise Principle A:

22)   *Binding Principle A (revised)*
        An anaphor must be bound in its binding domain.

This constraint says that anaphors must find an antecedent within the clause that immediately contains them.

4.   THE DISTRIBUTION OF PRONOUNS

Anaphors are not the only NP type with restrictions on their syntactic position. Pronouns are also restricted in where they may appear:

23)   a)   Heidi$_i$ bopped her$_j$ on the head with the zucchini.
        b)   *Heidi$_i$ bopped her$_i$ on the head with the zucchini.

Pronouns like *her* in the sentences in (23) may not be bound. (They may not be coindexed by a c-commanding NP.) The sentence in (23) may only have the meaning where the *her* refers to someone other than *Heidi*. Contrast this situation with the one in which the pronoun is in an embedded clause:

24)   a)   Heidi$_i$ said [$_{S'}$ that she$_i$ discoed with Art].
        b)   Heidi$_i$ said [$_{S'}$ that she$_k$ discoed with Art].

In this situation, a pronoun may be bound by an antecedent, but it doesn't have to be. It can be bound as in (24a), or not bound as in (24b). Unlike the case of anaphors, (which *must* be bound in a particular configuration), pronouns seem only to have a limitation on where they *cannot* be bound. That is, a pronoun cannot be bound by an antecedent that is a clause-mate (in the same immediate clause). You'll notice that this is exactly the opposite of where anaphors are allowed. This restriction is called **Principle B** of the binding theory. It makes use of the term free. **Free** is the opposite of bound.

25)   *Free*
        Not bound.

26)   *Principle B*
        A pronoun must be free in its binding domain.

Given that the binding domain is a clause, the ungrammaticality of (23b) is explained. Both *Heidi* and *her* are in the same clause, so they may not be bound to each other. The pronoun must be free. In (24) both indexings are allowed by Principle B. In (24b) the pronoun isn't bound at all (so is free within its binding domain). In (24a), the situation is a little trickier: The pronoun is bound, but it isn't bound within its binding domain (the embedded clause). Its binder lies outside the binding domain, so the sentence is grammatical.

5.   THE DISTRIBUTION OF R-EXPRESSIONS

R-expressions have yet another distribution. R-expressions don't seem to allow any instances of binding at all, not within the binding domain and not outside it either.

27)   a)   *Heidi$_i$ kissed Miriam$_i$.
       b)   *Art$_i$ kissed Geoff$_i$.
       c)   *She$_i$ kissed Heidi$_i$.
       d)   *She$_i$ said that Heidi$_i$ was a disco queen.[5]

In none of these sentences can the second NP (all R-expressions) be bound by a c-commanding word. This in and of itself isn't terribly surprising given the fact that R-expressions receive their meaning from outside the sentence (i.e., from the context). That they don't get their meaning from another word in the sentence (via binding) is entirely expected. We do have to rule out situations like (27). The constraint that describes the distribution of R-expressions is called ***Principle C***.

28)   *Principle C*
       An R-expression must be free.

Notice that Principle C says nothing about a binding domain. Essentially R-expressions must be free everywhere. They cannot be bound at all.

6.   CONCLUSION

In this chapter, we looked at a very complex set of data concerning the distribution of different kinds of NPs. We saw that these different kinds of NPs can appear in different syntactic positions. A simple set of Binding Principles (A, B, and C) governs the distribution of NPs. This set of binding principles is built upon the structural relations developed in the last chapter.

       In the next chapter, we are going to look at how we can develop a similarly simple set of conditions that will replace the complicated phrase structure rules set out in chapter 2. The constraints developed in this chapter have the shape of locality constraints (in that they require local, or nearness, relations between certain syntactic

---

[5] Note that this sentence is not a violation of Principle B. *Heidi* does not bind *she* here, even though they are coindexed. This is because *Heidi* does not c-command *she*. Note that *[Even her$_i$ enemies] love Heidi$_i$.* is well-formed, because neither NP c-commands the other, so there is no binding, even if they are coindexed. Remember coindexation is not the same thing as binding.

objects). In later chapters, we'll see a trend towards using locality constraints in other parts of the grammar.

IDEAS, RULES, AND CONSTRAINTS INTRODUCED IN THIS CHAPTER

i)   **R-expression**
      An NP that gets it meaning by referring to an entity in the world.

ii)   **Anaphor**
      An NP that obligatorily gets its meaning from another NP in the sentence.

iii) **Pronoun**
      An NP that may (but need not) get its meaning from another NP in the sentence.

iv)   **Antecedent**
      An NP that gives its meaning to a pronoun or anaphor.

v)   **Index**
      A subscript mark that indicates what an NP refers to.

vi)   **Coindexed**
      Two NPs that have the same index ($_i$, $_j$, $_k$, etc.) are said to be coindexed.

vii) **Corefer**
      Two NPs that are coindexed are said to corefer (refer to the same entity in the world).

viii) **Binds**
      A binds B if and only if
              A c-commands B *and*
              A and B are coindexed.

ix)   **Locality Constraint**
      A constraint on the grammar, such that two syntactic entities must be "local" or near to one another.

x)   **Binding Domain**
      The clause (for our purposes).

xi)   **Free**
      Not bound.

xii)   ***The Binding Principles***
    Principle A
        An anaphor must be bound in its binding domain.
    Principle B
        A pronoun must be free in its binding domain.
    Principle C
        An R-expression must be free.

FURTHER READING

Aoun, Joseph (1985) *A Grammar of Anaphora.* Cambridge: MIT Press.

Chomsky, Noam (1980) On Binding. *Linguistic Inquiry* 11, 1–46.

Chomsky, Noam (1981) *Lectures on Government and Binding.* Dordrecht: Foris.

Higginbotham, James (1980) Pronouns and bound variables. *Linguistic Inquiry* 11, 697–708.

Lasnik, Howard (1989) *Essays on Anaphora.* Dordrecht: Kluwer Academic Publishers.

Reinhart, Tanya (1976) The Syntactic Domain of Anaphora. Ph.D. dissertation, MIT.

PROBLEM SETS

1.   BINDING PRINCIPLES

Explain why the following sentences are ungrammatical:

a) *Michael$_i$ loves him$_i$.
b) *He$_i$ loves Michael$_i$.
c) *Michael$_i$'s father$_j$ loves himself$_i$.
d) *Michael$_i$'s father$_j$ loves him$_j$.
e) *Susan$_i$ thinks that John should marry herself$_i$.
f) *John thinks that Susan$_i$ should kiss her$_i$.

2.   JAPANESE

(Data from Aikawa 1994)

Japanese has a number of items that can be called pronouns or anaphors.
One of these is *zibunzisin*. For the purposes of this assignment assume that
any noun that has the suffix *-wa* c-commands any other NP, and assume
that any noun that has the suffix *-ga* c-commands any NP with the suffix *-o*.
Consider the following data:

a) Johnwa$_i$ [$_{S'}$ [$_S$ Maryga$_k$ zibunzisino$_{k/*i}$ hihansita] [$_C$ to]] itta.
    John   Mary   zibunzisin   criticized   that said
    "John said that Mary$_k$ criticized herself$_k$."
    "*John$_i$ said that Mary criticized himself$_i$."

Question 1: On the basis of only the data in (a) is *zibunzisin* an anaphor or a
pronoun? How can you tell?

Now consider this sentence:

b) Johnwa$_i$ [$_{S'}$ [$_S$ zibunzisinga$_i$ Maryo korosita] [$_C$ to]] omotteiru.
    John   zibunzisin   Mary killed   that think
    "John thinks that himself killed Mary."
        (*note:* grammatical in Japanese.)

Question 2. Given this additional evidence, do you need to revise your hypothesis from question 1? Is *zibunzisin* an anaphor, a pronoun or something
else entirely? How can you tell?

One more piece of data:

c) *Johnwa$_i$ [$_{S'}$[$_S$ zibunzisinga$_k$ Maryo$_k$ korosita] [$_C$ to]] omotteiru.
    John   zibunzisin   Mary killed   that think
    "*John thinks that herself$_k$ killed Mary$_k$."

Question 3. Sentence (c) is a violation of which binding principle? (A, B, or
C?) Which noun is binding which other noun in this sentence to cause the
ungrammaticality?

3.   WH-QUESTIONS

What problem(s) does the following sentence make for the binding theory?
Can you think of a solution? (Hint: consider the non-question form of this
sentence *John despises these pictures of himself.*)

Which pictures of himself$_i$ does John$_i$ despise?

Assume the following tree for this sentence:

4.   COUNTEREXAMPLES?[6]

Each of the following examples is problematic for the binding theory we formulated above. Briefly explain why. For data from languages other than English, your answer should be based on the facts of the target language, and not the English translations. Use the word-by-word glosses to determine whether the Dogrib and Modern Greek NPs should be analyzed as anaphors, pronouns or R-expressions. Your discussion of Dogrib should be based on consideration of both sentences.

a)   I have no money on me.

b)   John knew that there would be a picture of himself hanging in the post office.

c)   *Modern Greek*
      O Yanis$_i$ ipe stin Katerina   oti i Maria aghapa ton idhio$_i$.
      John   said to Catherin   that Mary loves   himself
      "John$_i$ told Catherine that Mary loves him$_{i/*k}$."

---

[6] This problem set was contributed by Betsy Ritter. The Dogrib data come from Saxon (1984).

d) *Dogrib*

   (i) John   ye-hk'è   ha

       John   3SG(=him)-shoot   future

      "John$_i$ is going to shoot him$_{k/*i}$."

   (ii) *ye-zha   shèeti

       3SG(=his)-son   ate

      "His son ate."

5. PERSIAN[7]

Does the binding theory account for the following data? Explain. (*Râ* means "the" when following object NPs. 3SG means "third person singular.")

a) Jân$_i$ goft [$_{S'}$ ke [$_S$ Mery$_k$ ketâb-â ro be xodesh$_{i/k}$ bargardune]].

    John said that   Mary book-PL râ to himself/herself return

    "John said that Mary (should) return the books to him/herself."

b) Jân$_i$ goft [$_{S'}$ ke [$_S$ Mery$_j$ ketâb-â ro be xodesh$_{i/j}$ barmigardune]].

    John said that   Mary book-PL râ to himself/herself return3SG.FUT

    "John said that Mary will return the books to him/herself."

Now consider (c) and (d): in these examples, *xod* 'self', instead of *xodesh* 'himself', is used. How do you explain the contrast between (a and b) and (c and d)? Note that (a and b) are taken from the spoken language, whereas (c and d) represent the formal written variant.

c) Jân$_i$ goft [ke [$_S$ Mery$_k$ ketâb râ barâye   xod$_{*i/k}$ bexânad]].

    John said that   Mary book râ for   self   read3SG

    "John said that Mary (should) read the book to *himself/herself."

d) Jân$_i$ goft [ke [$_S$ Mery$_k$ ketâb râ   barâye xod$_{*i/k}$ negahdârad]].

    John said that Mary book râ   for   self   keep3SG

    "John said that Mary (should) keep the books for *himself/herself."

6. C-COMMAND OR PRECEDENCE?

In the text above, we proposed that binding required both c-command and coindexation. Consider an alternative: binding requires that the antecedent precedes (rather than c-commands) and is coindexed with the anaphor or

---

[7] This problem set was contributed by Simin Karimi.

pronoun. Which of these alternatives is right? How can you tell? You might consider data such as the following:

a) [s' [sAlthough he$_i$ loves marshmallows] [s Art$_i$ is not a big fan of Smores]].
b) [s [NP His$_i$ yearbook picture] gives Tom$_i$ the creeps].

Part 2

The Base

chapter 5

X-bar Theory

0.   INTRODUCTION

As we saw in the last chapter, the theory of sentence structure that we've developed is quite powerful. It correctly predicts constituency and along with structural relations and the binding theory it also accounts for phenomena such as how we interpret nominals (nouns and noun phrases). This said, if we look a little more closely at sentence structure in many languages, we see that our theory has some empirical inadequacies. (It can't account for all the data.) Consider, for example, the subject NP in the sentence in (1):

1)   [The big book of poems with the blue cover] is on the table.

The structure our NP rule NP → (D) (AP+) N (PP+) assigns to this is:

2)

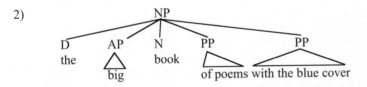

We can call this a *flat structure*. The PP *of poems* and the PP *with the blue cover* are on the same level hierarchically; there is no distinction between them in terms of dominance or c-command. In other words they are "flat" with respect to the head word *book*. From the point of view of constituency, we see that a number of tests point towards a more complicated structure. Consider first the constituency test of *replacement*. There is a particular variety of this process, called **one-*replacement***, that seems to target precisely a group of nodes that don't form a constituent in (2):

3)   I bought the big [book of poems with the blue cover] not the small [one].

Here, *one*-replacement targets *book of poems with the blue cover*, this group of words does not form a constituent in the tree in (2). Furthermore, *one*-replacement seems to be able to target other subgroups of words that similarly don't form constituents in (2):

4)   I bought the big [book of poems] with the blue cover not the small [one] with the red cover.

These facts seem to point to a more deeply embedded structure for the NP:

5)

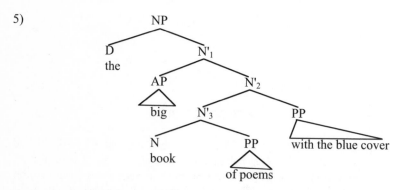

The *one*-replacement in (4) targets the node labeled N'$_3$. The *one*-replacement in (3) targets the node labeled N'$_2$. We have to change the NP slightly to get evidence for N'$_1$. If we change the determiner *the* to the determiner *that*, we can use *one*-replacement to target N'$_1$.

6)   I want [$_{NP}$ this [$_{N'}$big book of poems with the red cover]] not [$_{NP}$that [$_{N'}$one]].

         Similar evidence comes from conjunction:

7)   Calvin is [the [dean of humanities] and [director of social sciences]].
8)   Give me [the [blue book] and [red binder]].

We need these "intermediate" N' (pronounced "en-bar") categories to explain the items that are conjoined in these sentences.

         The flat structure seen in (2) is clearly inadequate and a more articulated structure is needed. This chapter is about these articulated trees. The theory that accounts for these is called X-bar theory.

Before getting into the content of this chapter, a few bibliographic notes are in order. The first presentation of X-bar theory appeared in Chomsky (1970). Jackendoff's (1977) seminal book *X-bar Syntax* is the source of many of the ideas surrounding X-bar theory. Perhaps the most complete description of X-bar theory comes from an introductory syntax textbook (like this one). This is Radford's (1988) *Transformational Grammar: A First Course*. That textbook presents one of the most comprehensive arguments for X-bar theory. This chapter draws heavily on all three of these sources. If you are interested in reading a more comprehensive (although slightly out-of-date) version of X-bar theory, then you should look at Radford's book.

1.   BAR-LEVEL PROJECTIONS

In order to account for the data seen above in the introduction, let us revise our NP rules to add the intermediate structure:

9)   NP → (D) N'
10)   N' → (AP) N' *or* N' (PP)
11)   N' → N (PP)

These rules introduce a new character to our cast of nodes, seen briefly above. This is the N' node. It plays the role of the intermediate constituent replaced by *one* above. The tree in (5) is repeated here showing how these rules (9–11) apply.

12)

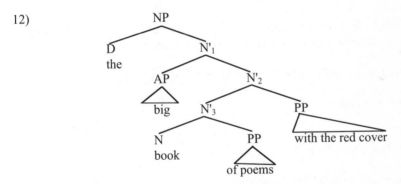

Rule (9) generates the NP node of this tree, with its daughters D and N'. The first version of rule (10) generates N'₁. The second version of rule (10) generates N'₂. Finally the last rule (11) spells out N'₃ as N and its PP sister.

We can now straightforwardly account for the *one*-replacement sentences. *One*-replacement is a process that targets the N' node:

13)   One-*replacement*
        Replace an N' node with *one.*

Without the intermediate N' node we would have no way of accounting for *one*-replacement or conjunction facts. With N', explaining these sentences is easy, since there is more structure in each phrase.

The rule system in (9–11) has a number of striking properties (including the facts that it is binary branching and the first N' rule is iterative or self-recursive). We will return to these properties in a later section and show how they account for a number of surprising facts about the internal structure of phrases. First, however, let's see if any other categories also have intermediate structure.

1.1   *V-bar*

There is an identical process to one-replacement found in the syntax of VPs. This is the process of **do-so-** (or **did-so-**) *replacement*. Consider first the VP in the following sentence, which has both an NP and a PP in it.

14)   I [eat beans with a fork].

The rule we developed for VPs in chapter 2 generates the following flat tree:

15)
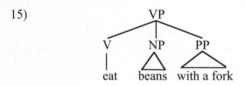

In this tree, there is no constituent that groups together the V and NP and excludes the PP. However, *do-so*-replacement targets exactly this unit:

16)   I [eat beans] with a fork but Janet [does so] with a spoon.

Let's formalize this rule as:

17)   Do-so-*replacement*
         Replace a V' with *do so*.

For this to work we need the following rules:

18)   VP → V' [1]
19)   V' → V' (PP)
20)   V' → V (NP)

The tree structure for the VP in (14) will look like:

21)

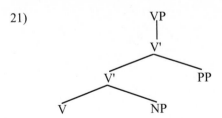

Rule (18) generates the VP and the V' under it; the next rule (19) expands the top V' into another V' and a PP. Finally, the lower V' is expanded into V and NP by rule (20).

The rule of *do-so*-replacement seen in (17) targets the lower V' and replaces it with *do so*. Evidence for the higher V' comes from sentences like (22).

22)   Kevin [ate spaghetti with a spoon] and Geordi [did so] too.

In this sentence, *did so* replaces the higher V' (which includes the V, the lower V', the NP, and the PP).

Similarly, conjunction seems to show an intermediate V' projection:

23)   The chef [eats beans] and [tosses salads] with forks.

The tree for a structure like this requires a V' node (a description of the conjunction rule can be found below in section 5):

---

[1] This rule may appear a little mysterious right now (since it appears to introduce a vacuous structure) but we will have need of it in a later chapter. For the moment, just assume that it is necessary, and we will provide additional justification for it later. You can note for now that in order to account for sentences like (22) below, we will need to assume that the entire replaced structure is a V', if we assume that *do-so*-replacement only targets V' nodes (and not VP nodes).

24)

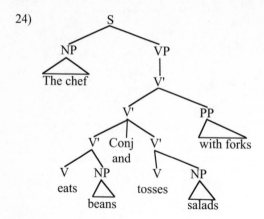

1.2   A-bar

The arguments for intermediate structure in APs are a little more tricky. As English seems to limit the amount of material that can appear in an AP. However, we do see such structure in phrases like (25):

25)   the [very [[bright blue] and [dull green]]] gown

In this NP, *bright* clearly modifies *blue*, and *dull* clearly modifies *green*. One possible interpretation of this phrase (although not the only one) allows *very* to modify both *bright blue* and *dull green*. If this is the case then the structure must minimally look like (26) (note: we will have reason to revise this tree later).

26)

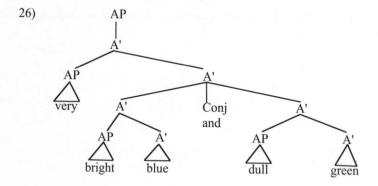

Under certain circumstances, some adjectives appear to allow prepositional modifiers to follow them:

27)   I am afraid/frightened of tigers.
28)   I am fond of circus performers.

These post-adjectival PPs have the "feel" of a direct object:

29)   I fear tigers.
30)   I like circus performers.

Consider now:

31)   I am [[afraid/frightened of tigers] and [fond of clowns] without exception].

Under one reading of this sentence, *without exception* modifies both *afraid of tigers* and *fond of circus performers*. Again this would seem to suggest that the sentence has the constituency represented by the above bracketing, which points towards an intermediate category of A'.

There is also a replacement phenomenon that seems to target A's. This is *so*-replacement:

32)   Bob is [very [serious about Mary]], but [less [so]] than Paul.

The adjective phrase here is *very serious about Mary*, but *so*-replacement only targets *serious about Mary*.

The rules that generate these structures are:

33)   AP → A'
34)   A' → (AP) A'
35)   A' → A (PP)

1.3   P-bar

The evidence for an intermediate P-bar projection is, if anything, weaker than that for APs. I'll admit this up front. But some small evidence does exist. Consider the following sentences:

36)   Gwen placed it [right [in the middle of the spaghetti sauce]].
37)   Maurice was [[in love] with his boss].
38)   Susanna was [utterly [in love]].

In these examples, we have what appear to be prepositional phrases (*in the middle of the spaghetti sauce, in love*) that are modified by some other element: *right, with his boss*, and *utterly* respectively. Note, however, that you can target smaller units within these large PPs with constituency tests:

39)   Gwen knocked it [right [off the table] and [into the trash]].
40)   Maurice was [[in love] and [at odds] with his boss].
41)   Susanna was [utterly [in love]], but Louis was only [partly [so]].

Examples (39) and (40) show conjunction of the two smaller constituents. Example (41) is an example of *so*-replacement. Let us call the smaller constituent here P' on a parallel with N', A', and V'. The rules that generate PPs are given below:

42)   PP → P'
43)   P' → P' (PP)
44)   P' → P (NP)

2.   GENERALIZING THE RULES: THE X-BAR SCHEMA

For each of the major phrase types (NPs, VPs, APs, and PPs) we have come up with three rules, where the second and third rules serve to introduce intermediate structure. Let's repeat all the rules here:

45)   NP → (D) N'
46)   N' → (AP) N' *or* N' (PP)
47)   N' → N (PP)
48)   VP → V'
49)   V' → V' (PP)
50)   V' → V (NP)
51)   AP → A'
52)   A' → (AP) A'
53)   A' → A (PP)
54)   PP → P'
55)   P' → P' (PP)
56)   P' → P (NP)

The evidence for some of these rules (like the N' rules) is quite strong. Evidence for some of the others is quite weak (such as VP → V', for which I've yet to present any evidence at all). However, let's consider the possibility that these are *all* reflective of our human language capability. We can now ask, are we missing any generalizations here?

Indeed we seem to be missing several. First, note that in all the rules above, the category of the rule is the same as the only element that is not optional. For example, in the NP rule, the element that isn't optional is N'. This is the same part of speech. Similarly, the only obligatory element in N' is either another N' or N. This is a very general notion in phrase structure; we call this headedness. All phrases appear to have **heads**. Heads are the most prominent element in a phrasal category and give their part of speech category to the whole phrase. Note that we don't have any rules of the form:

57)   NP → V AP

This rule not only seems meaningless, it is unattested in the system we've developed here. This property is called **endocentricity**, meaning that every phrase has a head. The only obligatory element in a phrase is the head.

Second, note that with the exception of the determiner in the NP rule, all non-head material in the rules is both phrasal and optional. We never find rules of the form:

58)   VP → A V

Any thing that isn't a head must be a phrase and optional.

Finally, notice that for each major category, there are three rules, one that introduces the NP, VP, AP and PP, one that takes a bar level and repeats it (e.g., N' → N' (PP)), and one that takes a bar level and spells out the head (e.g., N' → N (PP)). We seem to be missing the generalization that for each kind of phrase, the *same kinds of rules* appear. X-bar theory is an attempt to capture these similarities between rules.

We can condense the rules we've proposed into a simple set. To do this we are going to make use of variables (like variables in algebra) to stand for particular parts of speech. Let X be a variable that can stand for any category N, V, A, P. An XP is a catch-all term to cover NP, VP, AP, PP, similarly X' stands for N', V', A', P', and X represents N, V, A, and P. The Xs here are what give the theory its name.

Using this variable notation we can capture the generalizations that we have missed. Let's start with the NP, VP, AP, and PP rules:

59)   NP → (D) N'
60)   VP → V'
61)   AP → A'
62)   PP → P'

By using the variable notation we can summarize these rules with the single rule:

63)   XP → (YP) X' (*to be revised*)

Both X and Y here are variables for categories. This rule says that a phrase consists of some optional, phrasal[2] element followed by a node of *the same category* that is a single bar. Note that this last bit is crucial. If the X in XP stands for NP, then the bar level is an N'. This captures the endocentric property of our rules.

---

[2] The D in the NP rule is, of course, not phrasal. This is a problem we will return to in later chapters.

Now turn to the recursive N', A', V' and P' rules:

64)   N' → (AP) N' *or* N' (PP)
65)   V' → V' (PP)
66)   A' → (AP) A'
67)   P' → P' (PP)

For each of these rules, a category with a single bar level is iterated (repeated), with some optional material either on the right or the left. Again using X as a variable, we can condense these into a single rule:

68)   X' → (ZP) X' *or* X' (ZP) *(to be revised)*

Again the Xs here must be consistent in part of speech category. The material that is not the head (i.e., not X) must be phrasal and optional. Note that the categories of these non-head items is also indicated with variables (in this case: ZP).
      Finally, let's consider the rules that introduce the last layer of structure:

69)   N' → N (PP)
70)   V' → V (NP)
71)   A' → A (PP)
72)   P' → P (NP)

These rules can also be summarized into a single rule:

73)   X' → X (WP) *(to be revised)*

      The system we've come up with here is remarkably simple. We've reduced the number of rules to three (63, 68, 73). Because they use variables, these rules can generate most of the sentences of English. This analysis isn't without problems, however. Before we turn to resolving these problems and drafting a final version of the X-bar rules, we need to introduce some new terminology.

3.   COMPLEMENTS, ADJUNCTS, AND SPECIFIERS

Consider now the two prepositional phrases that are subconstituents of the following NP:

74)   the book [PP of poems] [PP with the glossy cover]

Using the X-bar rules,[3] we can generate the following tree for this NP:

---

[3] Specific instructions on drawing trees using the X-bar rules are found at the end of this chapter.

75)

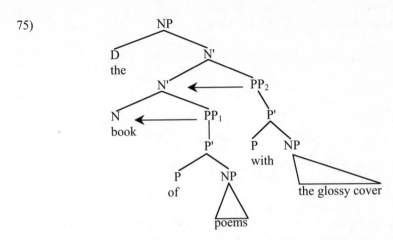

(I've used triangles in this tree to obscure some of the irrelevant details, but you should not do this when you are drawing trees, until you have a confident grasp of how tree notation works.) You'll note that the two PPs in this tree are at different levels in the tree. The lower PP_1 is a sister to the head N (*book*), whereas the higher PP_2 is a sister to the N' dominating the head N and PP_1. You'll also notice that these two PPs were introduced by different rules. PP_1 is introduced by the rule:

76) $X' \rightarrow X$ (WP)

and PP_2 is introduced by the higher level rule:

77) $X' \rightarrow X'$ (ZP)

Let's introduce some new terminology here to describe these two different kinds of PPs. An XP that is a sister to a head (N, V, A, or P) is called a ***complement***. PP_1 is a complement. Complements roughly correspond to the notion "object" in traditional grammar. XPs that are sisters to single bar levels (N', V', A', or P') and are daughters of an N' are called ***adjuncts***. PP_2 is an adjunct. Adjuncts often have the feel of adverbial or optional information.

78)   *Adjunct*
         An XP that is a sister to a single bar level (N', V', A', or P') and a daughter of a single bar level (N', V', A', or P').

79)   *Complement*
         An XP that is a sister to a head (N, V, A, P), and a daughter of a single bar level (N', V', A', or P').

The rules that introduce these two kinds of XPs get special names:

80)   *Adjunct rule*   X' → X' (ZP)
81)   *Complement rule*   X' → X (WP)

A tree showing the structural difference between these is given below:

82)

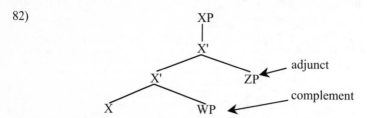

If there really are two different kinds of PP within an NP, then we expect that they will exhibit different kinds of behavior. It turns out that this is true. There are significant differences in behavior between adjuncts and complements.

3.1   Complements and Adjuncts in NPs

Take NPs as a prototypical example. Consider the difference in meaning between the two NPs below:

83)   the book of poems
84)   the book with a red cover

Although both these examples seem to have, on the surface, parallel structures (a determiner, followed by a noun, followed by a prepositional phrase), in reality, they have quite different structures. The PP in (83) is a complement and has the following tree:

85)

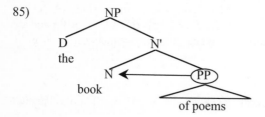

You'll note that the circled PP is a sister to N, so it is a complement. By contrast, the structure of (84) is:

86)

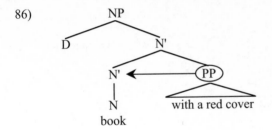

Here the PP *with a red cover* is a sister to N', so it is an adjunct. The differences between these two NPs is not one that you can *hear*. The difference between the two is in terms of the amount of structure in the tree. In (86), there is an extra N'. While this difference may at first seem abstract, it has important implications for the behavior of the two PPs. Consider first the meaning of our two NPs. In (83), the PP seems to complete (or complement) the meaning of the noun. It tells us what kind of book is being referred to. In (84), by contrast, the PP seems more optional and more loosely related to the NP. This is a highly subjective piece of evidence, but it corresponds to more syntactic and structural evidence too.

An easy heuristic (guiding principle) for distinguishing complements from adjunct PPs inside NPs, is by looking at what preposition they take. In English, almost always (although there are some exceptions) complement PPs take the preposition *of*. Adjuncts, by contrast, take other prepositions (such as *from, at, to, with, under, on*, etc.). This test isn't 100 percent reliable, but will allow you to eyeball PPs and tell whether they are complements or adjuncts for the vast majority of cases (such as (83) and (84) above). With this in mind, let's look at some of the other behavioral distinctions between complements and adjuncts.

Think carefully about the two rules that introduce complements and adjuncts. There are several significant differences between them. These rules are repeated here for your convenience:

87)   *Adjunct rule*   X' → X' (ZP)
88)   *Complement rule*   X' → X (WP)

First observe that because the complement rule introduces the head (X), the complement PP will always be adjacent to the head. Or more particularly, it will always be closer to the head than an adjunct PP will be. This is seen in the following data:

89)   the book   [of poems]   [with a red cover]
            head   *complement*   *adjunct*

90)   *the book   [with a red cover] [of poems]
            head   *adjunct*   *complement*

You can see how this is true if you look at the tree for sentence (89):

91)

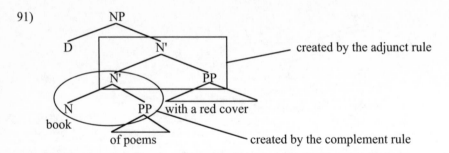

created by the adjunct rule

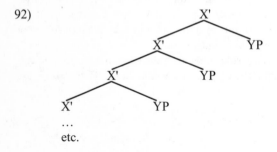

created by the complement rule

Since the adjunct rule takes an X' level category and generates another X' category, it will always be higher in the tree than the output of the complement rule (which takes an X' and generates an X). Since lines can't cross, this means that complements will always be lower in the tree than adjuncts, and will always be closer to the head than adjuncts.

There is another property of the rules that manifests itself in the difference between adjuncts and complements. The adjunct rule, as passingly observed above, is an iterative rule. That is, within the rule itself, it shows the property of recursivity (discussed in chapter 2): On the left-hand side of the rule there is an X' category, and on the right hand side there is another X'. This means that the rule can generate infinite strings of X' nodes, since you can apply the rule over and over again to its own output:

92)

```
                                    X'
                                   /  \
                             X'        YP
                            /  \
                       X'        YP
                      /  \
                  X'        YP
                  ...
                 etc.
```

The complement rule does not have this property. On the left side of the rule there is an X', but on the right there is only X. So the rule cannot apply iteratively. That is, it can only apply once within an XP. What this means for complements and adjuncts is that you can have any number of adjuncts (93), but you can only ever have one complement (94):

93)   the book [of poems] [with a red cover][from Blackwell][by Robert Burns]
              head *complement* *adjunct*   *adjunct*   *adjunct*

94)   *the book [of poems]   [of fiction]   [with a red cover]
              head *complement* *complement*   *adjunct*

The tree for (93) is given below; you'll note that since there is only one N, there can only be one complement, but since there are multiple N's, there can be as many adjuncts as desired.

95)

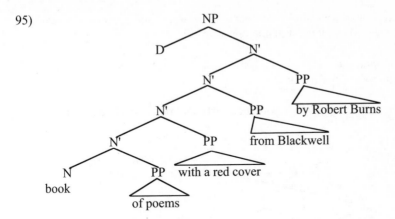

     Related to the facts that the number of adjuncts is unlimited, but only one complement is allowed, and complements are always adjacent to the head, observe that you can usually reorder adjuncts with respect to one another, but you can never reorder a complement with the adjuncts:

96)   the book of poems with a red cover from Blackwell by Robert Burns
97)   the book of poems from Blackwell with a red cover by Robert Burns
98)   the book of poems from Blackwell by Robert Burns with a red cover
99)   the book of poems by Robert Burns from Blackwell with a red cover
100)   the book of poems by Robert Burns with a red cover from Blackwell
101)   the book of poems with a red cover by Robert Burns from Blackwell
102)   *the book with a red cover of poems from Blackwell by Robert Burns
103)   *the book with a red cover from Blackwell of poems by Robert Burns
104)   *the book with a red cover from Blackwell by Robert Burns of poems
              (etc.)

     Note that adjuncts and complements are constituents of different types. The definition of adjuncthood holds that adjuncts are sisters to X'. Since conjunction (see under **_additional rules_** at the end of this chapter) requires that you conjoin elements of the same bar level, you could not, for example, conjoin an adjunct with a complement. This would result in a contradiction: Something can't be both a sister to X' and X at the same time. Adjuncts can conjoin with other adjuncts (other sisters to X'), and complements can conjoin with other complements (other sisters to X), but complements cannot conjoin with adjuncts:

105)   the book of poems with a red cover and with a blue spine[4]
106)   the book of poems and of fiction from Blackwell
107)   *the book of poems and from Blackwell

There is one final difference between adjuncts and complements that we will examine here. Recall the test of *one*-replacement:

108)   One-*replacement*
        Replace an N' node with *one*.

This operation replaces an N' node with the word *one*. Look at the tree in (109).

109)

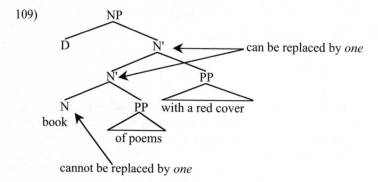

If you look closely at this tree you'll see that two possibilities for *one*-replacement exist. We can either target the highest N', and get:

110)   the one

or we can target the lower N' and get:

111)   the one with a red cover

But we cannot target the N head; it is not an N'. This means that *one* followed by a complement is ill-formed:

112)   *the one of poems with a red cover[5]

Since complements are sisters to X and not X', they cannot stand next to the word *one*. Adjuncts, by definition, can.

---

[4] If this NP sounds odd to you, try putting emphasis on the *and*.
[5] Not everyone finds this NP ill-formed. One possible explanation for this is that different dialects have different *one*-replacement rules. The dialect that finds this NP well-formed allows either N or N' to be replaced. The dialect that finds this ill-formed (or at least odd), only allows N' to be replaced.

A Common Error

Many beginning syntacticians, when faced with an NP like:

i)   The big banana

will make an easy mistake: They will treat the word *big* as a complement. That is, they draw the tree such that the word *big* is a sister to the N ba-nana. This is very wrong! *Big* here is an adjunct (you can test this yourself with the diagnostics we developed above) so it must be a sister to N'. The tree for this NP is:

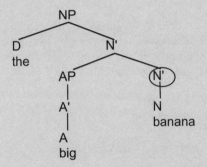

The circled N' here is crucial to make the AP an adjunct.

Complements and adjuncts don't have to follow the head. Material that pre-cedes an N head also shows the distinction between complements and adjuncts.

113)   the boring   linguistics   book
             adjunct   complement head

Boring is an adjunct but *linguistics* is a complement.[6] The tree for this NP is:

---

[6] Some linguists treat sequences such as linguistics book as a compound noun rather than as a complement adjective preceding a head noun. Can you figure out a way to distinguish these two possible analyses?

114)

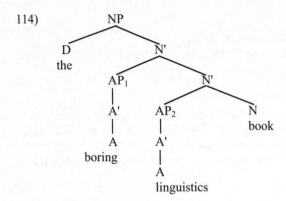

The first adjective phrase is an adjunct (sister to N'), the second is a complement (sister to N). The behavioral differences we saw above with post-nominal phrases hold here too. First there is the phenomenon of stacking: You are allowed to have more than one adjunct, but only one complement:

115)   the big red boring linguistics book
116)   *the boring linguistics fiction book

Complements always appear closer to the head than adjuncts:

117)   the red poetry book
118)   *the poetry red book

Adjuncts can be reordered with respect to one another, but complements are fixed in their position (adjacent to the head):

119)   the big boring red linguistics book
120)   ?[7]the boring big red linguistics book
121)   ?the red big boring linguistics book
122)   *the big boring linguistics red book
123)   *the big linguistics boring red book
124)   *the linguistics big boring red book

Adjuncts can be conjoined with adjuncts, and complements can be conjoined with complements, but adjuncts can't be conjoined with complements:

125)   the big and boring linguistics book
126)   the boring linguistics and anthropology book

---

[7] Most native speakers of English will find this example and the next one slightly odd. This is because there is a preferred order of adjectives in English. However, what is crucial here is that while these NPs seem odd (or "marked"), they are certainly better than the ones where the complement is reordered with the adjuncts: (122), (123), and (124).

127)   *the boring and linguistics book

Finally, adjuncts but not complements can stand next to the *one* of *one*-replacement:

128)   the boring book but not the interesting one
129)   *the linguistics book but not the anthropology one[8]

The complement/adjunct distinction clearly holds for modifiers that appear prenominally (before the noun) as well.

Before concluding our discussion of complements and adjuncts in NPs, I want to point out one area where the distinction makes an important advance over the theory of phrase structure we developed in chapter 1. Consider the following NP:

130)   the German teacher

This NP is actually ambiguous. It can mean either a teacher (say of math) who is German, or it can mean someone (of any nationality) who teaches the German language. In the old theory of phrase structure, we had no way of distinguishing these. With X-bar theory we do. When *German* refers to the subject being taught, it is a complement to the noun *teacher*. When it refers to nationality, it is an adjunct. We can see this if we apply various tests for distinguishing complements from adjuncts. Note that when we add an adjunct indicating a place of origin, then the NP is no longer ambiguous:

131)   the French German teacher

This can only mean "the teacher of German from France." The test of conjunction says that we can only conjoin adjuncts with adjuncts and complements with complements. If we conjoin German with another complement, the NP is again disambiguated:

132)   the math and German teacher *(can't mean she is from Germany)*

Finally, if we allow *one* insertion, only the adjunct (country) meaning is allowed:

133)   not the American teacher but the German one
         (can't mean "teacher of the German language")

In this chapter so far, we've covered a huge range of facts, so a quick summary is probably in order. In section 1, we saw that constituency tests pointed towards a more articulated structure for our trees than the one we developed in chapter 2. In section 2, we introduced the X' notation to account for this more complicated structure. In X-bar structure, there are three levels of categories. There are

---

[8] Again, some speakers find this grammatical. This presumably has to do with whether their dialect's *one*-replacement rule targets both N and N' or just N.

XPs, X's, and Xs. In this section – focusing exclusively on NPs – we introduced special terms for elements that are sisters to X' and X: *adjuncts* and *complements*. These
two different kinds of modifier have different properties. Adjuncts but not complements can be iterated and reordered and can stand next to *one*. Complements, by
contrast, must be located next to the head and can't be reordered. We also saw that
we could conjoin complements with complements and adjuncts with adjuncts, but
that we couldn't mix the two. All of these data provide support for the extra structure
proposed in X-bar theory. In the next subsection, we'll briefly consider evidence that
the complement/adjunct distinction holds for categories other than NP as well.

3.2   Complements and Adjuncts in VPs, APs, and PPs

The distinction between complements and adjuncts is not limited to NPs; we find it
holds in all the major syntactic categories. The best example is seen in VPs. The
direct object of a verb is a complement of the verb. Prepositional and adverbial
modifiers of verbs are adjuncts:

134)   I loved [the policeman] [intensely] [with all my heart].
            V   direct object   adverbial   PP phrase
                     complement   *adjunct*   *adjunct*

135)

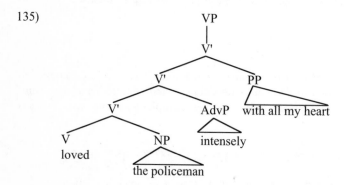

Direct objects must be adjacent to the verb, and there can only be one of them.

136)   *I loved intensely the policeman with all my heart.
137)   *I loved the policeman the baker intensely with all my heart.

This is classic adjunct/complement distinction. In general, complements of all categories (N, V, A, P, etc.) are the semantic objects of the head. Consider for example
all the complements below:

138)   John fears dogs.   *(verb)*
139)   John is afraid of dogs.   *(adjective)*
140)   John has a fear of dogs.   *(noun)*

In all these sentences, *(of) dogs* is a complement.

The evidence for the adjunct/complement distinction in adjective phrases and prepositional phrases is considerably weaker. Adverbs that modify adjectives have an adjunct flair – they can be stacked and reordered. Other than this, however, the evidence for the distinction in PPs and AdjPs, comes mainly as a parallel to the NPs and VPs. This may be less than satisfying, but is balanced by the formal simplicity of having the same system apply to all categories.

3.3   *The Notion* Specifier

In the section 3.1 above, we introduced two structural notions: adjuncts and complements. These correspond to two of the three X-bar rules:

141)   *Adjunct rule*   X' → X' (ZP) *or* X' → (ZP) X'
142)   *Complement rule*   X' → X (WP)

The third rule also introduces a structural position: the **specifier**.

143)   *Specifier rule*   XP → (YP) X'

We have only seen one specifier so far – the determiner in NPs:

144)   [the]   [book]   [of poems]   [with a red cover]
          specifier head   complement   adjunct

145)

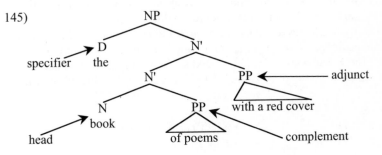

The specifier is defined as the daughter of XP and sister to X':

146)   *Specifier*
          An XP[9] that is a sister to an X' level, and a daughter of an XP.

---

[9] If you are being observant you'll notice that the single example we have of a specifier is not a phrase, but a word (the), so it may seem odd to say XP here. We return to this issue in later chapters.

We can show that specifiers are different from adjuncts and complements. Since the specifier rule is not recursive, you can only have one specifier:[10]

147)   *the these red books

The specifier rule has to apply at the top of the structure, this means that the specifier will always be the left-most element (in English anyway):

148)   *boring the book

The above example also shows that specifiers can't be reordered with respect to other adjuncts or complements. As the final difference between specifiers and other types of modifier, specifiers can only be conjoined with other specifiers:

149)   two or three books
150)   *two or boring books

On the surface, the usefulness of this position may seem obscure, since only determiners appear in it. But in later chapters we will have important use for specifiers. (In particular, we will claim that they are the position where subjects are generated in a variety of categories.)

4.   PARAMETERS OF WORD ORDER

In this chapter, and thus far in this book, we've been concentrating primarily on English. The reason for this is that, since you are reading this book, it is the language most accessible to you. However, syntacticians aren't interested only in English. One of the most interesting parts of syntax is comparing the sentence structure of different languages. The X-bar rules we've developed so far for English do an acceptable job of accounting for the order of constituents and hierarchical structure of English:

151)	*Specifier rule*	$XP \rightarrow (YP) X'$
152)	*Adjunct rule*	$X' \rightarrow X' (ZP)$ *or* $X' \rightarrow (ZP) X'$
153)	*Complement rule*	$X' \rightarrow X (WP)$

They don't account, however, well for other languages. Consider the position of direct objects (complements) in Turkish. In Turkish, the complement precedes the head:

---

[10] One possible exception to this is the quantifier *all*, as in *all the books*. In the next chapter, we discuss the idea that determiners head their own phrase (called a DP), which might provide a partial explanation for this exception.

154)   Hasan   kitab-i   oku-du.
        Hasan-SUBJ   book-OBJ   read-PAST
        "Hasan read the book."

If you look carefully at sentence (154) you notice that the word *kitabi* 'book' precedes the word *okudu* 'read.'

Not all languages put the complement on the right-hand side like English. Not all languages put the specifier before the head either. Our rules, while adequate for English, don't really get at the syntactic structure of languages in general. Remember, syntax is the study of the mental representation of sentence structure, and since we all have the same basic gray matter in our brains, it would be nice if our theory accounted for both the similarities and the differences among languages.

X-bar theory provides us with an avenue for exploring the differences and similarities among languages. Let's start by generalizing our rules a little bit. Let's allow specifiers and adjuncts to appear on either side of the head:

155)   *Specifier rule*   XP → (YP) X' *or* XP → X' (YP)
156)   *Adjunct rule*   X' → X' (ZP) *or* X' → (ZP) X'
157)   *Complement rule*   X' → X (WP) *or* X' → (WP) X

Each of these rules has two options, the specifier/complement/adjunct can all appear on either side of their head. Obviously, these rules are now too general to account for English. If these rules, as stated, were adopted straight out, they would predict the grammaticality of sentences like:

158)   *[NP Policeman the] [VP Mary kissed].
        (meaning *The policeman kissed Mary*.)

It would be a bad thing to do this. At the same time, constituent orders like the one in (158) are, in fact, seen the world's languages, so this clearly is an option. Our theory must capture both facts: The fact that the order in (158) is an option that languages use, and that it isn't the option used by English.

The way that generative syntacticians accomplish this is by claiming that the rules in (155), (156), and (157) are the possibilities universally available to human beings. When you acquire a particular language you select *one* of the options in the rule, based upon the input you hear from your parents. Take, for example, the complement rule. In English, complements of verbs follow the verbal head. In Turkish, they precede the head. There are two options in the rule:

159)   i)   X' → X (WP)
        ii) X' → (WP) X

The child learning English will adopt option (i), the child learning Turkish will adopt option (ii). These options are called ***parameters***. The proposal that word order is parameterized finds its origins in Travis (1984).

Here is an analogy that might help you understand this concept. Imagine that in your head you have a box of switches, just like the box of master breaker switches which controls the electricity in your house. These switches can be set *on* or *off*. The options in the X-bar rules are like these switches, they can be set in one direction or the other (and in some situations – such as adjuncts in English – allow both settings).

160)   *X-bar parameters switch box*

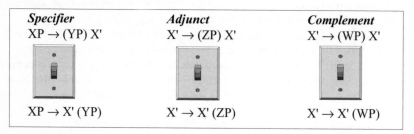

Specifier	**Adjunct**	**Complement**
XP → (YP) X'	X' → (ZP) X'	X' → (WP) X'
XP → X' (YP)	X' → X' (ZP)	X' → X' (WP)

When you are a child acquiring your language, you subconsciously set these switches, to tell you which version of the rules to use.

Notice that this gives us a very simple system for acquiring the word order of our languages. There are a finite set of possibilities, represented by the different settings of the parameters. English sets its complement parameter so that the complement follows the head. Turkish sets it the other way. The child only has to hear a small amount of data (perhaps even as little as one sentence) to know what side of the head complements go in their language. Once children have set the parameter, they can apply the right version of the rule and generate an unlimited number of sentences. In the problem sets at the end of this chapter, you have the opportunity of looking at some data from a variety of languages and determining how their X-bar parameters are set. For your reference, the English settings are give below:

161)   *Specifier*   specifier on left, head on right (XP → (YP) X')
                         e.g.,   *The* book

162)   *Adjunct*   Both options allowed (X' → (ZP) X' and X' → X' (ZP))
                         e.g.,   *Yellow* roses
                                    Books *from Poland*

163)   *Complement*   head on left, complement on right[11] (X' → X (WP))
                         e.g.,   Books *of Poems*
                                    John kissed *his mother*.

5.   X-BAR THEORY: A SUMMARY

Let's summarize the rather lengthy discussion we've had so far in this chapter. We started off with the observation that there seemed to be more structure to our trees than that given by the basic phrase structure rules we developed in chapter 2. In particular, we introduced the intermediate levels of structure called N', V', A', and P'. The evidence for these comes from standard constituency tests like conjunction, and from processes like *one*-replacement, and *do-so*-replacement. We also saw that material on different levels of structure behaved differently. Complements exhibit one set of behaviors and adjuncts a different set. Next we observed that our rules were failing to capture several generalizations about the data. First was the endocentricity generalization: all NPs, have an N head, all APs an A head, etc. There is no rule like NP → V A. Next, there was the observation that all trees have three levels of structure. They all have specifiers (weak evidence here), adjuncts and complements. In response to this, we proposed the following general X-bar theoretic rules:

164)   *Specifier rule*   XP → (YP) X' *or* XP → X' (YP)
165)   *Adjunct rule*   X' → X' (ZP) *or* X' → (ZP) X'
166)   *Complement rule* X' → X (WP) *or* X' → (WP) X

These rules use variables to capture cross-categorial generalizations. In order to limit the power of these rules, and in order to capture differences between languages, we proposed that the options within these rules were parameterized. Speakers of languages select the appropriate option for their language.

This is, you'll note, a very simple system. There are, of course, some loose ends, and in the next couple of chapters we'll try to tidy these up.

---

[11] The world is rarely as clean and tidy as we would like. We've already observed one exception to this principle. Some complements to N can appear before the head as in *poetry book*. There is an obvious way out of this problem. Each major part of speech has its own set of parameters (i.e., there is a different set of parameters for N than for V, etc.). This adds a layer of complication to the system not necessary for our purposes here, but you should keep this in mind.

Important Extra Rules
You'll need the following additional rules to do the homework in this chapter:

Sentence rules
> S' → (C) S
> S → NP (T) VP

Conjunction rules
> XP → XP Conj XP
> X' → X' Conj X'
> X → X Conj X

The first two rules are your sentence rule (S) and S' rule for introducing complementizers. The last three are the conjunction rules.

6.   DRAWING TREES IN X-BAR NOTATION

6.1   Important Considerations in Tree Drawing

In this section, we'll run through the steps for drawing trees in X-bar notation. The basics of tree drawing that you learned in chapter 2 hold here too:

i)   Write out the sentence and identify the parts of speech.
ii)   Identify what modifies what.
iii)   Start linking material together, it often helps to start at the right edge. I also recommend starting with APs, then NPs, then PPs, then NPs again, and then VPs.
iv)   Make sure you've attached everything according to the rules.
v)   Keep applying the rules until everything is linked up.
vi)   Apply the S and S' rules last.
vii)   Go back and check your tree against the rules.

These general principles, explored in depth in chapter 2, will also hold you in good stead here. But there are some additional points that are necessary when you are using X-bar theory.

viii)   When identifying what modifies what, it is also important to know whether it is a complement, adjunct, or specifier. This is important because you have to know whether to make it a sister to the head, to an X', etc.

ix)   We will need to slightly modify our golden rule of modification so that modifiers are always attached to a projection of the head they modify (N' and NP are *projections* of N).

x)   When linking material up, start with the modifiers closest to the head. Because X-bar structure is formulated the way it is, material closest to the head will be the most deeply embedded material – so it will have to attach to the head *first*.

xi)   Keep in mind that none of the X-bar rules are optional. That is, they must all apply. This results in a fair amount of vacuous or non-branching structure. Even if you have only a single word you will have *at least* the following structure:

xii)   Perhaps one of the most common errors of new syntacticians is in drawing trees for phrases with an adjunct and no complement. Consider the NP [notebook with a red cover]. *With a red cover* is an adjunct – that means that it has to be a sister to N' and a daughter to N' (by definition). This is seen in the following tree:

167)

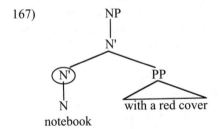

The circled N' here must be present in order to make the PP an adjunct. Be very careful to draw in these vacuous nodes that distinguish adjuncts from complements.

6.2   A Sample Tree

To get the full feel of tree drawing, let's do a sample tree. The sentence we'll draw is:

168)   The$_1$ man from Brazil found books of poems in the$_2$ puddle.

Our first step, as always, is to identify the parts of speech:

169)   D   N   P   N   V   N   P   N   P   D   N
        The₁ man from Brazil found books of poems in the₂ puddle.

Next, and most importantly, we have to identify what modifies or relates to what, and whether that modification is as an adjunct, complement, or specifier. This is perhaps the most difficult and tedious step, but it is also the most important. You will get better at this with practice. You can use the tests we developed above (stacking, coordination, etc.) to determine whether the modifier is a complement, adjunct, or specifier.

170)   [The₁] modifies [man] as a specifier.
        [Brazil] modifies [from] as a complement.
        [from Brazil] modifies [man] as an adjunct.
        [Poems] modifies [of] as a complement.
        [of Poems] modifies [books] as a complement.
        [books of poems] modifies [found] as a complement.
        [the₂] modifies [puddle] as a specifier.
        [the puddle] modifies [in] as a complement.
        [in the puddle] modifies [found] as an adjunct.

Keeping in mind the (revised) golden rule of modification, and the strict X-bar structure, we next start to build the trees. I suggest you generally start with APs. There are no APs in this sentence, so we'll start with NPs. We'll also start on the right hand side of the sentence. The first NP is *the puddle*, be sure to apply all three of the NP rules here. Don't forget the N' node in the middle. The determiner is the specifier of the NP, so it must be the sister to N' and daughter of NP.

171)

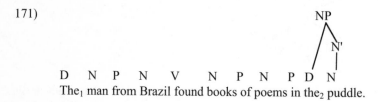

        D   N   P   N   V   N   P   N   P   D   N
        The₁ man from Brazil found books of poems in the₂ puddle.

There are two nouns in this sentence that aren't modified by anything (*Brazil* and *poems*). Let's do these next. Even though they aren't modified by anything they get the full X-bar structure, with NP, N' and N: This is because the rules are *not* optional.

172)

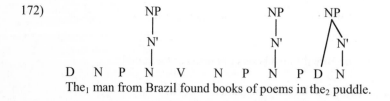

        D   N   P   N   V   N   P   N   P   D   N
        The₁ man from Brazil found books of poems in the₂ puddle.

There are two more nouns in this sentence (*man* and *books*), but if you look carefully at our list of modifications (170), you'll see that they are both modified by PPs. So in order to do them, we have to first build our PPs. There are three Ps in this sentence (and hence three PPs), each of them takes one of the NPs we've built as a complement. The objects of prepositions are always complements. That means that they are sisters to P, and daughters of P':

173)

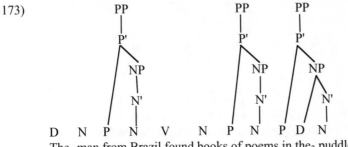

The₁ man from Brazil found books of poems in the₂ puddle.

Now that we've generated our PPs, we'll go back to the two remaining NPs. Let's first observe that the PP *in the puddle* does <u>not</u> modify an N (it modifies the V *found*, so it is <u>not</u> attached at this stage. Now, turn to the N *books*. This N is modified by *of poems* as a complement, that means that the PP will be the sister to the N head, and the daughter of N'. Again make sure you apply all three layers of structure.

174)

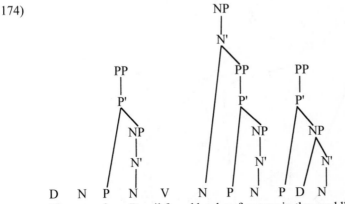

The₁ man from Brazil found books of poems in the₂ puddle.

Finally, we have the NP *the man from Brazil; from Brazil* modifies *man* as an adjunct. This means that it has to be a sister to N' and a daughter of N'. This will necessitate an extra layer of structure. (Note the difference between this NP and *books of poems*). The determiner is a specifier, which is a daughter of XP and a sister to X'.

175)

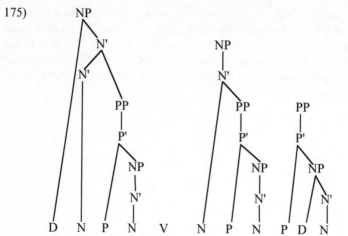

The₁ man from Brazil found books of poems in the₂ puddle.

Now we turn to the VP. The verb found has two modifiers. *Books of poems* is a complement, and *in the puddle* is an adjunct. *You should always start with the complement, and then follow with the adjuncts,* because complements are closer to the head. Remember, complements are sisters to V, and adjuncts to V'. Notice that the complement NP, which is closer to the head, is attached lower than the adjunct PP.

176)

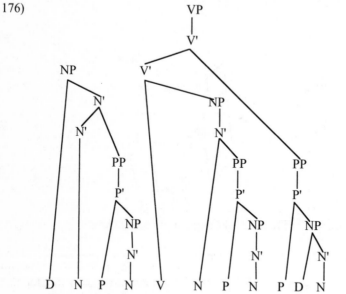

The₁ man from Brazil found books of poems in the₂ puddle.

Last, but not least, we apply the S rule, and then check the tree against the X-bar rules. Making sure that everything is attached; there are no crossing lines; adjuncts are sisters to a bar level, complements are sisters to a head; and finally every head has at least an X, X', and XP on top of it.

177)

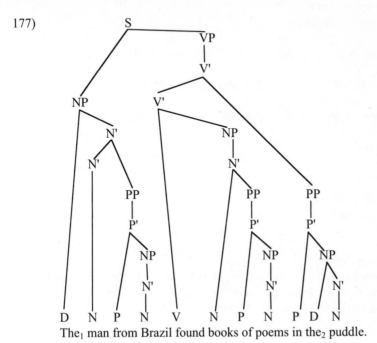

The₁ man from Brazil found books of poems in the₂ puddle.

Each tree will be different, of course, but with practice and patience you will develop the skill quite easily.

IDEAS, RULES, AND CONSTRAINTS INTRODUCED IN THIS CHAPTER

i)   ***Specifier***
        Sister to X', daughter of XP.

ii)   ***Adjunct***
        Sister to X', daughter of X'.

iii)   ***Complement***
        Sister to X, daughter of X'.

iv)   ***Head***
        The word that gives its category to the phrase.

v)   **One-*replacement***
          Replace an N' node with *one.*

vi)   **Do-so-*replacement***
          Replace a V' with *do so.*

vii)   ***Specifier Rule***   XP → (YP) X' or XP →X' (YP)

viii)   ***Adjunct Rule***   X' → X' (ZP) or X' → (ZP) X'

ix)   ***Complement Rule***   X' → X (WP) or X' → (WP) X

x)   ***Additional Rules***
          S' → (C) S
          S → NP VP
          XP → XP Conj XP
          X' → X' Conj X'
          X → X Conj X

xi)   ***Parameterization***
          The idea that there is a fixed set of possibilities in terms of structure (such
          as the options in the X-bar framework), and people acquiring a language
          choose from among those possibilities.

FURTHER READING

Baltin, Mark and Anthony Kroch (1989) *Alternative Conceptions of Phrase Structure.* Chicago: University of Chicago Press.
[This is a collection of papers about phrase structure theory.]

Borsley, Robert (1996) *Modern Phrase Structure Grammar.* Oxford: Blackwell.
[This book presents a different view of phrase structure (from the HPSG perspective).]

Carnie, Andrew (1995) Head Movement and Non-Verbal Predication. Ph.D. Dissertation, MIT.
[This work presents arguments against X-bar theory.]

Chametzky, Robert (1996) *A Theory of Phrase Markers and the Extended Base.* Albany: SUNY Press.
[This book presents a version of X-bar where the properties of the different rules are derived from other phenomena (advanced).]

Chomsky, Noam (1970) Remarks on Nominalization. In R. Jacobs and P. Rosenbaum (eds.) *Readings in English Transformational Grammar*. Waltham: Ginn.
pp. 184–221.
[The original proposal for X-bar theory.]

Jackendoff, Ray (1977) *X-bar Syntax: A Theory of Phrase Structure*. Cambridge:
MIT Press.
[This is the classic work on X-bar theory. The particular implementation of the theory is
slightly different than the one discussed here.]

Kayne, Richard (1994) *The Antisymmetry of Syntax*. Cambridge: MIT Press.
[This book discusses the possibility of deriving X-bar theory from deeper principles.]

Lightfoot, David (1991) *How to Set Parameters: Evidence from Language Change.*
Cambridge: MIT Press.
[This is an interesting read about how parameter setting might work.]

Radford, Andrew (1988) *Transformational Grammar: A First Course*. Cambridge:
Cambridge University Press
[This introductory syntax provides one of the most complete descriptions of X-bar the-
ory.]

Speas, Margaret (1990) *Phrase Structure in Natural Language*. Dordrecht: Kluwer
Academic Publishers
[The book argues for a derived notion of X-bar theory.]

Stowell, Tim (1981) Origins of Phrase Structure. Ph.D. dissertation, MIT.
[This thesis contains a significant development of Jackendoff's work.]

Travis, Lisa de Mena (1984) Parameters and Effects of Word Order Derivation.
Ph.D. dissertation, MIT.
[The proposal for parametric explanations for word order.]

PROBLEM SETS

1.   TREES

Draw the X-bar theoretic trees for the following sentences:

a)   Abelard wrote a poem about Héloïse.
b)   Abelard wrote a poem with Héloïse in mind.
c)   Abelard wrote a poem with Héloïse's pen.
d)   The red volume of obscene verse from Italy shocked the puritan
     soul of the minister with the beard quite thoroughly yesterday.

e) The biggest man in the room said that John danced an Irish jig
    from County Kerry to County Tipperary all night long.

2.   GERMAN NOUN PHRASES

Consider sentence (a) from German:[12]

a)   Die schlanke Frau aus Frankreich isst   Kuchen mit Sahne.
        the   thin   woman from France   eats cake with cream
        "The thin woman from France eats cake with cream."

The following sentences are grammatical if they refer to the same woman
described in (a):

b)   Die Schlanke aus Frankriech isst Kuchen mit Sahne.
        "The thin one from France eats cake with cream."

c)   Die aus Frankriech isst Kuchen mit Sahne.
        "The one from France eats cake with cream."

d)   Die Schlanke isst Kuchen mit Sahne.
        "The thin one eats cake with cream."

e)   Die isst Kuchen mit Sahne.
        "She eats cake with cream."

Now consider sentences (f–i):

f)   Die junge Koenigin von England liebte die Prinzessin.
        The young queen   of England loved the princess
        "The young queen of England loved the princess."

g)   Die junge liebte die Prinzessin.
        "The young one loved the princess."

h)   Die liebte die Prinzessin.
        "She loved the princess."

i)   *Die von England liebte die Prinzessin.
        "the one of England loves the princess."

---

[12] Thanks to Simin Karimi for providing the data for this question.

Assume the following things:
i)   *Der/Die* are always determiners, they are never nouns or pronouns
ii)   *Schlanke, junge,* are always adjectives, even in sentences (f) and (d)
        – assume they never become nouns. (Ignore the rules of German
        capitalization.)

The questions:
1) Describe and explain the process seen in (a–e) and (f–i), be sure to
    make explicit reference to X-bar theory. What English phenomenon (dis-
    cussed in this chapter) is this similar to? Make sure you analyze the
    German sentences not the English translations.

2) Draw the trees for sentences (a) and (f). Sentence (a) requires *two* dif-
    ferent trees.

3) Explain the ungrammaticality of (i) in terms of X-bar theory. In particular
    explain the difference between it and sentence (c). Draw trees to expli-
    cate your answer.

3.   JAPANESE

Consider the following data from Japanese:

a) Masa-ga kita.
    "Masa came."

b) Toru-ga shinda.
    "Toru died."

c) Kumiko-ga yonda.
    "Kumiko read."

d) Kumiko-ga hon-o yonda.
    "Kumiko read the book."

e) Toru-ga Kumiko-o mita.
    "Toru saw Kumiko."

f) Kumiko-ga Toru-o mita.
    "Kumiko saw Toru."

g) hon-ga akai desu.
    "the book is red."

h) Toru-ga sensei desu.
    "Toru is a teacher."

i)   Masa-ga ookii desu.
     "Masa is big."

j)   Sono hon-ga ookii desu.
     "that book is big."

k)   Toru-ga sono akai hon-o mita.
     "Toru saw that red book."

1)   What is the function of the suffixes -o and -ga?
2)   What is the word order of Japanese?
3)   Does the complement precede or follow the head in Japanese?
4)   Do adjuncts precede or follow the head in Japanese?
5)   Do specifiers precede or follow the X' node in Japanese?
6)   Draw the tree for sentence (k) using X-bar theory. Keep in mind your
answers to questions (1–5).

4.   PARAMETERS

Go back to the foreign language problems from the previous three chapters,
and see if you can determine the parameter settings for these languages.
You may not be able to determine all the settings for each language.

chapter 6

Extending X-bar Theory: CP, TP, and DP

0.   INTRODUCTION

In the last chapter, we looked at a very simple system of rules that accounted for a wide variety of data: X-bar theory:

1)   *Specifier rule*   XP → YP) X' *or* XP → X' (YP)
2)   *Adjunct rule*   X' → X' (ZP) *or* X' → (ZP) X'
3)   *Complement rule* X' → X (WP) *or* X' → (WP) X

These rules not only generate most of the trees we need for the sentences of the world's languages, they also capture the additional properties of hierarchical structure found within the major constituents.

This said, you may have noticed that this system isn't perfect. First, there is the status of specifiers. In particular, the specifier rule we proposed above requires that the specifier be a phrase (XP) level category. However, the only instances of specifiers we've looked at are determiners, which appear *not* to be phrasal. In this chapter, we will look at determiners, and specifiers, and propose a new category that fits X-bar theory: a determiner phrase (DP). We will see that determiners are not specifiers. Instead, we'll claim that the specifier position is used to mark a particular grammatical function: that of subjects. You'll see that specifiers (of all categories) are where subjects go.

Another troubling aspect of the X-bar theory is the exceptional rules that we've proposed:

4)   S' → (C) S
5)   S → NP (T) VP

These rules do not fit X-bar theory. In this chapter, we will look at how we can modify these so that they fit into the more general pattern.

1.   DETERMINER PHRASES (DPs)

In the last chapter, for lack of a better place to put them, we put determiners, like *the, a, that, this, those, these* in the specifiers of NPs. This however, violates one of the basic principles underlying X-bar theory: All non-head material must be phrasal. Notice that this principle is a theoretical rather than an empirical requirement (i.e., it is motivated by the elegance of the theory and not by any data), but it is a nice idea from a mathematical point of view, and it would be good if we could show that it has some empirical basis.

One thing to note about determiners is that they are heads. There can only be one of them in an NP (this isn't true cross-linguistically, but for now let us limit ourselves to English):

6)   *the that book

In other words, they don't seem to be phrasal.[1] If our requirement says that the only thing that isn't a phrase in an NP is the N itself, then we have a problem. One solution, perhaps not obvious, to this is to claim that the determiner is not actually inside the NP. Instead, it heads its own phrasal projection. This was first proposed by Abney (1987):

7)

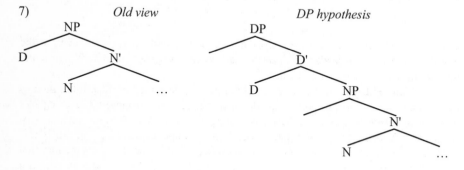

---

[1] In the last chapter we used this exact same piece of evidence to distinguish specifiers from adjuncts. As an exercise, you could try to construct an argument that distinguishes these two accounts of the same data.

Determiners, surprisingly, are not part of the NP. Instead the NP is the complement to the determiner head. This solution solves the theoretical problem, but we still need empirical evidence in its favor.

One piece of evidence comes from the behavior of genitive (possessive) NPs. There are two kinds of possessive NPs. The first is of less interest to us. This one is often called the *free genitive* or **of-*genitive***:

8)   the coat of the panther
9)   the roof of the building
10)   the hat of the man standing over there

The free genitive uses the preposition *of* to mark the possessive relation between the two NPs. More important in terms of evidence for DP is the behavior of the other kind of possessive: the ***construct*** or **'s-*genitive***.

11)   the panther's coat
12)   the building's roof
13)   the man standing over there's hat

There are a couple of important things to note about this construction. Notice first that the *'s* marker appears after the *full* possessor NP. For example, it attaches to the whole phrase *the man standing over there* not just to the head *man*:

14)   [the man standing over there]'s hat
15)   *the man's standing over there hat

This means that *'s* is not a suffix. Instead it seems to be a small word indicating possession. Next, note that it is in complementary distribution with (i.e., cannot co-occur with) determiners:

16)   *the building's the roof (cf. the roof of the building)
17)   *the panther's the coat (cf. the coat of the panther)
18)   *the man standing over there's the hat (cf. the hat of the man standing over there)

Unlike the *of*-genitive, the *'s*-genitive does not allow both the nouns to have a determiner. In other words, *'s* and determiners are in complementary distribution. In linguistics, when two items are in complementary distribution, they are instances of the same thing. (Take for example, phonology, where when two phones are found in different environments – in complementary distribution – then they are allophones of the same phoneme.) Determiners like *the* and *'s* and are different tokens of the same type. Assuming that *'s* is a determiner, and assuming the DP hypothesis holds true, we can account for the positioning of the *'s* relative to the possessor (see again (14) and (15)). The *'s* occupies the head D position, and the possessor appears in its specifier:

19)

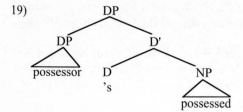

A tree for sentence (14) shows this:

20)

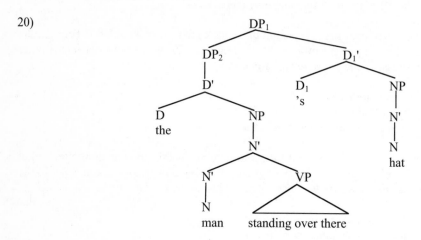

The possessor *[DP2 the man standing over there]* sits in the specifier of DP$_1$, which is headed by *'s*. So *'s* follows the whole thing. Notice that with our old theory, where determiners were specifiers of NP, there is no way at all to generate *'s* as a determiner and to also have the possessor NP proceeding it.

21)

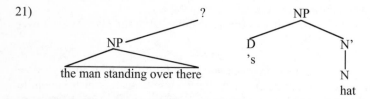

The X-bar rules don't provide any place to attach this pre-determiner NP, if determiners are specifiers.

Notice that in the tree in (20), there is a specifier of DP$_1$ (filled by DP$_2$). Note further that this specifier is phrasal (projects to an XP). Which means that it meets with our requirement that all non-head material be phrasal.

You might ask if by moving determiners out of the specifier we have completely destroyed the empirical justification for the specifier rule. Actually, we haven't, again if you look closely at the tree in (20) we still have a specifier, it just isn't a D, *instead* it is the DP possessor (DP$_2$). Further, as we will see below, there are other uses for the specifier positions. In particular, we will come to associate specifiers with subjects of various kinds of constituents.

2.   TPs (TENSE PHRASES) AND CPs (COMPLEMENTIZER PHRASES)

Next we turn to the S and S' rules which seemingly don't fit the X-bar pattern. First, we look at some terminology, then we turn to the form of the rules.

2.1   Clause Types

A *clause* is essentially a *subject* (usually a noun, which has the property indicated by the predicate; this is what the clause is about) and a *predicate phrase* (a group of words that assign a property to the subject). The most obvious kind of clause is the simple sentence. In the following examples, the subject is indicated in italics and the predicate phrase is in bold:

22)   *The boy* **ran**.
23)   *Howard* **is a linguistics student**.

As we'll see below, there are many other kinds of clauses. But we can use this as a working definition.

        A clause that stands on its own is called a *root, matrix,* or *main clause.* Sometimes, however, we can find examples of clauses within clauses. Examples of this are seen below:

24)   [Peter said [that Danny danced]].
25)   [Bill wants [Susan to leave]].

In each of these sentences there are two clauses. In sentence (24), there is the clause *(that) Danny danced* which is inside the root clause *Peter said that Danny danced.* In (25), we have the clause *Susan to leave* which has the subject *Susan*, and the predicate phrase *(to) leave*. This is contained within the main clause *Bill wants Susan to leave.*

        Both of these clauses within clauses are called *embedded clauses*. Another name for embedded clause is *subordinate clause*. The clause containing the embedded clause is still called the *main* or *root clause*. Using the S and S' rules we developed in chapter 2, the structure of a root clause containing an embedded clause is given below (I've obscured the irrelevant details with triangles):

26)

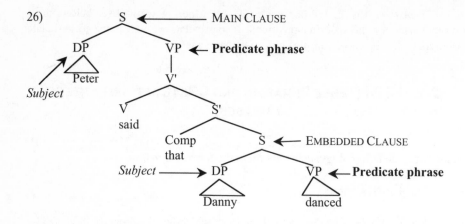

Embedded Clauses are Part of Main Clauses
A very common error among new syntacticians is to forget that embedded clauses are contained *within* main clauses. That is when faced with identifying what is the main clause in a sentence like

i)   Peter thinks that Cathy loves him.

most students will properly identify the embedded clause, as *(that) Cathy loves him*, but will claim that the main clause is only *Peter thinks*. This is completely incorrect. *Peter thinks* is not a constituent (look at the tree in (26)). The main clause is everything under the root S node. So the main clause is *Peter thinks that Cathy loves him*. Be very careful about this.

        In addition to the distinction between main and embedded clauses, there is another kind of distinction we can make along the lines of hierarchy. Embedded clauses can be specifiers, complements, or adjuncts. Here are some examples of *complement clauses*:

27)   Heidi said [that Art loves peanut butter].
28)   Colin asked [if they could get a mortgage].

These complement clauses (S's) are sisters to the verb, and thus complements. Clauses can also appear in adjunct positions. Relative clauses are one example of *adjunct clauses*:

29)   [The man [I saw get into the cab]] robbed the bank.

The relative clause in (29) *[I saw get into the cab]* modifies the head *man*. (Relative clauses are sometimes tricky, because they might appear to lack an overt subject.) *Specifier clauses* are ones that serve as the subject of a sentence (why these are specifiers will be made clear below):

30)   [[People selling their stocks] caused the crash of 1929].
31)   [[For Mary to love that boor] is a travesty].

To summarize, we have two basic kinds of clauses, main and embedded. Embedded clauses are contained within main clauses. Further, there are three types of embedded clauses: specifier clauses, complement clauses and adjunct clauses. This is summarized in the following table:

32)

Main clauses	Embedded clauses		
	specifier clauses	complement clauses	adjunct clauses

There is another way of dividing up the clause-type pie. We class clauses into two groups depending upon whether they are tensed or not.[2] Clauses with predicates that are tensed are sometimes called (obviously) *tensed clauses*, but you may more frequently find them called *finite clauses*. Clauses without a tensed verb are called *tenseless* or *non-finite clauses* (sometimes also *infinitival clauses*).[3]

33)   I said [that Mary signed my yearbook].   *tensed or finite*
34)   I want [Mary to sign my yearbook].   *tenseless or non-finite*

There are a number of tests for distinguishing finite from non-finite clauses. These tests are taken from Radford (1988). The embedded clause in sentence (35) is tensed, the one in (36) is untensed. I have deliberately selected a verb that is ambiguous between tensed and untensed in terms of its morphology (suffixes) here as an illustration:

35)   I know [you eat asparagus].   *finite*
36)   I've never seen [you eat asparagus]. *non-finite*

---

[2] There is a third kind of clause that we won't discuss here, called "small clauses." Small clauses don't have verbal predicates (that is, an NP, PP, or AP serves as the predicate. These generally don't get tense marking. An example is the embedded string in:

i)   [Maurice considers [Jason a fine upstanding gentleman]].

Small clauses are an important part of syntactic theory, but they are notoriously difficult to spot until you have some practice. For the purposes of this text we'll just ignore small clauses, but if you pursue syntax at a higher level you'll have to learn how to identify them.

[3] In many languages, the form of a verb found in a non-finite clause is called the *infinitive*. In English, infinitives are often marked with the auxiliary *to*, as in *to sign*.

One way to tell if a clause is finite or not is to look for agreement and tense morphology on the verb. These include the *-s* ending associated with third person nouns (*he eats̲*) and the past tense suffixes like *-ed*. The above examples don't show any such suffixes. However, if we change the tense to the past a difference emerges:

37)   I know you ate asparagus.   *finite*
38)   *I've never seen you ate asparagus.   *non-finite*

Finite clauses allow past tense morphology (the *ate* form of the verb *eat*), non-finite clauses don't. The same effect is seen if you change the person of the subject in the embedded clause. Third person subjects trigger the *-s* ending. This is allowed only in finite clauses.

39)   I know he eats̲ asparagus.   *finite*
40)   *I've never seen him eats̲ asparagus.   *non-finite*

The case on the subject of the noun is often a giveaway for determining whether or not a clause is finite. Case refers to the notions **nominative** and **accusative** introduced in chapter 1, repeated here:

41)

	Nominative		Accusative		Anaphoric	
	Singular	Plural	Singular	Plural	Singular	Plural
1st	I	we	me	us	myself	ourselves
2nd	you	you	you	you	yourself	yourselves
3rd masc	he		him		himself	
3rd fem	she	they	her	them	herself	themselves
3rd neut	it		it		itself	

If the clause is finite, then a subject pronoun will take the nominative case form:

42)   I know *he* eats asparagus.   *finite*

If the clause is non-finite then the subject will take the accusative form:

43)   I've never seen *him* eat asparagus.   *non-finite*

One test that works most of the time, but is not as reliable as the others, is to see if the subject is obligatory. If the subject is obligatory, then the clause is finite. If the subject is optional, or is not allowed at all, then it is non-finite. (Note: this test only works for English; in many languages, such as Spanish, subjects of finite clauses are optional.)

44)   I think that he eats asparagus. (cf. *I think that eats asparagus.) *finite*
45)   I want (him) to eat asparagus. (cf. I want to eat asparagus.)   *non-finite*

Another way to tell if a clause is finite or not is by looking at the complementizer. The complementizer *for* is only found with non-finite clauses. By contrast *that* and *if* are only found with tensed clauses:

46) I wonder if he eats asparagus.   *finite*
47) I think that he eats asparagus.   *finite*
48) [For him to eat asparagus] is a travesty.   *non-finite*
49) I asked for him to eat the asparagus.   *non-finite*

As a final test, we can note that finite and non-finite clauses take different kinds of T elements. The T in tensed clauses can contain auxiliaries and modals like *will, can, must, may, should, shall, is, have.* By contrast the only auxiliary allowed in non-finite clauses is *to.*[4]

50) I think [he *will* eat asparagus].
51) I want him *to* eat asparagus. (cf. *I want him will eat asparagus.)

This last property gets at the heart of the distinction between finite and non-finite clauses. In structural terms the difference between a finite and a non-finite clause lies in terms of what kind of T the clause has. If a clause is finite it bears some tense feature (like [±past] or [±future]). If it is non-finite, it doesn't have any of these features. The question of how this works for clauses where there is no auxiliary, we'll leave as a bit of a mystery for now, but will return to later in this chapter.

Let's summarize the discussion we've had thus far. We've been looking at a number of terms for describing various kinds of clauses. We defined clauses as a subject and a predicate phrase. We distinguished root or main clauses from embedded clauses. Embedded clauses come in three types: specifier clauses, complement clauses and adjunct clauses. The other dimension along which we can describe clauses is the finite/non-finite distinction.

With this terminology under our belts, we'll now turn to the structure of clauses, and see if we can make them fit better into X-bar theory.

2.2   S' vs. CP

We've observed that the S rule and the S' rule stand out alone, since they don't fit X-bar theory:

52) S' → (C) S
53) S → NP (T) VP

---

[4] English has two words *to*. One is a preposition, the other is non-finite T.

In fact, it is a fairly trivial matter to change these rules into X-bar theoretic format. Let us deal with the S' bar rule first. On a parallel to DPs, we might hypothesize that the complementizer itself is the head of S'. In this view, S' gets replaced with a *complementizer phrase* (CP). Complementizer phrases have C (complementizer) as their head, S as their complement and an empty specifier position. (This empty specifier position will become very important to us later, when we do *wh*-movement in chapter 11.) A tree showing a CP is given in (54).

54)

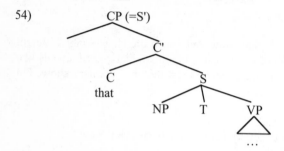

We can dispense with the special S' rule, and apply our X-bar rules to C, just as we do to N, V, A, and P.

We might ask how pervasive this rule is in our mental grammars. That is, do all clauses have CPs, or do only embedded clauses have CPs? On the surface, the answer to this question seems obvious: Only embedded clauses have CPs, since only embedded clauses appear to allow complementizers:

55)   John thinks that asparagus is yummy.
56)   *That asparagus is yummy. (cf. Asparagus is yummy.)

However, there is evidence that all clauses, even root clauses like (57), require some kind of complementizer.

57)   Asparagus grows in California.

In particular, we'll claim that some sentences have null complementizers. Don't assume that I'm crazy. No matter how strange this proposal sounds, there is actually some good evidence that this is correct. The tree in (58) shows one of these null complementizers.

58)

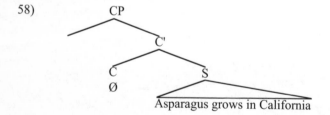

The evidence for this claim comes from cross-linguistic comparison of questions among languages. In particular, we'll focus on so-called ***yes/no questions*** (see chapter 8 for more discussion on these). These are questions that can be answered with either *yes, no* or *maybe*. Examples of yes/no questions in English are given below:

59)   Did John leave?
60)   Have you seen Louis?

In English, to form a yes/no question you either insert some form of the verb *do* (*do, does, did*) before the subject, or you invert the subject and the auxiliary (*You have seen Louis.* → *Have you seen Louis?*). This operation is called ***subject/aux inversion*** (more on this in chapter 8). In many other languages, however, yes/no questions are formed with a complementizer particle that precedes the verb. Take for example, Irish, which indicates yes/no questions with a special particle *Ar* (or its allomorph *An*):

61)   Ar thit Seán?
       Q   fall John
       "Did John fall?"

Languages like English that use subject/aux inversion don't have special complementizer question particles. The opposite also holds true. If a language has complementizer question particles, then it won't have subject/aux inversion. The phenomena are in complementary distribution. It seems reasonable to claim then, that question complementizers and subject/aux inversion are part of the same basic phenomenon. In order to make this concrete, let's make the following proposal: There is a question complementizer particle in English, just like there is in Irish. The difference is that in English this complementizer particle is null (has no phonological content). We will represent this ***null complementizer*** with the symbol $\emptyset_{[+Q]}$. It has no phonological content, but it must be realized or pronounced someway. The way English satisfies this requirement is by moving T into the C head:

62)

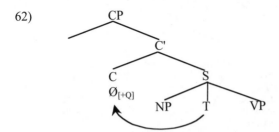

This results in the correct order, where the auxiliary (in T) now appears before the subject. By contrast, languages like Irish don't utilize this mechanism. Instead they have a particle that fills their [+Q] complementizer (like *Ar/An* in Irish).

English does, in fact, have an overt [+Q] complementizer, but it is only found in embedded questions. This complementizer is *if*. Unsurprisingly, subject/aux inversion is completely disallowed when *if* is present:

63)   Fabio asked if Claus had run a marathon.
64)   *Fabio asked if had Claus run a marathon.
65)   *Fabio asked had if Claus a perm.
66)   ?Fabio asked had Claus run a marathon.

if occupies the [+Q] complementizer, so no subject/aux inversion is required (or allowed).

Given the existence of overt root complementizers in other languages and the evidence that subject/aux inversion patterns like these overt root complementizers, we can conclude that, for questions at least, there are complementizers (and CPs) present, even in main clauses.

Of course, we haven't yet shown that non-question sentences have a root complementizer. For this, we need to add an extra step in the argument. Recall from chapter 5 that one can only conjoin elements that have the same bar level and the same category. If sentences showing subject/aux inversion use a null complementizer and if you can conjoin that question with non-question (such as a statement), then that statement must also include a (null) complementizer and CP. It is indeed possible to conjoin a statement with a question:

67)   [You can lead a horse to water] but [will it drink]?

Since the second clause here shows subject/aux inversion, we know there is a $\emptyset_{[+Q]}$ question complementizer present. By extension, we know that the clause it is conjoined with must also have a complementizer – this time, a non-question $\emptyset_{[-Q]}$.

68)

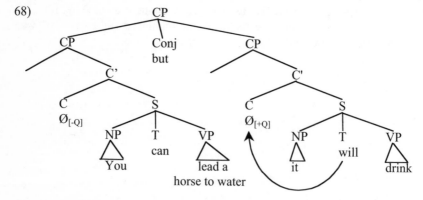

This is an argument for null complementizers attached to root clauses, even in simple statements. From this point forward, we will assume that there is a CP on top of every clause. For brevity's sake, I may occasionally leave this CP off my trees, but the underlying assumption is that it is always there. You should always draw it in when you are drawing your trees.

2.3 S vs. TP

The other rule that doesn't fit the X-bar pattern is our S rule:

69)   S → NP (T) VP

In order to make this fit X-bar theory, we're going to have to determine which element is the head of the sentence. If you look closely at (69), you'll notice that only one element is not itself phrasal: T. Remember that all non-head material must be phrasal. T seems to be a likely category for the head of the sentence. Let us then propose that the structure of the sentence looks like:

70)

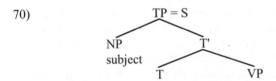

In this tree, S is replaced by TP; the subject NP sits in the specifier of TP, and the VP is the complement. (This is our first clear instance where the notion of specifier corresponds to the notion of subject. We will consider some other cases below.)

In chapter 2, we equated T with auxiliary verbs. But we might ask what happens in clauses where there is no auxiliary: Is there a TP? Is there a T? In order to answer this question, let's make the following observation: Tense inflection on a verb is in complementary distribution with auxiliaries (you never get both of them at the same time):

71)   The roadrunner walks funny.
72)   The roadrunner is walking funny.
73)   *The roadrunner is walks/walkings funny.

Recall that when two elements are in complementary distribution then they are instances of the same category. This means that T is both auxiliaries and inflectional endings on verbs. Similar evidence comes from coordination. Recall that you can only coordinate two items that are of the same category and bar level. In the following sentence, we are conjoining a T' that has an auxiliary with a T' that has a tensed verb. The tense inflection and auxiliary are italicized.

74)   [$_{TP}$ I [$_{T'}$[$_{T'}$ kiss*ed* the toad] and [$_{T'}$ *must* go wash my mouth now]]].

This evidence suggests that the two T's are identical in some deep sense: that is they both involve a T node: one an auxiliary, the other a tense inflectional ending.

If you think about the basic order of the elements we seem to have argued ourselves into a corner. Auxiliaries appear on the left of verbs, and inflectional suffixes (like *-ed*, and *-s*) appear on the right.

75)   He *will*   go.
76)   He   go*es*.

There are other differences between auxiliaries and inflectional suffixes, for example, auxiliaries, but not suffixes undergo subject/aux inversion. If we are to claim that inflectional suffixes and auxiliaries are both instances of T we have to account for these differences.

One possibility is to claim that both inflectional suffixes and auxiliaries are indeed generated under T. They differ, however, in terms of whether they can stand alone or not. Auxiliaries are independent words and can stand alone. By contrast, suffixes like *-s* and *-ed* have to be attached to a verb. Much like the case of moving T to C in order to pronounce $Ø_{[+Q]}$, we might hypothesize that endings like *-s* and *-ed* can't be pronounced in isolation, so they move to attach to the verb. In particular they seem to lower onto the verb: The following tree shows how this would work for the simple sentence *He walked*. This sentence starts out as *[he -ed walk]* then the *-ed* ending lowers to attach to the end of the verb:

77)

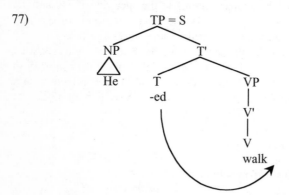

Notice that both the movements we have proposed (***T-affix lowering***, and T → C) have morphophonological motivations. Auxiliaries moves to $Ø_{[+Q]}$ to pronounce it, inflectional endings lower to V since they are verbal suffixes.

There is much more to the study of T and C and movement of these elements. (For example, the issue of what happens when you have both a $Ø_{[+Q]}$ and an inflectional suffix that need to be pronounced leaps to mind.) We will return to these issues in chapter 8.

T, Infl, Aux, AgrS, AgrO

In this chapter, we are using the category T to describe words like *is, may, can* and tense suffixes like *-s*. This is the standard practice now. In previous versions of the theory we are using, you can also find these words categorized as Aux (for auxiliary) or Infl (for Inflection). These are just other names for the same category. Some authors believe that auxiliaries are actually composed of three categories: T, AgrS (for subject agreement) and AgrO (for object agreement). For simplicity's sake, we'll stick to T here.

2.4   CP and TP Tree

Before moving on, here is the tree drawn in section 6.2 of chapter 5, this time with CP and TP instead of S' and S, and DP:

78)

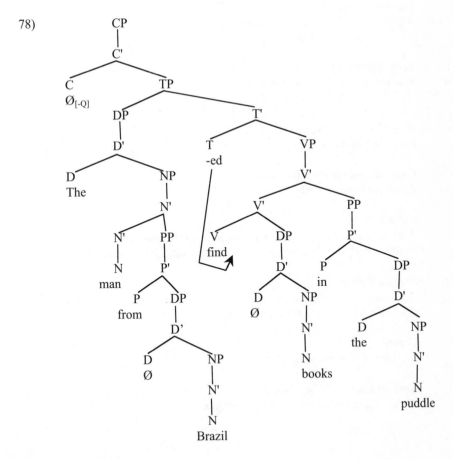

This tree has the subject DP in the specifier of TP. The past tense ending is in T, and lowers to the verb (we of course have to assume that there is some phonological or morphological readjustment that turns *finded* into *found*). You will also notice that we have a null $\emptyset_{[-Q]}$ complementizer. In addition you'll note that all NPs are complements to DPs. In a move parallel to having null Cs, I have drawn in null $\emptyset$ D heads as well, although this is a matter of some controversy.

IDEAS, RULES, AND CONSTRAINTS INTRODUCED IN THIS CHAPTER

i)   ***Determiner Phrase (DP)***
        Replaces D in NP. Uses X-bar theory: D heads its own phrase:
                [DP [D' D NP]]

ii)   ***Complementizer Phrase (CP)***
        Replaces S' rule. Uses X-bar theory:
                [CP [C' C TP]]

iii)   ***Tense Phrase (TP)***
        Replaces S rule. Uses X-bar theory:
                [TP NP$_{subject}$ [T' T VP]]

iv)   ***Free Genitive*/of-*Genitive***
        Possessed of the possessor

v)   ***Construct Genitive/'s-Genitive***
        Possessor 's possessed

vi)   ***Subject***
        A noun which has the property indicated by the predicate phrase. What the sentence is about. In most sentences, this is found in the specifier of TP.

vii)   ***Predicate Phrase***
        A group of word that attributes a property to the subject. (In most sentences this is the VP, although not necessarily so.)

viii)   ***Clause***
        A subject and a predicate phrase.

ix)   ***Root, Matrix,* or *Main Clause***
        A clause that isn't dominated by anything.

x)   **Embedded Clause/Subordinate Clause**
        A clause inside of another.

xi)   **Specifier Clause**
        An embedded clause in a specifier position.

xii)   **Adjunct Clause**
        An embedded clause in an adjunct position.

xiii)   **Complement Clause**
        An embedded clause in a complement position.

xiv)   **Tenseless** or **Non-finite Clause**
        A clause that isn't tensed (e.g., I want *[Mary to leave].*).

xv)   **Tensed** or **Finite Clause**
        A clause that is tensed.

xvi)   **T**
        The category that contains both inflectional suffixes and auxiliaries.

xvii)   **Root Ø Complementizers (Null Complementizers)**
        We claimed that all clauses are introduced by a complementizer, even main clauses.

xviii) **Yes/No Questions**
        A question that can be answered with either a *yes* or a *no*.

xix)   **Subject/Aux Inversion**
        A means of indicating a *yes/no* question. Involves movement of T to $Ø_{[+Q]}$ complementizer for morphophonological reasons.

xx)   **Affix Lowering**
        The lowering of inflectional suffixes to attach to their verb.

FURTHER READING

Abney, Steven (1987) The English Noun Phrase in its Sentential Aspect. Ph.D. dissertation, MIT.
[This dissertation introduced the notion DP.]

Chomsky, Noam (1991) Some notes on economy of derivation and representation. In R. Friedin (ed.), *Principles and Parameters in Comparative Grammar*. Cambridge: MIT Press. pp. 417–54.
[This paper introduced the notions of AgrS and AgrOP, which are variants of T.]

Emonds, Joseph (1980) Word order in Generative Grammar. *Journal of Linguistic Research* 1, 33–54.
[This is a classic paper that discusses the role of C in grammar.]

Pollock, Jean-Yves (1989) Verb-movement, Universal Grammar, and the structure of IP. *Linguistic Inquiry* 20, 365–424.
[This paper introduced the notion that Infl(T) might be composed of two categories: T and Agr.]

PROBLEM SETS

1. ENGLISH *THAT*[5]

Discuss the status of the word *that* in each of the following two sentences. Explain the differences between the two sentences. If you assign a different category status to *that* in each sentence, explain why. Draw the tree (use X-bar theory) for each of the sentences.

a) Robert thinks <u>that</u> students should eat asparagus.
b) Robert thinks <u>that</u> student should eat asparagus.

2. SUBJECTS AND PREDICATE PHRASES

In each of the following clauses identify the subject and the predicate phrase. Some sentences contain multiple clauses, be sure to identify the subjects and predicate phrases of all clauses.

a) The peanut butter has got[6] moldy.
b) The duffer's swing blasted the golf ball across the green.
c) That Harry loves dancing is evidenced by his shiny tap shoes.
d) The Brazilians pumped the oil across the river.

---

[5] Thanks to Eithne Guilfoyle for contributing this problem set.
[6] You may prefer *gotten* to *got* here. The choice is dialect-dependent.

3.   CLAUSE TYPES

The following sentences are "complex" in that they contain more than one clause. For each sentence, identify each clause. Remember main clauses include embedded clauses. Identify the complementizer, the T, and the subject of the clause; be sure to identify even *null* (Ø) complementizers and Ts with suffixes in them. State whether each clause is a finite clause or a non-finite clause.

a)   Stalin may think that Roosevelt is a fool.
b)   Lenin believes the Tsar to be a power-hungry dictator.
c)   Brezhnev had said for Andropov to leave.
d)   Yeltsin saw Chernyenko holding the bag.

4.   TREES

Draw the trees for the following sentences. Use X-bar theory, show all CPs, DPs, and TPs.

a)   The very young child walked from school to the store.
b)   Linguistics students like phonetics tutorials.
c)   John paid a dollar for a head of lettuce.
d)   Teenagers drive rather quickly.
e)   Martha said that Bill loved his Cheerios in the morning.
f)   Eloise wants you to study a new language. [assume *to* = T]
g)   For Maurice to quarrel with Joel frightened Maggie.
h)   John's drum will always bother me.

5.   TREES II

1)   Go back to chapter 2, problem set 4, and draw the trees using X-bar theory.
2)   Go back to chapter 3, problem set 2, and draw the trees using X-bar theory.

6.   HUNGARIAN

(Data from Szabolcsi 1994)

In the text above, we argued that the structure of genitive constructions in English looks like:

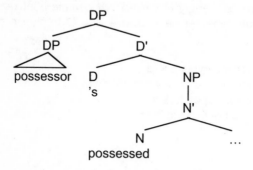

Consider the follow data from Hungarian. Does the possessor DP appear in the same place as the English ones?

a)   az en kalapom
        the I   hat
        "my hat"

b)   a   te   kalapod
        the you hat
        "your hat"

c)   a   Mari kalapja
        the Mary hat
        "Mary's hat"

Hungarian has another possessive construction, seen in (d).

        d)   Marinak a   kalapja
                Mary   the hat
                "Mary's hat"

Where is the possessor DP in (d)?

7.   ENGLISH MODALS AND AUXILIARIES

In traditional grammar, two different kinds of T are distinguished: modals and auxiliaries. Modals include words like *can, must, should, would, could, may,* and in some dialects *shall* and *will.* Auxiliary verbs, by contrast, include such words as *have* (and all its allomorphs such as *has* and *had*), and *be* (and all of its allomorphs: *is, are, been, was, were,* etc.) In this book, we've been treating modals and auxiliaries as both being members of the category T. Many linguists, believe that in fact, only modals are really of category T, and that auxiliaries are real verbs. They claim that an auxiliary and verb combination such as "is running" is actually a stacked set of VPs:

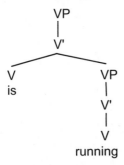

Construct an argument in favor of the idea that modals are of category T, but auxiliaries are really verbs. Assume the following: You may have as many V categories as you like, but there is only one T in any tensed clause's tree.

chapter 7

Constraining X-bar Theory: Theta Roles and the Lexicon

0.   INTRODUCTION

In chapters 5 and 6, we developed a very simple (only three rules) and general theory of phrase structure: X-bar theory. This theory accounts for the distinction between adjuncts, complements, and specifiers. It incorporates the more articulated view of sentence hierarchy required by constituency tests, and it captures cross-categorial generalizations (i.e., the fact that all kinds of phrases – NPs, VPs, APs, PPs, CPs, DPs, and TPs – have the same basic properties). Most importantly, it allows us to draw trees for most of the sentences of any language.

This said, there is a significant problem with X-bar theory: it also generates sentences that are not acceptable or grammatical. Take for example the following pairs of grammatical and ungrammatical sentences:

1)   a) Rosemary hates New York.
        b) *Rosemary hates.

2)   a) Jennie smiled.
        b) *Jennie smiled the breadbox.

3)   a) Traci gave the whale a jawbreaker.
        b) *Traci gave the whale.
        c) *Traci gave a jawbreaker.

Sentence (1b) should be perfectly acceptable (compare it to *Rosemary ran*). X-bar theory says that complements are optional. Therefore, direct objects, which are complements, should always be optional. The opposite type of fact is seen in the pair in (2). X-bar theory optionally allows a complement. So having a direct object here should be fine too. The same kind of effect is seen in (3), where both the direct object and indirect object are obligatory – contra X-bar theory.

What seems to be at work here is that certain verbs require objects and others don't. It appears to be a property of the *particular* verb. Information about the peculiar or particular properties of verbs is contained in our mental dictionary or **lexicon**. In this chapter, we'll look at how we can use the lexicon to constrain X-bar theory, so that it doesn't predict the existence of ungrammatical sentences.

1.   SOME BASIC TERMINOLOGY

Before launching into the structure of the lexicon, it is worth exploring some basic terminology that we use when describing the restrictions particular verbs place on their subjects and objects.

First, we need to refine the notion of predicate. The notion presented here is slightly different (and more narrow) than the definition we gave in the last chapter. We are going to base the notion of predicate on the mathematical notion of a "relation." The **predicate** defines the relation between the individuals being talked about and the real world – as well as with each other. The entities (which can be abstract) participating in the relation are called **arguments**. To see how this works, look at the following example:

4)   Gwen hit the baseball.

There are two arguments in this example, *Gwen* and *the baseball*. These are elements in the world that are participants in the action described by the sentence. The predicate here is *hit*. *Hit* expresses a relation between the two arguments: more precisely, it indicates that the first argument (*Gwen*) is applying some force to the second argument (*the baseball*). This may seem patently self-evident, but it's important to understand what is going on here on an abstract level.

We can speak about any particular predicate's **argument structure**. This refers to the number of arguments that a particular predicate requires. Take, for example, predicates that take only one argument. These are predicates like *smile, arrive, sit, run,* etc. and are called **intransitives**. Predicates that take two obligatory arguments are called **transitives**; some examples are *hit, love, see, kiss, admire,* etc. Finally predicates that take three arguments are called **ditransitives**. *Put* and *give* are the best examples of this class.

5)

Name	# of arguments	Example
intransitive	1 argument	smile, arrive
transitive	2 arguments	hit, love, kiss
ditransitive	3 arguments	give, put

In determining how many arguments a predicate has, we only consider complements and specifiers. Adjuncts are never counted in the list of arguments. Only obligatory elements are considered arguments.

Did You Run the Race?
The claim that only obligatory arguments are found in argument structure is not as straightforward as it sounds. Consider the verb *run*. It has both an intransitive use *(I ran)* and a transitive use *(I ran the race)*. A similar problem is raised by languages that can drop the subject argument (e.g. Spanish and Italian) or even imperative sentences in English (*Go home now!*). The subject is still an argument in these constructions, even though you can't hear it. We'll return to this issue in chapter 10

Predicates impose other restrictions on their arguments too. For example, they also place restrictions on the categories of their complements. A verb like *ask* can take either an NP or a CP as a complement:

6)   I asked [NP the question].
7)   I asked [CP if you knew the answer].

But a verb like *hit* can only take an NP complement:

8)   I hit [NP the ball].
9)   *I hit [that you knew the answer].

Restrictions on the categories that a verb can have as a complement are called **subcategorization restrictions**. In addition to these, we also find semantic restrictions on what can appear in particular positions:

10)   #My comb hates raisonettes.
11)   #A bolt of lightning killed the rock.

There is something decidedly strange about these sentences. Combs can't hate anything and rocks can't be killed. These semantic criteria are called **selectional restrictions**.

In the next section, we'll look at the theory of thematic relations, which is a particular way of representing selectional and subcategorizational restrictions.

2.   THEMATIC RELATIONS AND THETA ROLES

One way of encoding selectional restrictions is through the use of what are called **thematic relations**. These are particular semantic terms that are used to describe the role that the argument plays with respect to the predicate. This section describes some common thematic relations (this list is by no means exhaustive, and the particular definitions are not universally accepted).

The initiator or doer of an action is called the **agent**. Agents should be alive and capable of volition. In the following sentence, *Brad* is an agent.

12)   *Brad* hit Andrew.

Not every sentence has an agent; there is no agent in the following two sentences (13, 14). *A falling rock* is not alive and thus can't be an agent. Some scholars label arguments like *A falling rock* as **natural phenomena** or **non-volitional agents**. We won't distinguish between agent and non-volitional agents in this book, but some authors do. In (14), *Nancy* is not initiating or doing an action (see the experiencer thematic relation below), so she is *not* an agent.

13)   *A falling rock* hit Terry.
14)   *Nancy* loves Terry.

Agents must be capable of volition but they do not have to actually intentionally cause the action. In the following sentence, *Michael* is an agent, even though he didn't intentionally break the glass.

15)   *Michael* accidentally broke the glass.

Agents are most frequently subjects, but they can also appear in other positions.

Arguments that feel or perceive events are called **experiencers**. Experiencers can appear in a number of argument positions including subject and object:

16)   *Keziah* likes cookies.
17)   *Becki* saw the eclipse.
18)   Syntax frightens *Jim*.

Entities that undergo actions, are moved, experienced or perceived are called **themes**.

19)   Shelley kept *her syntax book*.
20)   The arrow hit *Michael*.
21)   The syntactician hates *phonology*.

The entity towards which motion takes place is called a **goal**. Goals may involve abstract motion:

22)   Millie went *to Chicago*.
23)   *Travis* was given the piña colada mix.

There is a special kind of goal called **recipient**. Recipients only occur with verbs that denote a change of possession:

24)   Julie gave *Jessica* the book.
25)   *Roy* received a scolding from Sherilyn.

The opposite of a goal is the **source**. This is the entity from which a motion takes place:

26)   *Bob* gave Steve the syntax assignment.
27)   Stacy came directly *from sociolinguistics class*.

The place where the action occurs is called the **location**:

28)   Andrew is *in Tucson's finest apartment*.
29)   We're all *at school*.

The object with which an action is performed is called the **instrument**:

30)   Patrick hacked the computer apart *with an axe*.
31)   *This key* will open the door to the linguistics building.

Finally, the one for whose benefit an event took place is called the **benefactive**:

32)   He bought these flowers for *Jason*.
33)   She cooked *Matt* dinner.

Notice that any given DP can have more than one thematic relation. In the following sentence, the DP *Jason* bears the thematic relations of agent and source (at the very least).

34)   *Jason* gave the books to Anna.

There is not a one-to-one relationship between thematic relations and arguments. However, linguists have a special construct called a **theta role** (or **θ role**), that does map one-to-one with arguments. Theta roles are bundles of thematic relations that cluster on one argument. In (34) above, *Jason* gets two thematic relations (agent and source), but only one theta role (the one that contains the agent and source thematic relations). Somewhat confusingly, syntacticians often refer to particular theta roles by the most prominent thematic relation that they contain. So you might hear a syntactician refer to the "agent theta role" of *[DP Jason]*. Strictly speaking, this is incorrect: Agent refers to a thematic relation, whereas the theta role is a bundle of thematic relations. But the practice is common, so we'll do it here. Remember, thematic relations are things like agent, theme, goal, etc., but theta roles are bundles of thematic relations assigned to a particular argument.

Let's now see how we can use these theta roles to represent the argument structure of a verb. Take a ditransitive verb like *give*. *Give* requires three arguments, a subject which must be an agent (the giver), a direct object, which represents the theme (the thing being given), and an indirect object, which represents a location or goal (the person to whom the theme is being given). Any variation from this results in ungrammaticality:

35)   John gave the book to Mary.
36)   *Gave the book to Mary.
37)   *John gave to Mary.
38)   *John gave the book.
39)   *John gave the book the pen to Mary.[1]
40)   *The rock gave the sky with the fork.

Examples (36–39) show that either having too many or two few arguments results in ungrammaticality. Example (40) shows that using DPs with the wrong theta roles does the same (*the rock* can't be an agent; *the sky* can't be a theme – it can't be given to anyone; and *with the fork* is an instrument, not a goal). It appears as if the verb *give* requires three arguments, which bear precisely the theta roles of agent, theme, and instrument. We represent this formally in terms of what is called a ***theta grid***.[2]

41)

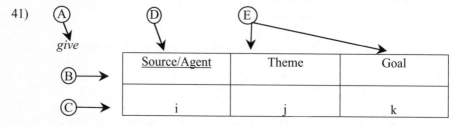

This grid consists of several parts. First of all, we have the name of the predicate (A). Next, for each argument that the predicate requires, there is a column (with two rows). Each of these columns represents a theta role. Notice that a column can have more than one thematic relation in it (but only one theta role). The number of columns corresponds exactly to the number of arguments the predicate requires. The first row (B) tells you the names of the theta roles. The second row (C), gives you what are called indices (singular: index) for each theta role. When a predicate appears in an actual sentence, we mark the DP bearing the particular theta role with

---

[1] This sentence would be OK if there were a conjunction between *the book* and *the pen*. What does this tell us about what conjunction does to theta roles?
[2] There are many ways to formalize theta grids, but I adopt here the indexing box method that Haegeman (1994) uses, since it seems to be the most transparent.

that index. Applying our grid to sentence (35), we get the following indexed sentence:

42)   John$_i$ gave [the book]$_j$ to [Mary]$_k$.

The $_i$ index maps the agent theta role to *John*. The $_j$ index maps the theme theta role to *the book*, etc.

Theta roles actually come in two types. The first is the ***external theta role*** (D). This is the one assigned to the subject. External theta roles are usually indicated by underlining the name of the theta role in the theta grid. The other kind are ***internal theta roles*** (E). These are the theta roles assigned to the object and indirect object. There is a semantic reason for the distinction between internal and external theta roles (see Marantz 1984 for extensive discussion), but we will leave that issue aside here. We will have use for the external/internal distinction in chapter 9, when we do NP/DP movement. For now, however, you should simply indicate which argument is the subject by underlining its name.

If you look carefully at the theta grid in (41), you'll notice that it only contains specifier (subjects) and complements (direct object and indirect object). There are no adjuncts listed in the theta grid. Adjuncts seem to be entirely optional:

43)   John put the book on the table (with a pair of tongs).   *instrument*
44)   (In the classroom) John put the book on the table.   *location*

This corresponds to our observation in chapter 5, that you can have as many or as few adjuncts as you like, but the number of complements and specifiers are more restricted. *Adjuncts are never arguments, and they never appear in theta grids.*

Up until now, we have been representing our grammar solely through the mechanism of rules (phrase structure, then X-bar rules). In order to stop X-bar rules from overgenerating, we need a constraint. Constraints are like filters. They take the output of rules, and throw away any that don't meet the constraint's requirements. In essence, we are going allow the X-bar rules to wildly overgenerate, and produce ungrammatical sentences. Those sentences, however, will be thrown out by our constraint. The constraint we are going to use is called the ***Theta Criterion***. The theta criterion ensures that there is a strict match between the number and types of arguments in a sentence and the theta grid.

45)   *The Theta Criterion*
       a)   Each argument is assigned one and only one theta role.
       b)   Each theta role is assigned to one and only one argument.

This constraint requires that there is a strict one-to-one match between argument DPs and theta roles. You can't have more arguments than you have theta roles, and you can't have more theta roles than you have DPs. Furthermore, since theta roles express particular thematic relations, the arguments will have to be of appropriate semantic types for the sentence to pass the constraint.

Let's look at some examples to see how this works. Consider the verb *love*. It has the theta grid given in (46). I haven't written in the indices here, because we'll add them when we compare the grid to a particular sentence.

46)   *love*

Experiencer	Theme

When a sentence containing the predicate *love* is produced, we apply indices to each of the arguments, and match those arguments to theta roles in the grid. The sentence in (47) is grammatical with the correct number of arguments. It is matched to the theta grid in (48). There is a one-to-one matching between arguments and theta roles. So the theta criterion is satisfied, and the sentence is allowed to pass through the filter and surface.

47)   Megan$_i$ loves Kevin$_j$.

48)   *love*

Experiencer	Theme
i	j

Contrast this with the ungrammatical sentence in (49)

49)   *Megan$_i$ loves.

This sentence lacks a theme argument, as seen in the following theta grid:

50)   *love*

Experiencer	Theme
i	

The theme theta role is not assigned to an argument (there is no index in its lower box). This violates the second condition of the theta criterion: Every theta role is assigned to an argument. There is not a one-to-one matching of the theta roles to the arguments in this sentence. Since the theta criterion is violated, the sentence is filtered out (marked as ungrammatical). Notice, our X-bar rules *can* generate this sentence; it is ruled as ungrammatical by our constraint.

The next sentence shows the opposite problem: A sentence with too many arguments.

51)   *Megan$_i$ loves Jason$_j$ Kevin$_k$.

52)   *love*

Experiencer	Theme	
i	j	k

Here, the argument *Kevin* doesn't get a theta role. There are only two theta roles to be assigned, but there are three arguments. This violates the first part of the theta criterion: the requirement that every argument have a theta role. Again, the theta criterion filters out this sentence as ungrammatical.

To summarize, we can constrain the output of the X-bar rules using a semantic tool: theta roles. The theta criterion is a constraint or filter that rules out otherwise well-formed sentences. The theta criterion requires that there is a strict one-to-one matching between the number and kind of theta roles and the number and kind of arguments.

3.   THE LEXICON

Let's take a step back from these details and look at the big picture. We have developed a model of grammar where we have three simple rules (the X-bar rules) that can generate a hierarchical constituent structure. These rules are constrained by the theta criterion, which uses the semantic notion of theta roles. Recall that our theory of syntax is meant to be a cognitive theory, so let's consider the question of where these rules and these theta roles are stored in the mind. Chomsky proposes that the part of the mind devoted to language is essentially divided into two parts. One part, which he calls the **computational component**, contains all the rules and constraints. This part of the mind does the work of building sentences and filtering out any ill-formed ones. The computational component can't work in a vacuum, however. It needs access to information about theta roles and the like. Chomsky claims that this information is stored in the **lexicon**, the other part of the human language faculty. The lexicon is your mental dictionary or list of words (and their properties). If you think about it, this is the obvious place for theta grids to be stored. Which theta roles are assigned to which argument is a property of each predicate. It is information that must be associated with that predicate and that predicate only. The obvious place to store information about particular words (or more properly **lexical items**) is in the lexicon.

The lexicon contains all the irregular and memorized parts of language. Each lexical entry (dictionary entry) must contain at least the following information):

- the meaning of the word
- the syntactic category of the word (N, V, A, P, T, C, etc.)
- the pronunciation of the word
- exceptional information of all kinds (such as morphological irregularities)
- the theta grid (argument structure).

When you learn a new word, you memorize all this information.

On an abstract level we can diagram the grammatical system as looking something like:

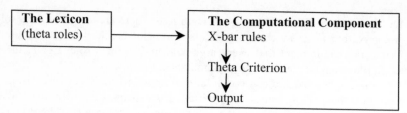

The lexicon feeds into the computational component, which then combines words and generates sentences. The fact that lexical information affects the form of the sentence is formalized in what we call the **Projection Principle**:

53)   *The Projection Principle*
         Lexical information (such as theta roles) is syntactically represented at all
         levels.

4.   EXPLETIVES AND THE EXTENDED PROJECTION PRINCIPLE

Before leaving the topic of the lexicon, I'd like to point out two special classes of predicates. Consider first the following "weather" verbs. These predicates don't seem to assign any theta roles:

54)   It rained.
55)   It snowed.
56)   It hailed.

What theta role does the pronoun *it* get in these sentences? If you are having a problem figuring this out, ask yourself what *it* refers to in the above sentences. It appears as if *it* doesn't refer to anything. In syntax, we refer to pronouns like this as *expletive* or *pleonastic pronouns*. These pronouns don't get a theta role (which of course is a violation of the theta criterion – a point we will return to below). The theta grid for weather verbs empty. They don't assign any theta roles.
         There is another class of predicates that take expletive pronouns. These are predicates that optionally take a CP subject:

57)   [cp That Bill loves chocolate] is likely.

The predicate *is likely* assigns one theta role. It takes one argument (the clause). (We will notate clausal arguments with the theta role *proposition*).

58)   *is likely*

proposition

You'll note that in (58) the theta role is not underlined. This is because the clause bearing the theta role of proposition is a complement. This can be seen in the following example:

59)   It is likely that Bill likes chocolate.

In this sentence, we again have an expletive *it*, which gets no theta role.

In order to maintain the theta criterion, we need to account for these expletive NPs without theta roles. Expletive pronouns usually appear in subject position. When *it* appears in other positions, it usually bears a theta role:

60)   I love *it*.   (*it* is a theme)
61)   I put a book on *it*.   (*it* is a goal or location)

Expletives seem to appear where there is no theta marked NP (or CP) that fills the subject position. This is encoded in a revised version of the Projection Principle: The ***Extended Projection Principle*** (EPP).

62)   *Extended Projection Principle* (EPP)
        All clauses must have subjects. Lexical information is syntactically represented

The EPP works like the theta criterion, it is a constraint on the output of the X-bar rules. It requires that every sentence have a subject. Next, we must account for the fact that expletives violate the theta criterion.

One way of doing this is by claiming that expletives are not generated by the X-bar rules. Instead they are inserted by a special ***expletive insertion*** rule:

63)   *Expletive insertion*
        Insert an expletive pronoun into the specifier of TP.

This rule applies when there is no other subject. If there is no theta marked subject and no expletive subject, then the EPP will filter the sentence out. The way in which we get around the theta criteria is by *ordering* the expletive insertion rule after the theta criterion has applied.

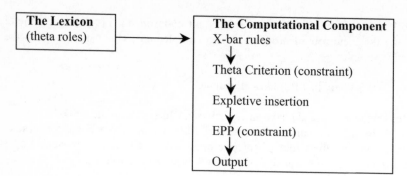

Since expletives are inserted *after* the theta criterion has applied, they can't be filtered out by it.

The model we've drawn here is very preliminary. In the next chapter, we will introduce a new kind of rule (the transformation – of which expletive insertion is a very special case) that will cause us to significantly revise this diagram.

Two Kinds of *It*

There are two *it* pronouns in English. One is the expletive found with weather verbs. The other is the neuter pronoun *it* found in sentences like:

i) It bit me on the leg.

If you contrast the *it* in (i) with the ones in the weather verbs, you'll see that the *it* in (i) does take a theta role (agent) and does refer to something (probably an insect or some other animal). Not every sentence with an *it* involves an expletive.

---

5.   SUMMARY

We started this chapter off with the observation that while X-bar rules capture important facts about constituency and cross-categorial generalizations, they overgenerate (that is they generate ungrammatical sentences). One way of constraining X-bar theory is by invoking lexical restrictions on sentences, such that particular predicates have specific argument structures, in the form of theta grids. The theta criterion rules out any sentence where the number and type of arguments don't match up one to one with the number and type of theta roles in the theta grid.

We also looked at one apparent exception to the theta criterion: theta role-less expletive pronouns. These pronouns only show up when there is no other subject, and are forced by the EPP. They escape the theta criterion by being inserted after the theta criterion has filtered out the X-bar rules.

By using lexical information (like theta roles) we're able to stop the X-bar rules from generating sentences that are ungrammatical. Unfortunately, as we'll see in the next chapter, there are also many sentences that the X-bar rules *cannot* generate. In order to account for these, we'll introduce a further theoretical tool: the transformational rule.

IDEAS, RULES, AND CONSTRAINTS INTRODUCED IN THIS CHAPTER

i)   The *predicate* defines the relation between the individuals being talked about and the real world – as well as with each other.

ii)   The *arguments* are the entities who are participating in the relation.

iii)   *Argument Structure*
        The number of arguments that a predicate takes.

iv)   *Intransitive*
        A predicate that takes only one argument.

v)   *Transitive*
        A predicate that takes two arguments.

vi)   *Ditransitive*
        A predicate that takes three arguments.

vii)   *Subcategorizational Restrictions*
        Restrictions on the syntactic category of an argument.

viii)   *Selectional Restrictions*
        Semantic restrictions on arguments.

ix)   *Thematic Relations*
        Semantic relations between a predicate and an argument – used as a means of encoding subcategorizational and selectional restrictions.

x)   *Agent*
        The doer of an action (under some definitions must be capable of volition).

xi)   *Experiencer*
        The argument that perceives or experiences an event or state.

xii)   *Theme*
        The element undergoing the action or change of state.

xiii)   **Goal**
         The end point of a movement.

xiv)   **Recipient**
         A special kind of goal, found with verbs of possession (e.g., give).

xv)   **Source**
         The starting point of a movement.

xvi)   **Location**
         The place an action or state occurs.

xvii)   **Instrument**
         A tool with which an action is performed.

xviii)   **Benefactive**
         The entity for whose benefit the action is performed.

xix)   **Proposition**
         The thematic relation assigned to clauses.

xx)   **Theta Role**
         A bundle of thematic relations associated with a particular argument (NPs/DPs or CPs).

xxi)   **Theta Grid**
         The schematic representation of the argument structure of a predicate, where the theta roles are listed.

xxii)   **External Theta Role**
         The theta role associated with subject NPs/DPs or CPs.

xxiii)   **Internal Theta Role**
         The theta role associated with objects or indirect objects.

xxiv)   **The Theta Criterion**
         a)   Each argument is assigned one and only one theta role.
         b)   Each theta role is assigned to one and only one argument.

xxv)   **Lexical Item**
         Another way of saying "word." A lexical item is an entry in the mental dictionary.

xxvi)   ***The Projection Principle***
Lexical information (like theta roles) is syntactically represented at all levels.

xxvii) ***Expletive (or Pleonastic) Pronouns***
A pronoun (usually *it* or *there*) without a theta role. Usually found in subject position.

xxviii) ***Extended Projection Principle (EPP)***
All clauses must have subjects, Lexical Information is syntactically represented.

xxix)   ***Expletive Insertion***
Insert an expletive pronoun into the specifier of TP.

xxx)   ***The Lexicon***
The mental dictionary or list of words. Contains all irregular and memorized information about language, including the argument structure (theta grid) of predicates.

xxxi)   ***The Computational Component***
The combinatorial, rule based, part of the mind. Where the rules and filters are found.

xxxii) ***The Model***

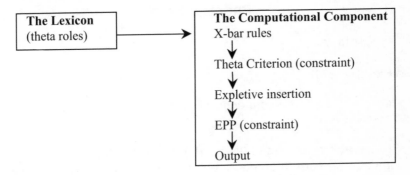

FURTHER READING

Grimshaw, Jane (1990) *Argument Structure.* Cambridge: MIT Press.

Gruber, Jeffrey (1965) Studies in Lexical Relations. Ph.D. dissertation, MIT.

Haegeman, Liliane (1994) *Introduction to Government and Binding Theory.* Oxford: Blackwell.

Levin, Beth (1993) *English Verb Classes and Alternations: A Preliminary Investigation.* Chicago: University of Chicago Press.

Marantz, Alec (1984) *On Grammatical Relations.* Cambridge: MIT Press.

Williams, Edwin (1981) Predication. *Linguistic Inquiry* 11, 203–38.

Williams, Edwin (1983) Semantic vs. syntactic categories. *Linguistics and Philosophy* 6, 423–46.

Williams, Edwin (1994) *Thematic Structure in Syntax.* Cambridge: MIT Press.

PROBLEM SETS

1.   SINHALA[3]

(Data from Gair 1970)

Two forms of the Sinhala verb appear in the data below and are identified in the glosses as A or B.

1) Provide a complete θ-grid (theta grid) for each of the verbs in the following data. Be sure to primarily look at the second line of each piece of data, not the English translation.
2) Indicate what theta role is assigned to what NP.
3) Discuss briefly (no more than 2 sentences) what kind of NP the suffix -ṭə attaches to.

---

[3] This problem is loosely based on one given to me by Barb Brunson. However, the data and questions have been altered. The data in this version of the problem set is taken directly from Gair, with some minor modifications to the glosses.

4) What is the difference between *mamə* and *matə*? (Hint: the answer to this question is related to the answer to question (3)).

5) In terms of θ roles, what is the difference between the A and the B verb forms?

a) Mamə   kawi   kiənəwa.
   I   poetry   tell-A
   "I recite poetry."

b) Matə   kawi   kiəwenəwa.
   I   poetry   tell-B
   "I started reciting poetry (despite myself)."

c) Lamea kataawə ahanəwa.
   child   story   hear-A
   "The child listens to the story."

d) Lameatə kataawə æhenəwa.
   child   story   hear-B
   "The child hears the story."

e) Mamə   natənəwa.
   I   dance-A
   "I dance."

f) Matə   nætəenəwa.
   I   dance-B
   "I dance (I can't help but do so)."

g) Hæmə irida   mə   mamə koləmbə yanəwa.
   every Sunday   EMPH   I   Columbo go-A
   "Every Sunday I deliberately go to Colombo."

h) Hæmə irida   mə   matə   koləmbə yæwenəwa.
   every Sunday   EMPH   I   Columbo go-B
   "Every Sunday I experience going to Colombo."

i) Malli   nitərəmə   aňdənəwa.
   brother   always   cries-A
   "Brother always cries."

j) Mallitə   nitərəmə   æňdənəwạ.
   brother   always   cries-B
   "Brother always bursts out crying without control."

k) Mamə   untə   baninəwa.
    I   them   scold-A
    "I deliberately scold them."

l) Maṭə   untə   bænenəwa.
    I   them   scold-B
    "I experienced scolding them."

m) Apiṭə pansələ   peenəwa.
    we   temple   see-B
    "We saw the temple."

2.   IRISH AND THE THETA CRITERION

What problems do each of the following sentences give for the theta criterion? (As a starting point, it may help to draw the theta grid for each verb
and show what NP gets what role.) Please, not more than 3–4 sentences of
discussion per example.

a) An fear a bhfaca mé é.
    the man who saw I him
    "The man who I saw."

b) Rinceamar.
    Dance.1PL
    "We danced."

c) Ba-mhaith liom an teach a thógail.
    COND-good with-me the house its building
    "I would like to build the house."

3.   WARLPIRI[4]

Consider the following data from Warlpiri:

a) Lungkarda ka   ngulya-ngka   nguna-mi.
    bluetongue AUX   burrow-A   lie-NON.PAST
    "The bluetongue skink is lying in the burrow."

---

[4]The data for this problem set comes from Ken Hale via Barb Brunson.

b) Nantuwu   ka   karru-kurra   parnka-mi.
    horse   AUX   creek-B   run-NON.PAST
    "The horse is running to the creek."

c) Karli   ka   pirli-ngirli   wanti-mi.
    boomerang AUX   stone-C   fall-NON.PAST
    "the boomerang is falling from the stone."

d) kurdu-ngku ka-jana pirli   yurutu-wana   yirra-rni.
    child-D   AUX   stone road-E   put.NON.PAST
    "the child is putting stones along the road."

What is the meaning of *each* of the affixes (suffixes) glossed with -A, -B, -C, -D, and -E. Can you relate these suffixes to theta roles? Which ones?

4.   OBJECT EXPLETIVES

In the text above, it was observed that theta-role-less expletives primarily appear in subject position. Consider the following sentence. Is it here an expletive?

    I hate it that you're always late.

How could you tell?

5.   PASSIVES

Part 1: Write up the theta grids for the verbs in the following sentences. Pretend as if there are two verbs *give* (give₁ is seen in (d), give₂ in (e)).

a) John bit the apple.
b) Susan forgave Louis.
c) The jockey rides the horse.
d) Phillip gave the medal to the soldier.
e) Phillip gave the soldier the medal.

Part 2: English has a suffix -*en*, which when attached to verbs changes the structure of the sentence associated with them. This is called the **passive** morpheme. The following sentences are the passive equivalents of the sentences in part 1. The bracketed PPs starting with *by* are optional.

f) The apple was bitten (by John).
g) Louis was forgiven (by Susan).
h) The horse was ridden (by the jockey).

i)   The medal was given to the soldier (by Phillip).
j)   The soldier was given the medal (by Phillip).

Describe in your own words what the -en passive suffix does to the theta grids of verbs. Pay careful attention to the last two examples, and to the optionality of the by-phrases.

6.   HIAKI -*WA*[5]

(Data from Escalante 1990 and Jelinek and Escalante forthcoming)

Part 1: Consider the function of the suffix –*wa* in Hiaki (also known as Yaqui), a language spoken in Southern Arizona and Mexico. Look carefully at the data below, and figure out what effect this suffix has on the theta grids of Hiaki verbs. What English phenomenon is this similar to?

(Notes: Sometimes when -*wa* attaches to a verb, the form of the root changes (usually /e/ becomes /i/). This is a morphophonological phenomenon that you don't need to worry about. ACC refers to accusative case, INST means instrument, and PERF means perfective aspect (aspect plays no role in the answer to this problem). There is no nominative suffix in Hiaki.)

a)   Peo Huan-ta chochon-ak.
      Pete John-ACC punch-PERF
      "Pete punched John."

a')   Huan chochon-wa-k.
      John punch-WA- PERF
      "John was punched."

b)   'Ume uusi-m uka kuchu-ta kuchi'i-m-mea bwa'a-ka.
      the children-PL the-ACC fish-ACC knife-PL-INST eat- PERF
      "The children ate the fish with knives."

b')   'U kuchu kuchi'i-m-mea bwa'a-wa-k.
      the fish knife-PL-INST eat-WA-PERF
      "The fish was eaten with knives."

c)   Peo bwiika.
      Pete sing
      "Pete is singing."

---

[5] Thanks to Heidi Harley for contributing this problem set.

c') Bwiik-wa.
   sing-WA
   "Singing is happening." or "There is singing going on." or "Someone is singing."

Part 2: Not all verbs allow -*wa*. Consider the following pairs of sentences that show verbs that don't allow -*wa*. In terms of theta grids, what do these sentences have in common with each other that differentiates them from the ones that allow -*wa* (above in part 1).

a) 'U wikia chukte.
   the rope come.loose
   "The rope is coming loose."

a') *Chukti-wa.
   come.loose-WA
   "Coming loose is happening." or "There is coming loose going on." or "Something is coming loose."

b) 'U kaaro nasonte.
   the car damage
   "The car is damaged."

b') *Nasonti-wa.
   damage-WA
   "Damage is happening." or "There is damage going on" or "Something is getting damaged."

c) 'U kari veete-k.
   The house burn-PERF
   "The house burned."

c') *Veeti-wa-k.
   Burn-WA-PERF
   "Burning happened." or "There was burning going on." or "Something is getting burned."

d) 'U vachi bwase'e.
   The corn cook
   "The corn is cooking."

d') *Bwase'i-wa.
   cook-WA
   "Cooking happened." or "There was cooking going on." or "Something is being cooked."

7. ANTIPASSIVES IN ENGLISH AND INUPIAQ

(Data from Seiler 1978)

In many languages there is an operation that changes the theta grid of certain verbs, this operation is called the *antipassive*.

Part 1: Here is some data from Inupiaq, an Inuit language of Canada and Alaska. Explain what adding the antipassive morpheme does to the theta grid of the verb. Verbs in Inupiaq agree with both their subjects and their objects. 3-3 means that the verb agrees with both a 3rd person subject and a 3rd person object. 3 means that the verb only agrees with a 3rd person subject.

Active

a) Aŋuti-m   umiaq   qiñig-aa   tirrag-mi.

    man-ERG   boat-ABS   see-3SUBJ.3OBJ   beach-at

    "The man sees the boat at the beach."

Antipassive

b) Aŋun   (umiag-mik)   qiñiq-tuq   tirrag-mi.

    man-ABS   boat-INST   see-3   beach-at

    "The man sees (with a boat) at the beach."

Part 2: The following is some data from English. This might also be called an antipassive construction. How is it similar or different from the Inupiaq antipassive?

c)   I ate a basket of apples.
d)   I ate.

Part 3

Transformations

chapter 8

Head-to-Head Movement

0.   INTRODUCTION

Consider the relation between a verb and its object: According to X-bar theory, an object is the complement to V (sister to V, daughter of V'). This means that *no* specifier or adjunct can intervene between the complement and the head (if they did, the object would no longer be a complement).

The following sentence is from Modern Irish Gaelic, this is a Verb-Subject-Object (VSO) word order language:

1)   Phóg Máire an lucharachán.
       Kissed Mary the leprechaun
       "Mary kissed the leprechaun."

In this sentence, the subject (a specifier) intervenes between the subject and the object: this sentence cannot be generated by X-bar theory. (Try to draw a tree where the specifier intervenes between the head and the complement – it's impossible.)

Now consider the following sentence from French:

2)   Je mange souvent des   pommes.
       I   eat   often   of.the apples
       "I often eat apples."

Souvent 'often' intervenes between the verb and the object. If *souvent* is an adjunct it is appearing between a head and its complement. X-bar theory can't draw the tree for this one either.

In sum, X-bar theory *undergenerates*, it does not produce all the possible grammatical sentences in a language.

Although based on very different problems than the ones in (1) and (2), Chomsky (1957) observed that a phrase structure grammar (such as X-bar theory) cannot generate all the sentences of a language. He proposed that what was needed was a set of rules that change the structure (in very limited ways) generated by phrase structure rules. These rules are called ***transformational rules***. Transformations take the output of X-bar rules (and other transformations) and change them into different trees.

The model of grammar that we are suggesting here takes the following form. You should read this like a flow chart. The derivation of a sentence starts at the top, and what comes out at the bottom is what you say.

3)   **The Computational Component**

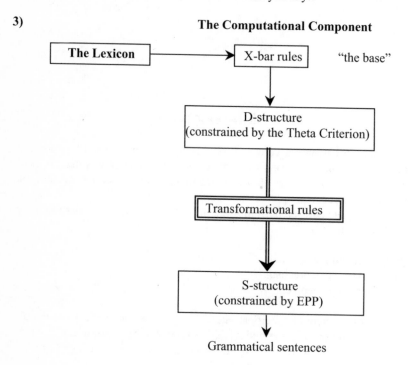

Grammatical sentences

X-bar theory and the lexicon conspire together to generate trees. This conspiracy is called ***the base***. The result of this tree generation is a level we call ***D-structure*** (this used to be called Deep Structure, but for reasons that need not concern us here, the name has changed to D-structure). You will never pronounce a D-structure. D-structure is also sometimes called the ***underlying form*** or ***underlying representation*** (and is similar in many ways to the underlying form found in phonology). The theta criterion filters out ungrammatical sentences at D-structure.

D-structure is then subject to the ***transformational rules***. These transformational rules can move words around in the sentence. We've actually already seen two of these transformational rules. In Chapter 6, we looked extensively at T to C raising in subject/aux inversion, and affix lowering, which gets inflectional suffixes to lower to their verb. (In this chapter, we're going to look in more detail at these last two rules.) The output of a transformational rule is called the ***S-structure*** of a sentence. The S-structure is filtered by the EPP, which ensures that the sentence has a subject. What are left are grammatical sentences.

In the version of Chomskyan grammar we are considering, we will look at two different kinds of transformations: movement rules and insertion rules. Movement rules move things around in the sentence. Insertion rules put something new into the sentence. This chapter is about one kind of movement rule: the rules that move one head into another, called ***head-to-head movement***. These transformational rules will allow us to generate sentences like (1) and (2) above. X-bar theory by itself cannot produce these structures.

Generative Power

Before we go any further and look at an example of a transformation, consider the power of this type of rule. A transformation is a rule that can change the trees built by X-bar theory. If you think about it, you'll see that such a device is extremely powerful; in principle it could do *anything*. For example you could write a changing rule that turns all sentences that have the word "red" in them to sentences with SOV order.

i) $[_{TP} \ldots red \ldots] \Rightarrow [_{TP} \, S \, [O \, V]]$

This rule would take a sentence like (ii) and change it into a sentence like (iii):

ii)   The red book bores me.
iii)   The red book me bores.

Similarly we could allow X-bar theory to generate sentences where the work "snookums" appears after every word, then have a transformation that deletes all instances of "snookums" (iv). (v) shows the D-structure of such a sentence. (vi) would be the S-structure (output) of the rule.

iv)   "snookums" $\Rightarrow \emptyset$
v)   I snookums built snookums the snookums house snookums.
vi)   I built the house.

These are crazy rules. No language has a rule of these types. However, in principle, there is no reason that rules of this kind couldn't exist. We thus need to restrict the power of transformational rules. We do this two ways:

vii)   *Rules must have a motivation*. Frequently these motivations are output constraints. like the EPP that we saw in the last chapter, or morphophonological, like the ones we will propose in this chapter.

viii)   Not only are rules motivated by output constraints, they are restricted by them. *You cannot write a rule that will create a violation of an output constraint*.

As we go along we will consider specific ways to constrain transformational rules so that they don't overgenerate.

1.   VERB MOVEMENT (V→T)

1.1   French

Let's return now to the problems we raised in the introduction to this chapter. Let's start with the sentence from French:

4)   Je mange souvent des   pommes.
        I eat   often   of.the apples
        "I often eat apples."

In this sentence, an adjunct surprisingly appears between the head of VP and its complement. Compare this sentence to the English sentence in (5):

5)   I often eat apples.

In the English sentence, the adjunct does not intervene between the verb and the complement. The tree for (5) would look like (6).

6)

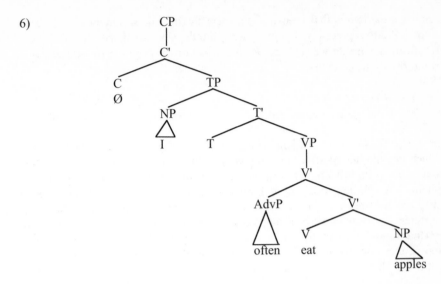

Notice the following thing about this structure. There is a head position that intervenes between the subject NP and the adverb *often*: this is the T position. T, you will recall, gives its inflection to the verb or surfaces as an auxiliary. Notice that in French (4), the thing that appears between the subject and the adverb is not T, but the tensed main verb.

Keeping this idea in the back of your mind now consider the following chart, which shows the relative placement of the major constituents of a French sentence with a tensed main verb (b), and English sentence with a tensed verb (a), and both languages with auxiliary constructions (c and d):

7)

a)	I	T	often	eat	apples
b)	Je	mange	souvent		des pommes
c)	I	have[1]	often	eaten	apples
d)	J'	ai	souvent	mangé	des pommes

There are several things to observe about this chart. Recall from chapter 5, that auxiliaries are instances of the category T; as such, V' adjuncts are predicted to invariably follow them. This seems to be the case (c and d). What is striking about the above chart is that tensed main verbs in French also seem to occupy this slot, whereas in English, they follow the adverb. How can we account for this alternation? Let's assume that the form which meets X-bar theory (and happens to be identical to the English tree in (6)) is what is generated in *both* French and English. The differ-

---

[1] In this chapter we aren't going to extensively discuss *have* and *be* in English. Instead we are simply going to generate them in T, as we have been doing up until now. This view is probably a bit naïve. Problem set 10 at the end of this chapter looks at the issue in more detail.

ence between the two is that French has a special *extra* rule which moves its verbs out of the VP. More precisely, it moves them into the slot associated with T. This is the transformational rule we will call $V \rightarrow T$ it is also known as **verb raising**. This rule is informally stated in (8).

8)   *V → T raising*
         Move the head V to the head T.

Before doing looking at an example, consider for a moment why this rule might apply. Much like the rule of affix lowering we introduced for English in chapter 6, this rule exists to get an inflectional affix on the verb. In fact, let's go one step further, let's claim that affix lowering and verb raising are really the same operation. Notice that they are in complementary distribution – a language either has one or the other. The difference between a verb raising language (French) and an affix lowering language (like English) might simply be one of a parameter. All languages have some version of this rule, some set the parameter to raise the verb to T, others set it to lower the T to the V.

9)   *Verb raising parameter*
         Verbs raise to T *or* T lowers to V.

This provides a simple account of the difference between English and French adverbial placement.
         Now, let's do a derivation for the French sentence (4) (*Je mange souvent des pommes*). The first step in the derivation is to build an X-bar structure, and insert all the words. This gives us the D-structure of the sentence:

10)

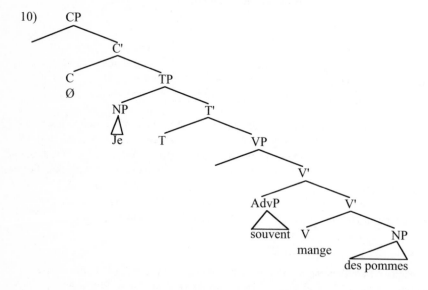

Notice that this D-structure is not a grammatical sentence of French (yet). In fact it has exactly the same word order as the English sentence in (5).

The next step in the deviation is to apply the transformation of Verb Movement. One typical way of representing a movement transformation is to draw a tree with an arrow.

11)

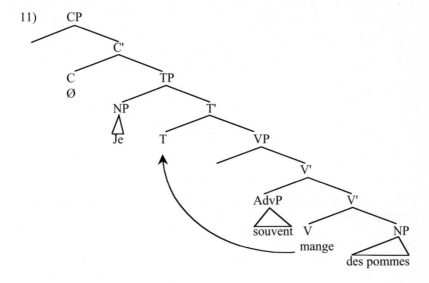

This results in the correct S-structure string:

12)   Je mange$_i$ souvent t_i des pommes.

yet at the same time allows us to maintain X-bar theory. The t_i here stands for "trace" and sits at the D-structure position of the verb.

Consider now the related derivation for the English sentence *He often eats apples*. The D-structure is the same, except with English words:

13)

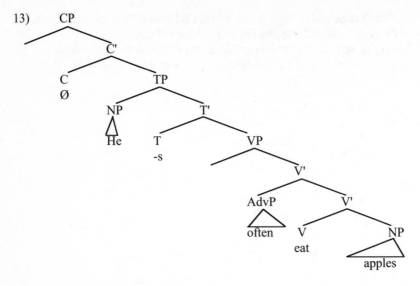

Since English is parameterized for affix lowering rather than verb raising, the inverse movement to French applies:

14)

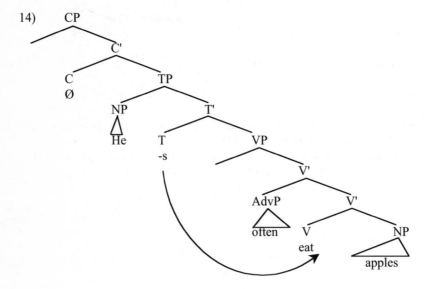

This results in the grammatical S-Structure:

15)   He often eats apples.

What we have seen so far is a rather technical solution to a relatively small problem. Now, I'm going to show you that this solution can be extended. Recall our chart with adverb above in (7). Consider now the identical chart with negatives:

16)

a)	I	do	not	eat	apples
b)	Je	ne-mange	pas		des pommes
c)	I	have	not	eaten	apples
d)	Je	n'ai	pas	mangé	des pommes

Ignore for the moment the French morpheme *ne-*, which is optional in spoken French in any case. Concentrate instead on the relative positioning of the negatives *pas* and *not* and the verbs. The situation is the same as with the adverb *often*. All auxiliaries in both languages precede negation, as does the main verb in French. But in English, the main verb follows the negation.[2]

We can apply the same solution to this word order alternation that we did for adverbs: we will move the verb around the negation. The tree here will be slightly different, however. Let us assume that *not* heads a projection called NegP, and this projection is the complement of TP, and dominates VP.

17)

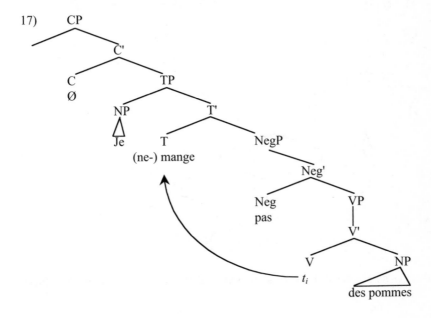

<hr/>

[2] For the moment, ignore the *do* verb. We will return to this below.

The transformation of verb movement then raises the verb around *pas* as represented by the arrow in (17).[3] Again this derives the correct word order.[4]

  Observe that the alternation in position between an auxiliary and a tensed verb is not limited to French. Many (if not most) languages show this same alternation. Take for example the language Vata, a Kru language of West Africa. The underlying word order of Vata is SOV (data from Koopman 1984).

18) a)   A   la   saka li.
          we   have rice eaten
          "We have eaten rice."

     b)   A   li   saka.
          we   eat   rice
          "We eat rice."

In the sentence with the overt auxiliary, the verb appears to the far right. When there is no auxiliary, the verb appears in the structural slot otherwise occupied by the auxiliary. This alternation can be attributed to verb raising. When there is an auxiliary (*la*), T does not require "support" from the verb, so the verb remains in its base generated position (19).

19)

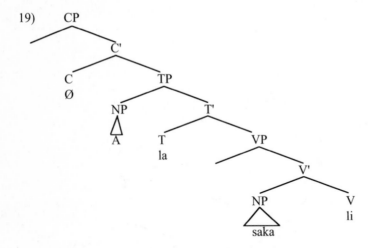

When there is no auxiliary, T requires support, and the verb raises around the object to T:

---

[3] An alternative to this is often found in the literature. In this alternative *ne-* heads the NegP and *pas* is in the specifier of NegP. The verb raises and stops off at the Neg head, (picking up *ne-* on the way) and then moves up to T. This alternative was presented in Pollock (1989).
[4] You might note that in English the comparable operation (affix lowering) does not apply around negation. We explore this issue in more detail below.

20)

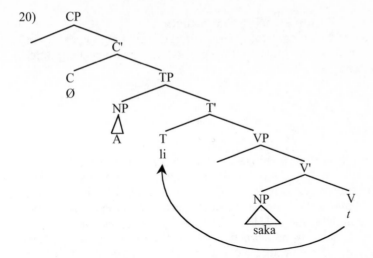

This, of course, is the correct word order (*A li saka*).

The transformational rule of V → T movement thus provides a simple, elegant and motivated account of cases where the verb shows up in the "wrong" position. The motivation for the verb to move (or the affix to lower) is intuitive: the need for the verb to get its inflection. This seems to correlate with the fact that in many languages there are positional alternations where auxiliaries (T) and tensed verbs are alternate and are in complementary distribution. This also gives a straightforward account of certain cross-linguistic differences. We can account for the fact that English and French consistently differ in the relative placement of adverbs and negation with respect to tensed verbs. We derived this difference by appealing to a parameter which either has the verb raise to T, or T-affixes lower to the verb.

1.2   Irish

Now we'll turn to the other (more difficult) problem raised in the introduction to this chapter. This is the Verb-Subject-Object (VSO) order of Irish.

21)   Phóg Máire an lucharachán.
        Kissed Mary the leprechaun
        "Mary kissed the leprechaun."

As we observed above, there is no way that X-bar theory can generate a sentence of this type. This is true of every basic sentence in Irish. VSO order is found in every tensed sentence in Irish. It is also the basic order of about 9 percent of the world's languages, including languages from many different language families such as Tagalog, Welsh, Arabic, Mixtec, Mayan, Salish, Turkana, Maasai (to name only a few).

Digression on Flat Structure

Up until the early 1980s, most linguists considered VSO languages to simply be exceptions to X-bar theory. They proposed that these languages had a **flat structure**:

i)

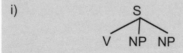

This structure is called "flat" because there are no hierarchical differences between subjects, object, and the verb. In other words, there are no structural distinctions between complements, adjuncts and specifiers. These sentences don't have a VP constituent. In (i) there is no single node dominating both the V and the second NP, but excluding the subject NP.

There is a delicate balance between a theory that is empirically adequate (one that accounts for all the data), like a theory that has *both* flat structure languages and X-bar languages, and one which is explanatorily adequate and elegant (like pure X-bar theory). By claiming that these languages were exceptions, linguists were left with a considerably less elegant theory. Thus the race was on to see if there was some way to incorporate these languages into X-bar theory. Notice, however, that pure elegance alone is not sufficient cause to abandon an empirically adequate but inelegant theory like flat structure – we must also have empirical evidence (data) in favor of the elegant theory.

Flat structure makes the following predications:

a)   There is no VP constituent.
b)   There is no evidence for a hierarchical distinction between subjects and objects – they both have the same mother and mutually c-command one another.

It turns out that both these predications are wrong. First, if VSO languages have no VP in simple tensed clauses they should have no VPs in other clause types either. McCloskey (1983) observed for Irish, and Sproat (1985) for Welsh, that this is false.

ii)   Tá   Máire [ag-pógail an lucharachán].
         Is   Mary   ing-kiss the leprechaun
         "Mary is kissing the leprechaun."

In auxiliary sentences in Irish, there is a plausible candidate for a VP: the words bracketed in (ii). If this V + O sequence is a constituent, it should obey a constituency tests. Two typical constituency tests from chapter 2, coordination and movement (clefting), show this:

iii)   Tá Máire [ag-pógail an lucharachán] agus [ag-goidú a ór].
        Is Mary [ing-kiss the leprechaun] and   [ing-steal his gold]
        "Mary is kissing the leprechaun and stealing his gold."

iv)   Is [ag-pógáil an lucharachán] atá Máire.
        It-is [ing-kiss the leprechaun] that.be Mary
        "it's kissing the leprechaun that Mary is."

These sentences show that the bracketed [V + O] sequence in (ii) is indeed a constituent, and a plausible VP.

        Now, turn to the second prediction made by flat structure, where all the NPs are on a par hierarchically. This too we can show is false. Recall from chapter 4, that there is at least one phenomenon sensitive to hierarchical position: the distribution of anaphors. Recall that the antecedent of an anaphor must c-command it. If flat structure is correct, then you should be able to have either NP be the antecedent and either NP be the anaphor, since they mutually c-command one another (they are sisters):

v)   S
                       ⟋ | ⟍
                      V   NP   NP

The data in (vi) and (vii) shows that this is false. Only the object NP can be an anaphor. This means that the object must be c-commanded by the subject. Further it shows that the subject cannot be c-commanded by the object. Flat structure simply can't account for this.

vi)   Chonaic Síle$_i$ í-fein$_i$.
        Saw   Sheila her-self
        "Sheila saw herself."

vii)   *Chonaic í-fein$_i$ Síle$_i$.
        Saw   her-self Sheila
        "Sheila saw herself."

The flat structure approach, if you'll pardon the pun, comes up flat. It makes the wrong predictions. The verb raising approach proposed in the main text doesn't suffer from these problems. It maintains X-bar theory so both has a VP and a hierarchical distinction between subjects and object.

The failure of X-bar theory to account for 9 percent of the world's languages is a significant one! However, the theory of transformations gives us an easy out to this problem. If we assume that VSO languages are underlyingly SVO (at D-structure), then a transformational rule applies which derives the initial order.

22)   SVO ⇒ VSO

How might we actually structurally implement this rule? Given the discussion in section 1.1 above, the answer should be obvious: we can use verb movement.

There is some straightforward evidence in favor of a verb movement approach to Irish word order: First, we see the same type of positional auxiliary/tensed verb word order alternations.

23)   Tá Máire ag-pógáil an lucharachán.
         Is Mary   ing-kiss   the leprechaun
         "Mary is kissing the leprechaun."

24)   Phóg Máire an lucharachán.
         kissed Mary the leprechaun
         "Mary kissed the leprechaun."

As in the French and Vata cases, with respect to a certain position (in Irish the initial position), auxiliaries and main verbs are in complementary distribution – evidence for V → T movement.

Unfortunately the situation here is not as straightforward as the French and Vata cases. If we try to draw the tree for (24), we immediately run into a problem.

25)

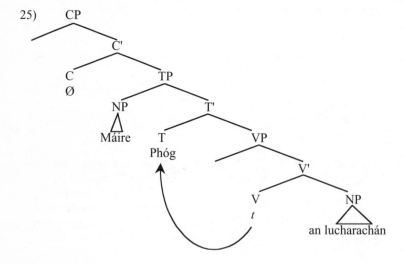

While moving the verb to T certainly accounts for the alternation between verbs and auxiliaries, it does not derive the correct VSO word order. Instead we get incorrect SVO order.

In all the sentences of Irish we've looked at, T (in the form either of an auxiliary or a raised tensed verb) seems to precede its specifier (the subject). One possibility to resolve this might be in exercising the parameters we looked at in chapter 5. So we might try putting the specifier of TP to the right in Irish:

26)

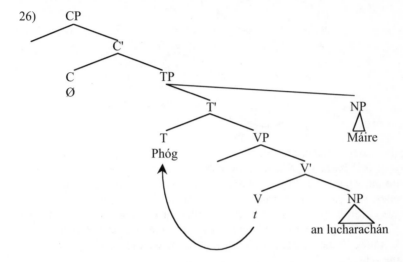

But this doesn't work, if you look carefully at the order of elements in (26) you'll see this results in VOS order, which is completely ungrammatical in Irish:

27)   *Phóg an lucharachán Máire.
          kissed the leprechaun Mary
          (ungrammatical with the reading "Mary kissed the leprechaun.")

So X-bar parameters clearly aren't the solution. The only alternative is to claim that we've been generating subjects in the wrong position. That is, subjects are not generated in the specifier of TP, like we have been assuming. Instead, they are *underlyingly* generated in the specifier of VP.

The idea that subjects are generated in the specifier of VP is called the **VP-internal subject hypothesis**, and was first proposed by Hilda Koopman and Dominique Sportiche (1991). The idea has some thematic motivation. By assuming that subjects are generated inside the VP we can make the strong claim that theta roles are assigned entirely within the VP.

If we assume the VP-internal subject hypothesis, the derivation of VSO order is trivial: It involves a straightforward instance of V → T raising:

28)

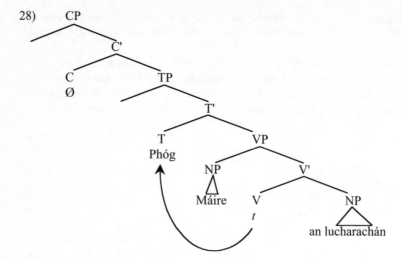

This derives the correct VSO order of Irish.

    Now at this point your head is probably spinning and you are saying to yourself "Hold on, what about English, French, and Vata! In all those languages the subject precedes T." Alas, this is true. The solution to the conundrum lies easily within our grasp, however. Perhaps it is the case that in English, French, and Vata (but not the VSO languages) subject NPs *move* from the specifier of VP to the specifier of TP. A simple French sentence then would have two movements, one of the verb, one of the subject:

29)

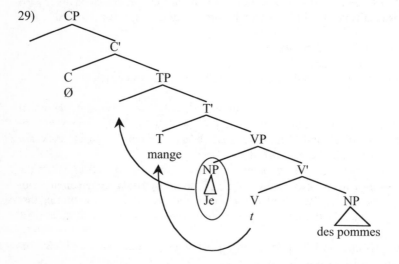

This second kind of movement is called **NP movement** and is the topic of the next chapter, where we'll discuss further evidence for VP-internal subjects. The correct formulation and motivations for NP movement are set out there. For now, we'll just observe that we have not argued ourselves into a corner; there is a way out.

Let us summarize the (quite complicated) discussion up to now. In section 0, we saw that there are instances where X-bar rules fail to generate the correct orders of sentences. To solve this problem, we looked at a new rule type: the transformation. Transformations take a structure generated by X-bar theory and change it in restricted ways. We've looked at one such transformation: V → T. This rule has the function of raising a verb to the T head. It does so in order that the verb can support inflection. We also looked at the mirror image of verb raising: affix lowering, which lowers an inflectional suffix to the verb. These are in complementary distribution, so serve as tokens of the same rule. A language is parameterized as to whether it takes the raising or the lowering variant. The difference in word order between French and English negatives and sentences with adverbials can be boiled down to this parameter. The rule of verb raising itself can explain the fact that an adjunct (the adverb) appears between a head and its complement. Taken together with the VP-internal subject hypothesis, verb raising can also explain the very problematic basic VSO word order. This simple straightforward tool thus allows us to account for a very wide range of complicated facts.

2.   T MOVEMENT (T → C)

Before leaving the topic of the movement of heads, we briefly return to a phenomena somewhat obliquely discussed in chapter 6. This is the phenomenon known as $T \rightarrow C$ movement or subject/aux inversion. In yes/no questions in English (questions that can be answered with either a *yes* or *no*), auxiliary verbs invert with their subject:

30)   You *have* squeezed the toilet paper.
31)   *Have* you squeezed the toilet paper?

In chapter 6, we claimed that this alternation is due to the presence of a special null question complementizer $Ø_{[+Q]}$. We observed that in many languages (such as Polish and Irish) yes/no questions aren't indicated with subject/aux inversion, but with a special form of the initial complementizer (recall Irish is VSO to start with, so subject/aux inversion would do nothing):

32)   An bhfaca tú   an madra?
        Q   See   you the dog
        "Did you see the dog?"

We claimed that subject/aux inversion is a special case of these question complementizers. English doesn't have an overt (pronounced) question complementizer like the Irish *an*. Instead, English has a null $Ø_{[+Q]}$ complementizer. Being phonologically null, however, is a bit of a problem, since the difference in meaning between a statement and a question is encoded in something you can't hear. English employs a mechanism (which we now know is a transformation), that gives phonological content to that $\emptyset_{[+Q]}$ by moving T to it, *around the subject*:

33)

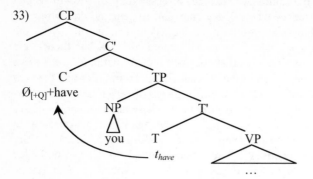

This kind of analysis is supported by the fact subject/aux inversion (T → C) is in strict complementary distribution with overt question complementizers as seen in the following embedded clauses:

34)   I asked *have* you squeezed the toilet paper.[5]
35)   I asked whether you *have* squeezed the toilet paper.
36)   *I asked whether *have* you squeezed the toilet paper.

So the process of subject/aux inversion must be a property triggered by complementizers. This rule is very similar to the rule of V → T raising. It is triggered by morphophonological requirements (such as the fact that something contentful must be pronounced, or that an affix needs a host). Both movements are instances of moving one head into another, so are considered instances of the same basic operation: **head-to-head movement**. This is a cover term for both V → T and T → C.

---

[5] For many people this sentence is not grammatical unless the embedded clause is a direct quote. (That is, it would properly be written with " " around it). This fact muddies the waters somewhat in this argument, as it may not be the case that T → C movement is allowed at all in embedded clauses in English. However, the same facts do hold true in other languages where subject/aux inversion in embedded clauses is more clearly instantiated.

VSO as Raising to C?

In the previous section we claimed that Irish VSO order involves raising the verb to T. We were also forced to claim that subjects were generated VP internally. Notice that in English, we also have a VS order, found in yes/no questions. These VS orders we analyze as T → C movement, with the subject remaining in its more typical place in the specifier of TP. Why don't we analyze Irish VSO order the same way? Instead of having VP-internal subjects, why don't we simply have verbs raise to T, then do T → C in *all* Irish clauses. This too would derive VSO order. There is a very good reason for this. Recall that in English T → C movement is blocked when there is an overt complementizer. (You don't move T into the C, because it already has phonological content.) If Irish VSO really involves raising to C, then it should be the case that you do *not* get VSO order when there is an overt complementizer. This is false. You get VSO order even when there is a complementizer.

i)   Duirt mé <u>gur</u> *phóg* **Máire** an lucharachán.
       Said I that kissed Mary the leprechaun
       "I said that Mary kissed the leprechaun."

This means that VSO must result from movement of the verb to some position lower than the complementizer. This is the analysis we argued for above, where V raises to T, and the subject is in the specifier of VP.

It appears as if V → T and T → C interact. In English, only auxiliaries ever occupy the T head as free-standing entities. Main verbs do not raise to T in English. So only auxiliaries under go T → C movement. Main verbs never do:

37)   Have you squeezed the toilet paper?
38)   *Squeezed you the toilet paper?

Contrast this to French. In French, main verbs undergo V → T movement. This means that when French does T → C movement, main verbs are predicted to also invert (because they are in T). This can be seen in the following tree:

39)

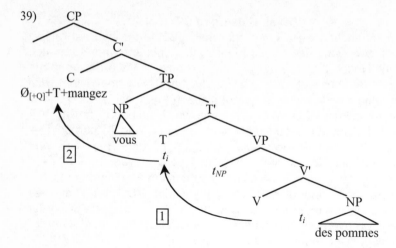

Movement ⒈ is V → T movement. Movement ⒉ is subsequent movement of the verb (in T) to C as part of T → C movement.

This prediction is borne out. Main verbs in French do invert in questions, but English main verbs do not.

40)   Mangez-vous des pommes?
41)   *Eat you the apples?

To summarize, we have looked (again) at the transformation of T → C movement in more detail. We saw that it has a phonological motivation, and is similar in some ways to V → T movement. We also noticed that in a language (such as French) where V → T movement applies main verbs as well as auxiliary verbs undergo T → C.

3.   *Do*-SUPPORT

In English, an interesting effect emerges when we try to question a sentence with no auxiliary:

42)   You eat apples.
43)   Do you eat apples?

In sentences with no auxiliary, we insert a dummy (=meaningless) auxiliary in yes/no questions. There must be a reason for this. We have argued that in English, T lowers to attach to V, at the same time in questions, the transformation of T → C movement forces the same T to raise. This is a contradiction: we want T to raise and lower at the same time. The phenomenon of *do*-support appears to be an escape hatch for T. If we insert a dummy (contentless) auxiliary to support the inflectional affixes, then this dummy can undergo T → C movement. This is an insertion trans-formation. This transformation is called **do-*insertion*** or **do-*support***:

44)   Do-*insertion*
        When there is no other option for supporting inflectional affixes, insert the
        dummy verb *do* into T.

What triggers this transformation is different than what triggers the movement trans-formations. The movement transformations are motivated (triggered) by morphophonological concerns. Insertion transformations apply only in the case that there is nothing else you can do. They are, in essence, operations of ***last resort***, you only apply them when you absolutely have to and when no movement transforma-tion can apply.

There are Two Verbs *Do* in English

Quite confusingly, English has two verbs *to do*. One is a main verb, meaning roughly "accomplish something," "perform an action." The other is a dummy (meaningless) auxiliary, which is inserted under "*do*-support." These are quite distinct entities. As can be seen by the fact that you can have both of them in one sentence:

i)   Did you do your homework?

Main verb *do* is not an auxiliary and is not in T, this can be seen by the fact that it cannot undergo T → C movement, and it follows *often* and *not*.

ii)   *Do you your homework?
iii)   You often do your homework.
iv)   You have not done your homework.

When invoking the *do*-insertion transformation, be careful that you only do it when dummy *do* is involved – not main verb *do*.

      Do-support doesn't apply only in questions; it also shows up in negative sentences.

45)   I ate the apple.
46)   I didn't eat the apple.

The negative morpheme *not* blocks the operation of affix lowering. The reasons for this are obscure. We will simply state it here as a stipulation.

47)   Affix lowering is *blocked* by the presence of *not* in English.

This is not a pretty condition, but is necessary. The issue of why this should be the case is still being hotly debated among syntacticians. We will leave the issue here with this stipulation.

4.   SUMMARY

In this chapter we've looked at a range of phenomena (subject/aux inversion, word order differences among languages, and *do*-support) that support the basic notion that we need more than X-bar rules. We have introduced the transformational movement rules of V → T and T → C and the insertion rule of *do*-support to account for these phenomena.

APPENDIX: TESTS FOR DETERMINING IF A LANGUAGE HAS V → T OR AFFIX LOWERING

The following are tests that you can use to determine if a particular language shows verb raising or not. These tests work well on SVO languages, but don't work with SOV languages (such as Japanese).

A)   If the language shows
                        Subj V *often* O
                order then it has V → T.

        If the language shows
                        Subj *often* V O
                order then it has affix lowering.

B)   If the language shows
                        Subj V *not* O
                order then it has V → T.

        If the language shows
                        Subj *not* V O
                order then it has affix lowering.

C)   If main verbs undergo T → C movement, then the language has V → T.

IDEAS, RULES, AND CONSTRAINTS INTRODUCED IN THIS CHAPTER

i)   **Transformation**
        A rule that takes an X-bar generated structure and changes it in restricted ways.

ii)   **D-structure**
        The level of the derivation created by the base, and has had no transformations applied to it.

iii)   **S-structure**
        The output of transformations. What you say.

iv)   **V → T raising**
        Move the head V to the head T (motivated by morphology).

v)   **Verb Raising Parameter**
        Verbs raise to T *or* T lowers to V.

vi)   **The VP-internal Subject Hypothesis**
        Subjects are generated in the specifier of VP.

vii)   **T → C Raising**
        Move T to C, when there is a phonologically empty $\emptyset_{[+Q]}$ complementizer.

viii)   **Do-*insertion* (Do-*support*)**
        When there is no other option for supporting inflectional affixes, insert the dummy verb *do* into T.

ix)   **Stipulation**
        Affix lowering is *blocked* by the presence of *not* in English.

x)   *The Model*

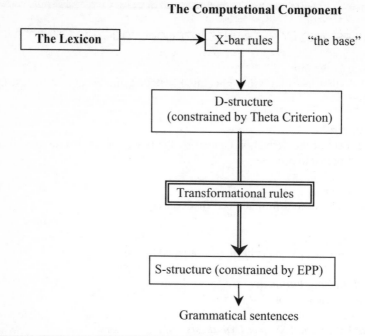

The Computational Component

FURTHER READING

Carnie, Andrew and Eithne Guilfoyle (2000) *The Syntax of Verb Initial Languages.* Oxford: Oxford University Press.

Emonds, Joseph (1980) Word order in Generative Grammar. *Journal of Linguistic Research* 1, 33–54.

Koopman, Hilda (1984) *The Syntax of Verbs: From Verb Movement Rules in the Kru Languages to Universal Grammar.* Dordrecht: Foris.

Koopman, Hilda and Dominique Sportiche (1991) The position of subjects. *Lingua* 85, 211–58.

Lightfoot, David and Norbert Hornstein (eds.) (1994) *Verb Movement.* Cambridge: Cambridge University Press.

McCloskey, James (1983) A VP in a VSO language. In G. Gazdar, G. Pullam, and I. Sag (eds.) *Order Concord and Constituency.* Foris, Dordrecht. pp. 9–55.

McCloskey, James (1991) Clause structure, ellipsis and proper government in Irish. *Lingua* 85, 259–302.

Ritter, Elizabeth (1988) A head movement approach to construct state noun phrases. *Linguistics* 26, 909–29.

PROBLEM SETS

1.   ENGLISH

Draw trees for the following English sentences, be sure to indicate all trans-formations with arrows. (Note the *-ed* suffix in (a) and (e) is <u>not</u> tense.)

a)   I have always loved peanut butter.
b)   I do not love peanut butter.
c)   Martha often thinks John hates phonology.
d)   Do you like peanut butter?
e)   Have you always hated peanut butter?
f)   Are you always so obtuse?

2.   AMERICAN VS. BRITISH ENGLISH VERB *HAVE*

English has two verbs *to have*. One is an auxiliary seen in sentences like (a):

a)   I *had* never seen this movie.

The other indicates possession:

b)   I never *had* a book.

You will note from the position of the adverb *never* that the possessive verb *have* is a main verb, whereas the auxiliary *have* is of category T.

Part 1: Consider the following data from American English. How does it sup-port the idea that auxiliary *have* is of category T, but possessive *have* is a main verb, and stays downstairs (i.e., has affix lowering apply)?

c)   I have had a horrible day.
d)   I have never had a pencil case like that!

e) Have you seen my backpack?
f) *Have you a pencil?

Part 2: Consider now the following sentence, which is grammatical in some varieties of British English:

g) Have you a pencil?

Does the possessive verb *have* in these dialects undergo V → T movement? How can you tell?

3.   VERB RAISING[6]

Based on the following data, do German and Persian exhibit V → T movement? Explain how you came to your answer.

German
a) Sprechen Sie Deutsch?
    speak   you German
    "Do you speak German?"

b) Ist er nach Hause geganen?
    is he to home gone
    "Has he gone home?"

c) Er sitzt nicht auf diesem Tisch.
    he sits not on this table
    "He does not sit on this table."

d) Sie soll nicht auf diesem Tisch sitzen.
    she must not on this   table sit
    "She must not sit on this table."

Persian
a) Rafti to madrese?
    went you school
    "Did you go to school?"

---

[6] Thanks to Simin Karimi for contributing this data.

b)   Bâyad un biyâd?
     must   he come
     "Must he come?"

c)   Man keyk na-poxtam.
     I   cake not-cooked
     "I did not bake cakes."

d)   Un na-xâhad âmad.
     he not-will come
     "He will not come."

4.   ITALIAN

(Data from Belletti 1994)

Consider the following data from Italian. Assume *non* is like French *ne-* and
is irrelevant to the discussion. Concentrate instead on the positioning of the
word *più*, 'anymore.'

a)   Gianni non ha più parlato.
        Gianni *non* has anymore spoken
        "Gianni does not speak anymore."

b)   Gianni non parla più.
        Gianni *non* speaks anymore
        "Gianni speaks no more."

On the basis of this very limited data, is Italian a verb raising language or an
affix lowering language?

5.   GERMANIC VERB SECOND

Background: Many of the languages of the Germanic language family exhibit
what is known as **verb second** order (also known as V2). With V2, the main
restriction on word order is that, in main clauses, the constituents may ap-

pear in essentially any order, as long as the verb is in the 2nd position in the sentence. This is seen in the following data from Dutch and German:

Dutch (Weerman 1989)
a) De man heeft een boek gezien gisteren.
     the man has   a   book seen   yesterday
     "The man has seen a book yesterday."

b) een boek heeft de man gezien gisteren.

c) gisteren heeft de man een boek gezien.

German (Vikner 1995)
d) Die Kinder haben diesen Film gesehen.
     the children have this   film seen
     "The children have seen this film."

e) Diesen Film haben die Kinder gesehen.

One analysis of this phenomenon uses the specifier of CP as a "topic" position. The most topical constituent (the bit under discussion) is put in the specifier of CP (i.e., is moved there – we'll discuss this kind of movement in chapter 11). Whatever is in T then moves to the C head by T → C movement:

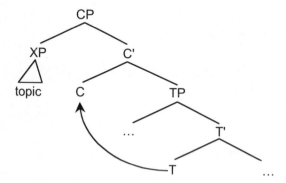

This puts T in second position.

Part 1: Now consider the following data from embedded clauses in German and Dutch.

Dutch

g) Ik geloof [dat de man een boek heeft gezien].
    I believe that the man a book   has   seen
    "I believe that the man has seen a book."

h) *Ik geloof [dat de man heeft een boek gezien].

German

i) Er sagt [daß die Kinder diesen Film gesehen haben].
    He said that the children this film saw   have
    "He said that the children saw this film."

j) *Er sagt [daß die Kinder haben diesen Film gesehen].

How does this data support the T →C analysis of V2? (Having trouble? Think about embedded *yes/no* questions in English).

Part 2. Consider now the following sentence of German and compare it to the embedded clauses in part 1 above.

k) Gestern sahen die Kinder den Film.
    Yesterday saw the children the film
    "The children saw the film yesterday."

Given what you now know about V2 and T → C movement in these languages, is German a V → T raising language or an affix lowering language?

Bonus: Is the data in part 1 above consistent with your answer? If not how might you make it consistent?

6.   HEBREW CONSTRUCT STATE (N → D)

(Based on the analysis of Ritter 1988, data from Borer 1999)

Background: In the text above we considered two variations on head movement: V → T, and T → C. In an influential article in 1988, Ritter proposed
that head movement might also apply inside NPs. More particularly she proposed that in many Semitic languages there is a rule of N → D movement.
This applies in a possessive construction called the construct state.

a) beit   ha-more
    house the-teacher
    "the teacher's house"

In the construct state, the noun takes on a special form (the construct):

b) *Free form*   bayit   'house'
    Construct   beit   'house'

Ritter proposes that the construct arises when the noun moves into the determiner. The construct morphology indicates that this noun is attached to
the determiner. A tree for sentence (a) is given below. The possessor noun
sits in the specifier of the NP, the possessed N head undergoes head
movement to D, where it takes on the construct morphology:

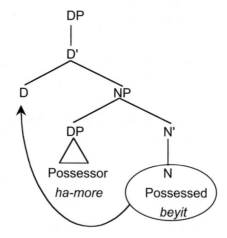

This results in the surface NP *[beyit ha-more]*.

Part 1: Consider now the following evidence, how does this support Ritter's N→D analysis?

c) *ha-beit ha-more
    the house the teacher
    "the house of the teacher"

Part 2: Now look at the positioning of adjectives. How does this support Ritter's analysis? Note in particular what noun the adjective modifies. (If you are having trouble with this question, trying drawing the tree of what the whole DP would look like before N → D movement applied.) M stands for "masculine", and F stands for feminine:

d) more   kita   xadaS
    teacher-M   class-F new-M
    "a class's new teacher" or "the new teacher of a class"
         but:
    "*a new class's teacher" or "*the teacher of a new class"

7.   ENGLISH[7]

Consider the italicized noun phrases in the following sentences:

a) I ate *something spicy.*
b) *Someone tall* was looking for you.
c) I don't like *anyone smart.*
d) I will read *anything interesting.*

One analysis that has been proposed for noun phrases like the ones above involves generating elements like *some* and *any* as determiners, and generating elements *one* and *thing* as nouns (under N), and then doing head-to-head movement of the Ns up to D. The tree below illustrates this analysis.

---

[7] Thanks to Jila Ghomeshi for contributing this problem set.

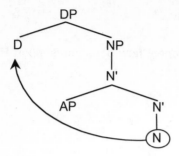

Give an argument in favor of this analysis, based on the order of elements within the noun phrase in general, and the order of elements in the noun phrases above.

8.   ENGLISH PROPER NAMES AND PRONOUNS

Consider the following data from English:

a) Lucy
b) *The Lucy
c) *Smiths
d) The Smiths
e) Him
f)   *The him
g) We linguists love a good debate over grammar.

Part 1: One possible analysis of proper names in English is that they involve head movement from an N position into a D position. How does the data in (a–d) above support this idea?

Part 2: Consider now the pronouns in (e–g). What category are they? N or D? Is there any evidence for movement?

9.   ITALIAN N→D[8]

(You may want to do question 8 before attempting this problem.)

In English, proper names cannot co-occur with determiners (e.g. *the John*). However, in Italian proper names of human beings *can* occur with determiners as the following example shows. (The presence or absence of the determiner seems to be free or perhaps stylistically governed.)

a)   i)   Gianni mi   ha   telefonato.
                Gianni me   has   telephoned
                "Gianni called me up."

        ii)   Il   Gianni   mi   ha   telefonato.
                the Gianni   me   has   telephoned
                "Gianni called me up."

Now, it has been argued that in the cases where the determiner does *not* occur, the proper name has moved from N to D. Provide an argument to support this view, based on the following examples. (Note: for the purposes of this question treat possessive pronouns such as *my* as adjectives.)

b)   i)   Il   mio   Gianni ha   finalmente   telefonato.
                the   my   Gianni has   finally   telephoned

        ii)   *Mio   Gianni ha   finalmente   telefonato.
                my   Gianni has   finally   telephoned

        iii)   Gianni mio   ha   finalmente   telefonato.
                Gianni my   has   finally   telephoned

c)   i)   E'venuto   il   vecchio   Cameresi.
                came   the   older   Cameresi

        ii)   *E'venuto   vecchio   Cameresi.
                came   older   Cameresi

        iii)   E'venuto   Cameresi   vecchio.
                came   Cameresi   older

d)   i)   L' antica   Roma
                the ancient   Rome
                "Ancient Rome"

---

[8] Jila Ghomeshi contributed this problem set based on data from Longobardi (1994).

ii)   *Antica   Roma
          ancient   Rome

iii)   Roma   antica
          Rome   ancient

10.   ENGLISH MODALS (REPRISE)

(In order to do this question, you should probably do problem set 7 (English modals and auxiliaries) in chapter 6 first.)

In problem set 7, chapter 6, you were asked to construct an argument that modal verbs, such as *can, may, must, should, would, could,* etc. are of category T, and auxiliary verbs, like *have* and *be*, are really verbs. Assume this to be the case; that is, assume modals have a structure like:

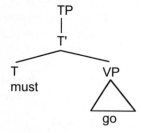

whereas auxiliaries have a structure like:

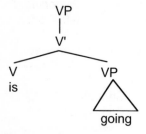

With this assumption in mind, your task is to determine whether English auxiliaries undergo verb movement, or have affix lowering of T to them. Use the diagnostics for verb movement discussed in this chapter. Explain your answer. Draw the trees for the following two sentences:

a)   Robert must be running.
b)   Robert is running.

If you claimed that English auxiliaries undergo verb raising, explain how this is possible when English main verbs do not. If you claimed that English auxiliaries have affix lowering, explain the word order of *yes/no* questions with auxiliaries.

chapter 9

NP/DP Movement

0. INTRODUCTION

In the last chapter, we looked at how certain basic word order facts could not be generated by X-bar theory alone. Instead, we saw that we need another rule type: the transformation. Transformations take X-bar trees and move elements around in them. The kind of transformation we looked at there moved heads into other heads. In this chapter, we are going to look at transformations that move NPs and DPs. (For the sake of convenience, I'm going to use NP to mean either NP or DP. Nothing turns on this usage. We could equally call the phenomenon DP-movement.)

Unlike head-to-head movement, where movement is motivated by word orders that cannot be generated using X-bar theory, the movement described here frequently takes X-bar generated trees and turns them into other acceptable X-bar generated trees. What motivates the movement is not a failure of X-bar theory, but instead the fact that certain NP/DPs can appear in positions we don't expect from a thematic (theta role) perspective.

1. A PUZZLE FOR THE THEORY OF THETA ROLES

Try to sketch out the theta grid for the verb *to leave*. *Leave* requires one obligatory argument: an agent:

1)   *leave*

agent
i

This can be seen from the following paradigm.

2)   a)   Bradley$_i$ left.
        b)   Stacy$_i$ left Tucson.
        c)   Slavko$_i$ left his wife.
        d)   *it left. (where *it* is a dummy pronoun, not a thing)

The only obligatory argument for the verb *leave* is the agent, which is an external (subject) argument. Other arguments are possible (as in 2b and c) but not required. Now, note the following thing about the obligatory agent role theta role. The agent role must be assigned to an argument *within the clause* that contains *leave*:

3)   a)   *[I want Bradley$_i$ [that left]].
        b)   *John$_i$ thinks [that left].

When you try to assign the theta role to an NP/DP that is outside the clause (such as the object *Bradley* or *John* in (3)) you get a stunningly ungrammatical sentence. There is thus the restriction on theta role assignment that an argument getting a theta role from a predicate must be local to (near by) the predicate. We call this a **locality condition.**

4)   *The locality condition on theta role assignment*:
        Theta roles must be assigned within the same clause as the predicate that assigns them.

This seems to be a reasonable condition on the lexicon and on theta theory.
        Now, look at the following sentence:

5)   [John$_i$ is likely [to leave]].

John here is the agent of *leaving*, but the NP/DP *John* appears in the main clause, far away from its predicate. Even more surprising is the fact that there seems to be no subject of the embedded clause. The solution to this problem is simple: there is a transformation that takes the noun *John* and moves it from the lower clause to the higher clause.
        Let's spell this out in more detail. The theta grid for *is likely* includes only one argument: the embedded clause. This is seen in the fact that it can appear as the sole theta marked argument:

6)   [[That John will leave]$_j$ is likely].
7)   It is likely [that John will leave]$_j$.
8)   *is likely*

proposition
j

If this is the case, then in sentence (5), *John* is definitely not receiving its theta role from *is likely*. This should be obvious from the meaning of the sentence as well. There is nothing about *John* that *is likely*, instead it is what *John* is doing (his leaving) that *is likely*. The sentence is a clear violation of the locality condition on theta role assignment in its surface form. In chapter 7, we argued that the theta criterion applies before the transformation of expletive insertion occurs. Translated into our new terminology, this means that the theta criterion holds of D-structure. This means that theta role assignment must also happen before all transformations. We can arrange for *John*'s theta role to be assigned clause internally, at D-structure. The D-structure of the sentence would then look like (9). (Theta marking is indicated with a dotted large arrow):

9)

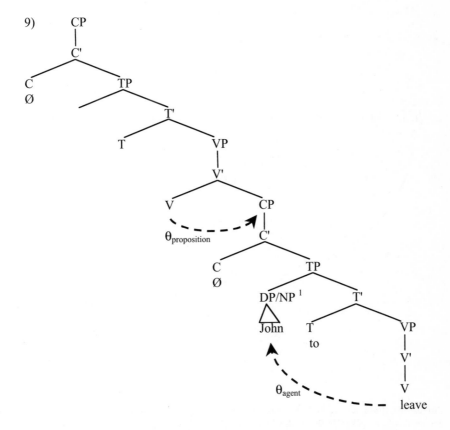

---

[1] For the moment, I'm abstracting away from the VP-internal subject hypothesis. We'll come back to this. Also I'm avoiding distinguishing DPs from NPs, and will use them interchangeably. This is fairly common in the literature on syntax.

The subject NP/DP is generated in the subject position of the embedded clause where it is assigned the agent theta role. How then do we derive the surface order? We need a transformation that moves this NP/DP to the specifier of the main clause TP. This transformation is called **NP movement** (or **DP movement**):

10)   *NP/DP movement*
        Move an NP/DP to a specifier position.

Notice that in the D-structure tree in (9) the specifier of TP is unoccupied. We can thus move the NP/DP *John* into that position resulting in the tree in (11):

11)

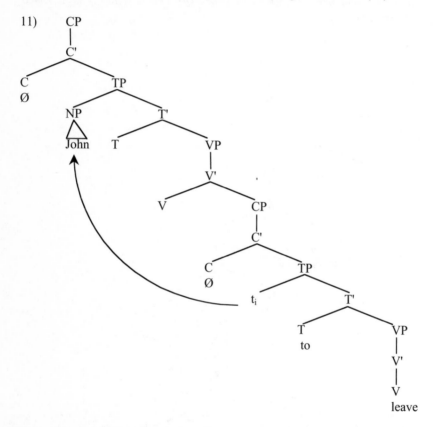

This particular instance of NP/DP movement is frequently called **raising**, because you are raising the NP/DP from the lower clause to the higher. Movement is indicated in this tree with an arrow and by placing the marker t_i in the D-structure position of the subject NP/DP. This *t* stands for 'trace'.

        As we stated in the last chapter, transformations are very powerful tools, and we want to limit their use. In particular we want to ensure that they only apply when required. Transformations thus need motivations or triggers. Look at the sentences in (12).

12)   a)   [That John will leave] is likely.
        b)   It is likely that John will leave.

Recall back to the chapter on the lexicon, the presence of the theta-role-less *it* in (b) is forced by the Extended Projection Principle (EPP) – the requirement that every sentence have a subject. We might speculate then that the absence of a subject in the D-structure of the main clause is the trigger for NP/DP movement. An NP/DP moves to the specifier of the main clause TP to satisfy the EPP. There are a number of important problems with this proposal. For example, it does not explain why we don't use expletives in these environments:

13)   *It is likely John to leave.

Nor does it explain why only the subject NP/DP of a embedded clause can satisfy the EPP, but not a moved object NP/DP:

14)   *Bill$_i$ is likely John to hit t_i.

We will return to these questions later in this chapter. However, it is a starting point and as a working hypothesis, we'll simply assume that the EPP is the motivation for NP/DP movement.

2.   PASSIVES

The sentence given in (15) is what is called an *active* sentence in traditional grammar.

15)   The policeman kissed the puppy.   *Active*

The sentence given in (16) by contrast is what is called a *passive*.

16)   The puppy was kissed by the policeman.   *Passive*

These two sentences don't mean exactly the same thing. The first one is a sentence about a policeman (*the policeman* is the topic of the sentence); by contrast (16) is a sentence about a puppy (*the puppy* is the topic). However, they do describe the same basic event in the world with the same basic participants: there is some kissing going on, and the kisser (agent) is *the policeman* and the kissee (theme) is *the puppy*. At least on the surface then, these two sentences seem to involve the same thematic information. On closer examination however, things change. Notice that in the passive sentence, the agent is represented by a prepositional phrase headed by *by*. This is an adjunct; as discussed in the chapter on the lexicon, adjuncts are not included in the basic theta grid and are not subject to the theta criterion. If the agent here is an adjunct and not subject to the theta criterion it should be optional. This is indeed the case:

17)   The puppy was kissed.

It thus seems that passives and actives have different thematic properties. Actives have an agent and a theme, whereas passives lack the agentive theta role in their theta grids.

The explanation for this is *not syntactic*, instead it is a morphological issue. The passive form of a verb takes special morphology. In English, there are two main passive suffixes. One is (unfortunately) homophonous with the past tense suffix *-ed*. The other is the *-en* suffix. These two are allomorphs of each other. We will use *-en* as the basic form, so as not to confuse the passive morpheme with the past tense. There is a simple morphological operation that derives a passive verb from an active one:

18)   kiss + en → kissed, beat + en → beaten, etc.

This morphological operation doesn't only affect the outward pronunciation of the word, it also affects the meaning. More particularly it affects the theta grid of the verb. By adding the passive suffix *-en*, we seem to delete the agent (or any external theta role) from the theta grid of the root verb. In essence, we create a new lexical entry with a different theta grid.

19)   *kiss*   + *en*   →   *kissed*

agent	theme

theme

The morphological operation changes thematic structures. (In many languages, there are other operations that do similar things to theta grids, for example in Japanese there is a morpheme *-sase* that adds a 'causer' theta role to the theta grid.)

Now, let's look at the word order in the passive and active. In the active, the theme argument appears in object position; in the passive it appears in the subject position. One possible analysis of this is to claim that the theme is generated in object position in both actives and passives, but then is moved to subject position in passives.

Here is a sample derivation. The D-structure of the passive sentence looks like (20). (Notice that the verb starts out in its passive form. The morphological operation happens in the lexicon and isn't seen in the syntax. Similarly, there is no underlying agent present in the D-structure of a passive (except in the optional *by*-phrase).) The thick arrow in this tree represents theta assignment, not movement.

20)

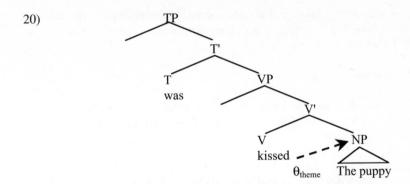

Now, like the raising sentences we looked at in section 1, the EPP is not satisfied here. There is nothing in the specifier of TP. The surface order of the passive can then be derived by NP/DP movement.

21)

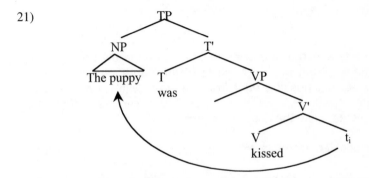

The NP/DP *the puppy* moves to satisfy the EPP.

     As mentioned above, passives often also occur with what appears to be the original external argument in a prepositional phrase marked with *by*.

22)   The puppy was kissed by the policeman

We treat these *by*-phrases as optional adjuncts which means they are not included in the theta grid. We draw these *by*-phrases in by adjoining them to V':

23)

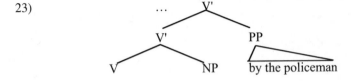

As in the case of raising, there are a couple of mysteries in the account we've presented here. For example, it isn't clear why it isn't simply permissible to satisfy the EPP by inserting an expletive:

24)   *It was kissed the puppy.[2]

Our theory predicts that such sentences should be acceptable. In order to explain why they are not, we are going to have to add a new theoretical tool: *Case*.

Movement or Underlying External Theme?

One might ask why it isn't simpler to say that the passive morpheme just deletes the agent and makes the theme an external argument in the theta grid.

i)

agent	theme		theme
		→	

(Compare the grids above to the ones in (19) where the theme is not an external argument.) Then the D-structure of the sentence will put the theme into the subject position right from the start with no movement. This is impossible, however, if you look at passives of sentences that take clausal complements. Take the active sentence in (ii):

ii)   Wilma considers [Fredrick to be foolish].

In this sentence, *Wilma* is the experiencer of *consider*, and *Fredrick* is the external theta role of the predicate *is foolish*. When *consider* is made into a passive, the subject of the lower clause raises to become the subject of the main clause:

iii)   Fredrick$_i$ is considered t_i to be foolish.

Notice that *Fredrick* is never theta-marked by the verb *consider*. As such there is no way to make it the external argument like in (i). Because of cases like (iii), the movement account is better.

---

[2] This sentence becomes grammatical if you put a big pause after *kissed*, but notice that in this circumstance, the *it* is not a dummy, but refers to the *puppy*.

3.   CASE

In many languages, nouns which bear particular grammatical relations take special forms. For example, in Japanese, subjects are marked with the suffix *-ga*, objects are marked with *-o* and indirect objects and certain adjuncts with *-ni*:

25)   Asako-ga   ronbun-o   kai-ta.
        Asako-NOM   article-ACC   wrote-PAST
        "Asako wrote the article."

26)   Etsuko-ga   heya-ni   haitte-kita.
        Etsuko-NOM   room-DAT   in-came
        "Etsuko came into the room."

These suffixes represent ***grammatical relations*** (see chapter 3). The three most important grammatical relations are **subject, object**, and **indirect object**. Notice that these are *not* the same as thematic relations. Thematic relations represent meaning. Grammatical relations represent how an NP/DP is functioning in the sentence syntactically. The morphology associated with grammatical relations is called ***case***. The two cases we will be primarily concerned with here are the ***nominative case***, which is found with subjects, and the ***accusative case***, found with objects.

English is a morphologically poor language. In sentences with full NP/DPs, there is no obvious case marking. Grammatical relations are represented by the position of the noun in the sentence:

27)   Jennifer swatted Steve.
28)   Steve swatted Jennifer.

There is no difference in form between *Jennifer* in (27), where the NP/DP is functioning as a subject, and (28), where it is functioning as an object. With pronouns, by contrast, there is a clear morphological difference, as we observed in chapter 1.

29)   She swatted him.
30)   He swatted her.

Most pronouns in English have different forms depending upon what case they are in:

31)   ***Nominative***   I   you he   she it   we   you they
32)   ***Accusative***   me   you him her it   us   you them

Can this be extended to full NP/DPs? Well, consider the general poverty of English morphology. The first and second persons in the present tense form of verbs don't take any overt suffix:

33)   I walk
34)   You walk
         (cf. He/She/It walk<u>s</u>. You walk<u>ed</u>)

But one wouldn't want to claim that (33) and (34) aren't inflected for tense. Semantically they are. These forms can only refer to the present, they can't refer to the past
or the future. We are thus forced to claim that there is an unpronounced or null present tense morpheme in English. It seems reasonable to claim that if there are null
tense suffixes, there are also null case suffixes in English. Indeed, in the system we
are proposing here all nouns get case – we just don't see it overtly in the pronounced
morphology. This is called **abstract Case**. (Abstract Case normally has a capital C to
distinguish it from morphological case.)

        Case, then, is a general property of Language. Furthermore it seems to be
associated with a syntactic phenomenon – the grammatical function (relations) of
NP/DPs. If it is indeed a syntactic property, then it should have a structural trigger.
In the case theory of Chomsky (1981), NP/DPs are given Case if and only if they
appear in specific positions in the sentence. In particular, nominative case is assigned
in the specifier of finite T, and accusative case is assigned as a sister to the verb
(prepositions also assign what is often called "dative" to their complement NP/DP): [3]

35)   NOMinative case   Specifier of finite T
         ACCusative case   Sister to transitive V
         DATive case   Assigned by a preposition.

        Case serves as our motivation for NP/DP movement. You can think of Case
as being like a driver's license. You can't drive without a license, and you can only
get a license at the Department of Motor Vehicles. So you have to go there to get the
license (OK, so the analogy isn't perfect). An NP/DP needs a license to surface in
the sentence, and it can only get a license (Case) in specific positions. If it isn't in
one of those positions, it must move to get Case. An NP/DP without Case can't
drive. This is called the **Case filter**:

36)   *The Case filter*
         All NP/DPs must be marked with a Case.
         If an NP/DP doesn't get Case the derivation will crash.

One standard way of implementing the Case filter is by using a mechanism known as
feature checking. This is based on a notion taken from phonology. The idea is that
words are composed of atomic features. A word like *he* is composed of features representing its person, its number, its gender etc. We can represent these features in a
matrix:

---

[3] This is an almost ridiculous oversimplification. There are many prepositional cases (loca-
tives, ablatives, jussives, etc.). We abstract away from this here. We are also ignoring the
genitive case normally associated with possessive constructions.

37)   *he*
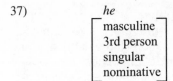
$$\begin{bmatrix} \text{masculine} \\ \text{3rd person} \\ \text{singular} \\ \text{nominative} \end{bmatrix}$$

Similarly, we will claim that Case assigners like T have a feature matrix:

38)   *is*
$$\begin{bmatrix} \text{present} \\ \text{3rd person} \\ \text{singular} \\ \text{nominative} \end{bmatrix}$$

You'll notice that both of these feature matrices have a feature [nominative]. The Case filter becomes a requirement that a noun like *he* be close enough to a Case assigner like *is*, to check that the noun has the right features. The noun must be close to its Case assigner:

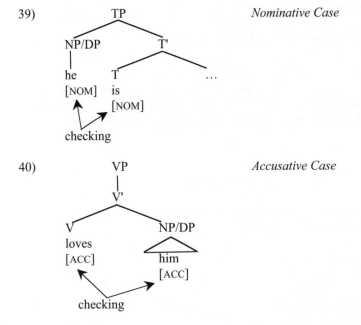

39)   *Nominative Case*

40)   *Accusative Case*

If the noun and the Case assigner are not local (that is, the noun is not in the specifier or complement of the Case assigner), then the feature won't be checked and the Case filter violated. We'll use this notion of locality in feature checking again in chapter 11, when we look at *wh*-movement.

Ergative/Absolutive Languages

In this book, we are looking exclusively at languages which take nominative and accusative cases. These are a fairly common kind of language in the western hemisphere. In nominative/accusative languages, the same case is assigned to the subjects of transitives and the subjects of intransitives (nominative case); a different case (accusative) is assigned to the objects of intransitives.

i)   *Nom/Acc languages*

	Nom	**Acc**
Trans	Subject	Object
Intrans	Subject	

However, there is a huge class of languages that does not use this case pattern, including many Polynesian, Australian, and Central American languages. These languages, called "Ergative/Absolutive" languages, mark the object of transitives and the subject of intransitives using the same case (absolutive); subjects of transitives are marked with a different case: ergative.

ii)   *Erg/Abs languages*

	Erg	**Abs**
Trans	Subject	Object
Intrans		Subject

From the perspective of structural case theory, these languages are a mystery and the subject of great debate. They don't fit the theory presented here. Even more mysterious are those languages that use *both* Nom/Acc and Erg/Abs case systems (under different circumstances).

4.   RAISING: REPRISE

Let's now return to the raising sentences we were looking at in section 1, and we'll expand the paradigm to include the following:

41)   It is likely that Patrick left.
42)   That Patrick left is likely.
43)   *Patrick is likely that t_i left.
44)   *It is likely Patrick to leave.
45)   *Patrick to leave is likely.
46)   Patrick is likely t_i to leave.

Sentences (41–43) involve a tensed (finite) embedded clause. Sentence (41) shows that one can satisfy the EPP with an expletive, provided the embedded clause is finite. Sentence (44) shows that an expletive won't suffice with a non-finite embedded clause. Sentence (42) shows that a tensed clause can satisfy the EPP, but a non-finite one cannot (45). Finally, we see that raising is possible with a non-finite clause (46) but not a finite one (43). This is quite a complicated set of facts, but it turns out that the distribution turns on a single issue. Above we saw that NP/DPs are assigned nominative Case only in the specifier of finite T. (In other words, non-finite T does not have a [NOM] feature, whereas finite T does.) Sentences (44–46) are *non-finite*. This means that the NP/DP *Patrick* cannot get nominative Case in the specifier of the embedded clause. The ungrammaticality of (44) and (45) are now explained: *Patrick* is not getting Case, so violates the Case filter. In sentence (46) by contrast, the NP/DP has moved to the specifier of the *finite* main clause T; it can receive Case here, so the sentence is grammatical:

47)

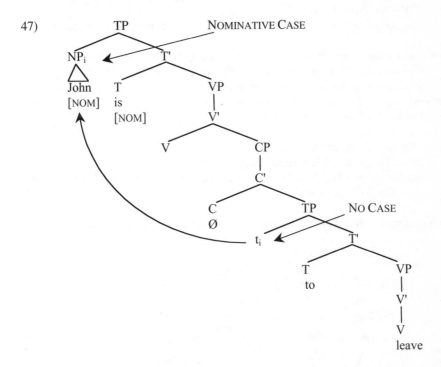

This is a pattern that is repeated over and over again. NP/DPs always move from positions that don't have Case (but where they get a theta role) to positions where they get Case.

    The distribution of raising in sentences (41), (42), and (43) is also now explained. These clauses have an embedded finite T. As such the NP/DP *Patrick* can get nominative Case in the specifier of embedded T. It does not have to move. If it did move, it would move without reason, as it already has Case.

5.   PASSIVES: REPRISE

Case theory also allows an explanation of passive constructions. However, this requires an additional piece of machinery to be added to the passive morphology. Only
active transitive verbs can assign accusative Case:

48)   He kissed her.

Passive verbs cannot:

49)   She was kissed.
50)   *She was kissed him.[4]
51)   *it was kissed her.   (where *it* is an expletive)

It thus appears that not only does the passive suffix absorb the verb's external theta
role, it also absorbs the verb's ability to assign accusative Case. This is rough version of what is called ***Burzio's Generalization*** (after Burzio 1986): *A predicate that
assigns no external theta role, cannot assign accusative Case.* The passive morpheme thus has the following two functions:

52)   The passive morpheme *-en*
         a)   absorbs a verb's external theta role.
         b)   absorbs a verb's ability to assign accusative Case to its sister. (Absorbs
              the [ACC] feature.)

With this in mind, reconsider the passive sentence we looked at in section 2:

53)

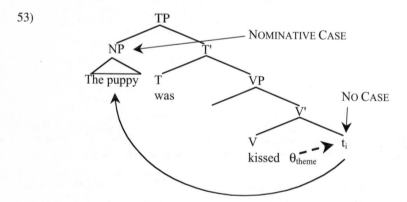

The passive form of *kiss (kiss + en → kissed)* cannot assign accusative Case to its
object. If the sentence was left as is, then this would result in a violation of the Case
filter. But this is not a disaster. The passive morphology has conspired to also elimi-

---

[4] This sentence is also a violation of the theta criterion.

nate the external theta role. This means that there is no NP/DP in the specifier of the finite T. There is a Case position open. Now we have the trigger for NP/DP movement in passives: An NP/DP moves to get Case from its Caseless theta position to the nominative Case assigning specifier of TP. Notice that this NP/DP now moves for two reasons. First it moves to satisfy the EPP, but it also must move to get Case.

Inherently Passive Verbs: Unaccusatives

One of the interesting discoveries of the 1980s was the fact that there are a set of verbs in many languages that are inherently passive. That is they have only an internal argument, and they don't assign accusative case. These are called *unaccusative verbs* (or less commonly *ergative verbs*). These were explored most thoroughly in the theory of grammar called Relational Grammar (a competitor to Transformational Grammar, but one whose ideas are easily transferable). Compare the two sentences in (i) and (ii)

i)   Stacy danced at the palace.
ii)   Stacy arrived at the palace.

The first sentence is a regular intransitive (often called *unergative*) where *Stacy* bears an external agent theta role. The sentence in (ii) by contrast has no external theta role. *Stacy* is a theme that originates in the object position of the sentence. *Stacy* then raised to subject position to satisfy the Case filter, just like a passive. These predicates are passive without having any passive morphology. The arguments for this are well beyond the scope of this textbook. But note the following two differences between the predicates in (i) and (ii). The unergative predicate in (i) can optionally take a direct object. Unaccusative predicates cannot (something that is predicted, if their subject is underlyingly an object):

iii)   Stacy danced a jig.
iv)   *Stacy arrived a letter.

Unaccusatives also allow an alternative word order (called **there** *inversion*) where the underlying object remains in object position. Since unergative subjects aren't generated in object position, they aren't allowed to appear there with *there* inversion.

v)   *There danced three men at the palace.
vi)   ?There arrived three men at the palace.

6.   CLOSING UP A LOOSE END

In the last chapter, we were forced to argue (on the basis of evidence from the VSO language Irish) that subject NP/DPs were generated in the specifier of VP not TP.

54)   TP   *Irish*

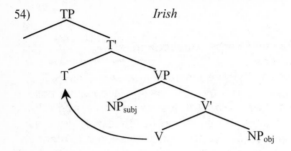

The problem, then, was why subject NP/DPs appear before T in languages like English. The solution should now be clear: All subject NP/DPs move to the specifier of finite T to get Case. In actives and intransitives, this is from the specifier of VP. In passives, from the underlying object position.

55)   TP   *English*

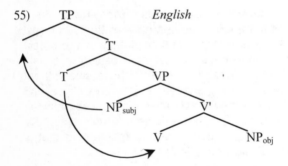

The difference between SVO languages like English and VSO languages is in where nominative Case is assigned. In SVO languages, nominative Case is assigned in the specifier of finite T. In VSO languages, nominative Case is assigned when the NP/DP is immediately c-commanded by finite T (which allows it to remain inside VP).

56)
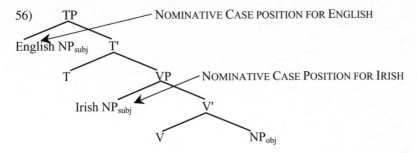

Sportiche (1988) observed that there is some evidence that English subjects start in the position occupied by Irish subjects, then they subsequently move to the specifier of TP. This evidence comes from the behavior of quantifier words like *all*. In English the following two sentences mean roughly the same thing:

57)   All the men have gone.
58)   The men have all gone.

In (58), the *all* word modifies *the men*. This means that at some point in the derivation they must have formed a constituent, even though *all* is separated from *the men* by the T element *have*. Sportiche suggests that the *all* word here reflects the D-structure or underlying position of the subject. Let us treat *all* as being of the category Q(uantifier), which like determiners heads its own projection. The D-structure of both sentences (57) and (58) is shown below:

59)
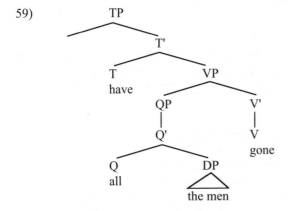

The QP *all the men* starts in the specifier of VP, as do all agents. In sentence (57), the whole QP moves to the specifier of TP:

60)

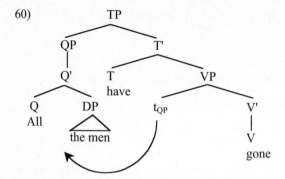

In sentence (58) by contrast, only the DP moves, stranding the Q head:

61)

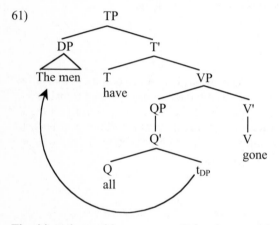

The idea that subjects start off in the specifier of VP (sometimes called the **VP-internal subject hypothesis**) thus accounts for how quantifiers like *all* can both modify subjects, yet at the same time be separated from them by elements like T.

7.   CONCLUSION

In this chapter, we've looked at situations where NP/DPs don't appear in the positions we expect them to (given our knowledge of theta theory). We have argued that these sentences involve movement of NP/DPs to various specifier positions. The motivation for this come from Case. The Case filter requires all NP/DPs to check a Case in a specific structural position. We looked at two situations where NP/DPs don't get Case in their D-structure position. In raising structures, an NP/DP is in the specifier of an embedded clause with non-finite T. In this position, it can't receive Case so it raises to the specifier of the finite T in the higher clause. We also looked at passive structures. The passive consists of two operations: one morphological and the other syntactic. The morphological operation adds the suffix *-en,* absorbs the external argument and absorbs the verb's ability to assign accusative Case. This results in a structure where there is no subject NP/DP, and the object cannot receive Case in its base position. The NP/DP must move to the specifier of T to get Case.

IDEAS, RULES, AND CONSTRAINTS INTRODUCED IN THIS CHAPTER

i)   **NP/DP Movement**
        Move an NP/DP to a specifier position.

ii)   **Raising**
        A specific instance of NP/DP movement. The NP/DP moves from the specifier of an embedded non-finite T to the specifier of a finite T in the main clause where it can get Case.

iii)   **Case**
        NP/DPs get a special morphological form depending on where they are in the sentence.

> Nominative is found on subjects (specifier of finite T).
> Accusative is found on objects (complement to V).

iv)   **The Case Filter**
        All NP/DPs must be marked with Case.

v)   **Passives**
        A particular verb form where the external argument (often the agent or experiencer) is suppressed and the theme appears in subject position. The movement of the theme is also an instance of NP/DP movement.

vi)   **The Morphology of Passives**
        The suffix -*en*:
        a) absorbs a verb's external theta role
        b) absorbs a verb's ability to assign accusative Case to its sister.

vii)   **The VP-internal Subject Hypothesis**
        The idea that all subjects (at least agents) start out in the specifier of VP, then move (in languages like English) to the specifier of TP.

viii)   **The Locality Condition on Theta Role Assignment**
        Theta roles must be assigned within the same clause as the predicate that assigns them.

ix)   **Unaccusatives**
        Inherently passive verbs like *arrive*.

x)   ***Burzio's Generalization***
       The idea that if a verb does not assign an external argument (i.e., is passive or unaccusative), then it can't assign accusative case.

FURTHER READING

Baker, Mark, Kyle Johnson, and Ian Roberts (1989) Passive arguments raised. *Linguistic Inquiry* 20, 219–51.

Burzio, Luigi (1986) *Italian Syntax*. Dordrecht: Reidel.

Chomsky, Noam (1995) *The Minimalist Program*. Cambridge: MIT Press.

Jaeggli, Osvaldo (1986) Passive. *Linguistic Inquiry* 17, 587–622.

Perlmutter, David and Paul Postal (1984) The 1-Advancement Exclusiveness Law. In David Perlmutter and Carol Rosen (eds.) *Studies in Relational Grammar*. Chicago: Chicago University Press. pp. 81–125.

Sportiche, Dominique (1988) A theory of floating quantifiers and its corollaries for constituent structure. *Linguistic Inquiry* 19, 425–49.

PROBLEM SETS

1.   ENGLISH

Draw the D-structure trees for the following sentences. Be explicit about what transformations derived the S-structure tree (if any). Recall that we have the following transformations: Expletive insertion, NP/DP movement (both raising and passive), affix lowering, verb movement, T → C movement, and *do*-support/insertion. Annotate the D-structure tree with arrows to show the derivation of the S-structure.

a)   Marie is likely to leave the store.
b)   The money was hidden in the drawer.
c)   Donny is likely to have been kissed by the puppy.
d)   It seems that Sonny loves Cher.
e)   Has the rice been eaten?

2.   ENGLISH UNGRAMMATICAL SENTENCES

Explain why the following sentences are ungrammatical. Some sentences may have more than one problem with them.

a)   *It seems Sonny to love Cher.
b)   *Bill was bitten the dog.
c)   *Donny is likely that left.

3.   PERSIAN ACCUSATIVE CASE[5]

In the text above, we claimed that some verbs have an accusative feature [ACC] that must get checked by a complement NP/DP. In English, we only see the realization of this feature on pronouns. This question focuses on the [ACC] feature in Persian.

Background: Persian is an SOV language. There is no Case distinction among Persian pronouns. For example, the pronoun *man* 'I, me' doesn't change whether it is a subject, object of a preposition or possessor (see (a) below). (iii) shows that possessors are linked to head nouns with a vowel glossed as EZ (for *Ezâfe*).

a)   i)   *Man*   ruznâme   xarid-am.
              I   newspaper   bought-1SG
              "I bought a newspaper."

        ii)   Simâ   az   *man*   ruznâme   xâst.
              Sima   from   me   newspaper wanted.3SG
              "Sima wanted a newspaper from me."

        iii) Ruznâme-ye   *man*   injâ-st.
              newspaper-EZ   me   here-is
              "My newspaper is here."

Hypothesis: It looks like the clitic *-râ* (which is realized as *-o* or *-ro,* depending on whether the preceding word ends in a vowel or not) is the realization of the [ACC] feature based on examples like the following:

b)   i)   Man   jiân-o   didam.
              I   Jian-RÂ   saw.1SG
              "I saw Jian."

---

[5] Thanks to Jila Ghomeshi for contributing this problem set.

    ii) * Man   jiân   did-am.
            I   Jian   saw-1SG

c) i)   Jiân   man-o   did.
         Jian   I-RÂ   saw.3SG
         "Jian saw me."

    ii) *Jiân   man   did.
         Jian   I   saw.3SG

d) i)   Jiân   in   ketâb-o   xarid.
         Jian   this   book+RÂ   bought.3SG
         "Jian bought this book."

    ii) *Jiân   in   ketâb   xarid.
         Jian   this   book   bought.3SG

One possible analysis is that Persian verbs have an [ACC] feature that gets checked by -râ. That is, -râ contributes the [ACC] feature to the NP/DP that can be used to check the feature of the verb.

The problem: Not all direct objects show up with -râ. Yet we don't want to say that the ones without -râ don't check the [ACC] feature of the verb.

e) i)   Jiân   ye   ketâb   xund.
         Jian   a   book   read.3SG
         "Jian read a book."

    ii) Jiân   ketâb-o   xund.
         Jian   book-RÂ   read/3SG
         "Jian read the book."

f) i)   Man   se-tâ   qalam   xarid-am.
         I   three   pen   bought-1SG
         "I bought three pens."

    ii) Man   se-tâ   qalam-o   xarid-am.
         I   three   pen+RÂ   bought-1SG
         "I bought the three pens."

g) i)   Jiân   pirhan   xarid.
         Jian   shirt   bought.3SG
         "Jian bought a shirt."

    ii)   Jiân   pirhan-o   xarid.
            Jian   shirt+RÂ   bought.3SG
            "Jian bought the shirt."

Suggest a solution to this problem.

4.   ARIZONA TEWA

(Data from Kroskrity 1985)

The following data is from Arizona Tewa:

a)   hẹ'i sen né'i 'enú mánk^{hw}ẹ́di.
      that man this boy 3.3.hit
      "That man hit this boy."

b)   né'i 'enú hẹ'i sen-di mánk^{hw}ẹ́di.
      This boy that man-DAT 3.PASS.hit
      "This boy was hit by that man."

c)   na:bí kwiyó hẹ'i p'o   mánsunt'ó.
      my   woman that water 3.3.drink
      "My wife will drink that water."

d)   hẹ'i p'o   nasunt'íi.
      that water 3.PASS.drunk
      "That water was drunk."

1) Determine the X-bar parameter settings for Tewa.
2) Draw trees for (a) and (c). Assume Tewa is an affix lowering language.
3) Describe in your own words the differences between (a) and (b) and between (c) and (d) in terms of theta roles and Case.
4) Draw the trees of (b) and (d) showing all the movements.

5.   MIDDLES, ACTIVES, CAUSATIVES, AND PASSIVES

Middles are English constructions that are little bit like passives. An example of an active/middle pair is seen below:

a) I cut the soft bread.
b) The soft bread cuts easily.

In (b), the theme appears in the subject position. One analysis of this order has the theme undergoing NP/DP movement to subject position.

Consider now the following triplet of sentences. The first sentence is called a middle, the second an active, and the third a causative.

d) The boat sank.   *middle*
e) The torpedo sank the boat.   *active*
f) The captain sank the boat (with a torpedo).   *causative*

Part 1: Describe the relationship between the active, middle, and causative in terms of their theta grids.

Part 2: Now consider the passives of sentences (d–f). Why should sentence (g) be ungrammatical, but (h) and (i) grammatical?

g) *Was sunk (by the boat).
     (also * It was sunk by the boat, where *it* is an expletive)
h) The boat was sunk by the torpedo.
i)   The boat was sunk by the captain (with a torpedo).

6.   TWO KINDS OF RAISING

In the text, we proposed that subjects of non-finite clauses can raise to the subject position of finite clauses in sentences like (a):

a) John$_i$ seems [t_i to have left].

This kind of raising is sometimes called **subject-to-subject raising**. Now consider the following sentence:

b) Bill wants John to leave.

This sentence should be ungrammatical, because *to* is a non-finite T, so can't assign Case to *John*. One hypothesis that has been proposed to account for this says there is also a process of **subject-to-object raising**:

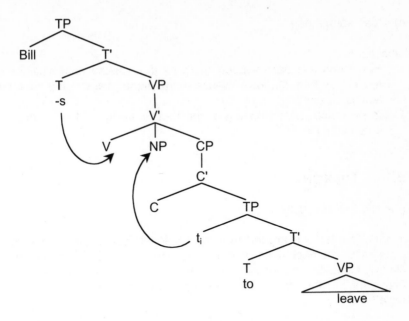

How does the following data support this analysis?

a)   John wants Bill to leave.
b)   John wants him to leave.
c)   John believes him to have been at the game.
d)   ?John$_i$ believes himself$_i$ to have been at the game.
e)   *John$_i$ believes him$_i$ to have been at the game.
f)   He is believed (by John) to have been at the game.

7.   HAITIAN CREOLE

(Data from Déprez 1992)

In the text, we suggested that NP/DP movement leaves what is called a trace
(*t*) at the D-structure position of the NP/DP. In English, you can't hear this
trace. Now consider the following data from Haitian Creole.

a)   Sanble   Jan   pati.
      seems   John   left
      "It seems that John left."

b)   Jan sanble li pati.
      John seems he leave
      "John seems he to have left."

c)   *Jan sanble pati.

Questions:
1) How does this data support the idea that raising constructions involve movement from the lower clause to the higher clause, and the movement leaves a trace?
2) Is sentence (b) a violation of the theta criterion? How might we make sure that it isn't ?

9.   TURKISH

(Data from Moore 1998)

In this chapter, we argued that the reason NP/DPs raise from embedded clauses to main clauses is that they cannot get Case in the embedded clause. Consider the following data from Turkish. What problems does this cause for our theory? Is there a simple way to explain why Turkish nouns raise?

a)   Biz süt   içiyoruz.
     we milk   drink
     "We are drinking milk."

b)   Biz$_i$ sana [$_{CP}$ t$_i$ süt içtik] gibi göründük.
     We you-DAT   milk drank like appear
     "We appear to you [$_{CP}$ drunk milk]."

10.   IMPERSONALS IN UKRAINIAN, KANNADA, AND IRISH

(The Ukrainian and Kannada data are taken from Goodall 1993. The Ukrainian data originally comes from Sobin 1985. The Kannada data is originally from Cole and Sridhar 1976.The Irish data is slightly modified from Stenson 1989.)

Many languages contain a construction similar to the passive called *the impersonal passive*. Consider the following data from Ukrainian, Kannada, and Irish. Pay careful attention to the Case marking on the various nouns.

Ukrainian
a)   Cerkvu   bulo zbudovano v 1640 roc'i.
     Church-ACC   was built   in 1640 year
     "The Church was built in the year 1640."

Kannada
b) Rama-nannu   kollalayitu.
    Ramma-ACC   kill.PASS
    "Rama was killed."

Irish
c) Buaileadh   iad   sa gcluife   deireanach.
    beat.PAST.PASS   them.ACC   in the game last
    "They were beaten in the last game."

What is the difference between these impersonal passive constructions and more traditional passives of English? Suggest a parameter that will account for the difference between languages like Ukrainian, Kannada, and Irish and languages like English. (Hint: the parameter will have to do with the way the passive morphology works.)

11.   UNACCUSATIVES AND PASSIVES

(Data from Perlmutter and Postal 1984)

In a textbox above, we mentioned the existence of a class of verbs that are essentially inherently passive. These are called unaccusatives. A surprising property of unaccusative verbs is that they don't allow passivization.[6]

a) The Shah slept in a bed.
b) The bed was slept in by the Shah.
c) Dust fell on the bed.   *unaccusative*
d) *The bed was fallen on by the dust.   *unaccusative*

Similar effects are seen in the following Dutch sentences. Sentence (e) is not unaccusative (we call these "unergatives"), while sentence (f) is. Both these sentences are impersonal passives. English doesn't have this construction, so they are difficult to translate into English.

e) In de zomer wordt er hier vaak gezwommen.
    "In the summer, there is swimming here."

f) *In de zomer wordt er hier vaak verdronken.
    "In the summer, there is drowning here."

---

[6] Strictly speaking, the data in (a–d) do not involve passivization, since the NP that is moved comes from inside a PP. The technical term for these constructions is pseudo-passivization. The differences between pseudo-passivization and passivization are not relevant to this problem set.

Your task is to figure out why passives of unaccusatives (like c, d, and f) are not allowed. The following data might help you:

g) Bill was hit by the baseball.
h) *Was been hit by bill by the baseball. (passive of a passive)
i) Bill gave Sue the book.
j) Sue was given the book by Bill.
k) *The book was been given by Bill by Sue. (passive of a passive)

12.   ICELANDIC QUIRKY CASE

(Data from Zaenen, Maling, and Thráinsson 1985)

In Icelandic, some verbs assign irregular case marking to particular arguments. For example, the verb *hjálpað* 'help' assigns dative case to its theme argument:

a) Ég hjálpaði honum.
    I   helped   him-DAT
    "I helped him."

This kind of irregular case marking is called **quirky Case** and it seems to be linked to the theta grid of the particular predicate. The dative case is obligatorily linked with whatever noun takes the theme role:

    hjálpað 'help'

agent	theme
i	k

                                    Dative Case

Now consider the following data from Icelandic NP/DP movement constructions.

b) Honum$_k$ var hjálpað t$_K$.
    him-DAT was helped
    "He was helped."

c) Ég tel honum$_k$ [t$_k$ hafa verið hjálpað t$_k$ i prófinu].
        I believe him-DAT have been helped   in the-exam
        "I believe him [to have been helped in the exam]."

What problem does this cause for the theory of NP/DP movement we have proposed above? Can you think of a solution? (A number of possibilities exist, be creative.)

13.   PASSIVES AND DOUBLE OBJECT CONSTRUCTIONS

(For more information on the phenomenon discussed in this problem set, see Larson 1988)

English has two constructions that surface with ditranstive verbs. One is called the prepositional construction, the other the double object construction:[7]

a)   I sent a book to Louis.   *prepositional*
b)   I sent Louis a book.   *double object*

It is possible to make passives out of these constructions. But some additional restrictions on how passives work are needed. Consider the following data and posit a restriction on NP/DP movement in passives to account for the ill-formedness of the ungrammatical sentences. Pay careful attention to sentence (g).

c)   A book was sent to Louis.
d)   *Louis was sent a book to.
e)   *To Louis was sent a book.[8]
f)   Louis was sent a book.
g)   *A book was sent Louis.

---

[7] There is a great deal of literature that tries to derive the double object construction from the prepositional construction using NP movement (see for example Larson 1988). The relationship between the two constructions is not relevant to the question in this problem set, but is an interesting puzzle in and of itself.

[8] This may be marginally acceptable in poetic or flowery speech. Assume for the purposes of this problem set that this is ungrammatical.

chapter 10

Raising, Control, and Empty Categories

0.   INTRODUCTION

The following two sentences look remarkably alike:

1)   Jean is likely to leave.
2)   Jean is reluctant to leave.

But these sentences are structurally very different. Sentence (1) is a raising sentence like those we saw in the last chapter. Sentence (2), however, is a different matter. This is what we call a ***control sentence***; it does not involve any NP movement. We will claim there is a special kind of null NP in the subject position of the embedded clause. Syntacticians call this special NP "PRO," which stands for "null pronoun." The differences between these two constructions are schematized below.

3)   Jean$_i$ is likely [t_i to leave].   *subject-to-subject raising*

4)   Jean is reluctant [PRO to leave].   *(subject) control*

The bracketed diagram in (3) shows the NP raising construction we looked at in chapter 9. The structure in (4), which has no movement, is the control construction. The evidence for this kind of proposal will come from the thematic properties of the various predicates involved. In addition to contrasting the sentences in (1) and (2), we'll also look at the differences between sentences like (5) and (6):

5)   Jean wants Brian to leave.
6)   Jean persuaded Brian to leave.

Again, on the surface these two sentences look very similar. But, again, once we look at these in more detail we'll see that they have quite different structures. We will claim that *Brian* in (5) raises to the object position of the verb *wants*. This is called **subject-to-object raising**, and was discussed in an exercise in the last chapter. The structure of the sentence in (6) parallels the structure of the control sentence in (2). Both *Jean* and *Brian* are arguments of the verb *persuade*, there is no raising, but there is a PRO in the subject position of the embedded clause.

7)   Jean wants Brian$_i$ [t$_i$ to leave].   *subject-to-object raising*

8)   Jean persuaded Brian [PRO to leave].   *object control*

The construction in (8) is called **object control** (because the object "controls" what the PRO refers to).
        This chapter ends with a short discussion of the various kinds of empty elements we've looked at so far (null heads, PRO, traces, etc.), and introduces a new one which is found in languages like Spanish and Italian.

1.   RAISING VS. CONTROL

1.1   Two Kinds of Theta Grids for Main Predicates

If you look at the following two sentences, you will see that the predicate *is likely* only takes one argument: a proposition.

9)   [That Jean left] is likely.   *clausal subject*
10)   It is likely [that Jean left].   *extraposition*

Sentence (9) shows the proposition *that Jean left* functioning as the predicate's subject. Sentence (10) has this embedded clause as a complement, and has an expletive in subject position. For reasons having to do with the history of generative grammar, but that need not concern us here, the first construction (9) is often called a **clausal subject** construction, and the second (10) an **extraposition** construction. The theta grid for the predicate is given in (11). As is standard (see chapter 7), expletives are not marked in the theta grid, as they don't get a theta role.

11)   *is likely*

proposition

We assume that the D-structure of the sentences given in (9) and (10) is identical. It has the embedded clause as a complement to the predicate, and nothing in the subject position: [1]

12)

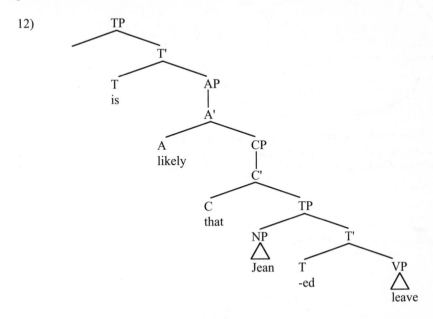

In the clausal subject construction, the embedded CP moves to the specifier of TP, presumably to satisfy the EPP requirement that every clause have a subject: [2]

---

[1] You'll notice that we represent the category of *likely* as an A, and *is* as T. Notice that X-bar theory allows us to do this. There is nothing in our system that requires that the predicate of a sentence be a verb.

[2] We haven't discussed the possibility of moving CPs before. Since this is movement for the EPP, it may well be a variant of NP movement. This analysis of clausal subjects (involving movement) is not uncontroversial. Some researchers generate these CPs directly in the specifier of TP at D-structure. We move it from the complement position to ensure parsimony with the analysis of expletive and raising constructions discussed below. We should also note that not all raising verbs allow the clausal subject construction. For example, *seem* and *appear* do not *[[that Jean left] seems]. I leave it as an exercise for you to figure out why this might be the case.

12')

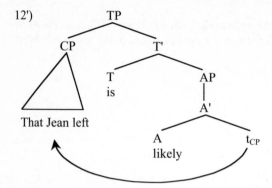

(12') shows the S-structure for sentence (9). Sentence (10) has a slightly different derivation, instead of moving the clause to satisfy the EPP, an expletive *it* is inserted into the specifier of TP as seen in the S-structure in (13):

13)

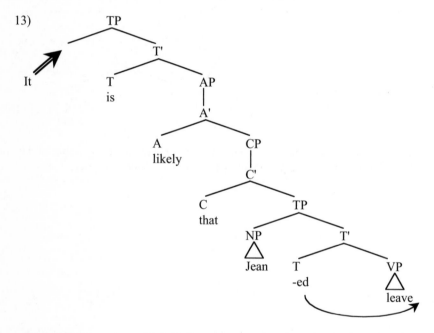

Observe that that the embedded clause is finite in both these sentences. This means that its subject gets nominative Case. As we saw in the last chapter, if the embedded clause is non-finite (as in 14), then the subject must move to get Case. Fortunately, *is likely* does not have an external (subject) theta role, but does have a nominative Case feature to check. This means that the specifier of the higher TP is available for Case feature checking. This is a typical raising construction.

14)   _____ is likely [Jean to leave].

15)

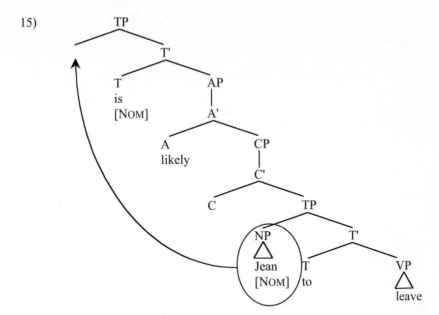

As we noted in chapter 9, the *Jean* in this sentence gets its theta role from *to leave*. *Jean* is going *to leave*, she isn't *likely*. What *is likely* is the whole proposition of Jean leaving. With *is likely* then, there is only one theta role assigned (to the embedded clause). Three possible sentences emerge with this structure: clausal subject, extraposition and raising.

Let's contrast this with the predicate *is reluctant*. If you think carefully about it, you'll notice that this predicate takes two arguments. The person who is reluctant (the experiencer) and what they are reluctant about (the proposition):

16)   *is reluctant*

experiencer	proposition

This means that, unlike *is likely*, *is reluctant* assigns a theta role to its subject. Because of this both clausal subject and extraposition (expletive) constructions are impossible. The specifier of TP of the main clause is already occupied by the experiencer, so there is no need to insert an expletive or move the CP for EPP reasons. This explains why the following two sentences (an extraposition and a clausal subject example) are ill-formed with the predicate *is reluctant*:

17)   *It is reluctant [that Jean left].   (where *it* is an expletive)
18)   *[that Jean left] is reluctant.

Both of these sentences seem to be "missing" something. More precisely they are both missing the external experiencer role: the person who is reluctant. Consider now the control sentence we mentioned above in the introduction:

19)   Jean is reluctant to leave.

Jean here is the experiencer, and the embedded clause is the proposition:

20)   a) *is reluctant*

experiencer	proposition
i	k

b) Jean$_i$ is reluctant [to leave]$_k$.

So *Jean* is theta marked by *is reluctant*. Note, however, that this isn't the only predicate in this sentence. We also have the predicate *leave*, with the following theta grid:

21)   *leave*

agent
m

Who is this theta role assigned to? It also appears to be assigned to the NP *Jean*:

22)   Jean$_{i/m}$ is reluctant [to leave]$_k$.

As we saw in chapter 7, the theta criterion only allows one theta role per NP. This
sentence seems to be a violation of the theta criterion, as its subject NP gets two
theta roles. How do we resolve this problem? The theta criterion says that there must
be a one-to-one mapping between the number of theta roles and the number of arguments in a sentence. This sentence has three theta roles (agent, experiencer, and
proposition), but only two arguments. The logical conclusion, if the theta criterion is
right – and we have every reason to believe it is, since it makes good predictions
otherwise – is that there is actually a third NP here (getting the surplus agent theta
role); you just can't hear it. This NP argument is called PRO (written in capital letters). PRO only appears in the subject positions of non-finite clauses. The structure
of a control construction like (19) is given below. Indexes mark the theta roles from
the theta grids in (20a) and (21):

23)

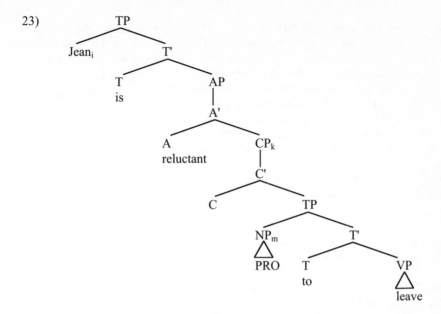

There is no raising or movement in this sentence. You'll notice that PRO is appearing in a position where no Case can be assigned. We return to this below, as well as to the question of why PRO must obligatorily refer to *Jean*.

Before looking at any more data it might be helpful to summarize the differences between control constructions and raising constructions. The main predicate in a raising construction does not assign an external theta role (it has an empty specifier of TP at D-structure). The subject of the embedded clause is Caseless, and raises to this empty position for Case checking (and to satisfy the EPP). In control constructions, the main clause predicate *does* assign an external argument. There is no raising; the external theta role of the embedded predicate is assigned to a null Caseless PRO. This is summarized in the following bracketed diagrams:

24)   a)   *no θ role*   *Agent*

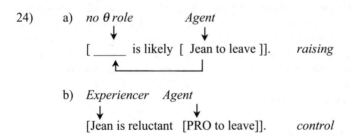

        b)   *Experiencer   Agent*

[Jean is reluctant   [PRO to leave]].   *control*

1.2   *Distinguishing Raising from Control*

One of the trials of being a syntactician is learning to distinguish among constructions that are superficially similar, but actually quite different once we dig a little deeper. Control and raising constructions are a perfect example. There are, however, some clear tests we can use to distinguish them. First, note that whether you have a raising or control construction is entirely dependent upon the main clause predicate. Some main clause predicates require raising, others require control (and a few rare ones can require both). The tests for raising and control then, mostly have to do with the thematic properties of the main clause's predicate.

To see this we'll contrast our two predicates *is likely*, which is a raising predicate, and *is reluctant,* which takes a control construction.

The most reliable way to distinguish raising constructions from control constructions is to work out the theta grids associated with the matrix predicates. If the matrix predicate assigns an external theta role (the one that is underlined, the one that appears in subject position), then it is not a raising construction. Take for example:

25)   a)   Jean is likely to dance.
        b)   Jean is reluctant to dance.

Contrast the role of *Jean* in these two sentences (as we did above in section 1.1). In the second sentence *is reluctant* is a property we are attributing to *Jean*. In (25a), however, there is nothing about *Jean* that *is likely*. Instead, what *is likely* is Jean's dancing.

One nice test that works well to show this is the behavior of idioms. Let's take the idiom *the cat is out of the bag*. This construction only gets its idiomatic meaning ("the secret is widely known") when the expression is a whole. When it's broken up, it can only get a literal interpretation ("the feline is out of the sack"). You can see this by contrasting the meanings of the sentences in (26)

26)   a)   The cat is out of the bag.
        b)   The cat thinks that he is out of the bag.

Sentence (26b) does not have the meaning "the secret is widely known." Instead our first reading of this sentence produces a meaning where there is actual cat-releasing going on. The subject of an idiom must at some point be local to the rest of the idiom for the sentence to retain its idiosyncratic meaning. We can use this as a diagnostic for distinguishing raising from control. Recall that in the D-structure of a raising construction the surface subject of the main clause starts out in the specifier of the embedded TP. Therefore in raising constructions, at D-structure, the subject of an embedded sentence is local to its predicate:

27)   [_____ is likely [Jean to dance]].

If D-structure is the level at which we interpret idiomatic meaning, then we should get idiomatic meanings with raising constructions.[3] With control constructions, on the other hand, the subject of the main clause is never in the embedded clause, so we don't expect to get idiomatic readings. This is borne out by the data.

28)   a)   The cat is likely to be out of the bag. *(idiomatic meaning)*
        b)   The cat is eager to be out of the bag. *(non-idiomatic meaning)*

We can thus use idiom chunks like *the cat* in (28) to test for raising versus control. If you get an idiomatic reading with a predicate, then you know raising is involved.

   Another test you can use to distinguish between raising and control constructions is to see if they allow the extraposition construction. Extraposition involves an expletive *it*. Expletives are only allowed in non-thematic positions, which are the hallmark of raising:

29)   a)   It is likely that Jean will dance.
        b)   *It is reluctant that Jean will dance.

At the end of this chapter, there is an exercise where you are asked to determine for a list of predicates whether or not they involve raising or control. You'll need to apply the tests discussed in this section to do that exercise.

1.3   What is PRO?

You may have noticed a fairly major contradiction in the story we've been presenting. In chapter 9, we claimed that NPs always need Case. However, in this section we've proposed that PRO can appear in the specifier of non-finite TP. This is not a Case position, so why are we allowed to have PRO here? Shouldn't PRO get Case too? It is, after all, an NP. Chomsky (1981) claims that the reason PRO is null and silent is precisely *because* it appears in a Caseless position. In otherwords PRO is a very special kind of NP, it is a Caseless NP, which explains why it can show up in Caseless positions, like the specifier of non-finite TP.

   Why do we need PRO? If we didn't have PRO, then we would have violations of the theta criterion. Notice that what we are doing here is proposing a null element to account for an apparent hole in our theory (a violation of either the theta criterion or the Case filter). There is good reason to be suspicious of this: It seems like a technical solution to a technical problem that is raised only by our particular formulation of the constraints. Nonetheless, it does have a good deal of descriptive power. It can account for most of the data having to do with embedded infinitival

---

[3] This is not an implausible hypothesis. Idioms have the feel of lexical items (that is, their meaning must be idiosyncratically memorized, just like the meanings of words). Remember that the lexicon is the source of the material at D-structure, so it makes sense that D-structure is when idiomatic meanings are inserted.

clauses. Until a better theory comes along, the PRO hypothesis wins because it can explain so much data.

2.   TWO KINDS OF RAISING, TWO KINDS OF CONTROL

2.1   Two Kinds of Raising

Up to this point we have been primarily looking at raising from the subject of an infinitive complement clause to the specifier of a main clause TP. This raising happens so the NP can get Case. However, raising doesn't have to target the specifier of TP; there are other instances of NP raising where the NP ends up in other positions. Consider the verb *want*. *Want* can take an accusatively marked NP:

30)   a)   I want cookies.
         b)   Jean wants Robert.
         c)   Jean wants him.

Want can also take an infinitive CP complement (sentence (31) is an instance of a control construction.)

31) I_i want [PRO$_i$ to leave].

This flexible verb can also show up with both an accusatively marked NP and an infinitive complement:

32) I_i want [Jean$_j$ to dance]$_k$.

Think carefully about the theta grids of the verbs here. *Jean* is the agent of *dance*, *I* is the experiencer of *want*, and the proposition *Jean to dance* takes up the second theta role of *want*.

33)   a)   *dance*

agent
j

         b)   *want*

experiencer	proposition
i	k

Notice that *Jean* does not get a theta role from *want*; it only gets one from *dance*. This means that this is not a control construction. You can see this if we apply our idiom test to the sentence: [4]

34)   I want the cat to be let out of the bag.

Although the judgment isn't as clear here, it is possible to get the idiomatic reading of *the cat to be let out of the bag*.
          Since this isn't a control construction, then how does the NP *Jean* get Case? The embedded TP is non-finite, so its specifier is not a Case position. The answer to this puzzle is the NP raises to the object position of *want*, where it can get accusative Case.

35)

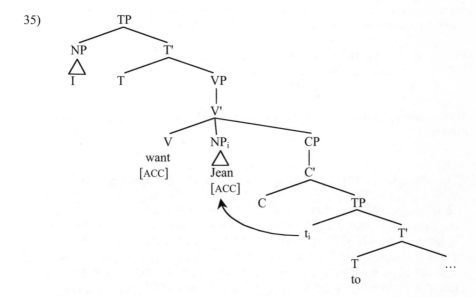

We can see that this is the right analysis of these facts by looking at the Case-marking a pronoun would get in these constructions. Since the NP shows up as a sister to a verb with an [ACC] Case feature, we predict it will take accusative Case. This is correct:

36)   a)   I want *her* to dance.
          b)   *I want *she* to dance.

Binding theory also provides us with a test for seeing where the NP is. Recall the fundamental difference between a pronoun and an anaphor. In the binding theory we

---

[4] The extraposition test will not work here. Remember expletives are usually only found in subject position (because of the EPP). *Jean* here is found in object position, so extraposition can't apply.

developed in chapter 4, an anaphor must be bound within its clause, whereas a pronoun must be free. What clause an NP is in determines whether it is an anaphor or a pronoun. We can use this as a test for seeing where an NP appears in the tree structure. We are considering two hypotheses: (37a) has the NP in the object position of *want* (just as in (35)), whereas (37b) has the NP in the subject position of the non-finite TP.

37)   a)   I want Jean$_i$ [t$_i$ to dance].
        b)   I want [Jean to dance].

If we can have a bound pronoun, instead of *Jean*, then we know that the pronoun must be in a different clause from its antecedent, since pronouns cannot be bound within their own clause. Similarly we predict that if an anaphor is OK, then the NP is within the same clause as its antecedent. The data supports (37a).

38)   a)   *Jean$_i$ wants her$_i$ to be appointed president.
        b)   Jean$_i$ wants her$_j$ to be appointed president.
        b)   ?Jean$_i$ wants herself$_i$ to be appointed president.[5]

These forms exhibit a second kind of raising, which we might call ***subject-to-object raising***.

Subject-to-object Raising = Exceptional Case Marking (ECM)
In the early work on Generative Grammar, in the 1960s and 1970s, the construction we have been looking at here was treated in a very similar manner to the analysis presented here. It was also called subject-to-object raising. In the 1980s and early 1990s (in what was called GB theory), there was period of time when these constructions got a different analysis. Instead of raising the infinitival subject to object position, the subject was left inside the embedded clause (in the specifier of TP), and the verb was allowed to "exceptionally" Case mark into the embedded clause. Thus for that period of time, these constructions were called *Exceptional Case Marking* (or *ECM*) constructions. Today, we have gone back to the original subject-to-object raising analysis. Can you think of some way that we can distinguish the ECM from subject-to-object raising analyses?

---

[5] This sentence isn't perfect. This is presumably because it means the same thing as [Jean wants to be appointed president]. Note, however, that it is better than (38a) when the pronoun is bound by the subject.

2.2   Two Kinds of Control

In section 1, we contrasted sentences like (39a) and (39b). These sentences differed in terms of their argument structure and in what movement if any applies. (39a) is a raising construction, where *Jean* gets its theta role only from *to leave*, and raises for Case reasons to the specifier of the main clause TP. In (39b), Jean gets a theta role from *is reluctant*, and there is no movement. Instead there is a null Caseless PRO in the specifier of the tenseless clause.

39)   a)   Jean$_i$ is likely [t_i to leave].
         b)   Jean$_i$ is reluctant [PRO$_i$ to leave].

In this subsection, we'll make a similar claim about the structures in (40)

40)   a)   Jean wants Robert$_i$ [t_i to leave].
         b)   Jean persuaded Robert$_i$ [PRO$_i$ to leave].

Sentence (40a) is an instance of subject-to-object raising. Sentence (40b), while on the surface very similar to (40a), is actually also a control construction. There are two major kinds of control constructions. To see this I'll put the two (b) sentences side by side in (41). (41a) is what we call **subject control**, because the subject NP of the main clause is co-referential with PRO. (41b) is **object control**, where the main clause object is co-referential with PRO.

41)   a) (=39b) Jean$_i$ is reluctant [PRO$_i$ to leave].   *subject control*
         b) (=40b) Jean persuaded Robert$_i$ [PRO$_i$ to leave].   *object control*

         Consider first the thematic properties of the raising construction:

42)   Jean$_i$ wants Robert$_j$ [t_i to leave]$_k$.

We are now well familiar with the theta grid for *to leave*, which takes a single agent argument. The theta grid for the subject-to-object raising verb *want* is repeated below:

43)   a)   *leave*

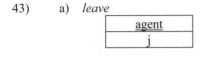

agent
j

         b)   *want*

experiencer	proposition
i	k

Robert is the agent of *leave*, but is not an argument of *want*. In section 2.1 above, we used the idiom test to show that this is the case. Now, contrast this situation with the object control verb *persuade*:

44)   Jean$_i$ persuaded Robert$_m$ [PRO$_j$ to leave]$_k$.[6]

The NP *Robert* in this sentence *is* theta marked by *persuade*. So in order not to violate the theta criterion we have to propose a null PRO to take the agent theta role of *leave*.

45)   a)   *leave*

agent
j

        b)   *persuade*

Agent	Theme	Proposition
i	m	k

We can see this again by comparing the idiomatic readings of subject-to-object raising vs. object control.

46)   a)   Jean wants the cat to get his/Bill's tongue.
         b)   #Jean persuaded the cat to get his/Bill's tongue.

Sentence (46a) is slightly odd, but it does allow the idiomatic reading, but (46b) only takes the literal (non-idiomatic) meaning.

Control = Equi

In early versions of Generative Grammar – in particular, the ones before the invention of theta roles – the phenomenon we are calling control was called **Equi-NP Deletion** or **Equi** for short. This is just another name for the same phenomenon.

2.3   Summary of Predicate Types

In this section we've argued for four distinct types of embedded infinite constructions: subject-to-subject raising, subject-to-object raising, subject control and object control. Which construction you get seems to be dependent upon what the main clause predicate is. For example, *is likely* requires a subject-to-subject raising construction whereas *is reluctant* requires a subject control construction. It should be noted that some verbs allow more than one type of construction. For example, the verb *want* allows either subject control, or subject-to-object raising:

---

[6] The indices on this sentence mark theta roles (as marked in the grid in (45)). They do not mark coindexing. In this sentence, the index $_m = _j$ (m and j are the same index).

47)   a)   Jean$_i$ wants [PRO$_i$ to leave].   *subject control*
        b)   Jean wants Bill$_i$ [t$_i$ to leave].   *subject-to-object raising.*

An example of these types is given in (48) and a summary of their properties in (49)

48)   a)   Jean is likely to leave.   *subject-to-subject raising*
        b)   Jean wants Robert to leave.   *subject-to-object raising*
        c)   Jean is reluctant to leave.   *subject control*
        d)   Jean persuaded Robert to leave.   *object control*

49)   a)   *subject-to-subject raising*
             • Main clause predicate has one theta role (to the proposition), and
               no external (subject) theta role
             • NP movement of embedded subject to the specifier of TP for EPP
               and Case
             • Allows idiomatic readings
             • Allows extraposition

        b)   *subject-to-object raising*
             • Main clause predicate assigns two theta roles (an external agent or
               experiencer and a proposition)
             • Main clause predicate has an [ACC] Case feature
             • NP movement of the embedded clause subject to the complement
               of V for Case reasons
             • Allows idiomatic readings

        c)   *subject control*
             • Main clause predicate assigns two theta roles (external agent or
               experiencer and proposition)
             • Caseless PRO in embedded clause
             • No NP movement
             • Does not allow idiomatic readings or extraposition

        d)   *object control*
             • Main clause predicate assigns three theta roles (external agent or
               experiencer, an internal theme and a proposition)
             • Caseless PRO in embedded clause
             • No NP movement
             • Does not allow idiomatic readings or extraposition

3.   CONTROL THEORY

In chapter 4, we developed a set of noun types (anaphors, pronouns, R-expressions)
that have different properties with respect to how they get their meanings.

R-expressions get their meaning from the discourse or context and can never be bound; anaphors are bound by antecedents within their clauses; and pronouns can either be bound by antecedents outside their clause or be free. In this section, we consider the troubling question of what kind of NP PRO is. Unfortunately, we are going to get a bit of a mixed answer.

Let us start by defining some terminology. This terminology is subtly similar to that of the binding theory (chapter 4), but it is different. If PRO gets its meaning from another NP, then PRO is said to be **controlled**. This is identical to the notion **coreferent** and very similar to the notion **bound** (we will make this distinction clearer below). The NP that serves as PRO's antecedent is called its **controller**.

We are going to contrast two different kinds of PRO. The first kind is called **arbitrary PRO** (or **PRO$_{arb}$**). The meaning of this pronoun is essentially "someone":

50)   [PRO$_{arb}$ to find a new mate], go to a dating service.

Arbitrary PRO is not controlled by anything. Arbitrary PRO is a bit like an R-expression or a pronoun, in that it can get its meaning from outside the sentence.

Non-arbitrary PRO (henceforth simply PRO) also comes in two different varieties. On one hand we have what is called **obligatory control**. Consider the sentence in (51). Here, PRO must refer to *Jean*. It can't refer to anyone else.

51)   Jean$_i$ tried PRO$_{i/*j}$ to behave.

There are other circumstances where PRO does not have to be (but can be) controlled. This is called **optional control**, and is seen in (52):

52)   Robert$_i$ knows that it is essential [PRO$_{i/j}$ to be well-behaved].

PRO here can mean two different things. It can either refer to Robert or it can have an arbitrary PRO$_{arb}$ reading (indicated in (52) with the subscript $_j$). You can see this by looking at the binding of the following two extensions of this sentence:

53)   a)   Robert$_i$ knows that it is essential [PRO$_i$ to be well-behaved on his$_i$ birthday].
        b)   Robert$_i$ knows that it is essential [PRO$_j$ to be well-behaved on one's$_k$ birthday].

(53a) has the controlled meaning (as seen by the binding of *his*), (53b) has the arbitrary reading (as seen by the presence of *one's*).

With this in mind let's return to the central question of this section. Is PRO an anaphor, a pronoun, or an R-expression? We can dismiss the R-expression option right out of hand. R-expressions must always be free. PRO is only sometimes free (= not controlled). This makes it seem more like a pronoun; pronouns can be both free or bound. The data in (52) seems to support this, PRO is behaving very much like a pronoun. Compare (52) to the pronoun in (54).

54)   Robert$_i$ knows it is essential [that he$_{i/j}$ is well-behaved].

You'll notice that the indexing on (54) which has a pronoun, is identical to the indexing on PRO in (52). We might hypothesize then that PRO is a pronoun. This can't be right, however. Recall that we also have situations where PRO must be bound (= controlled) as in the obligatory control sentence *Jean$_i$ tried PRO$_{i/*j}$ to be-have*. This makes PRO look like an anaphor, since anaphors are obligatorily bound. Williams (1980) suggests that in obligatory control constructions PRO must be c-commanded by its controller, just as an anaphor must be c-commanded by its antecedent. However, as should be obvious, this can't be right either. First, as noted above, we have situations where PRO is free (as in 52); anaphors can never be free. Second, if we take the binding theory we developed in chapter 4 literally, PRO and its controller *Jean*, are in different binding domains, violating Principle A.[7] We thus have a conundrum: PRO doesn't seem to be an R-expression, a pronoun, or an anaphor. It seems to be a beast of an altogether different color.

The PRO Theorem

Chomsky (1981) makes use of the contradictory nature of PRO to account for the fact that it must be null. This is found in his **PRO Theorem**. The details of this theorem need not concern us here, because they rely upon a notion we aren't pursuing in this book (*government*). He claims simply that PRO is both an anaphor and a pronoun at the same time. The contradiction here, he claims, can only be resolved by not pronouncing PRO (or more precisely ensuring that it doesn't get Case). For a more precise formulation of the PRO theorem, see Chomsky's original work, or the more accessible version found in Cowper's (1992) or Haegeman's (1994) textbooks.

Since the distribution of PRO does not lend itself to the binding theory, an entirely different module of the grammar has been proposed to account for PRO. This is called *control theory*. Control theory is the bane of professional theoreticians and students alike. It is, quite simply, the least elegant part of syntactic theory. We'll have a brief look at it here, but will come to no satisfying conclusions.

First let's observe that some parts of control are sensitive to syntactic structure. Consider what can control PRO in (55):

55)   [Jean$_i$'s father]$_j$ is reluctant PRO$_{j/*i}$ to leave.

---

[7] Recall from chapter 4, that our definition of binding domain as a clause is probably wrong. One might even hypothesize on the basis of data like *Jean is likely to behave herself* that the definition of binding domain requires some kind of tensed clause, rather than just any kind of clause. I leave as an exercise the implications of such a move.

If you draw the tree for (55), you'll see that while the whole NP *Jean's father* c-commands PRO, *Jean* by itself does not. The fact that *Jean* cannot control PRO strongly suggests that there is a c-command requirement on obligatory control, as argued by Williams (1980). This said, the structure of the sentence doesn't seem to be the only thing that comes into play with control. Compare now a subject control sentence to an object control one:

56)   a)   Robert$_i$ is reluctant [PRO$_i$ to behave].   *subject control*
      b)   Susan$_j$ ordered Robert$_i$ [PRO$_{i/*j}$ to behave].   *object control*

In both these sentences PRO must be controlled by *Robert*. PRO in (56b) cannot refer to *Susan*. This would seem to suggest that the closest NP that c-commands PRO must control it. In (56a), *Robert* is the only possible controller, so it controls PRO. In (56b), there are two possible controllers: *Susan* and *Robert*. But only *Robert*, which is structurally closer to PRO, can control it. This hypothesis works well in most cases, but the following example shows it must be wrong:

57)   Jean$_i$ promised Susan$_j$ [PRO$_{i/*j}$ to behave].   *subject control*

In this sentence it is *Jean* doing the behaving, not *Susan*. PRO must be controlled by *Jean*, even though *Susan* is structurally closer. So structure doesn't seem to be the only thing determining which NP does the controlling.

   One hypothesis is that the particular main clause predicate determines which NP does the controlling. That is, the theta grid specifies what kind of control is involved. There are various ways we could encode this. One is to mark a particular theta role as the controller:

58)   a)   *is reluctant*

experiencer controller	proposition

      b)   *persuade*

Agent	Theme controller	Proposition

      c)   *promise*

Agent controller	Theme	Proposition

In this view of things, control is a thematic property. But a very careful look at the data shows that this can't be the whole story either. The sentences in (59) all use the verb *beg*, which is traditionally viewed as an object control verb, as seen by the pair of sentences in (59a and b), where the (b) sentence shows an embedded tense clause paraphrase.

59)   a)   Louis begged Kate$_i$ [PRO$_i$ to leave her job].
        b)   Louis begged Kate that she leave her job.
        c)   Louis$_i$ begged Kate [PRO$_i$ to be allowed [PRO$_i$ to shave himself]].
        d)   Louis$_i$ begged Kate that he be allowed to shave himself.

Sentences (59c and d), however, show subject control. The PROs in (c) must be controlled by the subject *Louis*. The difference between the (a) and the (b) sentence seems to be in the nature of the *embedded* clause. This is mysterious at best. Examples like these might be used to argue that control is not entirely syntactic or thematic, but may also rely on our knowledge of the way the world works. This kind of knowledge, often referred to as **pragmatic** knowledge,[8] lies outside the syntactic system we're developing. The study of the interaction between pragmatics, semantics and syntax is one that is being vigorously pursued right now, but lies beyond the scope of this book. See the further reading section below for some places you can go to examine questions like this in more detail.

4.   ANOTHER KIND OF NULL SUBJECT: "LITTLE" *pro*

In chapter 7, we made the claim that all sentences require subjects, and encoded this into the EPP. However, many languages appear to violate this constraint. Take, for example, these perfectly acceptable sentences of Italian:

60)   a)   Parlo.
             speak.1SG
             "I speak."

        b)   Parli.
             speak.2SG
             "You speak."

The subject NP in these sentences seems to be missing. But there is no ambiguity here. We know exactly who is doing the talking. This is because the verbs are inflected with endings that tell us who the subject is. This phenomenon is called either **pro-drop** or **null subjects**. Ideally, we would like to claim that a strong constraint like the EPP is universal, but Italian (and many other languages) seem to be exceptions. One technical solution to this issue is to posit that sentences in (60) actually do have NPs which satisfy the EPP. Notice again that this is merely a technical solution to a formal problem.

          You might think that the obvious candidate for this empty NP would be PRO. But in fact, PRO could not appear in this position. Remember PRO only ap-

---

[8] See for example Landau's (1999) dissertation.

pears in Caseless positions. We know that Italian subject position is a Case position, because you can have an overt NP like *io* in (61).

61)   Io Parlo.
        I speak.1SG
        "I speak."

So linguists have proposed the category *pro* (written in lower-case letters). *pro* (called *little pro* or *baby pro*) appears in Case positions; PRO (called *big PRO*) is Caseless.

English doesn't have *pro*. This presumably is due to the fact that English doesn't have a rich agreement system in its verbal morphology:

62)   a) I speak.
        b) You speak.
        c) He/she/it speak<u>s</u>.
        d) We speak.
        e) They speak.

In English, only third person forms of verbs take any special endings. One of the conditions on *pro* seems to be that it often appears in languages with rich agreement morphology.[9] The means we use to encode variation among languages should now be familiar: parameters. We use this device here again in the *null subject parameter*, which governs whether or not a language allows *pro*. Italian has this switch turned on. English has it set in the off position.

5.   SUMMARY

We started this chapter with the observation that certain sentences, even though they look alike on the surface, can actually have very different syntactic trees. We compared subject-to-subject raising constructions to subject control constructions, and subject-to-object raising constructions to object control constructions. You can test for these various construction types by working out their argument structure, and using the idiom test. Next under consideration was the issue of what kind of NP PRO is. We claimed that it only showed up in Caseless positions. We also saw that it didn't meet any of the binding conditions, and suggested it is subject, instead, to control theory. Control theory is a bit of a mystery, but may involve syntactic, thematic, and pragmatic features. We closed the chapter by comparing two different kinds of null subject categories: PRO and *pro*. PRO is Caseless and is subject to the theory of control. On the other hand, *pro* takes Case and is often "licensed" by rich agreement morphology on the verb. This ends our look at NPs and NP movement. In

---

[9] This not a universally true statement. Many Asian languages allow *pro*-drop even though they don't have rich agreement systems. For discussion, see Huang (1989).

the next chapter we turn to the question of how we form questions that start with words like *who, which, when, where,* and *why,* etc.

IDEAS, RULES, AND CONSTRAINTS INTRODUCED IN THIS CHAPTER

i)   **PRO (big PRO)**
A null (silent) NP found in Caseless positions (the specifier of non-finite TP).

ii)   ***pro (Little pro or Baby pro)***
A null (silent) NP often found in languages with "rich" agreement. *pro* does get Case.

iii)   **Clausal Subject Construction**
A sentence where a clause appears in the specifier of TP. E.g., *[That Jean danced the rumba] is likely.*

iv)   **Extraposition**
A sentence (often an alternate of a clausal subject construction) where there is an expletive in the subject position and a clausal complement. E.g., *It is likely that Jean danced the rumba.*

v)   **Subject-to-subject Raising**
A kind of NP movement where the subject of an embedded non-finite clause moves to the specifier of TP of the main clause to get nominative Case. E.g., *Jean$_i$ is likely* t$_i$ *to dance.*

vi)   **Subject-to-object Raising** (*also called* **Exceptional Case Marking** *or* **ECM**)
A kind of NP movement where the subject of an embedded non-finite clause moves to the complement of the verb in the main clause to get accusative Case. E.g., *Jean wants Bill$_i$[t$_i$ to dance].*

vii)   **Control Theory**
The theory that governs how PRO gets its meaning. There appear to be syntactic factors (the controller must c-command PRO), thematic factors (what NP does the controlling is dependent upon what main clause predicate is present), and pragmatic factors involved.

viii)   **Pragmatics**
The science that looks at how language and knowledge of the world interact.

ix)   ***Subject Control*** *(also called* **Equi***)*
       A sentence where there is a PRO in the embedded non-finite clause that is
       controlled by the subject argument of the main clause. E.g., *John$_i$ is reluc-
       tant PRO$_i$ to leave.*

x)   ***Object Control***
       A sentence where there is a PRO in the embedded non-finite clause that is
       controlled by the object argument of the main clause. E.g., *John wants Bill$_i$
       PRO$_i$ to leave.*

xi)   ***Obligatory vs. Optional Control***
       Obligatory control is when the PRO must be controlled: *Jean$_i$ is reluctant
       PRO$_i$ to leave.* Optional control is when the NP can be controlled or not:
       Robert$_i$ knows that it is essential [PRO$_{i/j}$ to be well behaved].

xii)   ***PRO$_{arb}$***
       Uncontrolled PRO takes an "arbitrary" reference. That is, it means some-
       thing like *someone.*

xiii) ***Null Subject Parameter***
       The parameter switch that distinguishes languages like English, which re-
       quire an overt subject, from languages like Italian that don't, and allow *pro.*

FURTHER READING

Brame, Michael (1976) *Conjectures and Refutations in Syntax and Semantics.* Am-
       sterdam: Elsevier.

Bresnan, Joan (1972) Theory of Complementation in English. Ph.D. dissertation.
       MIT.

Chomsky, Noam (1965) *Aspects of the Theory of Syntax.* Cambridge: MIT Press.

Chomsky, Noam (1981) *Lectures on Government and Binding.* Dordrecht: Foris.

Hornstein, Norbert (1999) Movement and control. *Linguistic Inquiry* 30, 69–96.

Hyams, Nina (1986) *Language Acquisition and the Theory of Parameters.*
       Dordrecht: D. Reidel Publishing Company.

Jaeggli, Osvaldo and Kenneth Safir (eds.) (1989) *The Null Subject Parameter.*
       Dordrecht: Kluwer Academic Publishers.

Landau, Idan (1999) Elements of Control. Ph.D. dissertation. MIT.

Manzini, Maria Rita (1983) On control and control theory. *Linguistic Inquiry* 14, 421–46.

Petter, Marga (1998) *Getting PRO under Control*. The Hague: Holland Academic Graphics.

Postal, Paul (1974) *On Raising*. Cambridge: MIT Press.

Rizzi, Luigi (1982) *Issues in Italian Syntax*. Dordrecht: Foris.

Rosenbaum, P. S. (1967) *The Grammar of English Predicate Complement Constructions*. Cambridge: MIT Press.

Williams, Edwin (1980) Predication. *Linguistic Inquiry* 11, 203–38.

PROBLEM SETS

1. ENGLISH PREDICATES

(The idea for this problem set comes from a similar question in Soames and Perlmutter 1979)

Using your knowledge of theta theory and the tests of extraposition and idioms determine if these predicates are:

subject-to-subject raising,
subject-to-object raising,
subject control, or
object control.

Some predicates might fit into more than one category.

is eager	is believed	seems	is ready
persuaded	urged	requested	hoped
expect	force	tell	advise
ask	assure	imagine	promise
want	is likely	consent	imagine
encouraged	intended		

2.   TREES AND DERIVATIONS

Draw trees for the following sentences, annotate your trees with arrows so that they show all the movements, and write in all PROs with appropriate coindexing indicating control. You may wish to do this problem set *after* you have completed the problem set 1.

a) Jean wants Bill to do the Macarena.
b) Robert is eager to do his homework.
c) Jean seems to be in a good mood.
d) Rosemary tried to get a new car.
e) Susan begged Bill to let her sing in the concert.
f) Susan begged to be allowed to sing in the concert.
g) Christina is ready to leave.
h) Fred was believed to have wanted to try to dance.
i) Susan consented to try to seem to have been kissed.

3.   IS EASY

Consider the following sentences:

a) This book is easy to read.
b) John is easy to please.

Is *is easy* a raising or a control predicate or both? If it is a raising predicate, which argument is raised? If it is a control predicate, where is the PRO? What kind of PRO is it?

4.   THE EXISTENCE OF PRO

How does the following sentence provide support for the existence of PRO in the subject position of the non-finite clause?

a) [To behave oneself in public] is expected.

Consider now the following sentence. Does it provide support for the existence of PRO? How?

b) Robert$_i$ knew [$_{CP}$ that it was necessary [$_{CP}$ PRO$_i$ to behave himself$_i$]].

5.   ICELANDIC PRO AND QUIRKY CASE

(Data from Sigurðsson 1991)

Background. In order to do this question it will be helpful to have reviewed the discussion of floating quantifiers in chapter 9, and to have done the question on Icelandic quirky Case in chapter 9.

As discussed in chapter 9, in English, it is possible to "float" quantifiers (words like *all*) that modify subject arguments:

a)   The boys don't all want to leave.

Icelandic also allows floating quantifiers, but with a twist. The quantifier takes endings indicating that it has the same Case as the NP it modifies. Recall from the last chapter that certain verbs in Icelandic assign irregular or "quirky" Cases to their subjects. The verb *leiddist* 'bored' is one of these. In sentence (b), the subject is marked with its quirky dative Case. The floating quantifier *öllum* 'all' is also marked with dative.

b)   Strákunum leiddist öllum   í skóla.
     boys.DAT   bored all.DAT   in school
     "The boys were all bored in school."

We might hypothesize then, that floated quantifiers must agree with the noun they modify in terms of Case.

The question. Now consider the following control sentence. What problems does the following sentence hold for our claim that PRO does not get Case? Can you relate your solution to the problem of Icelandic passives discussed in the problem sets of the previous chapter? Note that the noun in the main clause here is marked with nominative rather than dative Case.

c)   Strákarnir vonast til að PRO leiðast ekki öllum í skóla.
     boys.NOM hope for to   bore not all.DAT in school
     "The boys hope not to be bored in school."

6.   CONTROLLERS

Williams (1980) claimed that obligatorily controlled PRO requires a c-commanding controller. What problem do the following sentences hold for that hypothesis?

a) To improve myself is a goal for next year.
b) To improve yourself would be a good idea.
c) To improve himself, Bruce should consider therapy.
d) To improve herself, Jane went to a health spa.

7.   IRISH *pro*

Irish is a null subject language.

a) Rinceamar.
   Dance.3PL.PAST
   "We danced."

Consider the following sentences and discuss how Irish *pro*-drop differs from that found in Italian:

b) Tá mé.
   Am I
   "I am."

c) Táim.
   Am.1SG
   "I am."

d) *Táim   mé.
   Am.1SG I
   "I am."

chapter 11

Wh-movement

0.   INTRODUCTION

In chapter 9, we looked at NPs which were appearing in positions where they didn't get theta roles. Instead, the NP surfaced in a derived position. That is, they were moved from the position where they got a theta role to a position where they could get Case. The trigger for this movement was the requirement that NPs check their Case feature, as Case can only be assigned in specific structural positions. In this chapter, we turn to another kind of phrasal movement, one where NPs already have Case. NPs (and other phrases) move for a different reason to form what is called a **wh-*question.***

There are several different kinds of questions, only two of which we are concerned with in this book. The first kind is the familiar ***yes/no question*** that we looked at in the chapter on head movement:

1)   Are you going to eat that bagel?
2)   Do you drink whisky?
3)   Have you seen the spectrograph for that phoneme?

The answers to these questions cannot be other than *yes, no, maybe* or *I don't know.* Any other response sounds strange:

1')   #Pizza/ ✓ yes
2')   #Scotch/ ✓ no
3')   #Syntactic tree/ ✓ no

The other kind of question is called a *wh*-question. These questions take their name from the fact that the words that introduce them (mostly) begin with the letters <wh> in English: *who/whom*, *what*, *when*, *where*, *why*, *which*, and *how*. The responses to these kind of questions cannot be *yes* or *no*. Instead they must be informative phrases.

4)   When did you do your syntax homework?   #yes / ✓ yesterday
5)   What are you eating?   #no/ ✓ a bagel
6)   How is Louise feeling?   #yes/✓ much better

How these questions are formed is the focus of this chapter.

> ### Who and Whom
> In traditional prescriptive grammar, there are two *wh*-words that refer to people: *who* and *whom*. *Who* is used when the *wh*-word originates in subject position and gets nominative Case. *Whom* is the accusative version. In most spoken dialects of Canadian and American English this distinction no longer exists, and *who* is used in all environments. For the sake of clarity, I use *who(m)* to indicate that the *wh*-word originated in object position, but you should note that from a descriptive point of view *who* is perfectly acceptable in object position for most speakers today.

1.   MOVEMENT IN *WH*-QUESTIONS

If you look closely at a statement and a related *wh*-question, you'll see that the *wh*-word appears in a position far away from the position where its theta role is assigned. Take for example:

7)   Becky bought the syntax book.
8)   What did Becky buy?

The verb *buy* in English takes two theta roles, an external agent and an internal theme. In sentence (7), *Becky* is the agent, and *the syntax book* is the theme. In sentence (8), *Becky* is the agent and *what* is the theme. In the first sentence, the theme is the object of the verb, in the second the theme is at the beginning of the clause. The situation becomes even more mysterious when we look at sentences like (9):

9)   What did Stacy say Becky bought?

In this sentence *what* is still the theme of *bought*, yet it appears way up at the beginning of the main clause. This would appear to be a violation of the locality condition on theta role assignment introduced in chapter 9.

      The situation becomes murkier still when we look at Case. Recall that accusative Case is assigned when an NP is the sister to a V:

10)   Matt kissed her.

But in *wh*-questions the accusative form (like *whom*) is not a sister to V:

11)   Whom did Matt kiss?

So it appears as if not only are these *wh*-words not in their theta positions, they aren't in their Case positions either

      Given what we've seen in the previous two chapters this looks like another case of movement, this one with different triggers again. Let's start with the question of where *wh*-words move to. One position that we've had for a while, but have not yet used, is the specifier of CP. We move *wh*-words to this position:

12)

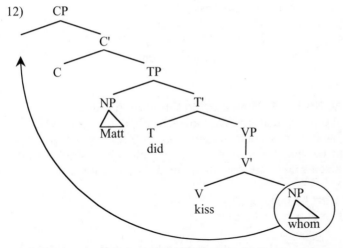

Notice that what moves here is an entire phrase. You can see this if you look at slightly more complex *wh*-questions:

13)   [To whom] did Michael give the book?
14)   [Which book] did Michael give to Millie?

When you move an entire phrase, it cannot be an instance of head-to-head movement (by definition), so this must be movement to a position other than a head, in this case we have the empty specifier of CP.

      The movement to the specifier of CP accounts for another fact about the word order of *wh*-questions: they also involve T → C movement (in main clauses):

15)   Who(m) are you meeting?
16)   *Who(m) you are meeting?

The *wh*-phrase appears to the left of the auxiliary in C. This means that the *wh*-phrase must raise to a position higher than C. The only position available to us is the specifier of CP:

17)   CP

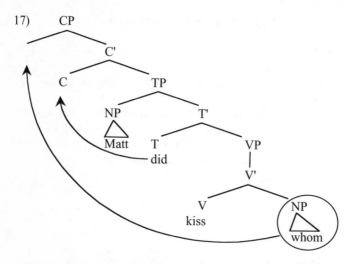

A Mystery: No T → C Movement in Embedded Clauses.
In the main text, we've noticed that *wh*-movement and T → C movement often go hand in hand. One surprising fact about English is that this is not true of embedded *wh*-questions. When a *wh*-question is embedded the subject does not invert with the auxiliary (i.e., no T → C movement):

i)   I wonder what he has done?
ii)   *I wonder what has he done?

Why you don't get T → C movement in embedded *wh*-clauses in English is a mystery. We don't have a good explanation for it.

        The fact that *wh*-movement is to the CP specifier position can also be seen in languages that allow both a *wh*-phrase and an overt complementizer, such as Irish:

18)   Cé   *a*^{L} bhí sa seomra?
        Who that-*wh* was in-the room
        "Who was in the room?"
                                                          Irish

In Irish, the *wh*-phrase *cé* 'who' appears to the left of the complementizer a^L, supporting the idea that the *wh*-phrase is in the specifier of CP, the only position available to it.

The English Doubly Filled CP Filter

While CPs containing *wh*-phrases allow complementizers to contain an inverted auxiliary: ([CP What did [IP she kiss]]?), they don't allow any other kind of complementizer:

i)   *I asked what that she kissed?
ii)   *I asked what whether she kissed?

Multiple *wh*-phrases are also not allowed:

iii)   *I asked what how she kissed?

There thus seems to be a constraint that disallows the CP having multiple pronounced contents. This constraint is called the **Doubly Filled CP Filter:**

iv)   *[CP *Wh-phrase* that/if/whether]

This constraint holds of English only. Other languages allow both a complementizer and the *wh*-phrase (data from Bavarian German, Bayer 1984):

v)   I woass ned *wann dass* da Xavea kummt.
        I know not when that the Xavea comes
        "I don't know when Xavea is coming."

See also example (18) from Irish in the main text.

Let's motivate *wh*-movement. In chapter 8, we triggered T → C movement with a [+Q] feature that was part of the complementizer. NP movement, in chapters 9 and 10, was triggered by a Case feature. We can do the same thing, here, for *wh*-questions, by proposing a feature that triggers the movement. Let's call this feature [+WH]. It resides in the C of a *wh*-sentence. A *wh*-phrase moves to the specifier of CP to be "near" the [+WH] feature. Another way to phrase this is to say that *wh*-words move into the specifier of CP to "check" the *wh*-feature, just like we moved NPs to the specifier of TP to check a [NOM] Case feature in chapter 9, and to the complement of V to check an [ACC] feature in chapter 10. We can formalize *wh*-movement the following way:

19)   Wh-*movement*
         Move a *wh*-phrase to the specifier of CP to check a *wh*-feature in C.

The existence of a [+WH] feature on C is not completely unmotivated. In some languages (such as Irish), there are special forms of complementizers that represent these features:

20)   [-Q, -WH]   *go*
         [+Q, -WH]   *an*
         [+Q, +WH]   *a*^{L}

You get the *go* complementizer when the sentence is not a *yes/no* or *wh*-question. You get the *an* complementizer in *yes/no* questions and *a*^{L} in *wh*-questions. The form of the complementizer is dependent upon the features it contains (McCloskey 1979).
         Let's do a derivation for the following sentence:

21)   Whom is Matt kissing?

The D-structure of this sentence will look like (22):[1]

22)

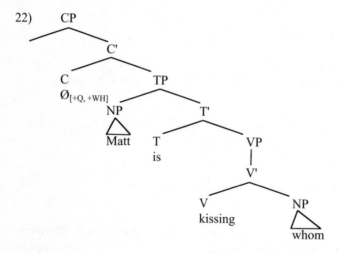

Matt and *whom* both get their theta roles in these D-structure positions. They also both get Case in these positions. We get T → C movement to fill the null [+Q] complementizer:

---

[1]For simplicity's sake, I'm abstracting away from the VP-internal subject hypothesis. If we assumed the VP internal subject hypothesis we'd have to move *Matt* from the specifier of VP to the specifier of TP for Case.

23)

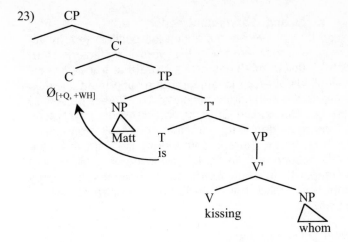

Wh-movement applies to check the [WH] feature:

24)

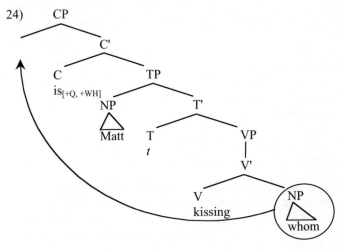

This results in the surface string in (25).

25)   Whom is Matt kissing?

Traces and *Wanna*-contraction

You may have noticed that I have been marking the position that move-ment occurs from with a *t* (coindexed with the word it replaces). The *t* here stand for "trace." Later in this chapter we'll see that traces are re-quired to block certain kinds of illicit movement. But an important question is whether there is any reality behind the notion "trace." This is especially important in a theory like Generative Grammar which claims psychologi-cal underpinnings. Finding evidence for something that isn't pronounced is remarkably difficult. However, there is some straightforward evidence for traces. First a little background: In spoken varieties of English (both standard and non-standard), function words often contract with nearby words. One such contraction takes non-finite T (*to*) and contracts it with a preceding verb like want:

i)   I want to leave → I wanna leave.

This phenomenon is called **wanna-*contraction***. Now consider what hap-pens when you have *wh*-movement and *wanna*-contraction going on at the same time. *Wanna*-contraction is permitted when the *wh*-movement applies to an object:

ii)   Who(m)$_i$ do you wanna kiss t$_i$.

But look what happens when you try to do *wanna*-contraction, when *wh*-movement targets the subject:

iii)   Who$_i$ do you want t$_i$ to kiss the puppy?
iv)   *Who do you wanna kiss the puppy?

English speakers have very strong judgments that *wanna*-contraction is impossible when the subject is *wh*-questioned. Why should this be the case? If we have traces, the explanation is simple: the trace intervenes between the *to* and the verb. It blocks the strict adjacency between the verb and the *to*, thus blocking contraction:

v)   Who$_i$ do you want t$_i$ to kiss the puppy?

The theory of traces, provides a nice explanation for this fact. For an al-ternate view see Pullum (1997).

Now let's do a more complicated example. This one involves NP move-ment, *wh*-movement and T → C movement:

26)   Who was kissed?

The D-structure of this sentence is given in (27). This sentence is a passive.

27)

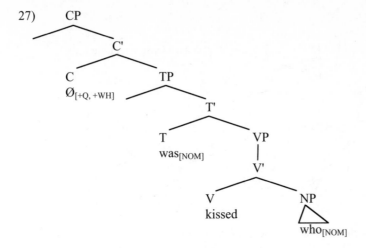

Who is the only argument in the sentence (a theme) and it starts out as a complement to the verb. Since this is a passive, however, it cannot get Case in this position. (Recall from chapter 9 that passive morphology suppresses the agent theta role, and the ability of the verb to assign accusative Case.) It must move to the specifier of TP to check nominative Case:

28)

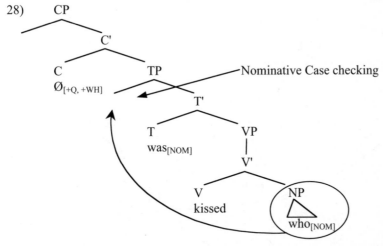

Once this NP has checked its Case features, it can move on to the specifier of CP for *wh*-feature checking. The auxiliary also undergoes T → C movement for the [+Q] feature. All these movements (including the NP movement seen in (28)) are represented in (29).

29)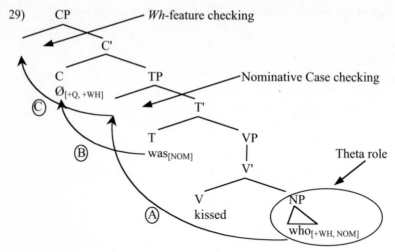

The NP starts in its theta position. There are then three movements in this structure, (A) NP movement, (B) T → C movement, and (C) *Wh*-movement. Wh-*movement only moves NPs that have already checked their Case features*. If we were simply to skip the NP movement as in the ill-formed tree in (30), the NP *who* would never check its Case feature, and thus would violate the Case filter. (30) is not an acceptable derivation.[2]

30)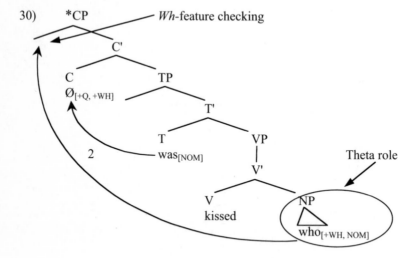

---

[2] If you are paying close attention, you may have noticed that the [NOM] feature is attached to T. T moves to C. This actually allows the [NOM] feature of the *wh*-phrase to be local to the [NOM] feature of T, since they are both inside the CP. This might mean that the NP doesn't have to stop off in the specifier of TP for Case reasons. The distinction between these approaches may well be notational.

Wh-movement can also apply across clauses. Next, we'll do a derivation of a sentence where the *wh*-phrase moves from an embedded clause to the specifier of a main clause CP.

31)   Who(m) did you think Jim kissed?

The D-structure of this sentence will look like (32). In this tree, *who(m)* is theta marked by the verb *kiss*, and gets its internal theme theta role in the object position of that verb. The two NPs in this sentence can also get Case in their D-structure positions, so there is no NP movement:

32)

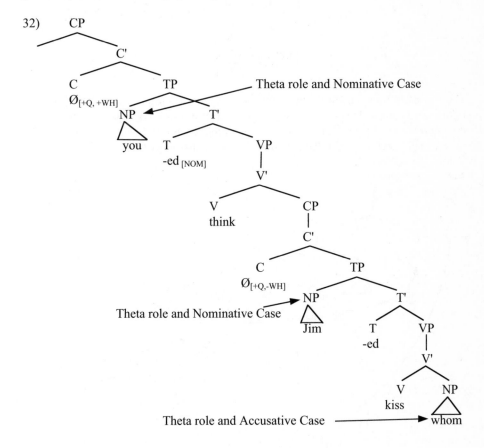

The T suffix *-ed* needs support, so it undergoes affix lowering:

33)

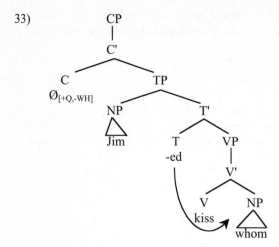

There is no NP movement in this sentence, but there is an unchecked [WH] feature in the main clause. This causes the phrase *who(m)* to move (A). In addition, there is the unpronounced [+Q] feature which triggers movement of T → C (B). Since there isn't an auxiliary in T, the rule of *do*-insertion must also apply (C):

34)

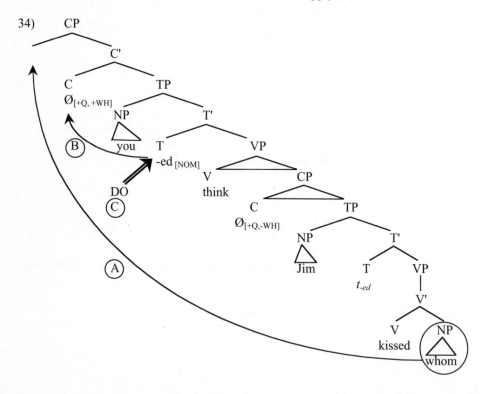

This derives the correct S-structure, where the *wh*-phrase is in initial position.[3]

The *That*-trace Effect

In English, *wh*-movement of objects seems to be free, you can do it either when there is a complementizer or when there is no complementizer:

i)   What$_i$ do you think Matt kissed t_i ?
ii)   What$_i$ do you think that Matt kissed t_i ?

This is not the case with subjects. *Wh*-movement from subject position is only possible when there is no overt *that* complementizer:

iii)   Who$_i$ do you think t$_i$ kissed Matt?
iv)   *Who$_i$ do you think that t_i kissed Matt?

This phenomenon is called the **that-*trace* effect**, from the constraint that is used to rule out sentences like (iv), the **that-*trace* filter**.

v)   [$_{CP}$* that *t*...]

The *that*-trace effect is not universal. Many languages (such as Italian), don't have it:

vi)   Chi credi   che *t*$_i$ venga?
         Who you-think that t$_i$ come
         "Who do you think is coming?" (Rizzi 1982)

The explanation for the *that*-trace effect was a central focus of the syntactic literature from the 1980s to about 1991, but lies beyond the scope of this text.

---

2.   CONSTRAINTS ON *WH*-MOVEMENT: BOUNDING THEORY

Wh-movement isn't without some limitations. There is a constraint on what categories you can move *out* of (the categories that contain the *wh*-word). Compare the following two sentences, one of which has *wh*-movement out of a simple complement CP (35). The other (36) moves a *wh*-phrase out of a clause that is contained *inside an NP* (a relative clause):

---

[3] In section 2, we will have reason to revise this tree somewhat, by having the *wh*-phrase stop off in the specifier of the embedded CP. We return to this below.

35)   What$_i$ did Bill claim [$_{CP}$ that he read t_i in the syntax book]?

36)   *What did Bill make [$_{NP}$ the claim [$_{CP}$ that he read t_i in the syntax book]]?

In sentence (35), we see that *wh*-movement ***out*** of a complement clause is grammatical. The nearly parallel sentence (36), on the other hand, shows that not all *wh*-movement out of a CP is acceptable. In particular it seems that you can't move a *wh*-word out of a CP contained within an NP. This phenomenon, first observed by Ross (1967), has come to be known as the **complex NP island** phenomenon. The word **island** here is meant to be iconic. Islands are places you can't get off of (without special means like a plane), they are surrounded by water, so you are limited in where you can move: You can only move about within the confines of the island. Islands in syntax are the same. You cannot move *out* of an island, but you can move around within it. Noun phrases are islands.

37)   *What did Bill make [$_{NP}$ the claim [$_{CP}$ that he read t_i in the syntax book]]?

                                      Complex NP Island

          There are other kinds of islands too. One of the most important is called a **wh-island**. First, observe that it is possible to move a *wh*-phrase to the specifier of an embedded CP:[4]

38)   I wonder [$_{CP}$ what [$_{TP}$ John bought t with the $20 bill]].

It is also possible to move (another) *wh*-phrase to the specifier of the main CP:

39)   [$_{CP}$ How do [$_{TP}$ you think [John bought the sweater]]]?

However, look at what happens when you try to do both (move one *wh*-phrase to the embedded specifier, and the other to the main CP specifier):

40)   *[$_{CP}$ How$_j$ do [$_{TP}$ you wonder [$_{CP}$ what$_i$ [$_{TP}$ John bought t_i t_j]]]]?

This sentence is wildly ungrammatical – even though we have only done two otherwise legitimate transformations. Now this isn't a constraint on having two *wh*-words in a sentence. Two *wh*-phrases are perfectly acceptable in other contexts:[5]

41)   How do you think John bought what?

42)   I wonder what John bought how?

---

[4] There is actually a restriction on this. *Wh*-movement to an embedded CP can only take place when the main verb selects (theta marks) a question clause. Verbs that do this are predicates like *wonder* and *ask*. Verbs like *think* don't allow embedded *wh*-questions. Since there will be occasions where we want to compare embedded *wh* and non-embedded *wh*, I'm going to play fast and loose with the choice of main verbs. I'll use *wonder* when I want an embedded question, but *think* when I want an embedded statement (with no [+WH] feature).

[5] If you have trouble with this judgment, try stressing the word *what* in (40) and *how* in (41).

It seems then to be a constraint on *moving* both of them. The same kind of example is seen in (43) and (44):

43)   I wonder what$_i$ John kissed t$_i$.
44)   Who$_j$ did you think/wonder t$_j$ kissed the gorilla?

Movement of either the subject (44) or the object (43) to the specifiers of CP is acceptable. However, movement of both results in terrible ungrammaticality:

45)   *Who$_j$ did you think/wonder what$_i$ t$_j$ kissed t$_j$?

The central intuition underlying an account of these facts is that once you move a *wh*-phrase into the specifier of a CP, then that CP becomes an island for further extraction:

46)   I asked [$_{CP}$ what$_i$ John kissed t_i].   *wh*-island

Movement out of this *wh*-island results in ungrammaticality.

We now have a descriptive statement about the restrictions on *wh*-movement. What we need is a formal description. In the ideal situation, we want our formal description to account for both types of islands (complex NP islands and *wh*-islands). In the 1970s and 1980s a theory of these facts was developed, called **bounding theory** (this is not to be confused with *binding* theory, which accounts for the distribution of anaphors and other NPs). Although currently a matter of great controversy, we will explore the most widely accepted version of bounding theory. A more recent alternative is presented in the next chapter.

The central idea underlying bounding theory is that certain kinds of nodes are boundaries for movement. These nodes are called **bounding nodes**. There are two bounding nodes: TP and NP.

47)   *Bounding nodes*: NP and TP.

Now it is clear that we can't simply say "Don't cross a bounding node". A simple *wh*-question like (52) violates this off the bat. In the following, the circled node with the thick line represents a bounding node. Crossing one of these nodes is perfectly grammatical:

48)   [$_{CP}$ who$_i$ did ([$_{TP}$)John see t_i]]?

Yet sentence (48) is completely grammatical. The account has to be more complicated. The answer lies in the **Subjacency Condition** (or **Subjacency Constraint**) of Chomsky (1973):

49)   *Subjacency Condition (or Subjacency Constraint)*
        Wh-movement may not cross more than one bounding node (but it may
        cross one).

Let's see how this works. First, consider the grammatical sentence in (48). The *wh*-movement there only crosses one bounding node, so the sentence meets the subjacency condition.
        Note that the subjacency condition forces us to make a stipulation on *wh*-movement across clauses:

50)   [$_{CP}$ What$_i$ did ([$_{TP}$) you think [$_{CP}$ that ([$_{TP}$) Millie said t_i]]]]?

Movement of this kind will necessarily cross two TPs, and thus should be a violation of the subjacency condition. However, the sentence is grammatical. Remember, *wh*-movement targets the specifier of CP. Fortunately, there is an unfilled specifier of CP between the two TPs

51)   [$_{CP}$ What$_i$ did [$_{TP}$ you think [$_{CP}$ _____ that [$_{TP}$ Millie said t_i]]]]?

If we allow the *wh*-phrase to stop off in this specifier on the way to the higher CP, we won't violate the Subjacency Constraint. We will have two movements, each of which will cross only one bounding node:

52)   [$_{CP}$ did ([$_{TP}$) you think [$_{CP}$ what$_i$ that ([$_{TP}$) Millie said t_i]]]]?

                                                                move # 1

53)   [$_{CP}$ What did ([$_{TP}$) you think [$_{CP}$ t_i that ([$_{TP}$) Millie said t_i]]]]?

                        move # 2

By allowing the *wh*-word to stop off in the intermediate CP's specifier, we have an "out" for the (grammatical) movement of *wh*-phrases across clause boundaries. This property of stopping off in intermediate specifiers of CP is sometimes called **cyclicity**. There are two cycles of movement in deriving a sentence like (51). The first cycle moves to the embedded CP specifier (51), the second to the higher one (52).
        Now that we've seen how grammatical sentences are generated, let's see if we can account for the island conditions with the Subjacency Condition. First, a complex NP island.

54)   *What$_i$ did Bill make the claim that he read t_i in the syntax book?

A pre-*wh*-movement structure for this sentence is given in (55) (this isn't the D-structure – I haven't bothered to undo any affix lowering, *do*-insertion, or T → C,

I've only undone the relevant *wh*-movement). I've marked the potential landing sites for the *wh*-word with an underline and the bounding nodes with a circle and a thick line:

55)

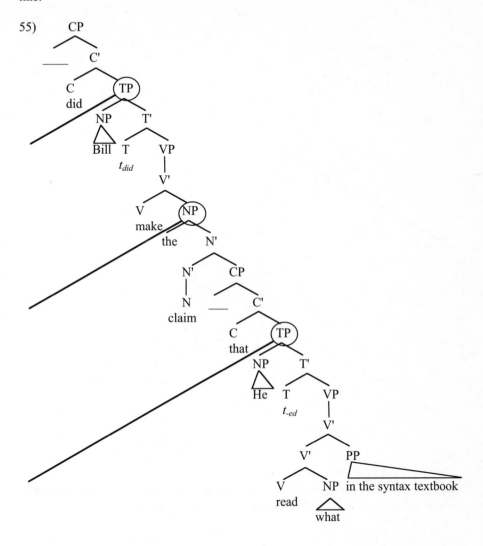

There are three bounding nodes in this tree: the matrix TP, the object NP, and the embedded TP. (Note that there are other NP nodes in this tree, but they do not count as bounding nodes as we are only concerned with what nodes you can move *out* of. So the only relevant NP nodes are those that *contain* (dominate) the *wh*-phrase.) The first step in the movement is to move the *wh*-phrase into the specifier of the embedded CP. This is a legitimate move, as it only crosses one bounding node.

56)

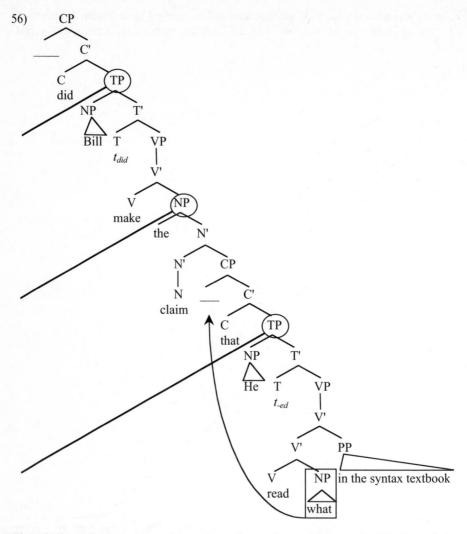

The *wh*-phrase here crosses only one bounding node, so this move is OK. Next, let's try to move to the next available node: the specifier of the higher CP:

57)

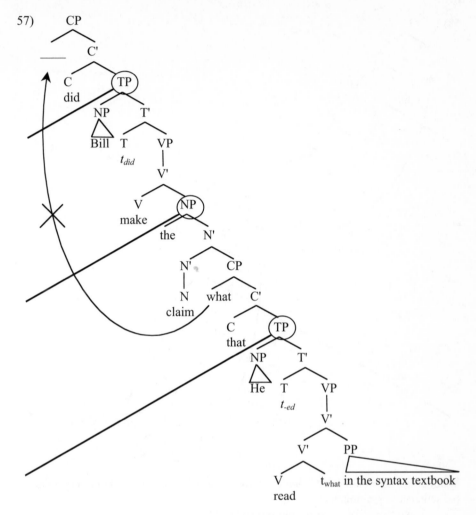

This move is illegitimate. It violates the Subjacency Condition by crossing two bounding nodes: the NP and the highest TP. This is the result we want, since the sentence is ill-formed. The Subjacency Condition correctly predicts that this sentence will be bad. Notice that we can't use the escape hatch we used with the grammatical sentence (51). There is no specifier of CP between the highest TP and the NP, so there is no stopping off place. For the sake of completeness, here is the tree for the comparable sentence without an NP island *(What did Bill claim that he read in the syntax book):*

58)

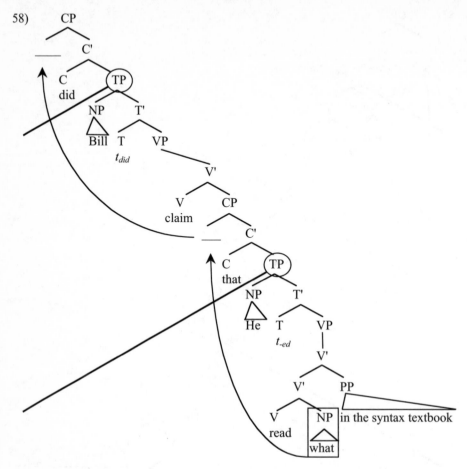

Without the dominating NP, each *wh*-movement only crosses one bounding node, so the sentence is grammatical.

Now, we'll do a *wh*-island sentence:

59)   *Who$_j$ did you wonder what$_i$ t$_j$ kissed t$_i$?

The D-structure for this sentence (again ignoring all extraneous transformations like T → C, etc.) is shown in (60).

60)

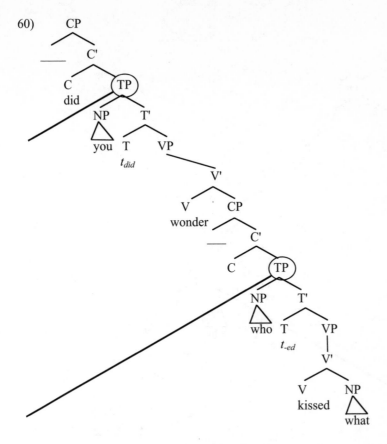

Here, there are only two bounding nodes, but there are also two *wh*-phrases to con-
tend with. First, we'll move *what* to the lower CP specifier:

61)

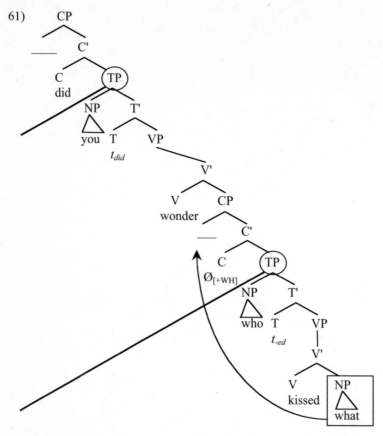

We know this kind of movement is OK, because of the grammaticality of sentences like *You wonder what John kissed*. This movement does not violate the Subjacency Constraint. It only crosses one bounding node. Now, we move the other *wh*-phrase.

62)

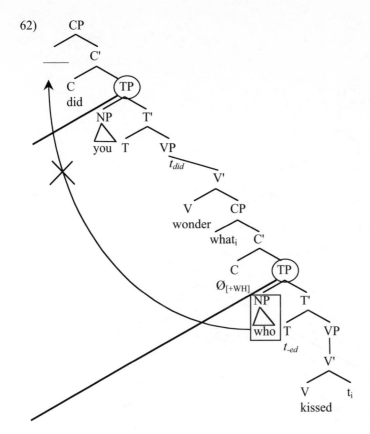

Movement of this second *wh*-phrase causes the violation. It can't stop off in the lower CP, *because this position is already occupied by the other* wh-*phrase. Who* is thus forced to cross two bounding nodes, resulting in a Subjacency violation. You might think that we could rescue this tree by simply ordering the movements differently, by moving the *who*-phrase first (thus allowing it to stop in the lower CP specifier), then moving the *what*-phrase. Due to the existence of traces, however, this is also ruled out. Using the same D-structure as before, let's move the *who*-phrase first, in two steps so that it doesn't violate Subjacency:

63)

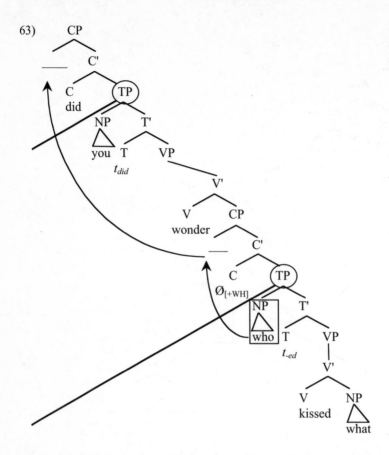

Since we only cross one bounding node at a time, each of these moves is acceptable. The sentence runs into trouble, however, when we try to move the other *wh*-phrase, *what*:

64)

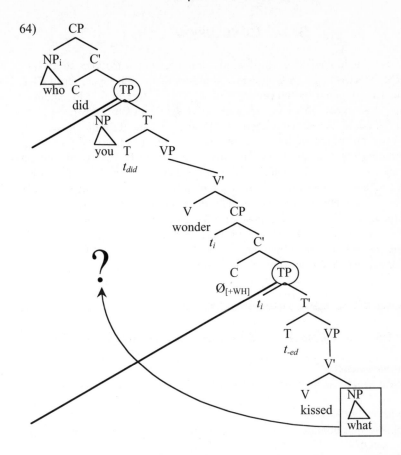

There is nowhere to move this NP to. The specifier of the lower CP is filled by the trace of the *who*-phrase, and the higher CP is filled by the *who*-phrase itself. There is no landing site for this NP. Moving it into the trace would result in having a doubly filled specifier (containing both the trace and the *what*-phrase). Just as you can't move an NP into another NP, you can't move a *wh*-phrase into a trace. The net result of all of this is that you can't save the ungrammatical sentence *Who did you wonder what kissed?* by moving the *who*-phrase first. No matter what you do, this sentence is going to be ill-formed as predicted by the Subjacency Constraint.

The arguments presented here are very complex, and the facts even more so. However, in the end a very simple pattern emerges with respect to islands. With the Subjacency Constraint, the range in which a *wh*-phrase can move is restricted. Apparent long-distance moves are the result of cyclic short movements. Cases where you can't make a short hop result in terrible ungrammaticality (such as the island violations).

3.   CONCLUSION

In this chapter, we looked at a third kind of movement transformation: *Wh-movement*. This process targets *wh*-phrases and moves them to the specifier of CPs. This movement is triggered by the presence of a [WH] feature in C. Movement is always from a Case position to the specifier of CP (a non-Case position). *Wh-movement* is not totally unrestricted; there is a locality constraint on the movement: Subjacency. Movement must be local, where local is defined as maximally crossing only one bounding node. In the boxes, we also saw that in English (and English alone) there are two additional constraints on *wh*-movement. One is the doubly filled CP filter: In English you can't have both a *wh*-word and an overt complementizer (although T → C movement is allowed). The other is the *that*-trace filter, which rules out *wh*-movement from a subject position adjacent to an overt complementizer.

Now that we have looked at three different kinds of movement, in the next chapter we are going to compare them and see what similarities and differences exist, and if there is a way to further simplify the system.

IDEAS, RULES, AND CONSTRAINTS INTRODUCED IN THIS CHAPTER

i)   **Wh-*movement***
        Move a *wh*-phrase to the specifier of CP to check a *wh*-feature in C.

ii)   ***Island***
        A phrase that contains (dominates) the *wh*-phrase, and that you may not move out of.

iii)   ***Bounding Nodes***: NP and TP.

iv)   ***Subjacency Condition (or Subjacency Constraint)***
        Wh-movement may not cross more than one bounding node (but it may cross one).

v)   ***Doubly Filled CP Filter*** *(English only)*
        * [$_{CP}$ WH that/if/whether]

vi)   **That-*trace Filter*** *(English only)*
        * *That* trace$_{wh}$

FURTHER READING

Baltin, Mark (1981) Strict bounding. In C. L. Baker and John McCarthy (eds.) *The Logical Problem of Language Acquisition*. Cambridge: MIT Press: 257–95.
[A classic work on bounding theory.]

Cheng, Lisa (1997) *On the Typology of Wh-Questions*. New York: Garland Press.
[A dissertation on the various kinds of *wh*-questions, with a focus on Chinese.]

Chomsky (1986) *Barriers*. Cambridge: MIT Press.
[A different view of bounding theory than that presented here.]

Chomsky, Noam (1977) On *wh*-movement. In Peter Culicover, Thomas Wasow, and Adrian Akmajian (eds.) *Formal Syntax*. New York: Academic Press. 71–132.
[A classic work on *wh*-movement and constraints on it.]

Chomsky, Noam and Howard Lasnik (1978) A remark on contraction. *Linguistic Inquiry* 9, 268–74.
[A paper on *wanna*-contraction.]

Cinque, Guglielmo (1981) *Types of A' Dependencies*. Cambridge: MIT Press.
[This is a very thorough examination of bounding theory and related topics.]

Koopman, Hilda (1984) *The Syntax of Verbs*. Dordrecht: Foris.
[One of the original sources of the idea that *wh*-movement targets the specifier of CP.]

Lasnik, Howard and Mamoru Saito (1984) On the nature of proper government. *Linguistic Inquiry* 15, 235–89.
[A paper that presents a different view of bounding theory.]

Lightfoot, David (1976) Trace theory and twice moved NPs. *Linguistic Inquiry* 7, 559–82.
[A paper on *wanna*-contraction.]

Manzini, Maria Rita (1992) *Locality: A Theory and Some of its Empirical Consequences*. Cambridge: MIT Press.
[An important book on bounding theory and related phenomena.]

Richards, Norvin (1997) What Moves Where When in Which Language? Ph.D. dissertation, MIT.
[An important dissertation on bounding theory and related phenomena.]

Rizzi, Luigi (1982) *Issues in Italian Syntax*. Dordrecht: Foris.
[This book contains discussion of the apparent differences between Italian and English in terms of bounding theory.]

Rizzi, Luigi (1989) *Relativized Minimality*. Cambridge: MIT Press.
  [A more modern view of bounding theory than the one presented in this chapter.]

Ross, J. R. (Haj) (1967) Constraints on Variables in Syntax. Ph.D. dissertation, MIT.
  [The classic work on island constraints.]

PROBLEM SETS

1.   ENGLISH TRANSFORMATIONS

For each of the following sentences, give the D-structure and annotate it with arrows indicating what transformations have applied. Be careful, since some of these sentences might have PRO in them.

a)   How was the plot discovered by the authorities?
b)   Which animals appear to have lost their collars?
c)   Alan told me who wanted to seem to be invincible.

2.   BOUNDING THEORY

Why is the following sentence ungrammatical?

   *Who$_j$ did [$_{TP}$ George try to find out [$_{CP}$ what$_i$ [$_{TP}$ t$_j$ wanted t$_i$]]]?

Draw a tree showing the exact problem with this sentence.

3.   PICTURE NPS

Why is the grammaticality of the following sentence surprising? Does the theory we have presented in this chapter predict this to be acceptable?

   Who(m) did you see a picture of?

4.   IRISH

(The idea behind this problem set is taken from McCloskey 1991)

Some dialects of English allow a kind of *wh*-construction, where the base position of the *wh*-word is filled a **resumptive pronoun**:

>This is the book$_i$ that the police are arresting everyone who reads it$_j$.

In Modern Irish, this kind of construction is very common. Modern Irish has two different *wh*-complementizers (notice that these are _not_ *wh*-words, which go in the specifier of CP, these are complementizers): a^L, a^N. The complementizer a^L is found in sentences like (a). Sentence (i) shows a simple sentence without *wh*-movement using the non-*wh*-complementizer *go*. Sentences (ii) and (iii) show two possible forms of the question. (ii) has the question moved only to an intermediate CP specifier. (iii) has the *wh*-phrase moved to the topmost specifier.

a) i)   Bíonn fios agat i gconaí [$_{CP}$ **go** bhuailfidh an píobaire an t-amhrán].
          be.HAB know at.2.S always that play.FUT the piper the song
          "You always know that the bagpiper will play the song."

    ii)   Bíonn fios agat i gconaí [$_{CP}$ caidé$_i$ **a^L** bhuailfidh an píobaire t$_i$].
          be.HAB know at.2.S always what$_i$ COMP play.FUT the piper t$_i$
          "You always know what the bagpiper will play."

    iii) [$_{CP}$ Cáidé$_i$ [$_{IP}$ **a^L** bhíonn fios agat i gconaí [$_{CP}$ t$_i$ **a^L** bhuailfidh an píobaire t$_i$]]?
          What COMP be.HAB know at.2.S always COMP play.FUT the piper
          "What do you always know the piper will play?"

Now the distribution of the complementizer a^N seems to be linked to the presence of a resumptive pronoun. Consider the (ii) sentences in (b) and (c). Both show resumptive pronouns and the complementizer a^N:

b) i)   Bíonn fios agat i gconaí [$_{CP}$ caidé$_i$ **a^L** bhuailfidh an píobaire t$_i$].
          be.HAB know at.2.S always what$_i$ COMP play.FUT the piper t$_i$
          "You always know what the bagpiper will play."

    ii)   [$_{CP}$Cén Píobaire$_j$ a^N [$_{TP}$ mbíonn fios agat i gconaí [$_{CP}$caidé$_i$ **a^L** bhuailfidh *sé$_j$* t$_i$]]?
          Which piper COMP be.HAB know at.2.S always what$_i$ COMP play.FUT he
          "Which bagpiper do you always know what he will play?"

c) i)   Tá máthair an fhir san otharlann.
          Be.PRES mother the man.GEN in.the hospital
          "The man's mother is in the hospital."

ii) Cé **a^N**   bhfuil **a_i** mháthair san otharlann?
who COMP be.PRES his mother in.the hospital
"Who is (his) mother in the hospital?"

The a^N complementizer and the resumptive pronouns are boldfaced in the above examples. Where precisely does the a^N-resumptive strategy appear? In what syntactic environment do you get this construction?

5. BINDING THEORY

In chapter 4, you were asked why the sentence below causes a problem for the binding theory. Remind yourself of your answer, and then explain how the model of grammar we have proposed in this chapter accounts for this fact.

Which pictures of himself does John despise?

6. ENGLISH

Do derivations for each of the following sentences. They may involve head-to-head movement, *do*-insertion, expletive insertion, NP/DP movement and *wh*-movement.

a) Car sales have surprised the stockbrokers.
b) Have you seen my model airplane collection?
c) Can you find the lightbulb store?
d) John was bitten by an advertising executive.
e) It is likely that Tami will leave New York.
f) Tami is likely to leave New York.
g) It seems that Susy was mugged.
h) Susy seems to have been mugged.
i) What did you buy at the supermarket?
j) I asked what Beth bought at the supermarket.
k) What is likely for Beth to have bought at the supermarket?
l) What is likely to have been bought at the supermarket?

7.   SERBO-CROATIAN[6]

(Data from Bošković 1997 as cited in Lasnik 1999a)

In this chapter, we have proposed that a *wh*-phrase appear in the specifier of CP, to check a [WH] feature. Our account of bounding theory requires that only one *wh*-phrase appear in the specifier of CP. Consider the following data from Serbo-Croatian (also known as Serbian or Croatian). Assume that Serbo-Croatian is SVO at D-structure.

a) Ko šta gdje kupuje?
   who what where buys
   "Who buys what where?"

b)   *Ko kupuje šta gdje?

c)   *Ko šta kupuje gdje?

d)   *Ko gdje kupuje šta?

What problems does this data raise for our analysis? Can you see a way around these problems?

8.   BINDING AND SCRAMBLING[7]

Modern Persian has a kind of movement often called **scrambling**. Your task in this problem set is to figure out whether scrambling is NP movement, head-to-head movement or *wh*-movement. The Persian word *hamdiga* means 'each other' and is an anaphor. Assume that anaphors are subject to the binding theory of chapter 4, and that they must be in argument positions to be bound. Sentence (a) shows the basic order. Sentences (b) and (c) show the surface word order after scrambling has applied. The scrambled sentences mean almost exactly the same thing as (a). HAB stands for "habitual".

---

[6] This problem set was contributed by Simin Karimi.
[7] This problem set was contributed by Simin Karimi.

a) Mo'allem-â_k fekr   mi-kon-an   [_{CP} ke [_{T'} [_{vP} bachche-hâ_i
   teacher-PL thought HAB-do-3PL   that   child-PL

[_{vP} aks - â -ye hamdiga_{i/*k} - ro be modir   neshun dâd-an]]].
picture-PL-EZ each other - RÂ to principal sign   gave-3PL
"The teachers_k think that the children_i showed [each other's]_{i/*k} pictures to
the principal."

b) Mo'allem-â_k [aks-â-ye hamdiga_{i/*k}-ro]_m fekr mi-kon-an [_{CP} ke [_{T'} [_{vP}
   [bachche-hâ_i] [_{vP} t_m be modir neshun dâd-an]]]].

c) [Aks-â-ye hamdiga_{i/*k}-ro]_m mo'allem-â_j fekr mi-kon-an
   [_{CP} ke [_{T'} [_{vP} bachche-hâ_i [_{vP} t_m be modir neshun dâd-an]]]].

9.   IRISH[8]

(The idea behind this problem set is taken from McCloskey 1979)

You may want to do problem 4 above before attempting this question.

Irish has a number of different complementizer forms. In declarative clauses
(statements), it uses the complementizer *go/gur*. As discussed in the text
above, when there is a question, this complementizer switches to the *wh*
form a^L:

a) Ceapann tú   go bhuailfidh an píobaire an t-amhrán
   think   you that play.FUT   the piper   the song
   "You think that the piper will play the song."

b) Caidé a^L cheapann tú a^L bhuailfidh an píobaire?
   What WH think   you WH play.FUT   the piper
   "What do you think the piper will play?"

Note carefully the number of a^L complementizers in sentence (b). (b) provides evidence that *wh*-phrases stop off in intermediate specifiers of CP (for
subjacency reasons). Explain why. You need to make the assumption that
the complementizer a^L only shows up when a *wh*-phrase has at one point
shown up in its specifier.

---

[8] This problem set was suggested by an anonymous Blackwell reviewer.

chapter 12

Towards Minimalism

0.   INTRODUCTION

Let's look at what we've done so far. At the beginning of this book, we looked at
rules that generate the basic phrase structure of human syntax. These rules generated
trees which represent hierarchical structure and constituency. These trees have particular mathematical properties which we investigated in chapters 3 and 4. In chapter
5, we saw that stipulated phrase structure rules missed some very basic generalizations, and developed the X-bar schema. The X-bar schema, being very general,
allows us (informed by parameter settings) to generate a wide variety of trees, and
capture structural differences between heads, complements, adjuncts, and specifiers.
In chapter 6, we extended the schema to various clause types, complementizers, and
DPs. In chapter 7, we saw that in fact the X-bar schema actually generated too many
structures, and that we had to constrain its power. The device we use to limit it is a
semantic one: the thematic properties of predicates (stored in the lexicon) and the
theta criterion. What results from the output of the X-bar schema and the lexicon is
called D-structure. The theta criterion holds of D-structures, as do the binding conditions. In chapters 8, 9, 10, and 11, we saw a variety of cases where lexical items
either could not be generated where they surfaced by X-bar theory (e.g., head-
adjunct-complement ordering in French) or appeared in positions other than the ones
predicted by theta theory. We developed a new kind of rule: the transformation,
which moves items around from their base position in the D-structure to the actual
position they appear in on the surface. There are three movement transformations:

Head-to-head movement (T → C and V → T), NP movement, and *wh*-movement. In each of these cases movement occurs because it *has* to. Each movement has a trigger or motivation. Heads move to fill empty [Q] features or to take an inflectional suffix. NPs move to check case features. *Wh*-phrases move to be near the [WH] feature. We also posited two insertion transformations: *Do*-support and expletive insertion. The output of the transformations is called S-structure, which is itself subject to several constraints: the Case filter, the EPP and the Subjacency Constraint. The model (flowchart) of the grammar looks like (1).

1)   **The Computational Component**

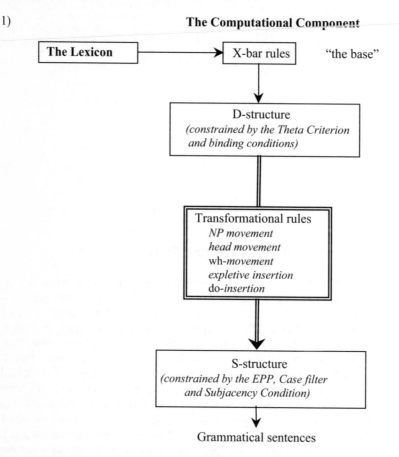

This straightforward model can generate a large number of sentence types. It is also a system with explanatory adequacy, which makes specific predictions about how a child goes about acquiring a language (via parameters).

This is a fairly complete and simple system, but we might ask if the system can be made even simpler. Are we missing any generalizations here? Recent work in syntactic theory answers this question with a resounding *yes*.

> ### The Minimalist Program
> The system of grammar described in this chapter is a very cursory look at some of the principles underlying the most recent version of generative grammar: The Minimalist Program (Chomsky 1993, 1995). The Minimalist Program is motivated not only by the search for explanatory adequacy but also for a certain level of formal simplicity and elegance. What is outlined here is by no means a complete picture, but is meant to give you a taste of what current work is striving towards.

1.   MOVE

In this book we've proposed the following motivations for transformations:

2)   a) Head movement   *to get a suffix or fill null* [+Q]
     b) NP movement   *to check case features*
     c) *Wh*-movement   *to check a* [+WH] *feature*

Notice that while there are significant differences between the motivations for the various types of movement, there is one overwhelming similarity. The movements all occur so that one item can appear near another. In the case of head movement the V or T head needs to appear as part of the same word as the place it moves to. With *wh*-movement, the *wh*-phrase needs to be near the [WH] feature, just as NP movement occurs so the NP can check its Case feature with T or V. All the motivations for movement then seem to be *locality constraint*s. That is, two items must be near or *local* to one another.

If this is the case, then there isn't really a significant difference between the rule types. Perhaps we can unify them into a single rule. This unified rule is called *Move*. Move says simply "move something" (but only if you have to):

3)   *Move (very informal version)*
       Move something somewhere.

Move actually predates Minimalism, but it an important part of the theory. Now of course, this is a bit vague and we'll have to sharpen it up in some way. In particular, we will want to constrain the rule so there isn't just random movement all over the sentence. So the next step is to formulate a constraint that motivates and forces this transformation to apply (in all the different circumstances).

Let's take *wh*-movement as our paradigm case. In *wh*-movement the *wh*-phrase moves to the specifier of CP so as to be local with a [WH] feature. Another way to think of this, as we suggested in chapter 11, is to say that both the *wh*-phrase and the complementizer have a [WH] feature, and they need to compare them, or *check* them. Checking of features can only occur in a local configuration. In this

case we have what is called a ***specifier/head configuration*** for reasons that should
be obvious from the following partial tree.

4)

```
                          CP
                  ┌───────┴───────┐
                 NP               C'
                  |            ┌───┴───┐
                  N        C         . . .
              [+WH] = [+WH]
                   ↘     ↗
```

                    checking configuration

The constraint that forces this movement to occur is called the ***Principle of Full Interpretation***[1] (Chomsky 1993, 1995).

5)   *Full Interpretation (FI)*
        Features must be checked in a local configuration.

6)   *Local Configuration*
        [WH] features: Specifier/Head configuration.

We can extend this to the other cases of movement too. As we suggested in chapter
9, imagine that Case is not simply an ending, but is also a feature. A subject NP
bears a [NOM] Case feature. Imagine also that the heads of the phrases that assign
case (T and V) also bear this feature (although they don't show it morphologically).

Case and Agreement

The notion that T bears some kind of Case feature often troubles people,
since Case is an inherently nominal kind of inflection and T seems to be
associated with verbal material. One clever solution to this problem is to
claim that verbal items like T do in fact bear Case; we just call case on
verbs "agreement." In fact, cross-linguistically, there does seem to be
some kind of correlation between the kinds of agreement markers that
are found on verbs and the case marking on the subjects. Languages
with ergative/absolutive case marking systems often also have erga-
tive/absolutive agreement. So we could claim that [NOM] when on a noun
is case, but when on T or a V is agreement, thus at least partly motivating
the structure in (7) and (8).

---

[1] The version of FI that I've given here is quite simplified. See Chomsky (1995) for a more
precise definition.

We can thus reduce the case filter to full interpretation: Nominative Case is feature checking like that in (7) and accusative Case is like that in (8):

7)

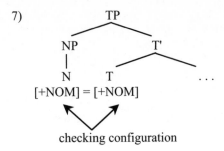

checking configuration

8)

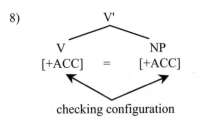

checking configuration

(Notice that this also allows a simple account of the passive. The passive morpheme absorbs the V's external theta role and its [ACC] feature). Because of the configuration in (8) we are going to have to slightly modify our definition of *local*:

9)   *Local Configuration*
        [WH] features: Specifier/Head configuration.
        [NOM] features: Specifier/Head configuration
        [ACC] features: Head/Complement configuration

Finally, we can extend this to the head movement cases. Instead of claiming that verbs move to pick up inflectional suffixes in V → T movement, let's claim that both the V and the T head bear some kind of abstract inflectional features (e.g., [±past]). When the verb and T check these features against one another then the suffix representing that tense feature (or agreement feature) is allowed to surface on the verb. The local configuration in this setting is within the head itself (a relationship which is called a head-head configuration):

10)   T

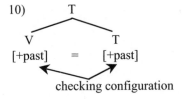

checking configuration

Similarly, both T and C bear a [+Q] feature, and they must be in a head-head checking relationship:

11)

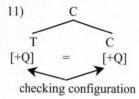

checking configuration

Of course, we must again massage the definition of local configuration somewhat:

12)   *Local Configuration*:
        [WH], [NOM] features: Specifier/Head configuration.
        [ACC] features: Head/Complement configuration
        [PAST], etc., [Q] features: Head-head configuration.

With this in place we actually have a very elegant transformational system. There is
one transformational movement rule (instead of three): Move; two constraints: full
interpretation and the Subjacency Constraint (and an admittedly stipulative definition
of local configuration).

2.   THE MINIMAL LINK CONDITION

The verbs *is likely* and *seem* both have empty subject positions and allow the subject-to-subject raising variant of NP movement.

13)   Mark$_i$ is likely [t$_i$ to have left].
14)   Mark$_i$ seems [t$_i$ to have left].

Consider now what happens when you embed one of these in the other. It is only
possible for NP movement to occur to the *lower* of the two case positions. (15)
shows the D-structure. (16) shows the grammatical S-structure where the NP shifts
to the lower position, and expletive insertion applies at the higher position. (17) and
(18) show ungrammatical forms, where the NP has shifted to the higher of the two
positions. This kind of movement is ungrammatical, whether or not (18 vs. 17) expletive insertion applies in the lower specifier of TP.

15)   ___ seems [that ___ is likely [Mark to have left]].
16)   It seems [that Mark$_i$ is likely [t$_i$ to have left]].
17)   *Mark$_i$ seems that is likely [t$_i$ to have left]].
18)   *Mark$_i$ seems that it is likely [t$_i$ to have left]].

When two Case positions are available you have to move to the closer (lower) one. In some ways this phenomenon is similar to *wh*-islands in bounding theory. *Wh*-movement, when it applies, must move to the first specifier of CP it comes across.

19)   *[CP Who did [TP Mark claim [CP what [TP t$_i$ loved t$_j$]]]]?

Recent work in the Minimalist framework (e.g., Chomsky 1995) has suggested that we can assimilate these two facts into a single constraint. Here is the observation: in both raising and *wh*-island constructions, ungrammaticality results when an element tries to move to a landing site higher than the closest *potential* one.

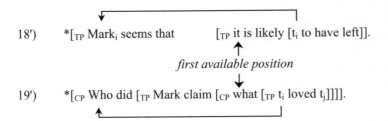

18')   *[TP Mark$_i$ seems that   [TP it is likely [t$_i$ to have left]].

                                first available position

19')   *[CP Who did [TP Mark claim [CP what [TP t$_i$ loved t$_j$]]]].

The constraint Chomsky proposes to account for this is called the **Minimal Link Condition** or **MLC**.

20)   *The Minimal Link Condition*
         Movement must target the closest potential position.

Sentences (18) and (19) are ungrammatical because the movement goes beyond the closest potential position into a higher position.

Economy Conditions and Shortest Move

The Minimalist program also has a set of constraints (called **economy constraints**) that don't hold of particular derivations of sentences or levels in a syntactic derivation, but hold across derivations. That is, if you have two possible derivations for the same surface sentence, the two derivations are compared with each other, and the one with the least movement or later movements is chosen over the one with more and earlier movements. In this book, we don't have the space to look at what economy constraints achieve for the theory of grammar (see some of the readings listed at the end of the chapter for more information). The proposal made in this subsection (the MLC) was originally conceived of in Chomsky (1993) as an economy condition called **Shortest Move**. Many researchers still think of the MLC in this way.

3.   EXPLAINING CROSS-LINGUISTIC DIFFERENCES

The system outlined above in sections 1 and 2, is extremely simple and elegant. It does however, make the unfortunate prediction that all languages will have exactly the same set of transformational rules (although they can still differ in phrase structure, due to the parameters). This is clearly not the case. English does not have V → T movement. Many other languages lack passive and raising. Still others appear to lack *wh*-movement. Take the case of Mandarin Chinese (data from Huang 1982; tone is omitted).

21)   a)   Ni xiang chi sheme?
              you want eat what
              "What do you want to eat?"

         b)   *Sheme ni xiang chi?
              what you want eat
              "What do you want to eat?"

         c)   Ni kanjian-le shei?
              you see-ASP who
              "Who did you see?"

         d)   *Shei ni kanjian-le?
              who you see-ASP
              "Who did you see?"

Chinese appears to have no *wh*-movement. Languages like this are called ***wh-in-situ*** languages because the *wh*-phrase remains in its base (theta) position. Why, then, is it the case that the [WH] features on the *wh*-phrases don't violate Full Interpretation? They are not in a local configuration with their C. Full Interpretation predicts that (21a) should be ungrammatical and (21b) should be grammatical – the exact opposite of the facts.

One possible solution to this problem is to slightly develop our model of grammar. Consider what actually happens when you say a sentence. Presumably after you construct the sentence in your head you pronounce it. So the next step after creation of S-structure is the phonological component of the grammar. Similarly, the sentence is not fully interpretable (or semantically comprehensible) until after S-structure. The semantic/interpretive part of the grammar must also follow S-structure. The name given to the phonological component in Minimalist approaches to grammar is ***Phonetic Form*** or ***PF***. The name given to the semantic/interpretive component is ***Logical Form*** or ***LF***. With these two additions the model of the grammar now looks like this:

22)   **The Lexicon** ————————————▶ X-bar rules   The Base

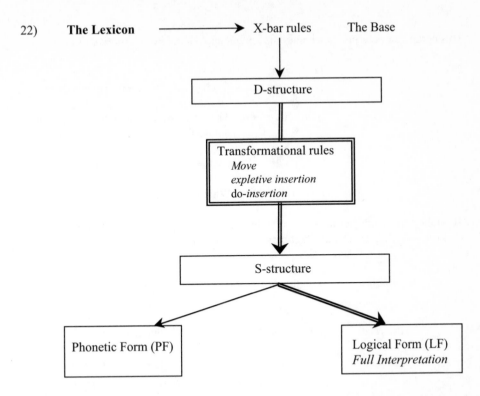

Chomsky (1993) makes two important claims. First he claims that Full Interpretation is a constraint that holds of sentences at LF, not S-Structure. Second, he claims that the operations that happen between D-structure and S-structure can also happen between S-Structure and LF. That means that transformations can apply on the left arrow between S-structure and LF in (22).

Some kinds of movement can happen *after* you say the sentence. At first glance this may seem very counter-intuitive, but it actually allows us to make the following remarkable claim about cross-linguistic variation: *All feature-checking movement happens in every single language.* The differences between languages are in when that movement occurs: before you start to say the sentence or after. Essentially there are two kinds of movement, movement that happens between D-structure and S-structure (called **overt** movement) and movement that happens between S-structure and LF (called **covert** movement). Since covert movement happens after the branching off to the PF (phonology) component you simply can't hear it happen. The differences between languages then, are in when they time specific instances of the general operation Move. English times those instances involving [WH] features overtly before S-structure, Chinese times those same movements covertly, after S-structure. This can be simply encoded in a parameter:

23)   Wh-*parameter*: Overt/Covert
        (English sets Overt, Chinese sets Covert)

This parameter determines whether movement applies before S-structure or after:

24)

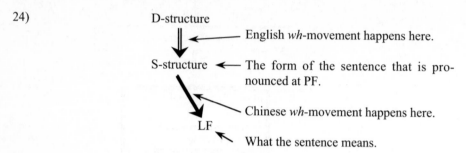

To make this clearer let us abstractly show each step of the derivation for Mandarin Chinese and English (I'm abstracting away from *do*-insertion, etc.):

25)

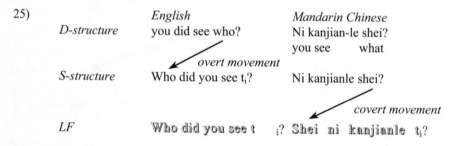

You'll notice that the LFs of this sentence are identical in both languages, but the S-structure is different. You never hear the LFs (in (25), this is indicated by writing the LFs in an outline font). You only hear the S-structures. The LFs are identical because the two sentences (in the two languages) mean the same thing.

This kind of story also allows us to get rid of the odd-man-out of transformations: Affix (T) lowering. This was the only movement that we looked at that went downwards. It also appeared to be in complementary distribution with V-movement. If a language has one, it doesn't have the other. This is suspicious; when we find items in complementary distribution, it suggests they are really instances of the same thing. With the system described above we can get rid of the affix lowering account of English. English doesn't have affix lowering. Instead, it has V → T movement like any other language, only in English it is timed covertly, so you never hear it.

26)   *French*   *English*
        D-structure Je souvent mange des pommes. I often eat apples.
                       I   often   eat   of.the apples

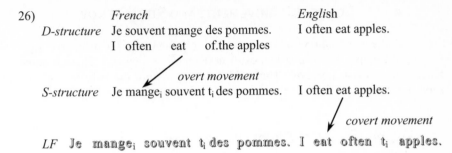

                              overt movement
        S-structure Je mange₍ᵢ₎ souvent t₍ᵢ₎ des pommes. I often eat apples.

                                    covert movement

LF Je mange₍ᵢ₎ souvent t₍ᵢ₎ des pommes. I eat often t₍ᵢ₎ apples.

Again, these sentences mean the same thing, so they have identical LFs. The word order in the two sentences is different, so the S-structures are different. Again this is encoded in a parameter:

27)   *Verb raising parameter*: Overt/Covert
        (French sets at Overt; English sets at Covert)[2]

In this view of things, differences in the word order of the world's languages reduce to a matter of timing in the derivation.

Strong vs. Weak Features

In this text, I've reduced timing effects like the covert/overt distinction to a parameter. This is actually a slightly different way of doing things than Chomsky (1993). Chomsky suggests that the overt/covert distinction is in fact encoded in the features that have to be checked, rather than in some parameter. English [WH] features are **strong** (that is they must be overtly checked); whereas Chinese [WH] features are **weak** (can be checked between S-structure and LF). Differences in languages thus become a lexical matter, as the features are associated with particular words. The differences between this account and the parameter one is relatively minor and need not concern us here. See Chomsky (1993 and 1995) for more discussion.

---

[2] Of course if you assume this, you can't claim that tense suffixes are generated in T, otherwise there is no way to get them onto the verb overtly. Chomsky (1993) gets around this problem by hypothesizing that the features that trigger movement aren't actual morphological items, like *-ed*, but instead are merely abstract features [+past]. The morphology on the verb is simply base generated on the verb in the lexicon and the features associated with it are checked at LF.

4.   Scope, LF Movement, and Subjacency

At first blush the whole notion of a movement you cannot hear seems pretty suspicious (just like empty words that you can't hear seems suspicious). There is some evidence it does exist, however. This evidence comes from the behavior of *wh*-questions in Chinese and from English sentences with quantifiers.

4.1   Subjacency/MLC Effects in Chinese

Let's compare two hypotheses. One is the covert movement hypothesis proposed above in section 3. That is, in Mandarin Chinese, *wh*-phrases move just as in English, but they move covertly, so that you don't hear the movement. The other hypothesis (on the surface less suspicious) is simply that *wh*-phrases don't move in Mandarin. Consider the predictions made by these two hypotheses with respect to island conditions and the Subjacency Condition (or MLC). Island effects are seen in English precisely because there is movement. Too long a movement (violating either subjacency or the MLC) causes the sentence to be ill-formed. When there is no movement, obviously, no violations of the MLC or Subjacency Constraint will occur. Now compare our two hypotheses about Chinese. The first hypothesis, according to which there is (covert) movement, predicts that Chinese will show subjacency violations. The other hypothesis predicts that no violations will appear since there is no *wh*-movement. Huang (1982) showed that Chinese does have *wh*-island (subjacency) effects. The following sentence is only ungrammatical with the meaning indicated (it is grammatical with other meanings).[3] This data is taken from Cheng (1997):

28)   Hufei xiang-zhi dao shei weishenme shengqi?
        Hufei want-know who why get angry
        *"For what reason(why)ᵢ does Hufei wonder who gets angry tᵢ?"

If this data can be explained by the Subjacency Constraint (or MLC), then we know that movement occurs – even if we can't hear it – because this constraint is sensitive to movement.

4.2   English Quantifiers and Scope

Let me introduce some concepts from formal logic. Words like *every* and *all* are often called **universal quantifiers** and are represented by the symbol $\forall$. Words like *some* are called **existential quantifiers** and are represented by the symbol $\exists$. In logic,

---

[3] For example, it can mean "Hufei wonders who gets angry why?" The distinction is subtle. Huang (1982) actually uses a slightly different mechanism for getting this result than the one I'm sketching out here, see the original work for more details.

quantifiers are said to hold *scope* over variables.[4] Variables are items that stand for arguments in the meaning of the sentence. The logical representation of an expression like *Everyone dances* is:

29) $\forall x$ [x dances]

This means that for any ($\forall$) person you choose (represented by x), then that person (x) dances. The quantifier $\forall$ has scope over the variable x.

An interesting phenomenon arises when we look at sentences with more than one quantifier. The following sentence is ambiguous in English:

30)   Everyone loves someone.

This can have two meanings. The first meaning is that for every person in the world there is some other person who they love: Mary loves John, Bill loves Susy, Rose loves Kim, ..., etc. The other meaning is that there is one person in the world that everyone else in the world loves: Mary loves John, Bill loves John, Rose loves John, ..., etc. Using a pseudo-logical paraphrase we can represent these two meanings as (30). The actual logical representations are given in (31):

31)   a)   For every person x, there is some person y, where x loves y.
        b)   For some person y, every person x loves y.

32)   a) $\forall x(\exists y[x \text{ loves } y])$
        b) $\exists y(\forall x[x \text{ loves } y])$

In logical notation, you'll notice that the difference between the two meanings lies in the order of the quantifiers, which reflects the embedding of the structure. The universal quantifier in (32a) is said to have *wide scope*, whereas in (32b) it has *narrow scope*.

In chapter 2, we claimed that if a sentence is ambiguous, then there are two tree structures for the sentence. It would be nice if we could draw two different trees that represent the two meanings of these sentences. One hypothesis about scope phenomena is that they reflect c-command. That is, a quantifier has scope over everything it c-commands.[5] Consider the meaning in (32a). We can easily see this scope when we draw the simplified tree (QP stands for Quantifier Phrase):

---

[4] This is a not entirely accurate statement. Quantifiers hold scope over constituents. Variables within a constituent that is in the scope of a particular quantifier are said to be bound by that quantifier. The distinction between quantifier binding and scope need not concern us here.
[5] A full discussion of the semantics and structure of scope lies well beyond the purview of this book. See Heim and Kratzer (1998) for more on this complicated topic.

33)

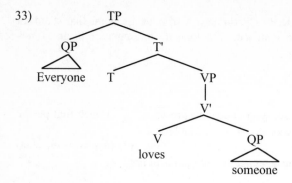

Everyone here c-commands *someone*, so the wide scope reading for the universal quantifier is derived. The narrow scope reading is more difficult, if this hypothesis is correct, then in the tree for (32b) *someone* must c-command *everyone*. The only way to get this fact is to move the quantifier. This kind of movement is called **quantifier raising** or **QR**.

34)

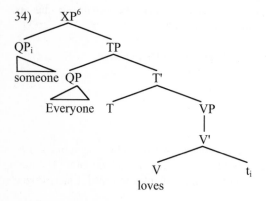

In this QR sentence, *someone* c-commands *everyone*, and so has scope over it. This derives the narrow scope reading for the universal quantifier. Obviously, this quantifier raising analysis cannot be overt. The surface string for this ambiguous sentence is *everyone loves someone* (not **someone everyone loves*). In order to get the second meaning for this sentence we need to propose movement you can't hear, in other words, covert movement. Covert movement thus has independent justification.[7]

---

[6] The landing site of QR is not clear, so I simply omit specification here.
[7] See Lasnik (1999a) for discussion of the possibility that there is no QR.

5. CONCLUSION

The story I've spun for you here covers a remarkable amount of material. It also unfortunately has many holes. This is partially because this is only meant to be an introductory textbook in syntactic structure. We couldn't possibly get into all the details of all the material, nor could we possibly consider all the possible arguments for (or against) a proposal like the overt/covert movement approach. In order to give such ideas their due, you'll need to take more advanced courses in syntax. Some good books that will take you on from where I've left you here are listed below, in the further reading section and the "Where to Go from Here" section at the end of the book. I hope that while other sections of this book have given you a firm foundation upon which you can build your syntactic knowledge, this chapter has given you a taste of current research in Minimalist syntax and the future of the discipline. This concludes our discussion of the Principle and Parameters/Minimalist model. In the final two chapters of this text, we discuss some related alternative approaches to syntax.

Some Other Features of Minimalism

The theory of Minimalism cannot all be contained in one chapter. Indeed, it would be hard to squeeze all the work done in this discipline into one book. However, I do want to mention in passing three other advances of Minimalism.

In this book, we looked extensively at X-bar theory. X-bar theory is one of the standard approaches to phrase structure. In Chomsky (1995), an alternative simpler approach, partially based on the work of Speas (1990) was proposed; this approach is called *Bare Phrase Structure* (BPS). In BPS, notions like XP and X' are not primitives and are not introduced by rules. Instead, they are read off of the tree. There is one simple rule, called *merge,* which takes two nodes and combines them into a third.

Another major trend in the minimalist literature has been over the number and nature of categories like T and C (called *Functional Categories*). Many different functional categories have been proposed and the question is hotly debated. Recent work has also focussed on deriving economy conditions from more general principles.

Minimalism has a particular programmatic and philosophical underpinning. I have not tried to explain this here. Please consult a book like Uriagereka (1998) for more on these issues.

For more on these questions, see the works in the further reading section at the end of this chapter.

IDEAS, RULES, AND CONSTRAINTS INTRODUCED IN THIS CHAPTER

i)   **Move** *(very informal version)*
        Move something somewhere.

ii)   **Full Interpretation**
        Features must be checked in a local configuration.

iii)   **Local Configuration**
        [WH], [NOM] features: Specifier/Head configuration.
        [ACC] features: Head/Complement configuration.
        [PST] etc, [Q] features: Head-head configuration.

iv)   **The Minimal Link Condition (MLC)**
        Movement must target the closest potential position.

v)   **Economy Conditions**
        Not looked at extensively in this book. These are conditions that hold be-
        tween derivations. If you have a pair of derivations where one has fewer
        movements, shorter movements, or later movements than the other, than the
        first is preferred. Shortest Move is the economy condition variant of the
        MLC.

vi)   **Logical Form (LF)**
        The semantic/interpretive system.

vii)   **Phonetic Form (PF)**
        The component of grammar where phonology occurs.

viii)   **Overt Movement**
        Movement between D-structure and S-structure (heard/pronounced move-
        ment).

ix)   **Covert Movement**
        Movement between S-structure and LF (silent movement).

x)   **Wh-***Parameter***:** Overt/Covert
        Verb raising Parameter: Overt/Covert

xi)   **Strong and Weak Features**
        Another way of encoding overt/covert parameters. Features are marked as
        strong if they need to be checked overtly, and weak if they are checked

covertly. This information is stored in the lexical entries of the words bearing the features.

xii)   ***Universal Quantifier ($\forall$)***
       Words such as *every, each, all, any.*

xiii) ***Existential Quantifier ($\exists$)***
       Words like *some,* or *a.*

xiv)   ***Scope***
       A quantifier's scope is the range of material it c-commands.

xv)   ***Wide vs. Narrow Scope***
       Wide scope is when one particular quantifier c-commands another quantifier. Narrow scope is the opposite.

xvi)   ***Quantifier Raising (QR)***
       A covert transformational rule that moves quantifiers.

xvi)   ***Bare Phrase Structure (BPS)***
       Not discussed beyond a mention in this textbook. This is a simplification of X-bar theory.

xvii) ***Merge***
       The name of the single phrase structure rule used in BPS. (Not discussed extensively in this chapter.)

xviii) ***Functional Categories***
       Categories like T, C, D, and P. These are the categories that hold the sentence together. (Not discussed extensively in this chapter.)

xix)   **Wh-*in-situ***
       When a *wh*-phrase stays in its case position. E.g., *what* in *Who loves what?*

FURTHER READING

(For information on textbooks that take you beyond the material contained in this book, please see "Where to Go from Here" at the end of the book.)

Cheng, Lisa (1997) *On the Typology of Wh-questions.* New York: Garland Press.
    [A dissertation on the various kinds of *wh*-questions, with a focus on Chinese.]

Chomsky, Noam (1991) Some notes on economy of derivation and representation. In
    R. Friedin (ed.) *Principles and Parameters in Comparative Grammar*. Cam-
    bridge: MIT Press. pp. 417–54.
    [The germs of the earliest work in Minimalism are found in this paper.]

Chomsky, Noam (1993) A Minimalist program for linguistic theory. In Kenneth L.
    Hale and Samuel J. Keyser (eds.) *The View from Building 20*. Cambridge: MIT
    Press. pp. 1–52.
    [The first Minimalist paper.]

Chomsky, Noam (1995) *The Minimalist Program*. Cambridge: MIT Press.
    [Chomsky's classic work on Minimalism. Not an easy read, but worth the effort.]

Heim, Irene and Kratzer, Angelika (1998) *Semantics in Generative Grammar*. Ox-
    ford: Blackwell.
    [This book is an introduction to semantics, and contains extensive discussion of quantifi-
    ers and quantifier scope.]

Huang, C.-T. James (1982) Logical Relations in Chinese and the Theory of Gram-
    mar. Ph.D. dissertation, MIT.
    [This dissertation examines the structure of Chinese *wh*-movement and the notion of LF.]

May, Robert (1985) *Logical Form*. Cambridge: MIT Press.
    [This book discusses at length quantifiers, scope, and quantifier raising.]

Radford, Andrew (1997a) *Syntactic Theory and the Structure of English: A Mini-
    malist Approach*. Cambridge: Cambridge University Press.
    [This is a fairly detailed introduction to Minimalism.]

Radford, Andrew (1997b*) Syntax: A Minimalist Introduction*. Cambridge: Cam-
    bridge University Press.
    [This is an accessible introduction to Minimalism.]

Saito, Mamoru and Howard Lasnik (1994) *Move Alpha: Conditions on its Applica-
    tion and Output*. Cambridge: MIT Press.
    [This work surveys the behavior of the rule Move (also known as Move-Alpha).]

Uriagereka, Juan (1998) *Rhyme and Reason: An Introduction to Minimalist Syntax*.
    Cambridge: MIT press.
    [This book, phrased as a dialogue between a syntactician and another scientist, explores
    many of the philosophical and technical issues underlying Minimalism.]

PROBLEM SETS

1. ENGLISH

In this chapter we proposed that the subjacency condition could be sub-sumed under the Minimal Link Condition (MLC). What problem do complex NP islands cause for this idea?

2. PF MOVEMENT

In the text above, we proposed that some movement was covert. That is, it happened between S-structure and LF. This movement affects meaning, but it doesn't affect how the sentence is pronounced. Can you think of any kind of movement that might occur just on the PF branch of the model? That is, are there any phenomena that affect only how the sentence is pronounced, but not its meaning?

3. SERBO-CROATIAN VS. ENGLISH *WH*-QUESTIONS

This is the same data that was in problem set 7 of chapter 11.

a) Ko šta gdje kupuje?
    who what where buys
    "Who buys what where?"

b) *Ko kupuje šta gdje?

c) *Ko šta kupuje gdje?

d) *Ko gdje kupuje šta?

Compare these sentences to the English:

e) *Who what where buys?
f) Who buys what where?
g) *Who what buys where?
h) *Who where buys what?

Using the terms "covert" and "overt movement," explain the difference in pa-rameter setting between Serbo-Croatian and English.

Part 4

Alternatives

chapter 13

Alternative Approaches: Lexical-Functional Grammar

0. ALTERNATIVE THEORIES

The first twelve chapters of this textbook are an introduction to syntactic theory from one particular perspective. That is the perspective of the Chomskyan Principles and Parameters (P&P) approach (and its descendant: Minimalism). While a large number of syntacticians (perhaps even a majority) operate using the assumptions and formalisms we've developed so far in this book, not everyone does. In this chapter and the next, we look at two other popular formalisms: *Lexical-Functional Grammar (LFG)* and *Head-Driven Phrase Structure Grammar (HPSG).*

In many ways, these theories have the same basic goals and assumptions as P&P syntax. LFG and HPSG are considered to be generative grammars, just like P&P or Minimalism. Where all these theories differ is in the precise formulation of the rules and constraints. We will have something to say about choosing among formalisms at the end of chapter 14, but to a great degree it comes down to a matter of the range of phenomena one wants to account for and one's preferred means of formal expression. My inclusion of these approaches is not meant to imply that they are better than P&P, nor to imply that P&P is better than them. They should simply be viewed as alternatives.

As a beginning syntactician, you might wonder why you should bother looking at alternative approaches. After all, a significant part of the literature and research being done in syntax uses the assumptions and formalisms developed in the first twelve chapters. Shouldn't we just pick one formalism and stick with it? To be honest, most researchers do just this; they do their work within only one formalism. For example, I do almost all of my research within the Minimalist approach. But this doesn't mean that I shouldn't be familiar with other formalisms too. An important body of work is conducted in these formalisms, and their results are often directly relevant to work being done in Chomskyan P&P or Minimalist syntax. Being able to interpret work done in these alternative approaches is a very useful skill (and unfortunately, one rarely taught to beginning syntacticians). The results found in other approaches to syntax have often affected the development of P&P theory. For example, the lexical approach to passives (whereby the passive morphology affects the thematic and case assigning properties of the underlying verbal morphology) replaced an earlier purely transformational approach to passives. This idea was borrowed from LFG. Similarly, the idea of feature checking is directly related to the notion of unification found in both LFG and HPSG. So I encourage you to keep an open mind and consider the advantages of being familiar with more than one formalism.

Even More Theories

In this book, we're only looking two alternatives to P&P theory. There are many other approaches to syntax that we're not going to look at in any detail. Several other theories that are generally considered to be part of the basic generative approach to grammar are Relational Grammar (RG), its descendant Arc Pair Grammar (APG), and Categorial Grammar. Other related formalisms include Autolexical Syntax and Tree Adjoining Grammar (TAG). These theories, although now quite different from one another, find their origins in early Generative Grammar. The approach known as Optimality Theory (OT), has a strong following among phonologists, and is growing in popularity among syntacticians.

Outside these formal approaches, there are a number of approaches to grammar that take a very different philosophical approach to the material than we do here. These are often called Functionalist theories of grammar. These include Cognitive Grammar (CG), Construction Grammar, Functional Grammar, Word Grammar, Stratificational Grammar, Systemic Grammar, and Role and Reference Grammar (RRG).

Obviously, we don't have room in a book like this to look at all these different approaches. The further reading section at the end of this chapter contains some pointers to books that look at these alternate approaches.

---

1.   THE ORIGINS OF LFG

The version of Chomskyan syntax current in the 1970s was called the Extended Standard Theory (EST); it was much more heavily reliant on transformations than P&P or Minimalism. Several researchers, including LFG founders Joan Bresnan and Ronald Kaplan, were dissatisfied with EST. First, they observed that a lot of syntactic information seems to extend beyond the basic phrase structure.[1] Take for example the issue of grammatical relations (subject, object, etc.). In EST (and P&P) grammatical relations are determined by the position an element takes in the tree. For example, subjects are in specifiers, objects are the complements to verbs, etc. In LFG, by contrast, grammatical relations are primitives. They are not read off the tree and instead are a basic tool for the grammar.

The other very significant departure from Chomskyan grammar is the fact that LFG does not use transformations. One argument for getting rid of (some) transformations comes from ***movement paradoxes***. The following data and arguments are taken from Bresnan (2001). Observe the following fact about the predicate *talked about*. This predicate requires an NP complement, and cannot take a CP complement:

1)   a)   We talked about [NP the fact that he was sick] for days.
     b)   *We talked about [CP that he was sick] for days.

When we move this complement,[2] however, this restriction is lifted:

2)   [CP That he was sick] we talked about___ for DAYS.

A similar effect is seen with verbal inflection. The auxiliary *will* requires a bare non-finite form of the following verb. The auxiliary *have*, by contrast, requires a participle, and disallows bare non-finite forms:

3)   a)   I will meet you.
     b)   *I will met you.
     c)   *I have meet him.
     d)   I have met him.

When you front the VP however, both auxiliaries can take the bare infinitive.

4)   a)   And meet you, I will.
     b)   And meet him, I have.

Finally, consider the inflection of the verb *to be* found with contracted negatives. In American English, the contracted form *amn't* is not allowed. In this dialect, there is no way to contract a negative with a first person form of the verb *to be*.

5)   I am not /*amn't/*aren't your friend.

---

[1] Many of the developments from the EST to Principles and Parameters, were in fact a response to this kind of criticism.

[2] We have not previously discussed the kind of movement seen in (2). This is often called topicalization. Topicalization may be a kind of *wh*-movement, where topics (the old information in the sentence) are fronted to the specifier of CP.

Somewhat surprisingly, once you do subject/auxiliary inversion, a contracted form is allowed. But even stranger, it takes the form normally found with second person pronouns: *aren't*.

6)   Aren't I your friend?/ *Amn't I your friend.

Notice from (5), that *aren't* is never found in non-questions with a first person pronoun. Bresnan reasons that if movement is actually deriving the word order, then we should find the same forms and the same kinds of restrictions on these forms in both the surface and base positions.[3]

In the next few sections, we sketch the basic mechanics of LFG. The treatment here is necessarily sketchy to keep this chapter to a reasonable length. The main points are presented here, but for a more complete view you should look at one of the introductory LFG sources listed in the further reading section below.

2.   C-STRUCTURE

One major part of LFG is almost identical to the approach taken in the rest of the book. This is the idea that the words of a sentence are organized into constituents, which are represented by a tree, and generated by rules. In LFG, these trees are called the *c-structure*, and are roughly equivalent to the S-structure in P&P.[4] Many LFG theorists adopt X-bar theory, but it is not as strictly applied to all languages. For example, LFG posits a flat (VP-less) structure for many VSO languages (Kroeger 1993) and "free word order" or "non-configurational" languages like Warlpiri (Simpson 1991). This said, most LFG c-structures look just like the S-structure trees we have built elsewhere in this book. There is one major exception to this, since there is no movement, there are (for the most part) no traces (nor are there any other null elements).

3.   FUNCTIONS

As you might guess from its name, there are two driving forces in Lexical-Functional Grammar: the lexicon (which we explore in section 4 below) and functions. The notion of function is borrowed from math and computer science. A

---

[3] One thing we haven't talked about extensively in this book is the interaction of the syntactic component with other parts of the grammar. The assumption Bresnan makes here is that morphology happens before syntax. In some versions of Minimalism (see for example Halle and Marantz 1993), morphology applies after the syntax has already constructed the tree. If this is the case, then Bresnan's argument doesn't necessarily go through.

[4] Because LFG doesn't use transformations, there is no D-structure. Phrase structure rules directly build the c-structure (= S-structure). Displaced items are dealt with in other ways. See below.

function is a rule that maps from one item to another.[5] There are really two kinds of functions in LFG, which can be a bit confusing. The first kind are called ***grammatical functions*** and are things like subject, object, etc. We called these grammatical relations in chapter 3. When a practitioner of LFG talks about functions, they are primarily talking about grammatical functions. The other kind of function is the principles which map between the different parts of the grammar, such as the mapping between the c-structure and the structure that represents the grammatical functions is called an ***f-structure***. We are going to look at grammatical functions here, then turn to the mapping relations in section 5.

In P&P syntax, grammatical functions or relations are read off of the tree. That is, you know what the subject of a sentence is by looking for the NP that is in the specifier of TP. Similarly, the object is defined as any NP that is the sister to a verb.

7)

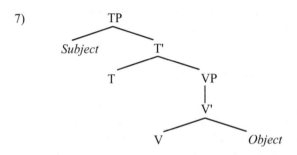

In LFG, grammatical functions are not defined by a tree; instead, they are primitive notions (meaning they can't be derived somehow). Every sentence has an f-structure which represents grammatical functions. In this structure, a particular NP will be identified as being the subject of the sentence, quite independent of the tree structure associated with the sentence. In the sentence *Diana loves phonology*, *Diana* is equated with the SUBJ grammatical function. This equation is usually represented in what is called an ***Attribute Value Matrix (AVM)***; the item on the left is the attribute or function, the item on the right is the value attributed to that function:

8)   [SUBJ   [PRED[6] 'Diana']]

Attributes can have various kinds of values, including other AVMs. For example, the value for the SUBJ function in sentence (9) is itself a matrix containing other functions:

9)   The professor loves phonology.

---

[5] If you are unfamiliar with this notion you might want to consult a good "mathematics for linguists" textbook, such as Allwood, Andersson and Dahl (1977).
[6] The term PRED here is a bit confusing, since 'Diana' is an argument of the clause. PRED here can be, very loosely, translated as the semantic head of the AVM.

10)

$$
\begin{bmatrix}
\text{...} & \\
\text{SUBJ} & \begin{bmatrix} \text{PRED} & \text{'professor'} \\ \text{DEF} & + \\ \text{NUM} & \text{sng} \end{bmatrix}
\end{bmatrix}
$$

In the embedded AVM, the function PRED tells you the lexical content of the subject NP, DEF tells you if it is definite or not, NUM tells you the number, etc. These are all properties of the subject. You'll notice that more than just grammatical functions are represented in these structures; various kinds of other features (like definiteness, etc.) are as well.

Once you combine all the AVMs for all the parts of a sentence you get the f-structure, containing all the sentence's featural and functional information. Where does all this featural information come from? Most of the information that is combined into the f-structure comes from the lexical entries of all the words in the sentence. The lexicon thus plays an important role in this theory.

4.   THE LEXICON

The lexicon is where a lot of the work in LFG is done. For example, the idea that we adopted in chapter 9 that passives involve a *lexical* morphological operation deleting the external argument is borrowed from the LFG literature. We return to operations like the passive, and how they work in LFG, in section 6 below. All the information that ends up in an f-structure starts out in the lexical entries of the words that compose the sentence.

The equivalent to a theta grid in LFG is the *a-structure* or argument structure.[7] As in P&P syntax, the a-structure is part of the lexical entry for the predicate. Simplifying somewhat, the lexical entry for the inflected verb *loves* is seen in (11). For the moment, ignore the arrows; I'll explain these below in section 5.

11)   *loves*:   V $(\uparrow\text{PRED}) = $ 'love $<(\uparrow\text{SUBJ}),(\uparrow\text{OBJ})>$'
                        $(\uparrow\text{TENSE}) = $ present
                        $(\uparrow\text{SUBJ NUM}) = $ sng
                        $(\uparrow\text{SUBJ PERS}) = $ 3rd

This lexical entry says that *love* is a verb which means 'love', and takes two arguments, an obligatory subject and an obligatory object (as contained within the $< >$ brackets). The parentheses here do *not* mean "optional" – as both arguments are, indeed, obligatory. It also tells us that *loves* is the present tense form. (The lexical

---

[7] This is a gross oversimplification, I'm ignoring a large number of mapping operations here. I'm also ignoring the complexities of inflectional morphology and how they interact with the featural structure. See Bresnan (2001) or Falk (forthcoming) for extensive discussion.

entry for *loved* would have a different value for TENSE.) And that the subject is third person singular. ((↑SUBJ NUM) means "my subject's number is ...")

All lexical items bring some information to the sentence, not just predicates. For example, we know that the determiner *the* is definite and such information is contained in its lexical entry.

12)   *the:*   D   (↑DEF) = +

Functional and featural information comes with the lexical item when it is inserted into the c-structure (as we will see below).

5.   F-STRUCTURE

F-structures, as noted above, are the set of all the attribute value pairs for a sentence. Perhaps the easiest way to see this is to look at an example. We use again the sentence *the professor loves phonology*. An f-structure for this sentence is given in (13):

13)

$$
\begin{bmatrix}
\text{PRED} & \text{'love <SUBJ, OBJ>'} \\
\text{TENSE} & \text{present} \\
\text{SUBJ} & \begin{bmatrix} \text{DEF} & + \\ \text{NUM} & \text{sng} \\ \text{PRED} & \text{'professor'} \end{bmatrix} \\
\text{OBJ} & [\text{PRED} \quad \text{'phonology'}]
\end{bmatrix}
$$

The topmost PRED function tells you what the predicate of the sentence is. It also contains information about the a-structure of the sentence. The TENSE feature tells you about the tense of the sentence. The SUBJ and OBJ functions have submatrices (containing information on their internal structure) as values.

C-structures must be related to f-structures somehow. This is accomplished with the use of variables. Consider the simple c-structure in (14), I am using an S here to avoid issues of head movement (which are discussed in section 6). Each lexical item is followed by the information it contributes by virtue of its lexical entry. Each node in the tree is marked with a *variable* (f_1, f_2, f_3, ..., etc.). These will be used in mapping to the f-structure. Again, ignore the arrows for the moment.

14)

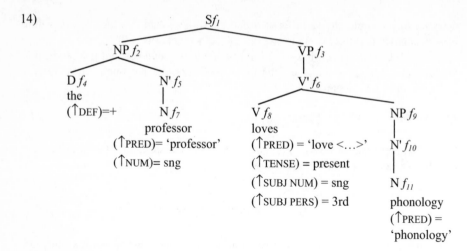

Each of these variables corresponds to a pair of matrix brackets in the f-structure. There is *no* one-to-one correspondence here. Multiple nodes in the tree can correspond to the same AVM:

14')

$$f_1, f_3, f_6, f_8, \begin{bmatrix} \text{PRED} & \text{'love <SUBJ, OBJ>'} \\[1em] \text{TENSE} & \text{present} \\[1em] \text{SUBJ} & f_2, f_4, f_5, f_7, \begin{bmatrix} \text{DEF} & + \\ \text{NUM} & \text{sng} \\ \text{PRED} & \text{'professor'} \end{bmatrix} \\[2em] \text{OBJ} & f_9, f_{10}, f_{11}, [\text{PRED} \quad \text{'phonology'}] \end{bmatrix}$$

This means that the information contained in nodes f_2, f_4, f_5, f_7 contribute the SUBJ features to the sentence. f_9, f_{10}, f_{11}, provide the OBJ info, etc.

The mapping formally happens through what is called an ***f-description***. The f-description is set out with ***functional equations***. These equations tell us, for example, that the subject of the sentence f_1 corresponds to the constituent f_2. This is written as:

15) $(f_1 \text{ SUBJ}) = f_2$

The fact that the subject NP (f_2) is definite is encoded in D node (f_4):

16) $f_2 = f_4$

When a node is a head, or simply passes information up the tree (e.g., V' or V), then a simple equivalence relation is stated:

17) $f_3 = f_6$

These functional equations control how information is mapped through the tree and between the tree and the f-structure. Each piece of information in the f-structure comes from (various places in) the tree as controlled by the functional equations in the f-description.

In order to make this clearer, as a notational device, c-structures are often annotated with their functional equations. There is a useful device that is used to clarify these annotations. These are ***metavariables***. Metavariables are variables that stand for other variables. There are two metavariables:

18)   a)   ↓ means "this node"
      b)   ↑ means "my mother" (immediately dominating node)

So the equation ↑=↓ means "all of the features I have also belong to my mother" – in other words, a head. The notation (↑SUBJ)=↓ means "I represent the subject function of my mother".

We also saw these arrows in lexical entries. They mean the same thing here. (↑PRED) = 'love' means "the terminal node that I fill has the predicate value of 'love'."

Here is the c-structure in (14) repeated with the functional equations annotated using metavariables:

14')

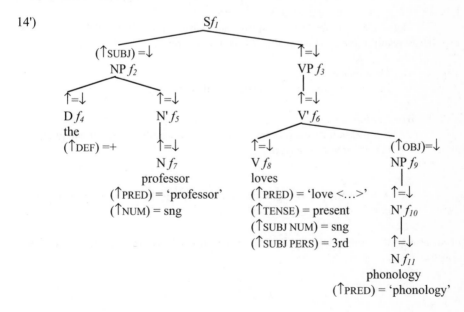

> **LFG as a Computational Model**
> You may have noticed that LFG is a very precise, mathematical model.
> There are strict rules controlling how information follows through the
> sentence and between levels. This has made it a favorite among com-
> puter scientists as a means of representing grammatical structure when
> they try to model human language.

     Unification is the idea that features and functions coming from disparate places in the tree must be compatible with one another. Take, for example, the fact that the verb specifies that its subject must be third person singular (as marked by the suffix *-s*). If the subject has number or person features, then those features must match the verb's subject features in the f-structure. This is forced by the fact that the f-structure (in mathematical terms) solves for, or is the solution to, the set of functional equations known as the functional description. If the features didn't match, then the f-structure wouldn't unify. Notice that this is a very similar notion to the idea of feature checking, discussed in chapters 9, 11, and 12. Feature checking also ensures compatibility of features coming from different parts of the sentence. Minimalism simply uses movement, rather than functional equations, to guarantee this. Both systems have their advantages; LFG's system has a certain mathematical precision and elegance that P&P movement and feature checking does not. By contrast, P&P/Minimalism is able to derive word order differences between languages from feature checking and movement. Minimalism thus provides a slightly more elegant theory of word order than LFG, which uses language-specific phrase structure rules. It is not at all clear which approach is preferable.

     There are a number of constraints on f-structures. Three of these conspire together to result in the LFG equivalent of the theta criterion:

19)   a)   *Uniqueness*
             In a given f-structure, a particular attribute may have at most one value.

        b)   *Completeness*
             An f-structure must contain all the governable grammatical functions that its predicate governs.

        c)   *Coherence*
             All the governable grammatical functions in an f-structure must be governed by a local predicate.

(19a) is also the constraint that forces unification. All f-structures must meet these constraints.

5.1   Why F-structures?

We now have a fairly detailed sketch of the basics of LFG. Before turning to some implementations of the model dealing with some of the empirical issues we've looked at elsewhere in this book, it is worth considering why the LFG model uses f-structures. The answer is fairly straightforward: Information about a particular grammatical function may come from more than one place in the tree and, more importantly, the sources of information do not have to be constituents. Falk (forthcoming) gives the example of the pair of following sentences:

20)   a)   The deer are dancing.
        b)   The deer is dancing.

The form of the subject noun is identical in both of these sentences. However, in terms of meaning, it is plural in (20a) and singular in (20b). Let's assume that the lexical entry for the form 'deer' lacks any specification for number:

21)   *deer*   N   ($\uparrow$PRED) = 'deer'

The number associated with the subject function in the sentences in (20) comes from the auxiliary:

22)   a)   *are* T   ($\uparrow$TENSE) = present
                             ($\uparrow$SUBJ NUM) = pl
        b)   *is*   T   ($\uparrow$TENSE) = present
                             ($\uparrow$SUBJ NUM) = sg

While the number comes from the auxiliary, it is only really a property of the subject. The NUM feature still gets mapped to the SUBJ function, because of the functional annotation ($\uparrow$SUBJ NUM)=pl. You can see this in the following simplified representations, where the mapping between c-structure and f-structure is informally represented with arrows.

23)   a)

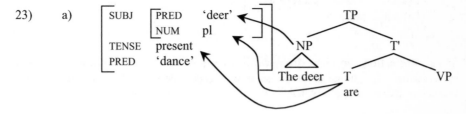

b)
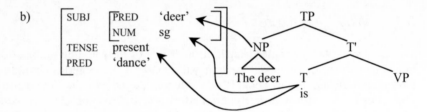

Similar facts are seen in "free[8] word order" or "non-configurational" languages, like the aboriginal Warlpiri language spoken in Australia. Contra the Golden Rule of constituency we discussed in chapter 2, in Warlpiri, words that modify one another do not have to appear as constituents on the surface. In the following sentence (data taken from Simpson (1991), argument from Bresnan (2001)), the adjective *wita-jarra-rlu* 'small' modifies *kurdu-jarra-rlu* 'two children.' Similarly, *yalumpu* 'that' modifies *maliki* 'dog.' Notice that these do not form contiguous strings of words and there are no obvious constituents here. We know what the modification relations are because of the case marking (ERG or ABS) on the various words. We can see that the information that maps onto the subject or object functions comes from various parts of the sentence:

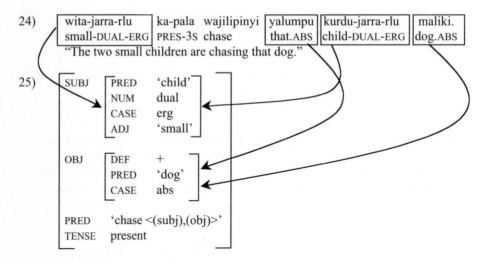

24)

wita-jarra-rlu	ka-pala	wajilipinyi	yalumpu	kurdu-jarra-rlu	maliki.
small-DUAL-ERG	PRES-3S	chase	that.ABS	child-DUAL-ERG	dog.ABS

"The two small children are chasing that dog."

25)

SUBJ   [PRED   'child'
         NUM   dual
         CASE   erg
         ADJ   'small']

OBJ   [DEF   +
         PRED   'dog'
         CASE   abs]

PRED   'chase <(subj),(obj)>'
TENSE present

Since information can come from various parts of the tree, this points towards a system where functional information is not read directly off the tree; instead, an f-structure-like level is motivated.[9]

---

[8] It isn't at all clear that the word order of these languages is actually "free"; indeed, the order may reflect discourse factors such as what is topical (old information) and what is focused (new information).

[9] It is worth briefly mentioning how P&P deals with these same facts. At D-structure, these units do form constituents. A transformation, known as **scrambling** (see the exercises in

6.   ASSORTED PHENOMENA

Having now quickly laid out the fundamentals of LFG (c-structure, f-structure, the lexicon, etc.), we turn to how various phenomena discussed in other parts of this book are treated in LFG.

6.1   Head Mobility

In chapter 8, we analyzed alternations between the position of a tensed verb and the position of auxiliaries in languages like French, Vata, or Irish as involving head-to-head movement. Recall the data from French and English:

26)

a)	I	T	often	eat	apples
b)	Je	mange	souvent		des pommes
c)	I	have	often	eaten	apples
d)	J'	ai	souvent	mangé	des pommes

In French, the main verb alternates in its position relative to the adverb *souvent*, depending upon the presence or absence of an auxiliary. When an auxiliary is present, the verb stays in its base position. When there is no auxiliary, the verb moves to T. Although LFG has no movement, it has a related account of these phenomena. LFG simply posits that tensed verbs and untensed participial forms belong to different categories. This is called **head mobility**. Tensed verbs are of category T, whereas untensed forms are of category V:

27)   a) *mange* T $(\uparrow \text{PRED}) = $ 'eat $<(\uparrow \text{SUBJ}), (\uparrow \text{OBJ})>$'
                      $(\uparrow \text{TENSE}) = $ present
         b) *mangé* V $(\uparrow \text{PRED}) = $ 'eat $<(\uparrow \text{SUBJ}), (\uparrow \text{OBJ})>$'
         c) *ai*   T $(\uparrow \text{TENSE}) = $ present[10]

(26b) uses the lexical entry in (27a), and has a c-structure as in (28a). (26d) uses the two lexical entries in (27b and c) and gives the c-structure in (28b):

---

chapter 11), then reorders the elements so they don't surface as constituents. Both approaches achieve essentially the same results with different underlying assumptions.

[10] The sentence *J'ai souvent mangé des pommes* also bears what are called aspect features. We leave these aside here.

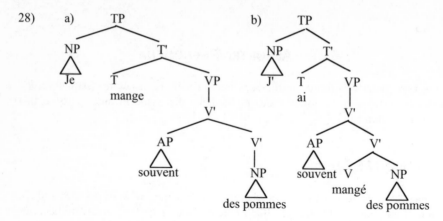

You'll notice that in (28a) the VP has no head V. This is allowed in LFG, but not in P&P theory (as it violates the endocentric properties of X-bar theory).

In English, both participles and tensed verbs are of the category V; only auxiliaries are of category T:

29)   a) *eat*   V   ($\uparrow$PRED) ='eat <($\uparrow$SUBJ), ($\uparrow$OBJ)>'
                          ($\uparrow$TENSE) = present
       b) *eaten*   V   ($\uparrow$PRED) ='eat <($\uparrow$SUBJ), ($\uparrow$OBJ)>'
       c) *have*   T   ($\uparrow$TENSE) = present

This means that both the participle and the tensed form will appear in the VP and no outward appearance of head movement will arise.

As an aside we can briefly note that these two approaches to position alternations actually make different predictions. First, let's pull together some threads from chapters 8 and 12. In chapter 12, we proposed the Minimal Link Condition, by which movement must always occur to the closest potential landing site. Consider what this means when we look at questions with auxiliaries in French. Recall that French main verbs can undergo T → C movement if they are tensed. If you think carefully about the MLC, you'll see that they must stop off in the T head before proceeding to C, as T is the closest potential landing site:

30)

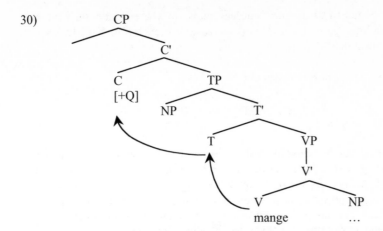

This means that movement can't skip a head on the way up. You can either move through all the heads, or move just the highest head but there is no skipping. The movement approach thus correctly predicts that (30a and b) will be grammatical, but (31c) where the V head has skipped the T (as indicated by the presence of the auxiliary) will be ill-formed:

31)   a)   Mangez-vous t_T t_V des pommes?

      eat you   of.the apples
      "Do you eat the apples?"

    b)   Avez-vous t_T mangé des pommes?

      have you   eaten of.the apples
      "Have you eaten the apples?"

    c)   *Mangé-vous [$_T$ avez] t_v des pommes?

      eat you   have of.the apples
      "Have you eaten the apples?" (Lit: "Eat you have the apples?")

Movement of the verb around an auxiliary is predicted to be ill-formed by the MLC.

In LFG, by contrast, there is no *a priori* reason why we couldn't allow a verb to be of category C (without tense) and have an auxiliary of category T. So, in a sense, LFG predicts (31c) could be well-formed. To be fair, however, LFG has other ways of ruling out sentence (31c). For example, LFG could stipulate that French verbs that are of category C must also contain the sentence's tense information. Notice, however, that while LFG can mechanically churn out the facts with such a stipulation, the facts don't fall out from anything principled as they do in P&P.

Also to be fair to LFG, there is at least one case where head movement may appear to skip an intervening head: This is the case of French *pas* 'not.' If *pas* is a head, then head movement skips it:

32)   Je ne-mange [$_{NEG}$ pas] t$_V$ des pommes.

I   eat   not   of.the apples
"I don't eat apples."

In LFG, this fact is straightforwardly dealt with. The P&P literature gets around this problem by treating *pas* as the specifier of NegP, and *ne* (which is attached to the verb) as the head. As the verb moves through the Neg head, on its way to T, it picks up *ne*. Since *pas* is in the specifier position, it stays in place, and can be skipped by the head movement. This analysis is controversial even among practitioners of P&P. Other potential counterexamples, include the so-called "long head movement" found in Breton and the Slavic Languages (see Rivero 1991).

6.2   Passives

In chapter 9, the analysis of passives we proposed involved two parts. The first is a morphological operation that changes the argument structure of the verb and steals the verb's ability to check accusative case. The second part of the passive is syntactic: The object moves from the complement to the VP to the subject position for Case reasons. As we noted above, one of the crucial differences between LFG and P&P is in their treatment of grammatical functions. LFG's basic grammatical functions allow us to do passives in just one step, which all happens in the lexicon. In LFG there is no syntactic component to passives. Instead there is a simple lexical change associated with the passive morphology:

33)   a)   *kiss*   V   ($\uparrow$PRED) ='kiss <($\uparrow$SUBJ), ($\uparrow$OBJ)>'

             +en

        b)   *kissed*$_{pass}$ V   ($\uparrow$PRED) ='kiss <   Ø   ($\uparrow$SUBJ) >'

When the lexical entry in (33b) is inserted into a c-structure, the original object is directly placed into the subject position. There is no movement.

> **Movement or Grammatical Function Changing?**
> It is hard to decide which approach is better. On one hand, LFG has a simpler account of passives than P&P; it involves only one operation. On the other hand, this simplicity comes at the expense of having primitive (that is non-derived) grammatical functions/relations. The elegance of LFG's analysis of the passive involves a complication to the underlying machinery of the system.

6.3   Raising and Control

Before getting into LFG's analysis of raising and control constructions, we need to introduce the theory's treatment of non-finite complements. In most versions of LFG, these are not treated as CPs. Instead, they are most often treated as VP constituents. The special category VP' has been created to host *to*. The c-structure for a typical raising construction is seen in (34):

34)

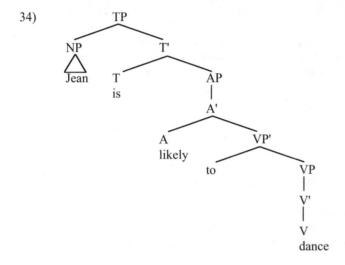

An almost identical c-structure is used in control constructions:

35)

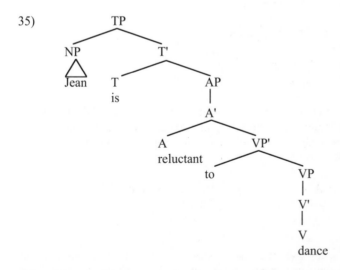

The differences between control and raising constructions are expressed in lexical entries and f-structures, not in the phrase structure (c-structure) as in P&P.

Let's start with control constructions.[11] LFG uses a special grammatical function to represent non-finite complements. Since embedded predicates in these constructions don't have their subject expressed overtly, they are considered ***open functions*** (that is, they are missing an argument). The grammatical function used to represent open functions is XCOMP (or XAJU in the case of adjuncts). Predicates like *is likely* and *is reluctant* select for XCOMPS in their lexical entries. The lexical entry for *reluctant* is given in (36):

36)   *reluctant*   A $(\uparrow\text{PRED}) = $ 'reluctant $<(\uparrow\text{SUBJ}), (\uparrow\text{XCOMP})>$

Reluctant takes a thematic subject and an open function as its arguments. When we combine this with a predicate such as *dance*, we get an f-structure like the following for the sentence *Jean is reluctant to dance*:

37) $*\begin{bmatrix} \text{SUBJ} & [\text{ PRED } \text{ 'Jean' }] \\ \\ \text{PRED} & \text{'reluctant } <(\uparrow\text{SUBJ}), (\uparrow\text{XCOMP})>' \\ \text{TENSE} & \text{present} \\ \text{XCOMP} & \begin{bmatrix} \text{SUBJ} & ?????? \\ \text{PRED} & \text{'dance } <(\uparrow\text{SUBJ})>' \end{bmatrix} \end{bmatrix}$

This f-structure is ill-formed, because it violates the principle of completeness: The subject function of the XCOMP is not filled. This is resolved using the LFG equivalent of control: ***functional control***. Functional control is indicated with a curved line linking the two functions.

38) $\begin{bmatrix} \text{SUBJ} & [\text{ PRED } \text{ 'Jean' }] \\ \\ \text{PRED} & \text{'reluctant } <(\uparrow\text{SUBJ}), (\uparrow\text{XCOMP})>' \\ \text{TENSE} & \text{present} \\ \text{XCOMP} & \begin{bmatrix} \text{SUBJ} & [\quad] \\ \text{PRED} & \text{'dance } <(\uparrow\text{SUBJ})>' \end{bmatrix} \end{bmatrix}$

This indicates that the subject of the main clause is also the subject of the non-finite complement. Functional control is licensed by the lexical entry of the main clause verb. Here is a revised lexical entry for *reluctant* that contains a control equation (a statement that licenses the curved line in (38):

36')   *reluctant*   A $(\uparrow\text{PRED}) = $ 'reluctant $<(\uparrow\text{SUBJ}), (\uparrow\text{XCOMP})>$
                                         $(\uparrow\text{SUBJ}) = (\uparrow \text{ XCOMP SUBJ})$

---

[11] I am simplifying the situation here. The range of phenomena P&P theory groups as "control" constructions divide into two groups in the LFG analysis: functional control and anaphoric control, which have different properties. We won't distinguish these here. See Falk (forthcoming) or Bresnan (2001) for explanations of the difference.

In English, the second line of this entry stipulates that the subject of the main predicate is identical to the subject of the XCOMP. Notice that this is essentially the equivalent of the thematic analysis of control discussed in chapter 10, and suffers from the same empirical problems as a thematic analysis (see the discussion in chapter 10 to remind yourself of these facts).

In control constructions, the controller must *f-command* the controllee. One node f-commands another if it is less deeply embedded in the f-structure (inside fewer square brackets).

Interestingly, raising constructions have a similar analysis. They also involve functional control. The difference between them and more traditional control constructions is simply that the subject argument of the raising predicate is non-thematic (doesn't get a theta role – indicated by writing it outside the < > brackets), and it is linked to a particular argument in its complement's argument structure (as indicated by the second line of the lexical entry). To see this, consider the lexical entry for *likely*:

39)   *likely*   A $(\uparrow\text{PRED}) =$ 'likely $<(\uparrow\text{XCOMP})>(\uparrow\text{SUBJ})$'
                                 $(\uparrow\text{SUBJ}) = (\uparrow\text{XCOMP SUBJ})$

The first line of this lexical entry puts the subject argument outside the angle brackets (< >), indicating that it doesn't get a theta role. The second line specifies that the argument which fills this function is the thematic subject of the open function. Again, in the f-structure this is indicated with a curved line. The following is the f-structure for *Jean is likely to dance*:

40)
$$
\begin{bmatrix}
\text{SUBJ} & [\text{PRED} \quad \text{'Jean'}] \\
\\
\text{PRED} & \text{'likely} <(\uparrow\text{XCOMP})>, (\uparrow\text{SUBJ})\text{'} \\
\text{TENSE} & \text{present} \\
\text{XCOMP} & \begin{bmatrix} \text{SUBJ} & [\quad] \\ \text{PRED} & \text{'dance} <(\uparrow\text{SUBJ})>\text{'} \end{bmatrix}
\end{bmatrix}
$$

The difference between the raising and the control sentence simply reduces to a matter of argument structure.

6.4   Wh-*movement: Long Distance Dependencies*

The sharing of feature structures (as expressed by the curved line) is also used to define long distance dependencies such the relationship between a *wh*-phrase and the gap (or trace) it is associated with. There is a special grammatical function: FOCUS, which is found in *wh*-constructions. I'll abstract away from the details, but in English, this function is associated with the specifier of CP. The element taking the FOCUS function must share features with some argument (this is forced on the sentence by the constraint of coherence). The following is the f-structure for the sentence *Which novel do you think Anne read?* (COMP is the function assigned tensed embedded clauses.)

41)

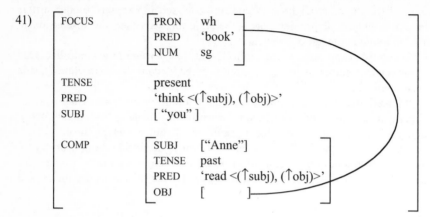

The FOCUS shares the features of the OBJ function of the complement clause, indicating that they are identical.

There is much more to *wh*-dependencies in LFG than this simple picture. For example, LFG has an account of island conditions based on f-structures. There is also an explict theory of licensing *wh*-dependencies. For more on this see the readings in the further reading section at the end of the chapter.

7.   CONCLUSION

This concludes our whirlwind tour of Lexical-Functional Grammar. A single chapter does not give me nearly enough space to cover the range and depth of this theory, and as such doesn't give LFG the opportunity to really shine. I've glossed over many details and arguments here, but I hope this chapter gives you enough information to pursue further reading in this alternative framework. Remember that the results derived in frameworks like LFG can give us insights about the way human language works. If we're clever enough, we should be able to incorporate these insights into the P&P or Minimalist framework, too. Similarly, a student of LFG should be able to use the insights of Minimalism or P&P to inform their theorizing. Remember that syntactic theories are only hypotheses about the way syntax is organized. We really don't know which approach, if any of these, is right. So by looking at other theoretical approaches we question our basic assumptions, and consider new alternatives.

IDEAS, RULES, AND CONSTRAINTS INTRODUCED IN THIS CHAPTER

i) **Movement Paradoxes**
When the form or behavior of a moved item is not identical to the form or behavior of the item in its base position.

ii) **C-structure**
Constituent structure. The tree in LFG. Roughly equivalent to S-structure in P&P.

iii) **Grammatical Function**
Same thing as a grammatical relation. Common grammatical functions:

SUBJ   subject
OBJ   object
PRED   predicate
XCOMP   open complement (non-finite clause)
COMP   closed complement (finite embedded clause)
FOCUS   the function associated with *wh*-phrases

iv) **F-structure**
The level of representation where grammatical functions are unified.

v) **Attribute Value Matrix (AVM)**
A matrix that has an attribute (or function) on the left and its value on the right. The set of all AVMs for a sentence form the sentence's f-structure.

vi) **A-structure**
Argument structure. The LFG equivalent of the theta grid.

vii) **Variables**
LFG uses variables $(f_1, f_2, f_3, \ldots,$ etc.) for each node on the c-structure which are used in the mapping between c-structure and f-structure.

viii) **Functional Equation**
An equation that maps one variable to another (e.g., $(f_1 \text{ SUBJ}) = f_2$ says that f_2 maps to f_1's SUBJ function).

ix) **F-description**
The set of all functional equations. Defines the mapping between c-structure and f-structure.

x)   ***Annotated C-structure***
        A c-structure annotated with the functional equations which map it to the f-structure.

xi)   ***Metavariable***
        A variable over variables. $\uparrow$ = my mother's variable, $\downarrow$ = my variable.

xii) $\uparrow=\downarrow$
        "All the functional information I contain, my mother also contains."

xiii) $(\uparrow SUBJ)=\downarrow, \ (\uparrow OBJ)=\downarrow$
        "I am the subject of the node that dominates me" or "I am the object of the node that dominates me."

xiv)   ***Unification***
        All the features and functions associated with the f-structure must be compatible. (Similar to feature checking in Minimalism.)

xv)   ***Uniqueness***
        In a given f-structure, a particular attribute may have at most one value.

xvi)   ***Completeness***
        An f-structure must contain all the governable grammatical functions that its predicate governs.

xvii)   ***Coherence***
        All the governable grammatical functions in an f-structure must be governed by a local predicate.

xviii) ***Head Mobility***
        The idea that lexical items can take different categories depending upon their features. E.g., a tensed verb in French is of category T, whereas an untensed one is a V. This derives head-to-head movement effects.

xix)   ***Lexical Rule of Passives***
        Passives in LFG are entirely lexical. There is no syntactic movement:

$$(\uparrow PRED) = \text{`}<(\uparrow SUBJ), (\uparrow OBJ)>\text{'}$$

+en $\Downarrow$ $\Downarrow$

$$(\uparrow PRED) = \text{`}< \quad \varnothing \quad (\uparrow SUBJ) >\text{'}$$

xx)   ***Open function*** (XCOMP)
        A function with a missing argument (e.g., a non-finite clause).

xxi)   ***Functional Control***
        The LFG equivalent of control, indicated with a curved line linking two
        AVMs in a f-structure.

xxi)   ***Raising vs. Control***
        In LFG raising vs. control reduces to a lexical difference. The SUBJ function
        in raising constructions isn't thematic, but is in control constructions:
        a)   *reluctant*   A   ($\uparrow$PRED) = 'reluctant <($\uparrow$SUBJ), ($\uparrow$XCOMP)>'
        b)   *likely*   A   ($\uparrow$PRED) = 'likely <($\uparrow$XCOMP)> ($\uparrow$SUBJ)'
                                  ($\uparrow$SUBJ) = ($\uparrow$XCOMP SUBJ)

FURTHER READING

Further reading on LFG:

Bresnan, Joan (2001) *Lexical-Functional Syntax*. Oxford: Blackwell.
    [This is a very detailed and comprehensive outline of LFG.]

Dalrymple, Mary, Ronald Kaplan, John Maxwell and Annie Zaenen (eds.) (1995)
    Formal Issues in Lexical-Functional Grammar. Stanford: CSLI Publications.
    [A collection of important papers in LFG.]

Falk, Yehuda N. (forthcoming) *Lexical-Functional Grammar: An Introduction to
    Parallel Constraint-Based Syntax*. Stanford: CSLI Publications.
    [A very accessible introduction to LFG.]

Kaplan, Ronald (1995) The formal architecture of Lexical-Functional Grammar. In
    Dalrymple, Mary et al. (eds.), *Formal Issues in Lexical-Functional Grammar*.
    Stanford: CSLI Publications. pp. 7-27.
    [This paper outlines the formal properties of LFG.]

Kaplan, Ronald and Joan Bresnan (1982) Lexical-Functional Grammar: A formal
    system for grammatical representation. In Joan Bresnan (ed.), *The Mental Rep-
    resentation of Grammatical Relations*. Cambridge: MIT Press. pp. 173–281.
    [The seminal paper on LFG.]

A lot of material on LFG can be found on the web:
    http://www-lfg.stanford.edu/lfg
    http://clwww.essex.ac.uk/LFG

Further reading on other theories:

Edmondson, Jerold and Donald A. Burquest (1998) *A Survey of Linguistic Theories.*
    (3rd ed.) Dallas: Summer Institute of Linguistics.

Sells, Peter (1985) *Lectures on Contemporary Syntactic Theories.* Stanford: CSLI
    Publications.

PROBLEM SETS

1.   ENGLISH

Draw the annotated c-structures and f-structures for the following sentences:

a)   Susie loves the rain.
b)   Joan thinks that Norvin is likely to write a paper.
c)   What have you read?

2.   ICELANDIC (AGAIN)

Go back to the questions on quirky case in Icelandic in chapters 9 (question
12) and 10 (question 5) and review the data. These data caused problems
for us with our case driven theory of movement and our theory of PRO. Do
these same problems arise in LFG? Why or why not?

3.   TRANSFORMATIONS OR NOT?

Construct the design for an experiment that would distinguish between a
transformational approach, and a non-transformational approach like LFG.

4.   *WANNA*-CONTRACTION

How might LFG account for *wanna*-contraction (see chapter 11) if it doesn't
have movement or traces?

chapter 14

Alternative Approaches: Head-Driven Phrase Structure Grammar

0. INTRODUCTION

Another major formalism for syntactic theory is ***Head-Driven Phrase Structure Grammar*** or ***HPSG***. HPSG is also a generative theory of grammar. It shares with P&P and LFG the goal of modeling how human Language is structured in the mind. HPSG actually finds its sources with a variety of theoretical approaches, including an early version of P&P. The most direct ancestor of HPSG is the theoretical approach called ***Generalized Phrase Structure Grammar*** (or ***GPSG***) which was developed by Gazdar, Klein, Pullum and Sag (1985). GPSG was an early attempt to do syntax without transformations. Unlike LFG, which focused on enriching the lexicon, GPSG emphasized the phrase structure component. GPSG got around having transformations by having an enriched set of phrase structure rules, which themselves could be generated by other rules (called metarules). GPSG was conservative in the claims it made about Universal Grammar: Each language had its own set of rules. HPSG, by contrast, is a theory of human Language and makes specific claims about language universals and variation. HPSG and LFG have many things in common. For example they both make use of a highly enriched lexicon, and the Attribute Value Matrix (AVM) notation we saw with LFG. [1]

    As with our discussion of LFG, a short chapter like this cannot hope to properly cover the rich variety of work done in HPSG. In order to get a fuller picture

---

[1] With some significant differences in notation and assumptions.

you'll need to look at some of the primary sources of material listed in the further reading section at the end of this chapter; in particular, Sag and Wasow (1999) is a very accessible work. Another small caveat is in order before we launch into the details of the theory. For pedagogical reasons, I have couched the presentation here so that someone who has read the first 13 chapters of this book can relate the material here to what they already understand. Sometimes in order to do this, I've had to use metaphors and analogies that many practitioners of HPSG would disagree with. For example, I often state that some theoretical device in HPSG is the "equivalent" of something else in P&P or LFG. By this, I generally mean "does roughly the same kind of work;" I do not mean that they are necessarily notationally or empirically equivalent – as they are not. See section 6 at the end of this chapter for discussion of if and how we might evaluate different theories of grammar.

1.   FEATURES

The basic tool of linguistic description in HPSG is *features*. There are a couple of notational systems for features; I adopt here the one used in Sag and Wasow (1999).[2] Much of the argumentation in this chapter is also taken from that book.

Features enable linguistics to talk about such information as the category of a word, what other words it must appear with (i.e., its theta grid), and what level in the tree the node is (in HPSG, bar levels are treated as features). As in LFG, features are paired with a value in an AVM:

1)   [NUM   pl]

and again like LFG, features can take feature structures as values:

2)   [AGR   [NUM   pl]]

The AVM in (2) says that the agreement feature for the word involves a number feature which is plural in value.

Feature structures come of a variety of types. First we have types that indicate the *word* vs. *phrase* status of every constituent in a tree (thus roughly equivalent to the notion of bar level). The features for a node are next divided into three major classes: the values of the feature SYN are structures relevant to the syntax, ARG-ST (argument structure) feature structures represent the theta grid, and the value of a SEM feature structure represents the semantic properties of the node.

Let us first talk about SYN feature structures. SYN feature structures tell us about the formal grammatical properties of the node. They tell us the syntactic category of the node, any inflectional properties of the node, what other elements the

---

[2] It should be noted that many of the ideas in Sag and Wasow (1999) diverge from the conception of HPSG presented in Pollard and Sag (1994); many HPSG researchers would disagree with the particulars presented here. In particular see Richter (2000) for discussion of the differences among various kinds of HPSG.

node must combine with, etc. The feature that determines the category of the node and its inflectional properties is called the HEAD feature. The feature that restricts what kind of nodes appear in the specifier position is called the SPR feature, and the feature that restrict what kind of nodes appear in the complement position is the COMPS feature. To see how this works, let us take a partial lexical entry for the word *letter*. This example is taken from Sag and Wasow (1999: 132).

3)

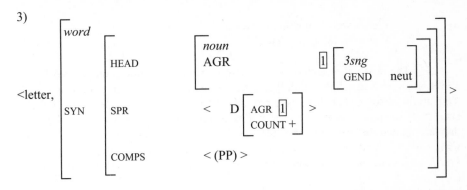

This looks much more intimidating than it actually is. The lexical entry is an ordered list of the form of the word and the large AVM. Ordered lists are represented with angled brackets (< >). At the top we have *word*, which tells us, obviously, that this is a word and not a phrase. Below this we have the SYN feature whose value is described by the AVM containing the HEAD, SPR, and COMPS features. The HEAD feature tells us what kind of lexical item this is. It is a *noun*, it triggers neuter and third person agreement. The SPR feature gives us an ordered list of the items that may or must appear in the specifier position of any projection of this noun. The ordered list in this lexical entry contains only one item: a count noun determiner. The boxed number found both in the HEAD feature and in this SPR feature (1) is called a *(coreference)* **tag**. Tags are used to indicate that certain substructures of an overall structure are identical. The tag [1] in the description of the HEAD feature refers to the object described by the AVM that follows it. The [1] in the SPR feature indicates that whatever the agreement features of the head are, they must be identical for the specifier. This means that since the noun is 3rd person singular, the determiner must also be singular:

4)   a)   this (sg) letter (sg)
       b)   *these(pl) letter (sg)

The idea of structural identity (as expressed by coreference tags) does much of the work that Functional Control does in LFG and feature checking does in P&P – and more. For instance, it allows HPSG to have a non-transformational analysis of raising and to eliminate PRO in control constructions.

Notice that the specifier is not optional in this lexical entry. In English, with singular count nouns, specifiers are not optional:

5)   a) I gave her the letter.
        b) I gave her a letter.
        c) *I gave her letter.

Finally, we have the COMPS feature, which says that we may have an optional PP complement:

6)   a) a letter about computer software
        b) a letter from the president

The next major feature is the ARG-ST feature. Its value is an ordered list of all the arguments associated with the word and represents the theta grid of the word. You might observe that there is a redundancy between ARG-ST features, and the SPR/COMPS features. As we will see below in section 2, this is acceptable because they are treated differently by the rules which combine words into sentences. As we will see, we need the ARG-ST feature for binding reasons, independent of the SPR/COMPS features.[3] An example of the ARG-ST feature for the verb *love* is given in (7):

7)   <*love*,   [ARG-ST < NP, NP>]>

We can impose various kinds of selectional restrictions on this representation, of course. For example, the verb *loves* requires that its subject be third person singular. We can encode this by inserting an AVM with this specification into the first NP slot in the ARG-STR list.

8)   <*loves*, [ARG-ST < [NP [AGR 3s]], NP>]>

The last major class of feature structures are the SEM (semantic) features. These give us information about how the word and sentence are to be interpreted. For example, MODE tells us the semantic type of the node (proposition, interrogative, directive, referential item). The INDEX features are like the indices we used in chapter 4: They mark the various participants or situations described in the sentence. Last, we have the RESTR (restriction) feature, which tell us the properties that must hold true for the sentence to be true. Again, this looks a bit like our theta grids from chapter 7. Unfortunately we don't have the space to cover this interesting aspect of HPSG in any detail, see Sag and Wasow (1999) for more discussion.

The complete lexical entry for the noun *letter* is given in (9), showing all these features. The largest AVM in this structure is known as the noun's *SYN-SEM structure*.

---

[3] Other arguments for distinguishing ARG-STR from COMPS and SPR can be found in Manning and Sag (1998).

9)

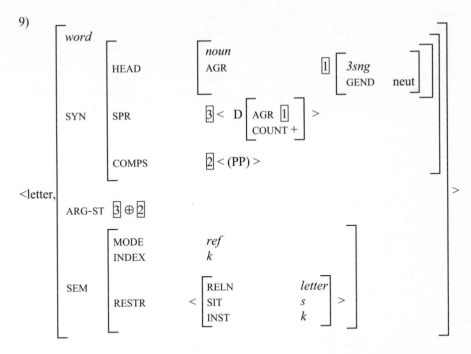

Each word in the lexicon has a rich lexical entry like this which specifies the features and feature structures it brings to the sentence. This lexical entry tells us that this item is a *word*; its SYN feature specifies that it is a *noun* with a 3sng, neuter HEAD feature. Since it is a count noun, the SPR feature requires that it take a count determiner, which must agree with the HEAD | AGR feature (indicated by the tag 1) It may also take an optional PP COMPS (complement). The specifier and complement features are related in the ARG-ST feature by the tags 3 and 2 (I'll discuss the ⊕ symbol below). The SEMantic features, which don't really concern us much here, indicate that the item is REFerential and is assigned the index *k*. The RESTR feature tells us what the word means and what context it can appear in. (Again see Sag and Wasow (1999) for a more complete description of all these features.)

2.   THE LEXICON

Needless to say, there is a lot of information stored in lexical entries in HPSG grammars. In many cases this information is redundant or predictable. For example, for any count noun (such as *letter* or *ball* or *peanut*), there are two forms: a singular form and a plural form. Ideally we don't really want two complete lexical entries, as the information in one is predictable from the other. While memory is cheap, it

would be nice to reduce the amount of redundancy or predictable information contained in each lexical entry. HPSG does this in a number of ways.[4]

First, like LFG, HPSG has lexical rules that can change the shape of lexical
entries. Take for example the plural rule that derives the lexical entries for plurals
out of uninflected nouns. (The F_{NPL} notation refers to a function that does the actual
morphology. For example, F_{NPL} applied to *cat*, will result in *cats*, but F_{NPL} applied to
child will give you *children*.)

10)   *Plural Rule*

$$< \boxed{1}, \begin{bmatrix} noun \\ \text{ARG-ST} < [\text{count +}]> \end{bmatrix} > \Rightarrow < F_{NPL}(\boxed{1}), \begin{bmatrix} word \\ \text{SYN [HEAD [AGR [NUM pl]]]} \end{bmatrix} >$$

This rule says that given any basic count noun root $\boxed{1}$, you can create a plural lexical
item that has an identical feature structure, except with plural number.

Similar rules can be applied to do derivation (such as deriving the noun
dancer from the verb *dance*), or to do grammatical function-changing operations like
the passive. In the following rule (taken from Sag and Wasow 1999: 235) the symbol
⊕ means "an append of lists." For more on this notion, see the references below, but
for our purposes it roughly corresponds to an ordering of the AVMs. You'll see that
the rule does three things: (i) it puts the verb (⑴), into a passive form; (ii) it puts the
first argument (NP$_i$) into an optional *by*-phrase. (Don't worry about the details of the
feature structure for the *by*-phrase); (iii) it moves all the other arguments (ⓐ) up in
the ARG-ST list, the ⊕ symbol showing that the arguments are strictly ordered with
respect to one another. The big gray arrows in the following rule are not part of the
rule itself; I've just written them in to point out the important parts of the rule.

11)   *Passive Rule*

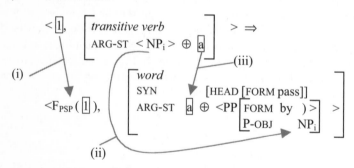

There is one further area of redundancy in the lexicon, which we already
noted in section 1 above. The information about the number of arguments a word
takes appears twice in the SYN-SEM structure. It appears once in the ARG-ST feature
and once in the SPR/COMPS features. This redundancy is solved by the ***Argument***

---

[4] One of which we don't have the space to discuss here: *inheritance hierarchies*. These are
discussed at length in Sag and Wasow (1999) and other sources on HPSG.

Realization Principle (12), which builds the SPR and COMPS features out of the ARG-ST feature:

12)   *Argument Realization Principle (ARP)*
        A word structure satisfies the following feature structure description:

$$
\begin{bmatrix}
\text{SYN} & \begin{bmatrix} \text{SPR} & \boxed{1} \\ \text{COMPS} & \boxed{2} \end{bmatrix} \\
\text{ARG-ST } \boxed{1} \ \oplus \ \boxed{2}
\end{bmatrix}
$$

The equivalence of the SPR/COMPS features and the ARG-ST feature is indicated by the tags $\boxed{1}$ and $\boxed{2}$. The first argument is mapped to the SPR feature, the second to the COMPS feature. This principle says that you map the first argument of the argument structure into the SPR position, and the second one into the COMPS position.

        HPSG, then, shares with LFG a rich lexicon with many lexical rules. This is where the similarities end, however. In LFG, we used functions and functional equations to map constituency (c-structure) onto the functional representation (f-structure). In HPSG, like P&P theory and as we'll see below, functional (= featural) information is read directly off the constituent tree instead of using mapping principles.

3.   RULES, FEATURES, AND TREES

HPSG differs from LFG in at least one significant regard: it is **compositional**. By that we mean that the way in which the meaning of the sentence is determined is by looking at the constituent structure associated with the sentence. HPSG shares this assumption with P&P. The meaning of a sentence in HPSG and P&P/Minimalism can be calculated by taking each node, and using constituency to determine what modifies what. Relationships between words are directly encoded into constituency. In LFG, we instead used functional equations to calculate the relationships between words.

        In all three theories (HPSG, LFG, and P&P/Minimalism), the end of the sentence should involve a **saturation, satifaction**, or **unification** of the features introduced by the words.[5] In Minimalism, this was accomplished by feature checking

---

[5] The exact characterization of how this works is a matter of some debate in HPSG, with various formal proposals in different versions of the theory. In early HPSG this was done with unification (see chapter 13), as is the version found in Sag and Wasow (1999). In Pollard and Sag (1994) well-formed feature structures are licensed by *conjunction* (or more accurately the conjunctive satisfaction of all the principles of the grammar). The distinctions between these approaches need not concern us here, which is why I've adopted the neutral term *satisfaction* (or *saturation*) to get at the underlying idea. See Richter (2000) for a discussion of the formal apparatus underlying these issues.

via the construction of the phrase structure tree and via movement. In LFG, this is accomplished by functional equations that map to an f-structure. In HPSG, by contrast, all feature satisfaction occurs by combining words into constituents. Constituency is introduced by phrase structure rules.[6] These rules look a little different than the ones we used in chapters 2, 5, and 6, but they do the same work. There are three basic rules (which are roughly equivalent to the complement rule, the adjunct rule and the specifier rule of X-bar theory). The first of these is the *Head Complement Rule*. This takes a head (marked with H) word, and if it is in sequence with a number of arguments that match its COMPS requirements, licenses a phrase with an AVM like its own, except that those COMPS features have been checked off and deleted.[7]

13)   *Head Complement Rule*

$$\begin{bmatrix} phrase \\ \text{COMPS} <> \end{bmatrix} \quad \rightarrow \quad H \begin{bmatrix} word \\ \text{COMPS} < \boxed{1}, \ldots, \boxed{n} > \end{bmatrix} \boxed{1} \quad \ldots \quad \boxed{n}$$

Notice that the tags $\boxed{1}, \ldots, \boxed{n}$ on the head must be identical to the tags of the phrases that follow. This means that the element(s) on the right hand side of the head must be selected for in the COMPS portion of the head word. The resulting category (the *phrase*) has had it's COMPS features erased. (Thus making the satisfaction of features like COMPS very much like feature checking.) The output of this rule – when applied to an transitive verb and an NP – is seen in (14). For ease of exposition, I've omitted most of the featural information here, leaving just the relevant features present.

---

[6] Phrase structure rules are actually a shorthand notation for more complicated principles. See Pollard and Sag (1994) for more discussion.

[7] For expository ease, I'm occasionally lapsing into the metaphors and terminology of Minimalism, which are not accepted by practitioners of HPSG. I do this so that you can relate the ideas of HPSG to what you have previously seen in this book; this doesn't mean that the ideas are entirely equivalent. For example, the notions of checking and deletion suggest a derivational approach to syntax which is not necessarily a part of HPSG. For more on the philosophical and methodological assumptions underlying HPSG see Pollard and Sag (1994).

14)

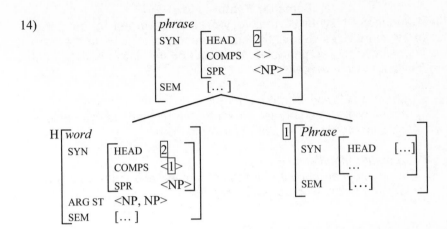

The resulting phrase is what we would label a V' in P&P syntax. The rule combines a head with an item that satisfies one of its COMPS requirements. It then licenses a phrase lacking that COMPS requirement.

One thing to notice about (14) is that the head features of the head word become the head features of the entire phrase, just like the syntactic category of a head is passed up the tree to the phrase level in the X-bar theory of chapter 5. In HPSG this due to the ***Head Feature Principle***:

15)   *Head Feature Principle(HFP)*
        The HEAD value of any headed phrase is identical to the HEAD value of the
        head daughter.

You'll also notice that the SPR feature of the head daughter is also transferred up to the mother node. This is triggered by the ***Valence Principle*** (Sag and Wasow 1999):

16)   *Valence Principle*
        Unless the rule says otherwise, the mother's SPR and COMPS values are
        identical to those of the head daughter.

Semantic Feature Flow

The distribution of syntactic feature values is governed by our three phrase structure rules. Semantic feature values also flow up the tree. This is governed by two principles. We won't go into these in detail, but here they are for your reference:

i)   *Semantic Compositionality Principle*
        In any well-formed phrase structure, the mother's RESTR value is the sum of the RESTR values of the daughters.

ii)   *Semantic Inheritance Principle*
        In any headed phrase, the mother's mode and index values are identical to those of the head daughter.

Adjuncts are introduced by the ***Head Modifier Rule***. This rule makes reference to the special feature MOD. The MOD feature is contained in the SYN-SEM structure of the modifier and is linked to the thing it modifies with a tag, allowing modifiers to impose selectional restrictions on the phrases they modify. The rule takes a *phrase* (equivalent to our X' level) and licenses another *phrase* (X').

17)   *Head Modifier Rule*
        [*phrase*]   →   H $\boxed{1}$[*phrase*] $\begin{bmatrix} phrase \\ \text{HEAD [MOD } \boxed{1}] \end{bmatrix}$

Specifiers are introduced using the third rule, which also takes a *phrase* (X') and licenses a *phrase* (however, this time equivalent to our XP). The S node in HPSG is a projection of the verb (i.e., is licensed as a mother of the VP by this rule). Just as in X-bar theory, the HFP allows this rule to be non-category specific.

18)   *Head Specifier Rule*
        $\begin{bmatrix} phrase \\ \text{SPR} <> \end{bmatrix}$ → $\boxed{1}$ H $\begin{bmatrix} phrase \\ \text{SPR} <\boxed{1}> \end{bmatrix}$

This rule takes a phrase with a non-empty SPR value and combines it with an item that satisfies that value, and generates a phrase without a SPR value.

On an intuitive level, these rules take as inputs the lexical entries for words and output sentences where the information has been combined into a meaningful whole. In the next two sections, we turn to a variety of phenomena discussed in this book and look at how HPSG accounts for them.

4.   BINDING

HPSG does not use the notion c-command to determine binding relations. Instead, binding makes reference to the ARG-ST list in the SYN-SEM structures. Because of the rules discussed above in section 3, arguments on the left side of an ARG-ST ordered list will always be higher in the tree than ones further to the right on the list. As such the binding conditions in HPSG are based on precedence in the ARG-ST list. This is accomplished with the notion *outrank* (all definitions taken from Sag and Wasow 1999).

19)   *Outrank*
        A phrase A *outranks* a phrase B just in the case where A's SYN-SEM struc-
        ture precedes B's SYN-SEM structure on some ARG-ST list.

Anaphors are marked with a special feature: ANA. [ANA +] nodes are subject to the HPSG equivalent of principle A:

20)   *Principle A*
        An [ANA +] SYN-SEM structure must be outranked by a co-indexed SYN-SEM
        structure.

Pronouns, which are [ANA −] are subject to principle B.

21)   *Principle B*
        An [ANA −] SYN-SEM structure must not be outranked by a co-indexed SYN-
        SEM structure.

Because of the direct mapping between the ARG-ST and the tree, this will give us essentially the same results as the c-command analysis given in chapter 4. For a discussion of the important differences between a c-command analysis and an ARG-ST analysis, see Pollard and Sag (1992).

5.   LONG DISTANCE DEPENDENCIES

In this section, we look briefly at how HPSG deals with long distance dependencies between the surface position of *wh*-phrases and the position with which they are thematically associated. P&P uses movement to capture this relation. LFG uses functional control. HPSG uses a feature: GAP.[8] This is a feature like COMPS or SPR that indicates that an argument is required by the SYN-SEM structure and is missing. The presence of a non-empty GAP feature indicates that an argument is not filling the expected complement position. This is encoded in a revised version of the argument realization principle, where the sequence ②⊖③ is a list where the elements on the list ③ have been removed from ②. This principle allows you to optionally map an argument to the GAP feature rather than the COMPS feature.

---

[8] Also called SLASH.

22)   *Revised ARP*[9]

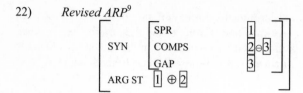

This guarantees that any argument that could appear on the COMPS list can appear on the GAP list instead. Just as we needed principles for passing head features, valence features and semantic features up the tree, we also need a principle to make sure GAP features make it up to the top of the tree: ***The GAP Principle***. (Formulation again taken from Sag and Wasow 1999: 344.)

23)   *The GAP Principle*

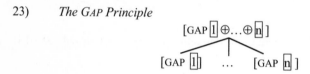

This principle encodes the idea that a mother's GAP feature represents the union of all the GAP values of its daughters.

Let's do an example. Because we don't have the space to introduce HPSG analyses of head movement or *do*-support, we'll use topicalization, rather than a *wh*-question as an example of a long distance dependency. Topicalization has the same basic properties as other *wh*-movement (subject to island constraints, etc.). The sentence we'll do is seen in (24). This sentence is grammatical if we put contrastive stress on the first NP.

24)   <u>That boy</u>, we saw …

In a normal sentence, an NP (filled by *that boy*) occupies the COMPS position of the verb *saw*. In this sentence, by contrast, the COMPS position is empty. Instead there is an NP in the GAP feature. The NP *we* satisfies the verb's SPR feature. The GAP value is percolated up the tree by the GAP principle which results in a tree like (25): [10]

---

[9] This particular formulation only allows *wh*-extraction from object position. As something to think about, you might consider how HPSG would go about dealing with subject extraction (as seen in the Irish data in chapter 11).
[10] You might consider whether gap feature percolation is really different from movement or is simply a notational variant. What kind of evidence might you propose to distinguish the two approaches?

25)

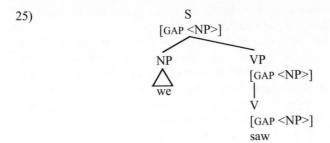

The GAP feature associated with the S node must be satisfied someway. This is accomplished with the **Head Filler Rule**.

26)   *The Head Filler Rule*

$$\begin{bmatrix} phrase \\ \text{GAP} <> \end{bmatrix} \rightarrow \boxed{1}\begin{bmatrix} phrase \\ \text{GAP} <> \end{bmatrix} \quad \text{H}\begin{bmatrix} phrase \\ \text{FORM fin} \\ \text{SPR} <> \\ \text{GAP} < \boxed{1} > \end{bmatrix}$$

This rule satisfies the GAP feature, by adding the missing NP at the top of the tree:

27)

                    S
                [GAP < >]
         ┌──────────┘
        NP   S
        △   [GAP <NP>]
    That boy   ┌──────┘
                   NP   VP
                   △   [GAP <NP>]
                   we   │
                               V
                          [GAP <NP>]
                               saw

6.   CHOOSING AMONG THEORIES

Once again, this survey has been too brief to get a full appreciation for the theory of HPSG, but it should be enough to give you a feel for how the system works.

We briefly turn now to the very thorny question of which theoretical approach is right. If you ask this question at any major syntax conference you are likely to get lynched. Most linguists hold to their theories the way religious fanatics follow their beliefs or the way nationalists feel about their countries. I admit that I personally am guilty of this at times. As you can see from the number of chapters in this book devoted to P&P compared to the number of chapters devoted to other approaches, my heart lies squarely in the P&P/Minimalist camp.

Unfortunately, there is rarely rational dialog on the question of what theoretical approaches are the best. At the same time, the theories quite liberally borrow from one another. Feature checking in P&P is borrowed from HPSG features satisfaction, grammatical function changing lexical rules are borrowed from LFG, etc. Now it is true that to a greater or lesser degree the different theories make different empirical predictions. One might think that on empirical grounds alone, you should be able to choose the right theory. However, if you take this approach you are treading on dangerous ground, for two reasons. First, while one theory provides a nice account of one part of the syntax, another theory will do better at a different component, so you have to carefully balance what parts of syntax are the most important. Second, some theoretical approaches are better worked out than others. More people work in P&P/Minimalism than in the other approaches, so the empirical coverage of that theory is unsurprisingly greater. You might think instead that we can compare the theories on the grounds of elegance or precision. For example, HPSG is considerably more precise than P&P, and has more extensive internally consistent fragments of the grammars of particular languages. But this doesn't cut it either: Precision or elegance does not necessarily mean that the theory is an accurate representation of human Language. In fact, the only real grounds along which we could ever accurately gauge the correctness of a theory is on the basis of how well it models how Language works in the mind or brain. Despite some scholars' claims to the contrary, we are a long way from being able to test such modeling reliably. I suspect that when we do, we'll discover that **all** of our theories are wrong in many important respects. In the meantime, we're left with a number of theoretical approaches that do roughly the same range of work, for the same basic goals. Instead of trying to determine which one is "right" (probably a fruitless task), it is better to understand the advantages of each approach, and the insights they give us into the nature of human Language.

IDEAS, RULES, AND CONSTRAINTS INTRODUCED IN THIS CHAPTER

(Some of the definitions below are taken from Sag and Wasow 1999.)

i)   ***Features***
         These do the work of determining what can combine with what.
      a)   Bar-level-like features tell us what hierarchical level the node is at.
      b)   The SYN feature structures gives us the syntactic info about the node.
         i)   The HEAD feature gives the category and inflectional info.
         ii) The COMPS feature tells us what complements appear in the structure.
         iii) The SPR feature tells us what appears in the specifier.

iv) The GAP feature tells us if there is a long distance dependency.

   c) The ARG-ST feature is the HPSG equivalent of the theta grid. Binding relations are defined against this. It takes the form of an ordered list <...>.

   d) The SEM feature structures tell us the semantic information about the constituent, and come in a variety of types.

ii) ***SYN-SEM Structure***
The set of AVMs for a node, containing all the SYN, SEM and ARG-ST features.

iii) ***(Coreference) Tags***
Numbers written in boxes (e.g., ☐1) that show that two items are identical in a SYN-SEM structure or between SYN-SEM structures.

iv) ***Argument Realization Principle*** *(revised)*

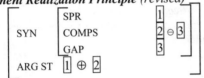

$$
\begin{bmatrix}
\text{SYN} & \begin{bmatrix} \text{SPR} & \boxed{1} \\ \text{COMPS} & \boxed{2} \ominus \boxed{3} \\ \text{GAP} & \boxed{3} \end{bmatrix} \\
\text{ARG ST} & \boxed{1} \oplus \boxed{2}
\end{bmatrix}
$$

v) ***Plural Rule***

$$
< \boxed{1}, \begin{bmatrix} noun \\ \text{ARG-ST} < [\text{count} +] > \end{bmatrix} > \Rightarrow < F_{NPL}(\boxed{1}), \begin{bmatrix} word \\ \text{SYN [HEAD [AGR [NUM pl]]]} \end{bmatrix} >
$$

vi) ***Passive Rule***

$$
< \boxed{1}, \begin{bmatrix} transtive\ verb \\ \text{ARG-ST} < NP_i > \oplus \boxed{a} \end{bmatrix} > \Rightarrow
$$

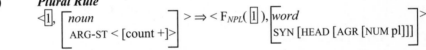

$$
< F_{PSP}(\boxed{1}), \begin{bmatrix} word \\ \text{SYN} & [\text{HEAD [FORM pass]}] \\ \text{ARG-ST} & \boxed{a} \oplus < (\begin{bmatrix} \text{PP} & \text{FORM} & \text{by} \\ \text{P-OBJ} & & NP_j \end{bmatrix}) > \end{bmatrix} >
$$

vii) ***Compositional***
The idea that the semantics of the sentence can be read off of the constituency tree. This idea is shared by P&P and HPSG, but is rejected by LFG.

viii) ***Feature Satisfaction*** *(sometimes loosely called* **Unification**)
The idea that all the features in a SYN-SEM structure must match. The rough equivalent of feature checking in P&P/Minimalism.

ix)   **Head Complement Rule**

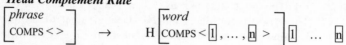

$$\begin{bmatrix} phrase \\ \text{COMPS} <> \end{bmatrix} \rightarrow \quad \text{H} \begin{bmatrix} word \\ \text{COMPS} < \boxed{1}, \dots, \boxed{n} > \end{bmatrix} \boxed{1} \ \dots \ \boxed{n}$$

x)   **Head Feature Principle**

The HEAD value of any headed phrase is identical to the HEAD value of the head daughter.

xi)   **Valence Principle**

Unless the rule says otherwise, the mother's SPR and COMPS values are identical to those of the head daughter.

xii)   **Semantic Compositionality Principle**

In any well-formed phrase structure, the mother's RESTR value is the sum of the RESTR values of the daughters.

xiii)   **Semantic Inheritance Principle**

In any headed phrase, the mother's mode and index values are identical to those of the head daughter.

xiv)   **Head Modifier Rule**

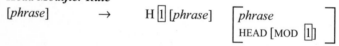

$$[phrase] \rightarrow \quad \text{H} \boxed{1} [phrase] \quad \begin{bmatrix} phrase \\ \text{HEAD} [\text{MOD} \ \boxed{1}] \end{bmatrix}$$

xv)   **Head Specifier Rule**

$$\begin{bmatrix} phrase \\ \text{SPR} <> \end{bmatrix} \rightarrow \quad \boxed{1} \quad \text{H} \begin{bmatrix} phrase \\ \text{SPR} < \boxed{1} > \end{bmatrix}$$

xvi)   **Outrank**

A phrase A outranks a phrase B just in the case where A's SYN-SEM structure precedes B's SYN-SEM structure on some ARG-ST list.

xvii)   **Principle A**

An [ANA +] SYN-SEM structure must be outranked by a co-indexed SYN-SEM structure.

xviii)   **Principle B**

An [ANA −] SYN-SEM structure must not be ranked by a co-indexed SYN-SEM structure.

xix)   **The G*AP* Principle**

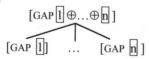

$$[\text{GAP} \ \boxed{1} \oplus \dots \oplus \boxed{n}]$$

$$[\text{GAP} \ \boxed{1}] \quad \dots \quad [\text{GAP} \ \boxed{n}]$$

xx)   ***The Head Filler Rule***

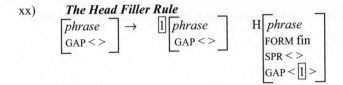

$$\begin{bmatrix} phrase \\ \text{GAP} <> \end{bmatrix} \rightarrow \boxed{1}\begin{bmatrix} phrase \\ \text{GAP} <> \end{bmatrix} \quad \text{H}\begin{bmatrix} phrase \\ \text{FORM fin} \\ \text{SPR} <> \\ \text{GAP} < \boxed{1} > \end{bmatrix}$$

FURTHER READING

Borsley, Robert (1996) *Modern Phrase Structure Grammar*. Oxford: Blackwell.
[This is a textbook that surveys various approaches to phrase structure, including GPSG and HPSG.]

Gazdar, Gerald, Ewan Klein, Geoffrey Pullum and Ivan Sag (1985) *Generalized Phrase Structure Grammar*. Cambridge: Harvard University Press.
[The seminal work on GPSG.]

Manning, Christopher and Ivan Sag (1998) Argument structure, valence and binding. *The Nordic Journal of Linguistics* 21, 107-44.

Pollard, Carl and Ivan Sag (1992) Anaphors in English and the scope of Binding Theory. *Linguistic Inquiry* 23, 261-303.

Pollard, Carl and Ivan Sag (1994) *Head-Driven Phrase Structure Grammar*. Stanford: CSLI Publications and Chicago: The University of Chicago Press.
[The seminal work on HPSG.]

Richter, Frank (2000) A Mathematical Formalism for Linguistic Theories with an Application in Head-Driven Phrase Structure Grammar. Ph.D. Dissertation. University of Tübingen.

Sag, Ivan and Thomas Wasow (1999) *Syntactic Theory: A Formal Introduction*. Stanford: CSLI Publications.
[A very accessible textbook for HPSG.]

PROBLEM SETS

1.   ENGLISH

Create an HPSG-style lexicon for the following words:

> the, kitten, tore, toilet, paper.

And then draw a tree using the rules and lexical entries for the sentence:

> The kitten tore the toilet paper.

You may abbreviate your SYN-SEM structures using tags.

2.   SUBJECT/AUX INVERSION

How might HPSG go about doing subject/aux inversion? (Hint: consider a lexical rule.) Assume that auxiliary verbs select for other verbs in their ARG-ST features.

3.   ISLAND CONSTRAINTS

In this chapter, we didn't talk at all about how HPSG might account for island constraints. Propose a constraint on the GAP principle that might account for them.

Conclusions

We started this textbook out with the question of what a person needs to know about their language in order to understand a simple sentence. We hypothesized that some of language is innate and other parts are parameterized. In the first twelve chapters of this book, we sketched out some of the major research threads in one approach to syntax: the principles and parameters (P&P) view. In part 1, we looked at how rules generate hierarchical tree structures. These structures are geometric objects with mathematical properties. We looked at one set of phenomena (binding) that is sensitive to those properties. In part 2, we looked at a more sophisticated view of tree structures, developing X-bar theory, and the thematic (lexical) constraints on it such as theta theory. In part 3, we looked extensively at how problematic word orders, such as passives, raising, VSO languages, and *wh*-questions could all be accounted for using movement. In chapter 12, we brought these threads together and started looking at the minimalist approach to grammar. Part 4 of this book changed direction slightly. We looked, ever so briefly, at two popular alternatives to P&P/Minimalism. This was so that you could read papers and books written in those alternatives, as well as giving you a taste for other, related, ways we can approach topics in syntax.

Congratulations for getting through all this material. I hope this book has whetted your appetite for the study of syntax and sentence structure and that you will pursue further studies in syntactic theory. To this end, I've appended a list of books that can take you to the next level.

Where to Go from Here

Baltin, Mark and Chris Collins (2000) *The Handbook of Contemporary Syntactic Theory*. Oxford: Blackwell.

Bresnan, Joan (2001) *Lexical-Functional Syntax*. Oxford: Blackwell.

Cook, V. J. and Mark Newson (1996) *Chomsky's Universal Grammar: An Introduction* (2nd ed.). Oxford: Blackwell.

Cowper, Elizabeth (1994) *A Concise Introduction to Syntactic Theory: The Government and Binding Approach*. Chicago: Chicago University Press.

Culicover, Peter W. (1997) *Principles and Parameters: An Introduction to Syntactic Theory*. Oxford: Oxford University Press.

Haegeman, Liliane and Jacqueline Guéron (1999) *English Grammar: A Generative Perspective*. Oxford: Blackwell.

Haegeman, Liliane (1994) *Introduction to Government and Binding Theory*. Oxford: Blackwell.

Lasnik, Howard (1999a) *Minimalist Analyses*. Oxford: Blackwell.

Ouhalla, Jamal (1990) *Introducing Transformational Grammar* (2nd ed.). London: Edward Arnold.

Radford, Andrew (1997a) *Syntactic Theory and The Structure of English: A Minimalist Approach*. Cambridge: Cambridge University Press.

Radford, Andrew (1997b) *Syntax: A Minimalist Introduction*. Cambridge: Cambridge University Press.

Roberts, Ian (1997) *Comparative Syntax*. London: Edward Arnold.

Sag, Ivan and Thomas Wasow (1999) *Syntactic Theory: A Formal Introduction*. Stanford: CSLI Publications.

Webelhuth, Gert (1995) *Government and Binding Theory and the Minimalist Program*. Oxford: Blackwell.

References

Aarts, Bas (1997) *English Syntax and Argumentation*. New York: St. Martin's Press.

Abney, Steven (1987) The English Noun Phrase in its Sentential Aspect. Ph.D. dissertation, MIT.

Aikawa, Takako (1994) Logophoric use of the Japanese reflexive *zibun-zisin* 'self-self'. *MIT Working Papers in Linguistics* 24, 1–22.

Aissen, Judith (1987) *Tzotzil Clause Structure*. Dordrecht: Reidel.

Allwood, Jens, Lars-Gunnar Andersson, and Östen Dahl (1977) *Logic in Linguistics*. Oxford: Oxford University Press.

Anderson, Stephen and Paul Kiparsky (eds.) (1973) *A Festschrift for Morris Halle*. New York: Holt, Rinehart and Winston.

Aoun, Joseph (1985) *A Grammar of Anaphora*. Cambridge: MIT Press.

Baker C. L. and John McCarthy (eds.) (1981) *The Logical Problem of Language Acquisition*. Cambridge: MIT Press.

Baker, Mark, Kyle Johnson, and Ian Roberts (1989) Passive arguments raised. *Linguistic Inquiry* 20, 219–51.

Baltin, Mark (1981) Strict bounding. In C. L. Baker and John McCarthy (eds.), *The Logical Problem of Language Acquisition*. Cambridge: MIT Press. pp. 257–95.

Baltin, Mark and Chris Collins (2000) *The Handbook of Contemporary Syntactic Theory*. Oxford: Blackwell.

Baltin, Mark and Anthony Kroch (1989) *Alternative Conceptions of Phrase Structure*. Chicago: University of Chicago Press.

Bard, Ellen G., Dan Robertson and Antonella Sorace (1996) Magnitude estimation of linguistic acceptability. *Language* 72, 32–68.

Barsky, Robert (1997) *Noam Chomsky: A Life of Dissent*. Cambridge: MIT Press.

Bayer, J. (1984) COMP in Bavarian syntax. *The Linguistics Review* 3, 209–4.

Belletti, Adriana (1994) Verb positions: Evidence from Italian. In David Lightfoot and Norbert Hornstein (eds.), *Verb Movement*. Cambridge: Cambridge University Press. pp. 19–40.

Borer, Hagit (1999) Deconstructing the construct. In Kyle Johnson and Ian Roberts (eds.) *Beyond Principles and Parameters*. Dordrecht: Kluwer Academic Publishers. pp. 43–89.

Borsley, Robert (1996) *Modern Phrase Structure Grammar*. Oxford: Blackwell.

Bošković, Zeljko (1997) Superiority and economy of derivation: Multiple *wh*-fronting. Paper presented at the 16th West Coast Conference on Formal Linguistics.

Brame, Michael (1976) *Conjectures and Refutations in Syntax and Semantics*. Amsterdam: Elsevier.

Bresnan, Joan (1972) Theory of Complementation in English. Ph.D. dissertation, MIT.

Bresnan, Joan (ed.) (1982). *The Mental Representation of Grammatical Relations*. Cambridge: MIT Press.

Bresnan, Joan (2001) *Lexical-Functional Syntax*. Oxford: Blackwell.

Burzio, Luigi (1986) *Italian Syntax*. Dordrecht: Reidel.

Carnie, Andrew (1995) Head Movement and Non-Verbal Predication. Ph.D. dissertation, MIT.

Carnie, Andrew and Eithne Guilfoyle (2000) *The Syntax of Verb Initial Languages*. Oxford: Oxford University Press.

Chametzky, Robert (1996) *A Theory of Phrase Markers and the Extended Base*. Albany: SUNY Press.

Cheng, Lisa (1997) *On the Typology of Wh-Questions*. New York: Garland Press.

Chomsky, Noam (1957) *Syntactic Structures*. The Hague: Janua Linguarum 4.

Chomsky, Noam (1965) *Aspects of the Theory of Syntax*. Cambridge: MIT Press.

Chomsky, Noam (1970) Remarks on nominalization. In R. Jacobs and P. Rosenbaum (eds.) *Readings in English Transformational Grammar*. Waltham: Ginn. pp. 184–221.

Chomsky, Noam (1973) Conditions on transformations. In Stephen Anderson and Paul Kiparsky (eds.), *A Festschrift for Morris Halle*. New York: Holt, Rinehart and Winston. pp. 232–86.

Chomsky, Noam (1975) *The Logical Structure of Linguistic Theory*. New York: Plenum.

Chomsky, Noam (1977) On *wh*-movement. In Peter Culicover, Thomas Wasow, and Adrian Akmajian (eds.), *Formal Syntax*. New York: Academic Press. pp. 71–132.

Chomsky, Noam (1980) On Binding. *Linguistic Inquiry* 11, 1–46.

Chomsky, Noam (1981) *Lectures on Government and Binding*. Dordrecht: Foris.

Chomsky, Noam (1986) *Barriers*. Cambridge: MIT Press.

Chomsky, Noam (1991) Some notes on economy of derivation and representation. In Robert Friedin (ed.), *Principles and Parameters in Comparative Grammar*. Cambridge: MIT Press. pp. 417–54.

Chomsky, Noam (1993) A minimalist program for linguistic theory. In Kenneth L. Hale and Samuel J. Keyser (eds.), *The View from Building 20: Essays in Honor of Sylvain Bromberger*. Cambridge: MIT Press. pp 1–52.

Chomsky, Noam (1995) *The Minimalist Program*. Cambridge: MIT Press.

Chomsky, Noam and Howard Lasnik (1978) A remark on contraction. *Linguistic Inquiry* 9, 268–74.

Cinque, Guglielmo (1981) *Types of A' Dependencies*. Cambridge: MIT Press.

Cole, Peter and S. N. Sridhar (1976) Clause union and relational grammar: Evidence from Hebrew and Kannada. *Studies in the Linguistic Sciences* 6, 216–27.

Cook, V. J. and Mark Newson (1996) *Chomsky's Universal Grammar: An Introduction* (2nd ed.). Oxford: Blackwell.

Cowper, Elizabeth (1994) *A Concise Introduction to Syntactic Theory: The Government and Binding Approach*. Chicago: University of Chicago Press.

Culicover, Peter (1997) *Principles and Parameters: An Introduction to Syntactic Theory*. Oxford: Oxford University Press.

Culicover, Peter, Thomas Wasow and Adrian Akmajian (eds.) (1977) *Formal Syntax*. New York: Academic Press.

Dalrymple, Mary, Ronald Kaplan, John Maxwell, and Annie Zaenen (eds.) (1995) *Formal Issues in Lexical-Functional Grammar*. Stanford: CSLI Publications.

Dedrick, John and Eugene Casad (1999) *Sonora Yaqui Language Structures*. Tucson: University of Arizona Press.

Déprez, Vivienne (1992) Raising constructions in Haitian Creole. *Natural Language and Linguistic Theory* 10, 191–231.

Derbyshire, Desmond (1985) *Hixkaryana and Linguistic Typology*. Dallas: Summer Institute of Linguistics.

Edmondson, Jerold and Donald A. Burquest (1998) *A Survey of Linguistic Theories*. (3rd ed.) Dallas: Summer Institute of Linguistics.

Emonds, Joseph (1980) Word order in Generative Grammar. *Journal of Linguistic Research* 1, 33–54.

Escalante, Fernando (1990) Voice and Argument Structure in Yaqui. Ph.D. dissertation, University of Arizona.

Fabb, Nigel (1994) *Sentence Structure*. London: Routledge.

Falk, Yehuda N. (forthcoming) *Lexical-Functional Grammar: An Introduction to Parallel Constraint-Based Syntax*. Stanford: CSLI Publications.

Friedin, Robert (ed.) (1991) *Principles and Parameters in Comparative Grammar*. Cambridge: MIT Press.

Gair, James (1970) *Colloquial Sinhalese Clause Structure*. The Hague: Mouton.

Garrett, Merrill (1967) Syntactic Structures and Judgments of Auditory Events. Ph.D. dissertation, University of Illinois.

Gazdar, Gerald, Ewan Klein, Geoffrey Pullum, and Ivan Sag (1985) *Generalized Phrase Structure Grammar*. Cambridge: Harvard University Press.

Gazdar, G., G. Pullam, and I. Sag (eds.) (1983) *Order Concord and Constituency*. Dordrecht: Foris.

Goodall, Grant (1993) On case and the passive morpheme. *Natural Language and Linguistic Theory* 11, 31–44.

Grimshaw, Jane (1990) *Argument Structure*. Cambridge: MIT Press.

Gruber, Jeffrey (1965) Studies in Lexical Relations. Ph.D. dissertation, MIT.

Haegeman, Liliane (1994) *Introduction to Government and Binding Theory*. Oxford: Blackwell.

Haegeman, Liliane and Jacqueline Guéron (1999) *English Grammar: A Generative Perspective*. Oxford: Blackwell.

Hale, Kenneth L. and Samuel Jay Keyser (eds.) (1993) *The View from Building 20: Essays in Honor of Sylvain Bromberger*. Cambridge: MIT Press.

Halle, Morris and Alec Marantz (1993) Distributed morphology and the pieces of inflection. In Kenneth L. Hale and Samuel Jay Keyser (eds.) *The View from Building 20: Essays in Honor of Sylvain Bromberger*. Cambridge: MIT Press. pp. 111–76.

Heim, Irene and Kratzer, Angelika (1998) *Semantics in Generative Grammar*. Oxford: Blackwell.

Higginbotham, James (1980) Pronouns and bound variables. *Linguistic Inquiry* 11, 697–708.

Higginbotham, James (1985) A note on phrase markers. *MIT Working Papers in Linguistics* 6, 87–101.

Holzman, Mathilda (1997) *The Language of Children* (2nd ed.). Oxford: Blackwell.

Hornstein, Norbert (1999) Movement and control. *Linguistic Inquiry* 30, 69–96.

Huang, C.-T. James (1982) Logical Relations in Chinese and the Theory of Grammar. Ph.D. dissertation, MIT.

Huang, C.-T. James (1989) PRO-drop in Chinese. In Osvaldo Jaeggli and Kenneth Safir (eds.), *The Null Subject Parameter*. Dordrecht: Kluwer Academic Publishers. pp. 185–214

Hyams, Nina (1986) *Language Acquisition and the Theory of Parameters*. Dordrecht: D. Reidel.

Jackendoff, Ray (1977) *X-bar Syntax: A Theory of Phrase Structure*. Cambridge: MIT Press.

Jackendoff, Ray (1993) *Patterns in the Mind*. London: Harvester-Wheatsheaf.

Jacobs, R. and P. Rosenbaum (eds.) (1970) *Readings in English Transformational Grammar*. Waltham: Ginn.

Jaeggli, Osvaldo (1986) Passive. *Linguistic Inquiry* 17, 587–622.

Jaeggli, Osvaldo and Kenneth Safir (eds.) (1989) *The Null Subject Parameter*. Dordrecht: Kluwer Academic Publishers.

Jelinek, Eloise and Fernando Escalante (forthcoming) Unergative and unaccusative verbs in Yaqui. In Gene Casad and Thomas L. Willett (eds.), *Uto-Aztecan: Structural, Temporal and Geographic Perspectives: Papers in Honor of W. Miller*. Hermosillo: Universidad Autonoma de Sonora.

Johnson, Kyle and Ian Roberts (eds.) (1991) *Beyond Principles and Parameters*. Dordrecht: Kluwer Academic Publishers.

Kaplan, Ronald (1995) The formal architecture of Lexical-Functional Grammar. In Mary Dalrymple, et al. (eds.), *Formal Issues in Lexical-Functional Grammar*. Stanford: CSLI Publications.

Kaplan, Ronald and Joan Bresnan (1982) Lexical-Functional Grammar: A formal system for grammatical representation. In Joan Bresnan (ed.), *The Mental Representation of Grammatical Relations*. Cambridge: MIT Press. pp. 173–281.

Kayne, Richard (1994) *The Antisymmetry of Syntax*. Cambridge: MIT Press.

Koopman, Hilda (1984) *The Syntax of Verbs: From Verb Movement Rules in the Kru Languages to Universal Grammar*. Dordrecht: Foris.

Koopman, Hilda (1992) On the absence of case chains in Bambara. *Natural Language and Linguistic Theory* 10, 555–94.

Koopman, Hilda and Dominique Sportiche (1991) The position of subjects. *Lingua* 85, 211–58.

Kroeger, Paul (1993) *Phrase Structure and Grammatical Relations in Tagalog*. Stanford: CSLI Publications.

Kroskrity, Paul (1985) A holistic understanding of Arizona Tewa passives. *Language* 61, 306–28.

Landau, Idan (1999) Elements of Control. Ph.D. dissertation, MIT.

Larson, Richard (1988) On the double object construction. *Linguistic Inquiry* 19, 335–91.

Lasnik, Howard (1989) *Essays on Anaphora*. Dordrecht: Kluwer Academic Publishers.

Lasnik, Howard (1999a) *Minimalist Analyses*. Oxford: Blackwell.

Lasnik, Howard (1999b) On feature strength. *Linguistic Inquiry* 30, 197–219.

Lasnik, Howard and Mamoru Saito (1984) On the nature of proper government. *Linguistic Inquiry* 15, 235–89.

Levin, Beth (1993) *English Verb Classes and Alternations: A Preliminary Investigation*. Chicago: University of Chicago Press.

Lightfoot, David (1976) Trace theory and twice moved NPs. *Linguistic Inquiry* 7, 559–82.

Lightfoot, David (1991) *How to Set Parameters: Evidence from Language Change*. Cambridge: MIT Press.

Lightfoot, David and Norbert Hornstein (eds.) (1994) *Verb Movement*. Cambridge: Cambridge University Press.

Longobardi, Giuseppi (1994) Reference and proper names: A theory of N-movement in syntax and Logical Form. *Linguistic Inquiry* 25, 609–65.

Manning, Christopher and Ivan Sag (1998) Argument structure, valence and binding. *The Nordic Journal of Linguistics* 21, 107–44.

Manzini, Maria Rita (1983) On control and control theory. *Linguistic Inquiry* 14, 421–46.

Manzini, Maria Rita (1992) *Locality: A Theory and Some of Its Empirical Consequences*. Cambridge: MIT Press.

Marantz, Alec (1984) *On Grammatical Relations*. Cambridge: MIT Press.

Marcus, Gary, Steven Pinker, Michael Ullman, Michelle Hollander, T. J. Rosen, and Fei Xu (1992) Overregularization in language acquisition. *Monographs of the Society for Research in Child Development* 57.

May, Robert (1985) *Logical Form*. Cambridge: MIT Press.

McCloskey, James (1979) *Transformational Syntax and Model Theoretic Semantics: A Case Study in Modern Irish*. Dordrecht: Reidel.

McCloskey, James (1983) A VP in a VSO language. In G. Gazdar, G. Pullam, and I. Sag (eds.), *Order Concord and Constituency*. Dordrecht: Foris. pp. 9–55.

McCloskey, James (1991) Clause structure, ellipsis and proper government in Irish. *Lingua* 85, 259–302.

Moore, John (1998) Turkish copy raising and A-chain locality. *Natural Language and Linguistic Theory* 16, 149–89.

Ouhalla, Jamal (1990) *Introducing Transformational Grammar* (2nd ed.). London: Edward Arnold.

Perlmutter, David and Paul Postal (1984) The 1-Advancement Exclusiveness Law. In David Perlmutter and Carol Rosen (eds.) *Studies in Relational Grammar*. Chicago: University of Chicago Press: 81–125.

Perlmutter, David and Carol Rosen (eds.) *Studies in Relational Grammar*. Chicago: University of Chicago Press.

Petter, Marga (1998) *Getting PRO under Control*. The Hague: Holland Academic Graphics.

Pinker, Steven (1995) *The Language Instinct*. New York: Harper Perennial.

Pollard, Carl and Ivan Sag (1992) Anaphors in English and the scope of binding theory. *Linguistic Inquiry* 23, 261–303.

Pollard, Carl and Ivan Sag (1994) *Head-Driven Phrase Structure Grammar*. Stanford: CSLI Publications and Chicago: University of Chicago Press.

Pollock, Jean-Yves (1989) Verb-movement, Universal Grammar, and the structure of IP. *Linguistic Inquiry* 20, 365–424.

Postal, Paul (1974) *On Raising*. Cambridge: MIT Press.

Pullum, Geoffrey K. (1997) The morpholexical nature of English *to*-contraction. *Language* 73, 79–102.

Radford, Andrew (1988) *Transformational Grammar: A First Course*. Cambridge: Cambridge University Press.

Radford, Andrew (1997a) *Syntactic Theory and The Structure of English: A Minimalist Approach*. Cambridge: Cambridge University Press.

Radford, Andrew (1997b) *Syntax: A Minimalist Introduction*. Cambridge: Cambridge University Press.

Reinhart, Tanya (1976) The Syntactic Domain of Anaphora. Ph.D. dissertation, MIT.

Reinhart, Tanya (1983) *Anaphora and Semantic Interpretation*. London: Croom Helm.

Richards, Norvin (1997) What Moves Where When in Which Language? Ph.D. dissertation, MIT.

Richter, Frank (2000) A Mathematical Formalism for Linguistic Theories with an Application in Head-Driven Phrase Structure Grammar. Ph.D. Dissertation, University of Tübingen.

Ritter, Elizabeth (1988) A head movement approach to construct state noun phrases. *Linguistics* 26, 909–29.

Rivero, Maria-Louisa (1991) Long head movement and negation: Serbo-Croatian vs. Slovak and Czech. *The Linguistic Review* 8, 319–51.

Rizzi, Luigi (1982) *Issues in Italian Syntax*. Dordrecht: Foris.

Rizzi, Luigi (1989) *Relativized Minimality*. Cambridge: MIT Press.

Roberts, Ian (1997) *Comparative Syntax*. London: Edward Arnold.

Rosenbaum, P. S. (1967) *The Grammar of English Predicate Complement Constructions*. Cambridge: MIT Press.

Ross, J. R. (Haj) (1967) Constraints on Variables in Syntax. Ph.D. dissertation, MIT.

Sag, Ivan and Thomas Wasow (1999) *Syntactic Theory: A Formal Introduction*. Stanford: CSLI Publications.

Saito, Mamoru and Howard Lasnik (1994*) Move Alpha: Conditions on Its Application and Output*. Cambridge: MIT Press.

Sampson, Geoffrey (1997) *Educating Eve: The Language Instinct Debate*. London: Cassell.

Sapir, Edward and Morris Swadesh (1939) *Nootka Texts, Tales, and Ethnological Narratives, with Grammatical Notes and Lexical Materials*. Philadelphia: Linguistic Society of America.

Saxon, Leslie (1984) Disjoint anaphora and the binding theory. *Proceedings of WCCFL* 3, 2242–51.

Seiler, Wolf (1978) The modalis case in Iñupiat. *Work Papers of the Summer Institute of Linguistics* 22, 71–85.

Sells, Peter (1985) *Lectures on Contemporary Syntactic Theories*. Stanford: CSLI Publications.

Sigurðsson, Halldór Ármann (1991) Icelandic case-marked PRO and the licensing of lexical arguments. *Natural Language and Linguistic Theory* 9, 327–65.

Simpson, Jane (1991) *Warlpiri Morpho-Syntax: A Lexicalist Approach*. Dordrecht: Kluwer Academic Publishers.

Soames, Scott and David M. Perlmutter (1979) *Syntactic Argumentation and the Structure of English*. Berkeley: University of California Press.

Sobin, Nicholas (1985) Case and agreement in the Ukrainian morphological passive construction. *Linguistic Inquiry* 16, 649–62.

Speas, Margaret (1990) *Phrase Structure in Natural Language*. Dordrecht: Kluwer Academic Publishers.

Sportiche, Dominique (1988) A theory of floating quantifiers and its corollaries for constituent structure. *Linguistic Inquiry* 19, 425–49.

Sproat, Richard (1985) Welsh syntax and VSO structure. *Natural Language and Linguistic Theory* 3, 173–216.

Stenson, Nancy (1989) Irish autonomous impersonals. *Natural Language and Linguistic Theory* 7, 379–406.

Stowell, Tim (1981) Origins of Phrase Structure. Ph.D. dissertation, MIT.

Szabolcsi, Anna (1994) The noun phrase. In *Syntax and Semantics 27: The Syntax of Hungarian*. New York: Academic Press. pp. 179–279.

Travis, Lisa de Mena (1984) Parameters and Effects of Word Order Derivation. Ph.D. dissertation, MIT.

Uriagereka, Juan (1998) *Rhyme and Reason: An Introduction to Minimalist Syntax*. Cambridge: MIT Press.

Vikner, Sten (1995) *Verb Movement and Expletive Subjects in the Germanic Languages*. Oxford: Oxford University Press.

Webelhuth, Gert (1995) *Government and Binding Theory and the Minimalist Program*. Oxford: Blackwell.

Weerman, Fred (1989) *The V2 Conspiracy*. Dordrecht: Foris.

Williams, Edwin (1980) Predication. *Linguistic Inquiry* 11, 203–38.

Williams, Edwin (1983) Semantic vs. syntactic categories. *Linguistics and Philosophy* 6, 423–46.

Williams, Edwin (1994) *Thematic Structure in Syntax*. Cambridge: MIT Press.

Zaenen, Annie, Joan Maling, and Hoskuldur Thráinsson (1985) Case and grammatical functions: The Icelandic passive. *Natural Language and Linguistic Theory* 3, 441–83.

Index

∃, *see* existential quantifier
↑, *see* metavariable
↓, *see* metavariable
∀, *see* universal quantifier
[+NOM] 235, 317
[+ACC] 235, 317
[+Q] 153–4, 205–8, 318
[+WH] 286–93, 316

A' 112–13
absolutive (Abs) 236
abstract Case, *see* Case
accusative 9, 21, 233–5, 282, *see also*
 [+ACC]
acquisition 12–13, 22, 25
actives 247–8
adjective phrase (AP) 35–6, 112–13,
 126–8
adjectives 28–30, 36, 55
adjunct 116–28, 137, 138, 171
adjunct clause 148, 159
adverb phrase (AP) 35–6, 112–13, 126–8
adverbs 28–30, 36, 55, 192–6
affix lowering 156, 159, 193–9, 210–11,
 322–3
agent 168, 177
agreement 158, 318
AgrO 157
AgrS 157
ambiguity 49–51, 60
anaphor 7, 21, 90, 98
anaphora 7–10, 21, 26, 90–4, 200–1
antecedent 8, 91–2, 98
antipassive 186
ARG-ST, *see* features
Argument Realization Principle 365, 370,
 373
argument structure 166, 177
arguments 166, 177
Arizona Tewa 247
asterisk 7, 21
a-structure 340, 355
asymmetric c-command 76–7, 82
Attribute Value Matrix 339–40, 355
Aux, *see* auxiliary

auxiliary 56, 151, 155–7, 163, 193–9,
 205–10, 222–3
AVM, *see* Attribute Value Matrix
axioms of dominance 69
axioms of precedence 74

Bambara 62
bar levels 109–11
Bare Phrase Structure 327, 329,
BAR-LEVEL features, *see* features
base 185–6, 190
Bavarian German 285
benefactive 169, 178
bind 92–4, 98
binding domain 94–6, 98
binding principles, *see* principles A, B,
 and C
binding theory 89–103, 269–70, 310–11,
 313, 368
bounding nodes 295, 306
bounding theory 293–306
BPS, *see* Bare Phrase Structure
bracketed diagrams 32, 48, 56
branch 66, 80
Burzio's generalization 238, 244
by-phrases 231

Case 233–53, 283, 316–17
case 9, 21
Case filter 234–43, 290, 314, 316
categories, *see* parts of speech
causatives 247–8
c-command 75–8, 80–7, 97–8, 100, 103,
 201, 240, 271–2, 275
Chinese, *see* Mandarin Chinese
Chomsky, Noam 6
clausal subject construction 256, 259, 275
clause 33, 39–41, 95, 143–64, 174, 178
click experiment 31
closed class parts of speech 56–7
cognitive science 4–5
Coherence 344, 354, 356
coindex 91–2, 98
complement 116–28, 137, 143
complement clause 149, 159
complementizer 56, 151, 153, 160, 205,
 286, 308–10, 312